FORCE AND TOUCH
FEEDBACK
FOR VIRTUAL REALITY

FORCE AND TOUCH FEEDBACK FOR VIRTUAL REALITY

GRIGORE C. BURDEA
Electrical and Computer Engineering Department
Rutgers—The State University of New Jersey

A Wiley-Interscience Publication

JOHN WILEY & SONS, INC.

New York / Chichester / Brisbane / Toronto / Singapore

Copyright © 1996 by John Wiley & Sons, Inc.

Library of Congress Cataloging-in-Publication Data:
Burdea, Grigore.
    Force and touch feedback for Virtual Reality / Grigore C. Burdea.
        p.   cm.
    Includes bibliographical references and index.
    ISBN 0-471-02141-5 (alk. paper)
    1. Human-computer interaction.   2. Virtual reality.   I. Title.
QA76.9.H85B86   1996
006—dc20   95-15428
                                                             CIP

Printed in the United States of America

10 9 8 7 6 5 4 3 2 1

To Gregory, my little prince

CONTENTS

FOREWORD

It is no accident that we routinely speak of "having a good grasp" of a subject, or of "having a good feel for" the behavior of a complex system. These very metaphors attest to the power of our haptic senses for understanding the real world. These haptic senses, although not so highly resolved as vision or audition, feed our consciousness and subconscious in ways that are very deep.

We should reasonably expect, therefore, that haptic displays will enhance our perception of computed worlds. This has been shown indeed to be true.

So far as I can tell, the generalized concept of virtual worlds with which people can interact was first enunciated by Ivan Sutherland in his great address, "The Ultimate Display" at the 1965 IFIP Congress in New York. He challenged his hearers to think of a graphical display as a window through which one looks into a virtual world. Equally startling, he also proposed the general use of kinesthetic displays for virtual worlds with normal or idiosyncratic physics, analogous to the force displays long used in flight simulators. I was in the audience, and Sutherland's speech electrified my imagination, and ultimately my own research program.

It is therefore a special joy now to have a book describing the state of the art of haptic displays for virtual worlds, and the development of that art. Prior work has been scattered widely over publications in many disciplines. This monograph is surprisingly comprehensive in both its subject-matter coverage and in the range of relevant work that is cited. I expect to use it not only as a snapshot of the current state of the art, but as reference compendium, useful for its collection of the relevant physiology, psychology, control theory, and mathematics long after those particular devices and systems described have fallen into obsolescence.

It is encouraging to see a treatment start with the haptic senses themselves, not with gadgetry. Virtual-world builders are illusionists by trade, and our first task as illusionists is to understand perception and understanding as mediated by our senses. *Immersion* in other worlds, visually, aurally, and haptically is the ideal we pursue. *Interaction* with the virtual worlds aids powerfully in making the experiences seem real.

To these well-known concepts, Burdea insightfully adds a third, *imagination*, that willing suspense of disbelief that Coleridge defined to constitute poetic faith. Too often we overlook the power of imagination to enhance our virtual world experiences. All too often we have to admit a necessity for imagination, occasioned by our adolescent technologies. We often dream of achieving such technological virtuosity that our travelers in virtual worlds will no longer need imagination. That dream is, I think, the illusionist's own illusion: we shall never achieve it, and if we did, we should be immeasurably impoverished by our loss.

Virtual worlds, or synthetic environments, technology holds great promise for medicine, for design, for training, and for science. It is an irony sadly characteristic of our culture that these promising uses will be enabled, if at all, as byproducts of our desire to be entertained. God help us.

I am convinced that virtual worlds techniques, both for work and for play, will be made more effective and more delightful by the ability to feel, as well as to see and hear, the imaginary. To that end this book contributes significantly.

Chapel Hill, North Carolina   Frederick P. Brooks, Jr.

PREFACE

Virtual Reality as a high-end user-computer interface has matured in recent years and produced applications in areas ranging from mechanical design to entertainment and medical training. The usefulness and realism of present-generation VR simulators are hampered by a lack of force and tactile feedback to the user. Thus, we can navigate through virtual worlds, grasp and manipulate objects, but we cannot feel their weight, surface smoothness, compliance, or temperature. The general public, and even some VR specialists are not aware that devices capable of providing such very useful sensorial feedback do exist. This book is intended to bridge this knowledge gap and provide a unified and complete source of information on the novel force/tactile feedback technology and its use in VR simulations. The coverage and level of detail make it especially useful to the engineer, computer scientist, human-factors specialist and application developer. The book may also be used in universities as a second-semester text for design courses in Virtual Reality.

The literature search part of this book was done when I was on Sabbatical leave at the Computer Science Department of the University of North Carolina at Chapel Hill. I want to thank Professor Frederick Brooks, Jr. for inviting me there and agreeing to write the Foreword to the book despite a very busy schedule. My gratitude also goes to Captain Christofer Hasser from Wright-Patterson AFB and Professor Edward Colgate from Northwestern University who reviewed my manuscript and provided very useful suggestions. The production of this book in a timely manner was made possible by the CAIP Center at Rutgers University who allowed me to use their computer and printing resources during the second part of my Sabbatical. The book coverage of the worldwide state-of-the-art in force/tactile feedback interfaces for VR could not have been done without the help of hundreds of companies and researchers who graciously provided relevant material.

Finally, on a personal note, I should add that the birth of this virtual "child" of mine happily coincided with our first real baby. My wife, parents, and in-laws provided help and encouragement without which my manuscript may not have seen a timely completion. This book is an expression of my affection for them.

Piscataway, New Jersey   GRIGORE C. BURDEA

FORCE AND TOUCH
FEEDBACK
FOR VIRTUAL REALITY

CHAPTER 1

INTRODUCTION

We live in an era of increased computer usage in all fields of life ranging from personal finance, to healthcare, to manufacturing, and entertainment. Today computers are not only faster and less expensive, but communicate with us in more sophisticated ways. Compact disk (CD)-based multimedia has allowed human-comptuer interaction through text, compressed graphical animation, stereo sound and live video images. A technological revolution is now taking place in which the user's interaction with computers is mediated by an artificial or "virtual reality" [Krueger, 1991; Pimentel and Teixeira, 1994; Burdea and Coiffet, 1994].

Virtual Reality is superior to other forms of human–computer interaction since it provides a real-time environment integrating several new communication modalities. These include stereo graphics [Akka, 1992], three-dimensional sound [Wenzel, 1992a,b], tactile feedback [Burdea et al., 1992a; Marcus, 1993], and even taste and smell [Bardot et al., 1992; Keller et al., 1995].

By providing such a rich and real-time sensorial interaction Virtual Reality makes the user feel immersed in the simulation or application he is running. As opposed to looking at the computer, the user feels surrounded by a synthetic world with which he can interact and modify. Sheridan refers to this compelling feeling as:

> In some ideal sense, and presumably with sufficiently good technology, a person would not be able to distinguish between actual presence, telepresence, and virtual presence.
> —Sheridan [1992b]

What results is a far more natural interface, and one in which the user can be more productive and more creative. Therefore Virtual Reality may also be defined as an integrated trio of immersion–interaction–imagination, as illustrated in Figure 1.1 [Burdea and Coiffet, 1994].

1

VIRTUAL REALITY TRIANGLE

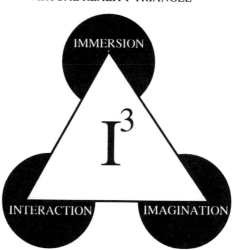

Figure 1.1 Virtual Reality immersion–interaction–imagination. Reprinted by permission from [Burdea and Coiffet, 1994] © Éditions Hermès.

The above benefits of Virtual Reality make it very attractive for research and development, as well as for the commercial market. The need for better simulation has led to applications ranging from surgical training and execution [McDonald et al., 1995], to entertainment [Virtual World Entertainment, 1991], military training [Gembicki and Rousseau, 1993], or arts and education [Miller et al., 1992]. These various applications have pushed an incipient market of only $50 million [Donovan, 1993] to grow by more than an order of magnitude by 1995.

Yet, there still exist at least two aspects that prevent Virtual Reality (VR) from reaching its full potential. The first involves complexity of the scene graphics, which creates the level of visual realism of the virtual world. At present, scene complexity is limited by computer performance. It is still not possible to have both real-time and complex worlds in the same simulation, forcing designers to sacrifice visual realism for high frame-update rates. Real-time graphics require at least 15 frames/sec [Piantanida et al., 1993], and preferably 30 frames/sec, limiting scene complexity to between five and ten thousand polygons, depending on the computer used. The doubling in processor power that occurs every few years is expected to solve the need for visual realism, although it will take time to reach the required 40 million triangles/sec/eye estimated by some researchers [Fuchs et al., 1989].

The realism of current simulations is also impacted by a second factor, namely the lack of good physical simulation. Touch and force feedback are very important sensations in our daily life. Cutt states that:

> People use tactile feedback to perform tasks in various ways. One way is to explore some portion of the environment and thus achieve tactile identification of objects, positions, and orientations. Secondly, to actively use tactile feedback to manipulate or move an object to perform a task. The lack of tactile feedback in virtual environments removes

a major source of information "display" to the user. Currently most data acquisition in virtual environments is with vision and with non-contact sensors such as sound. The information requirements of many tasks needing dextrous manipulation and the sense of touch (such as remote control of a robot to locate and feel surface contours of objects) is not met without tactile feedback. —Cutt [1993]

In today's commercial VR simulations, users can usually pass through walls, lift but not feel the weight and compliance of grasped objects, and so on. Physical characteristics can be neglected in simple "fly-by" simulations or video games; however, they become critical in applications where the user actively manipulates the simulated world, a typical example being surgical simulators. It is difficult and unreasonable to train a doctor to properly execute a given procedure, without giving him the feel of the organ being cut, of an artery pulse, or of a malignancy's harder consistency within its softer surrounding tissue.

To provide sufficient realism, the simulation must include physical constraints [Papper and Gigante, 1993] such as object rigidity, mass and weight, friction, dynamics, surface characteristics (smoothness or temperature), and so on. Adding physical characteristics to virtual objects in turn requires both powerful computing hardware (preferably a distributed system) and specialized input/output (i/o) tools. These i/o devices are worn by the user and provide tactile and force feedback in response to the VR simulation scenario.

A second class of simulations where providing tactile and force feedback is essential for successful completion of the task performed are dark virtual environments. In such simulations users need to rely on other senses to supplement the visual feedback that is lacking or nonexistent.

1.1. TERMINOLOGY

Before starting our discussion on the history of virtual tactile and force feedback technology and its applications, it is better to define the terminology of this new field. We find this necessary because, even within the technical community, terms are intermixed and may lead to confusion.

Tactile and force feedback do differ in several aspects such as physiology, control requirements, and functionality. Tactile feedback is sensed by receptors placed close to the skin, with the highest density being found in the hand. These high-bandwidth receptors (50 – 350 Hz) sense the initial contact with the environment, its fine surface geometry, rugosity, surface temperature, and slippage. Force feedback is sensed by low-bandwidth receptors placed deeper in the body, typically on muscle tendon attachments to bones and joints. These receptors provide information on the total contact force, as well as grasped object compliance and weight. When referring to a VR simulation the "Virtual Lexicon" gives the following definitions:

Tactile Feedback:

Sensation applied to the skin, typically in response to contact or other actions in a virtual world. Tactile feedback can be used to produce a symbol, like Braille, or simply a sensation that indicates some condition.

Force Feedback:

The sensation of weight or resistance in a virtual world. Force feedback requires a device which produces a force on the body equivalent (or scaled) to that of a real object. It allows a person in cyberspace to feel the weight of virtual objects, or the resistance to motion that they create. —*CyberEdge Journal*, [1993b]

These terms differ also in functionality, namely the ability to oppose actively the user volitional hand movement [Burdea and Langrana, 1993]. Force feedback (at large levels) can stop the user's motion, whereas tactile feedback cannot. It therefore cannot prevent virtual or robotic hands from possibly destroying remotely grasped objects.

Haptic feedback. From the Greek *haptesthai*, meaning to touch, is synonymous with tactile feedback [Webster, 1985]. This author and others extend its meaning to that of force feedback.

Kinesthetic feedback. Synonymous with proprioception, it refers to *kinesthesia*, a sense mediated by end organs located in muscles, tendons, and joints and stimulated by bodily movements and tensions [Webster, 1985]. Some authors use kinesthetic feedback to group both tactile and force feedback in a single definition, but this is somewhat incorrect.

Proprioceptive feedback. Relates to stimuli arising within the organism. It provides information related to body posture and is based on receptors located at the skeletal joints, in the inner ear, and on impulses from the central nervous system (memory effect).

1.2. FROM PROTOTYPES TO COMMERCIAL APPLICATIONS

Specialized devices to provide virtual haptic feedback are the result of decades of active research in both industry and university laboratories. In the 1950s and 1960s, when Virtual Reality did not exist, research was aimed at developing and improving telerobotic systems. In such systems, the operator controls a "master" arm that transmits his commands to a remote slave. Sheridan [1992b] defines the master–slave teleoperator system as follows:

> In a teleoperation sense, a master-slave teleoperator system has two subsystems: (1) the *master device*, which typically is a multi-degree-of-freedom, more-or-less anthropomorphic (having a serial-kinematic form like a human arm) mechanical device, positioned directly by a human operator; and (2) a *slave device*, which typically is isomorphic to (having the same form as) the master. The latter is often equipped with an end effector (a hand for grasping, or a specialized tool to perform some specialized task...
> —Sheridan, [1992b]

The slave follows the master input and interacts with a (usually) harmful environment (such as nuclear, outer-space, or underwater sites). The first teleoperator systems had purely mechanical linkages so that the slave was in close proximity to the master arm. A newer electrical servomechanism was developed in 1954 by Goertz and Thompson [1954] at Argonne National Laboratory and is illustrated in Figure 1.2.

What makes this system relevant to this book is the presence of electrical servoactuators in the master arm. These actuators received feedback signals from slave sensors and applied forces to the user's hand grasping the master. In this way, the user felt as if he was manipulating the remote environment directly. In 1965, the well-known pioneer of Computer Graphics, Ivan Sutherland, put forward the vision of an "ultimate display" to a virtual world that included haptic feedback from simulation [Sutherland, 1965]. Frederick Brooks, Jr. and his colleagues at the University of North Carolina at Chapel Hill were so emboldened by Sutherland's vision of interactive computer graphics with force feedback that in 1967, they embarked on the project GROPE. Its ambitious aim was real-time simulation of three-dimensional molecular docking forces. It proved to be the longest research project in virtual force feedback. By 1971, GROPE-I demonstrated a two-dimensional continuous force field simulation [Batter and Brooks, 1971]. Later, the research team used a surplus Argone Arm donated by Goertz to simulate three-dimensional collision forces [Kilpatrick, 1976]. GROPE II used the manipulator to interact with wireframe models of virtual

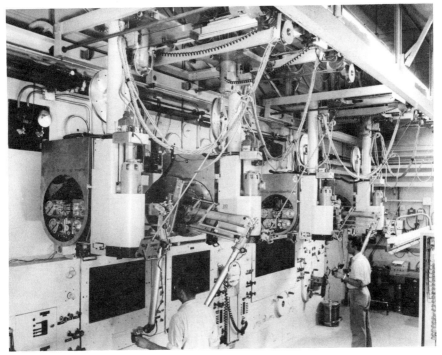

Figure 1.2   The master-slave telemanipulation system developed by Goertz and Thompson at Argonne National Laboratory. Photo courtesy of Argonnne National Laboratory.

child's blocks on a virtual table. Finally, after more than 20 years, much faster computing hardware allowed Brooks and his colleagues to reach their original goal of a three-dimensional molecular docking simulation [Brooks et al., 1990].

In the mid-1960s and early 1970s another group of researchers at the Cornell Aeronautical Laboratory, and later at General Electric constructed an exoskeleton master, so that input from the user was obtained from both arms and legs. This master was placed inside a larger exoskeleton slave used to amplify the power of the user. This complex prototype, called "Hardiman" consisted of 30 hydraulically powered servo joints, as shown in Figure 1.3 [Makinson, 1971].

Whereas the Hardiman was designed to lift and carry loads up to 340 kg (750 lb), the weight fed back to the user limbs was reduced by a factor of 25 to a maximum of 13 kg. The drawback was unstable control at normal operating speeds, because control

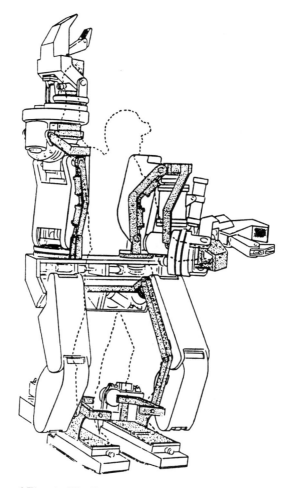

Figure 1.3 General Electric "Hardiman" power-amplifying exoskeleton. Reprinted by permission from Makinson [1971]. © General Electric Co.

technology was not as well-developed at the time. Additionally, the possibility of a leak in the hydraulics was potentially hazardous to the user enclosed in the Hardiman. Hydraulic exoskeleton technology was subsequently refined by researchers at the University of Utah Center for Engineering Design to produce the Utah-NOSC Arm [Jacobsen et al., 1989].

A much simpler and safer design using pneumatic bladders was developed by Jones and Thousand, who in 1966 patented one of the first dextrous master manipulators. As opposed to the previous Argonne Arm or Hardiman which provided feedback to the user's wrist, a dextrous master measures user hand commands (usually through sensing gloves) and provides feedback to independent fingers. This concept is illustrated in Figure 1.4. The user's hand position was measured by a sensing glove and transmitted to a slave robot gripper. Errors between user and robot hands could appear when the robot grasped objects. In that case a pressure proportional to the measured position error was used to inflate pneumatic bladder actuators placed in the palm of the master. Thus the user received a very natural sensation, as if he was grasping the object directly. Twenty-five years later a similar concept was used by researchers at Advanced Robotics Research Ltd. in the United Kingdom for their Teletact I and II gloves [Stone, 1991, 1992].

A more complex dextrous master with feedback to each finger phalange was subsequently patented by Zarudiansky [1981]. His design uses a rigid external shell and an inner glove worn by the user, as shown in Figure 1.5. The external shell (22) houses a number of actuators (28) connected to several rings (24–27) which are attached to the user's inner glove. These actuators provide force feedback to the fingers as well as to the palm and wrist. The patent mentions as application the teleoperation of dextrous slave robotic hands; however, to our knowledge a prototype has never been built.

During the mid and late 1980s, researchers at the National Aeronautics and Space Administration (NASA) and Jet Propulsion Laboratories (JPL) were also developing master arms for teleoperation, as space repair missions were coming of age. Thus they created a teleoperation testbed using the Salisbury/JPL arm [Bejczy and Salisbury, 1980; Hannaford et al., 1989], a six-degree-of-freedom generalized master with force feedback. Earlier joint-based servo control required kinematic similarity between master and slave. Masters were therefore bulky and could be used to control only one type of slave. The advance brought by the Salisbury/JPL arm was the introduction of computer-based Cartesian control, allowing the master to be more compact and to be able to teleoperate slaves with different kinematic configurations. The full potential of the generalized master flexibility was attained later when real robot slaves were replaced by virtual counterparts, allowing a very flexible training environment [Kim and Bejczy, 1991].

All the above masters were developed originally for telerobotic applications and not to serve as i/o devices for VR, a field that appeared in the late 1970s. Researchers then started to develop special-purpose tactile/force feedback hardware. One of the first prototypes to provide tactile feedback from a graphics simulation was the "Sandpaper" system developed at the Massachussetts Institute of Technology Media Laboratory [Minsky et al., 1990]. The prototype, illustrated in Figure 1.6,

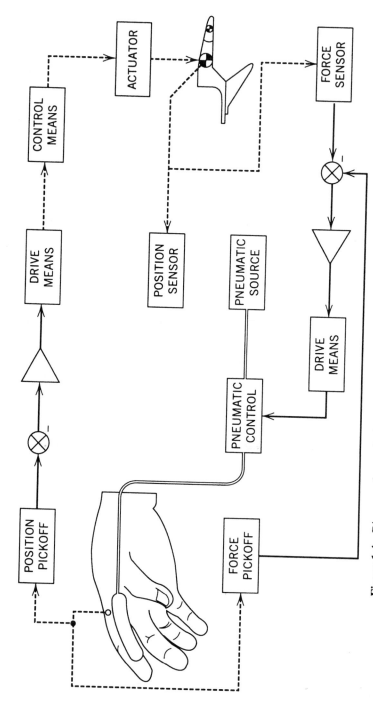

Figure 1.4 Diagram of an early dextrous master using pneumatic actuators. Jones and Thousand [1966]. Courtesy of Northrop Grumman Corporation.

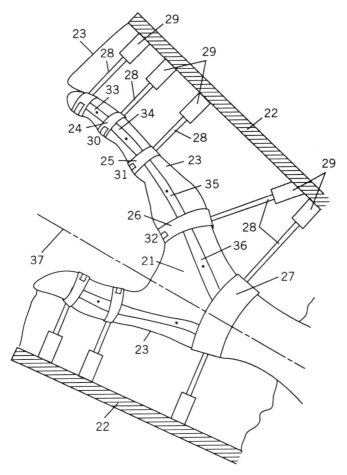

Figure 1.5   Diagram of the nonportable dextrous master patented by Zarudiansky [1981]. Reprinted by permission.

consisted of a two-degree-of-freedom joystick with large electrical actuators in an enclosure placed by the computer. The high bandwidth of the feedback loop (500 to 1000 Hz) allowed for both force and tactile feedback in a single simple and easy to use device. It was thus possible to move a cursor over various samples of virtual sandpaper and feel their surface texture. Inertia and damping were also modeled in a two-dimensional simulation.

Desk-top systems such as feedback joysticks have the advantage of using high-bandwidth bulky actuators whose weight is supported by the desk. The drawback is a significant reduction in the user's freedom of motion, since his hand has to stay on the joystick. Thus large-volume gesture-based interactions with the virtual environment are out of the question. In order to allow natural freedom of motion of the user hand, and still provide tactile and force feedback, masters have to be portable and light.

Figure 1.6   The "Sandpaper" system developed by Margaret Minsky at the MIT Media Laboratory. (Photograph credit: Alan Blount).

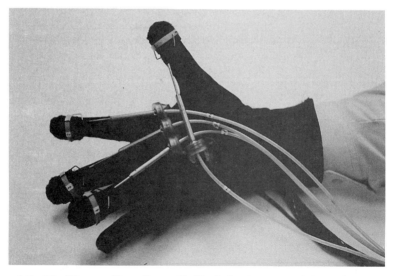

Figure 1.7   The "Rutgers Master" portable i/o device (courtesy of CAIP Center, Rutgers University).

One such device was demonstrated in 1992 at the Rutgers University CAIP Center. The Rutgers Master [Burdea et al., 1992a] shown in Figure 1.7 uses four pneumatic microactuators placed in the palm to give users the feel of the hardness of virtual objects being manipulated. It weighs only 100 grams (2.5 ounces), therefore does not tire users during prolonged simulations.

The first commercial systems designed for virtual i/o became available at the end of 1993 through the introduction of the Touch Master and SAFIRE Master [EXOS Inc., 1995]. These were followed by the recent introduction of lower-cost masters such as the PHANToM Arm [Massie and Salisbury, 1994] and the Impulse Engine [Jackson and Rosenberg, 1995]. With these new devices, developers have the tools to complement the visual and sound feedback created by earlier i/o devices. It is expected that the price of commercial tactile and force feedback systems will drop further in the years to come, which will allow widespread acceptance and integration

TABLE 1.1   Abbreviated History of Research on Virtual Tactile/Force Feedback in the United States

Project	Year			
	1960	1970	1980	1990
Argonne National Lab. (Goertz, 1954)	Argonne Arm			
General Electric Co. (Mosher, 1964)		Handiman Exoskeleton		
Jones and Thousand (1966)		Servo manipulator		
Kilpatrick (1976) Brooks et al. (1990)			GROPE–UNC	
Zarudzianski (1981)			Dextrous Master	
NASA-JPL (Hannaford et al., 1989)			Salisbury-JPL Master	
MIT Media Lab. (Minsky et al., 1990)				Tactile joystick
Rutgers University (Burdea et al., 1992)				Rutgers Master I, II
EXOS Co., (Marcus, 1995)				SAPHIRE Arm
MIT AI Lab. (Massie and Salisbury, 1994)				PHANToM Arm
Immersion Co., (Jackson and Rosenberg, 1995)				Impulse Engine

with most of today's virtual simulations. New applications will of course follow. Table 1.1 summarizes the history of the U.S. tactile/force feedback research described here.

Outside the United States, research on haptic feedback for VR simulations has been pursued by groups in various countries, notably Japan [Iwata 1990, 1993], England [Stone, 1991], France [Bouzit et al., 1993], and Italy [Bergamasco et al., 1994a]. All of these projects will be described in more detail later in this book.

1.3. CHAPTER OUTLINE

The next chapter in this book is dedicated to human kinesthetic sensing for various receptors and areas of the body. Results of human-factors experiments are used to determine what are the optimal signal characteristics for tactile and force feedback (magnitude, bandwidth, resolution, accuracy) that need to be applied by the i/o hardware on the user body. Chapter 3 is dedicated to the technology available to provide this feedback, including miniature and hybrid type actuators. Coverage of force feedback masters is divided into desk-top systems (Chapter 4) and newer portable masters for both hand and full-body feedback (Chapter 5), and Chapter 6 reviews tactile feedback systems. When appropriate we include examples of haptic masters that provide both tactile and force feedback, and better address the human sensorial requirements. Chapter 7 details the physical modeling aspects of virtual haptic feedback including collision detection, surface deformation, hard and soft contact simulation, and so on. Interface control issues, such as bandwidth, system stability, and time delays, are discussed in Chapter 8. Human-factor studies, described in Chapter 9, aim at quantifying the advantages of haptic feedback in terms of task error rates, subject learning time, user comfort, and safety. The integration of tactile/force feedback in VR simulations has made possible a host of new applications ranging from medical training in surgery, to home entertainment, to single-soldier training and telerobotics. These applications are described at length in Chapter 10. A look at the future of virtual haptic feedback concludes this book.

CHAPTER 2

HAPTIC SENSING AND CONTROL

Touch can be defined as the sensation evoked when the skin is subject to mechanical, thermal, chemical, or electrical stimuli [Cholewiak and Collins, 1991]. A discussion of human tactile psychophysics is complicated by a number of factors, such as the temporal and spatial characteristics of the receptors involved, their saturation (or adaptation) that influences perceived sensations, and the lack of understanding of some related neural paths and cortex mapping. No consensus exists concerning such fundamental aspects as spatial tactile resolution, maximal force exertion, or proprioception resolution. Rigorous testing to elucidate these aspects using modern computing hardware have only recently begun [Jones and Hunter, 1992]. These tests are typically done on small groups, which reduces the statistical significance of the results.

Despite these difficulties, it is paramount to present here the human tactile/force sensing-and-control characteristics, because these are key to the successful design of associated human–computer interfaces:

> Clearly, anyone wishing to construct a device to communicate the sensation of remote touch to a user must be fully aware of the dynamic range of the touch receptors, with particular emphasis on their adaptation to certain stimuli. It is only too easy to disregard the fundamental characteristics of the human body.
>
> —Kalawsky [1993]

Hence our discussion starts by presenting the human tactile, proprioceptive, kinesthetic, thermal- and nocious- (pain) sensing characteristics. This is followed by a description of the sensory–motor (forces and torques) and human hand mechanical impedance. These parameters are subsequently used to provide quantitative guidelines for optimal design of the associated human–machine interface hardware.

2.1. HAPTIC SENSING

Tactile sensing is the result of a chain of events that starts with a stimulus (such as heat, pressure, or vibration) applied to the body. Depending on type, magnitude, and location on the skin, this stimulus triggers a response from specialized receptors. Thermoreceptors respond to a change in skin temperature, mechanoreceptors to mechanical action (force, vibration, slip), whereas nocioreceptors convey the sensation of pain. If the stimulus is larger than the threshold of its corresponding receptor, a response is triggered and an electrical discharge (or "action potential") is generated in the afferent nerve fiber. Second-order neurons transmit the signal further up the spine and into the thalamus region of the brain. Here third-order neurons complete the path to the somesthetic area of the cortex where the corresponding sensations of pressure, temperature, or pain are registered [Seow, 1988].

2.1.1. Physiology of Touch

The most active role in tactile explorations is played by hairless (glabrous) skin covering the palmar and fingertip regions of the body. Fingers have a high sensorial density of specialized receptors that corresponds to a large sensory cortex surface. Mapping the hand receptors to nearly a quarter of the (total) cortex surface results in great sensitivity to external stimuli. This sensorial mapping is dynamic, so that accidental finger loss results in a realocation of the "vacated" cortex area to serve adjacent healthy fingers [Shreeve, 1993].

The glabrous skin has five major types of receptors: free receptors (or nerve endings), Meissner corpuscles, Merkel's disks, Pacinian corpuscles, and Ruffini corpuscles. Hairy skin has an additional type of receptor, namely the hair-root plexus (or follicle) that detects movement on the surface of the skin. The various tactile receptors and their location in hairless and hairy skin are illustrated in Figure 2.1 [Seow, 1988].

The free nerve endings are located close to the surface of both glabrous and hairy skin. These free neurons respond to distributed pain (injury), as opposed to encapsulated neurons that respond to mechanical stimuli. *Meissner corpuscles* represent over 40 percent of the hand tactile receptors and lie just below the epidermis. Since they move with the ridges of the skin, these receptors can best detect the movement across the skin and function as velocity detectors.

Merkel's disks form 25 percent of the receptors in the hand and have a disk-like nerve ending. These receptors respond best to pressure, but can also provide vibration information. *Pacinian corpuscles* are the largest of the skin corpuscle receptors and represent 13 percent of the hand receptors. They are placed deeper in the skin (dermis) and function as acceleration detectors. Pacinian corpuscles detect light touch as well as vibrations (being most sensitive at approximately 250 Hz). Finally, *Ruffini corpuscles* have a fusiform structure and make up approximately 19 percent of the hand receptors. They detect pressure and skin shear as well as thermal changes.

Sensorial Adaptation. The process of "sensorial adaptation" quantifies the temporal variation in the number of potential discharges produced by a given receptor

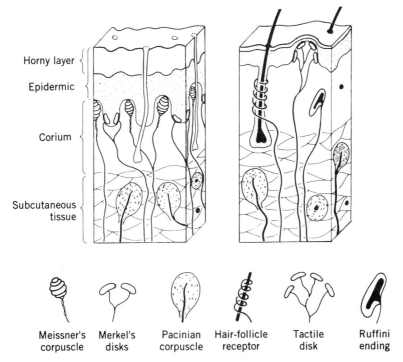

Horny layer

Epidermic

Corium

Subcutaneous
tissue

| Meissner's corpuscle | Merkel's disks | Pacinian corpuscle | Hair-follicle receptor | Tactile disk | Ruffini ending |

Figure 2.1   The structure and location of tactile receptors in the skin. From Seow, *Physiology of Touch, Grip, and Gait*, © 1988 John Wiley & Sons, Inc. Reprinted by permission.

in response to a constant stimulus. Some sensors exhibit a very slow rate of decay of their discharge rate (measured in impulses per second). These are *slow adapting* (SA) receptors. Figure 2.2 illustrates the decay in impulse rate for an SA receptor corresponding to stimuli of three intensities, 1.55 N, 5.25 N, and 9.95 N [Seow, 1988]. As can be seen, the discharge rate drops logarithmically over a period of 40 sec, with the largest drop corresponding to the stimulus of smallest intensity (1.55 N).

Rapidly adapting (RA) receptors have such a fast impulse rate of decay that in a very short time the stimulus becomes undetected. A familiar example is that of people wearing gloves or glasses. Their tactile receptors have adapted and the gloves or glasses are not consciously felt on the skin.

The four encapsulated touch receptors mentioned previously can be further classified according to their adaptation rate. Merkel disks are SA type I receptors, which produce a long but irregular discharge rate in response to forces applied to the skin [LaMotte and Srinivasan, 1987a]. Ruffini corpuscles are of type SA-II and produce a regular discharge rate for a steady load. This discharge rate increases linearly with the logarithm of the force, as shown in Figure 2.2. Meissner corpuscles are RA-I receptors that discharge mostly at the onset of the stimulus [LaMotte and Srinivasan, 1987b]. Therefore, they respond best to velocity. Finally, Pacinian corpuscles discharge only once for each stimulus application, thus are not sensitive to constant pressure on

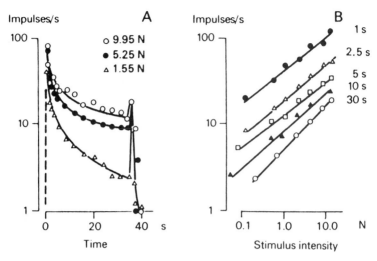

Figure 2.2 Sensorial adaptation for a "slow adapting" receptor, for three stimulus intensities. From Seow, *Physiology of Touch, Grip, and Gait,* © 1988 John Wiley & Sons, Inc. Reprinted by permission.

the skin. They serve best as acceleration or vibration detectors. Experiments have shown that they respond best to frequencies near 200 Hz, which is the lowest stimulus amplitude threshold [Schmidt, 1977].

A number of psychophysical studies have been conducted to quantify the intensity of touch sensation. The minimal touch energy felt by the hand determines the so-called "absolute threshold." Although this threshold varies from person to person, the literature cites absolute threshold values of 80 mg on the fingertips and 150 mg on the palm [Sherrick and Craig, 1982]. The intensity of the vibrotactile stimulus applied to the fingertips is normally 5 to 10 times greater than the absolute threshold, depending on the vibration frequency. As stated previously, Pacinian corpuscles have the smallest mechanical threshold corresponding to a vibration frequency of 200 to 250 Hz.

A recent study by Ino and his colleagues [Ino et al., 1993a] quantified the influence of grasped surface characteristics, such as temperature, on the absolute threshold. They used a Peltier heat pump (described in more detail in Chapter 6) to vary the temperature of a platform moving under the subject's index fingertip. Results showed that the best sensitivity to skin strain was obtained when the platform temperature was 32°C. Sensitivity degraded markedly as fingertip temperature increased past 40°C.

The *Weber ratio* is defined as the just-detectable intensity increment (or decrement) divided by the intensity that already exists (the baseline intensity). This ratio, sometimes called the *differential limen* (DL) was determined to be about 0.14 for static pressure and about 0.20 for impulse stimuli (tap) and vibrations. The static pressure DL, or pressure *just-noticeable-difference* (JND) is a function of the area over which the pressure is applied. Tan and colleagues [1994] studied the variation of the pressure JND for the forearm (as the most likely location for the attachment of a force feedback device). They used three weights (2.2, 8.9, and 35.6 N) and three corresponding contact areas (1.27 cm^2, 5.06 cm^2, and 20.27 cm^2), resulting in a constant pressure of 1.8 N/cm^2. Experimental data showed that the pressure JND decreased as the contact area increased, so that subjects were most sensitive to pressure changes when the contact area was largest. The location of the stimulus on the forearm (wrist or elbow) was determined to be less important in the change of pressure JND. These test results are summarized in Table 2.1.

Spatiotemporal Resolution. Another way to characterize mechanoreceptors is according to their receptive field size. The receptive field of a receptor is the area within which a given intensity stimulus can excite the receptor. It can vary from 1–2 mm^2 up to 45 cm^2 depending on the receptor type and location on the body. In general, determining the receptive field of a single receptor is difficult since there is both crosstalk (several receptors responding to a single stimulus) or enclosure of one field into another. The hand SA–II and RA–II receptors (Pacinian and Ruffini corpuscles) have large receptive fields and therefore low spatial resolution. Conversely, the SA–I and RA–I receptors (Meissner corpuscles and Merkel disks) have much smaller receptive fields and provide a more accurate spatial localization.

Tests have been done to determine the fingertip spatial resolution using the so-called *two-point limen.* As illustrated in Figure 2.3 [Sherrick and Craig, 1982], the subjects' skin was simultaneously touched by two sharp objects (such as the tips of a draftsman's compass). The distance between the compass tips was progressively decreased while the subjects were asked whether they felt one or two stimulus points. The average separation distance (two-point limen) above which subjects always discriminated two points was found to be 2.5 mm. Other tests determined the spatial localization error to be a circle of 1.5–mm radius about the point of contact. Skin on other parts of the body has much less spatial resolution than on the fingertip. The palm cannot discriminate two points that are less than 11 mm apart [Shimoga, 1993],

TABLE 2.1 Average Pressure JND as a Function of Contact Area

Body site	Contact Area (cm^2)		
	1.27	5.06	20.27
	Pressure JND		
Elbow (Volar)	0.167	0.062	0.040
Elbow (Dorsal)	0.113	0.052	0.033
Wrist (Dorsal)	0.188	0.044	—
Overall Average JND	0.156	0.053	0.037

Adapted from Tan et al. [1994]

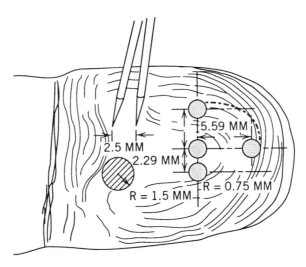

Figure 2.3 Two-point spatial discrimination for the fingertip. Sherrick and Craig, [1982]. Reprinted with the permission of Cambridge University Press.

whereas the two-point discrimination for the thigh is 67 mm [Seow, 1988]. Warm temperature improves discrimination, whereas older age is a detriment to it. Table 2.2 summarizes the characteristics of skin mechanoreceptors in terms of sensorial adaptability, receptive fields, and functionality.

Mechanoreceptor resolution is both spatial and temporal. When two events are presented to the skin close in time, a subject may feel that he received only one stimulus. The *successiveness limen* (SL) is the time threshold for which subjects are able to detect two consecutive stimuli. Mechanoreceptors have an SL value of

TABLE 2.2 Characteristics of Skin Mechanoreceptors

Receptor Type	Rate of Adaptation	Stimulus frequency, Hz	Receptive Field	Function
Merkel Disks	SA–I	0–10	Small, well defined	Edges, intensity
Ruffini Corpuscles	SA–II	0–10	Large, indistinct	Static force, skin stretch
Meissner Corpuscles	RA–I	20–50	Small, well defined	Velocity, edges
Pacinian Corpuscles	RA–II	100–300	Large, indistinct	Acceleration, vibration

Adapted by permission from Seow [1988]; Cholewiak and Collins [1991]; and Kalawsksy [1993].

approximately 5 msec, which is much smaller than the corresponding SL for the eye (25 msec). To perceive the order of stimuli (i.e., which event occurred first on the skin), the same time interval between successive stimuli grows to 20 msec. Although the temporal limen for touch is relatively short, it does not reflect the time spent by higher centers in the nervous system (cortex) processing the information. An example is the time required by blind people to recognize Braille characters. Studies using a tachistotactometer measured character (or character group) identification times of 0.87 to 1.56 sec [Fulke, 1982]. Welch and Warren [1986] reported a tactile response to stimuli of 0.110 to 0.120 sec.

The above-mentioned spatial and temporal thresholds are adversely affected by *masking*, a condition in which one stimulus interferes with the detection (or recognition) of another. When stimuli are close together on the skin, increasing the time interval between the test and masking stimuli will reduce masking. Additionally, as the number of vibrators in a pattern increases, so does the masking effect on a single test vibrator. When the time interval is larger than 150 to 200 msec the masker stimulus produces little interference. Designers of dynamic tactile displays would like high information transmission rates. This in turn requires rapid patterns (small temporal separation) and compactness (small spatial separation) both of which unfortunately produce masking!

2.1.2. Thermoreceptors and Nociceptors

Human temperature sensing is assured by thermoreceptors located in the skin. These receptors are divided into those preferentially receptive to cold, which are located in or just beneath the epidermis, and warmth-sensitive receptors located in the dermis (corium). These nerve endings have a receptive field of approximately 1 to 2 mm in diameter and a spatial resolution that is less than that of pain receptors (nociceptors) or that of mechanoreceptors. Spatial accuracy for detection of thermal stimuli increases when it is coupled with skin deformation. The thermoreceptor density varies, the hand having 1 to 5 cold-sensitive receptors/cm^2 versus only 0.4 warmth-sensitive receptors/cm^2 [Schmidt, 1977].

Tissue-damaging (or noxious) stimuli trigger nociceptors, which detect pain. These free nerve endings respond also to mechanical or thermal stimuli, provided they have great intensity. Nociceptors have a receptive field of approximately 25 mm^2. An applied force or temperature above the nociceptor threshold (above 45°C or below −15°C) triggers a pain response in the cortex. The response to such a stimulus is faster than normal tactile responses due to a faster signal transmission (mediation) in the brain [Shreeve, 1993].

Another interesting aspect related to pain perception is the stimulus after-effect. A burning sensation, for example, persists long after the (high) temperature stimulus had disappeared. The length of time that the after-effect sensation is perceived depends on the initial stimulus magnitude and can be shortened with local compensatory stimulation. One applies ice at the location of a skin burn to alleviate pain.

2.1.3. Proprioception and Kinesthesia

Proprioception refers to the human perception of one's own body position and motion. The sense of position and movement is complemented by the sense of force within muscles and tendons. The sense of position refers to the angle of various skeletal joints, whereas change in angle per unit of time represents velocity (or movement). The sense of force also plays a role in motion detection. Motion in free space compensates for one's limbs' weight, whereas contact with an obstacle in the environment produces contact forces.

There are three types of joint position receptors, namely free nerve endings, as well as Ruffini and Pacinian corpuscles located at skeletal articulations. Motion of the body determines changes in the pressure applied on these receptors. The compression or stretching of the receptor capsules changes the amplitude of the receptor potential discharge that is subsequently interpreted by the central nervous system as position. Conversely, a change in impulse frequency corresponds to a change in joint velocity.

The sensitivity (resolution) of joint position sensing determines the accuracy with which we control the position of body extremities (fingers or toes). A given angular joint error at the shoulder will produce a much larger positioning error at the hand than the same joint error at the wrist. In fact joint position sensitivity (JND) is not constant for all joints in the human body. The smallest JND corresponds to the hip joint (0.2°), whereas the largest is at the toe (6.10°) [Kalawsky, 1993]. Recent tests measured the JNDs for the wrist, elbow, and shoulder joints using a protractor and a digital angle meter (with an accuracy of 0.2°) [Tan et al., 1994]. Over 300 trials done on three subjects showed that the JND decreases from 2.0° at the wrist to 0.8° at the shoulder. Table 2.3 summarizes the joint JNDs for the arm.

Joint position errors, discussed above, result in Cartesian positioning errors between various body extremities. Fingertip position JND is of most interest to haptic interface research, as interaction with the virtual world takes place in Cartesian space. A study on the manual resolution of length between the thumb and forefinger was performed by Tan et al. [1992]. The researchers used a modified digital vernier caliper that had two rectangular pads where the fingers were placed. The experiments used a single-interval, forced-choice methodology with correct-answer feedback. The subjects had to choose between two answers corresponding to randomly presented reference length L_o and reference length plus increment $L_o + \Delta L$. Subjects had no direct visual feedback from the caliper, but were told the correct answer at the completion of each trial (correct-answer feedback). Results showed that the length JND increased monotonically when the reference length L_o increased. Specifically, JND grew from 1.0 mm for $L_o = 10$ mm to 2.4 mm for $L_o = 80$ mm.

TABLE 2.3   **Average Position JND for Various Arm Joints**

Joint	Finger	Wrist	Elbow	Shoulder
Position JNDs	2.5°	2.0°	2.0°	0.8°

Adapted from Tan et al. [1994].

The central nervous system integrates position information from joint sensors with data received from other sensors such as Golgi tendon organs and muscle spindles discussed below. The Golgi organs are located between muscles and their corresponding tendons and play a role of proprioceptors/kinesthetic (or force) sensors. As kinesthetic sensors, they have the function of localized tension detectors, which regulate muscle co-contraction, playing an important role in fine motor control.

The second type of receptors are muscle spindles located between individual fibers throughout the muscle. Muscle spindles are excited by the stretching of neighboring muscle fibers (both passive and active). Although the Golgi tendon organs measure the muscle tension, the spindles can determine the rate of increase (stretch) in muscle length. The Golgi tendon organs and muscle spindles are mechanoreceptors that play the most important part in kinesthesia. Force sensation is also a function of muscle fatigue, which increases the *perceived* force magnitude, even when the force actually produced by the muscle stays constant [Jones and Hunter, 1992].

Additional kinesthetic and proprioceptive sensing may be provided by skin mechanoreceptors (discussed previously) due to cutaneous stretching associated with body motion. This is true especially for cutaneous receptors located in the skin covering our hands, feet, and face. Jones and Hunter [1992] in their review article state, however, that the precise contribution of signals arising from joint and cutaneous receptors to proprioception remains unclear because inconsistencies in present experimental results have been reported in the literature.

2.2. SENSORY–MOTOR CONTROL

Humans use a combination of position and kinesthetic sensing to perform motor (or force) control as part of daily living activities. Srinivasan and Chen [1993] state that:

> In addition to the tactile and kinesthetic sensory channels, the human haptic system also includes the motor subsystem which enables control of body postures and motions together with the forces of contact with objects... In performing manual tasks in real or virtual environments, contact force is perhaps the most important variable that affects both tactual sensory information and motor performance.
> —Srinivasan and Chen, [1993]

Exploratory tasks, such as shape detection, are dominated by the sensorial part of the sensory–motor control loop. Conversely, manipulation tasks aimed at (actively) modifying the environment are motor-dominant tasks [Jandura and Srinivasan, 1994].

The force exertion mechanism is adaptable and involves both a higher (volitional) level loop and a lower (reflex) loop. The volitional control loop is utilized when maximum force exertion takes place. The reflex loop tends to minimize the applied forces to reduce physical fatigue.

One example of force control adaptation is the fingertip grasping of slippery objects. Here the applied force depends on both the load being lifted and on the object surface coefficient of friction. The minimal grip force/load ratio required to prevent slip is the *slip ratio*. Johansson and Westling [1984] showed that the rate of change in the grip force and the final grip force value increased with the degree of surface smoothness. The weight of the grasped object did not affect the slip ratio, but increased the duration to attain steady-state force. Thus the grip force increased as the load increased, but the final steady-state force for each load depended on the surface friction. Local anesthesia was subsequently used to block tactile information from fingertip receptors. The resulting deterioration of the grip force control and induced object slippage illustrate the importance of tactile sensing during grasping.

The key aspects of human sensory–motor control are maximum force exertion, force tracking, torque, compliance and viscosity resolution, finger mechanical impedance, and force control bandwidth. These will now be discussed.

2.2.1. Maximum and Sustained Force Exertion

Finger contact forces depend on the way objects are grasped (geometry), as well as on individual gender, age, motor handicaps, and skill. Grasping geometry has been classified by two categories, namely power and precision grasps [Cutkosky and Howe, 1990]. Power grasps have high stability and force, because the whole hand and palm are used, but they lack dexterity (fingers are locked on the grasped object). Conversely, precision grasps exert less force but have higher dexterity since only the fingertips are used. Typical power and precision grasping configurations are illustrated in Figure 2.4.

Maximum Force Exertion. Several studies have been conducted to measure the controllable manual maximum force exertion. An et al. [1986] found a maximum power grasping force of 400 N for males and 228 N for female subjects. Power and precision hand grasping force measurements are illustrated in Table 2.4.

Sutter et al. [1989] studied the maximum force exerted by the pointer, index, and ring fingers as a function of metacarpal (MCP) joint angle (0° corresponding to a flat palm and fingers). Tests done on six subjects showed that maximum finger force was about 50 N for the pointer and index fingers and 40 N for the ring finger. These forces were determined to remain almost constant over MCP joint angles of 0° to 80°. At larger angles, force exertion required the bending of both the MCP and proximal-inter-phalangeal (PIP) joints and maximum forces dropped slightly.

Tan et al. [1994] extended the study of maximum controllable force output to include the PIP and MCP joints, as well as the wrist, elbow, and shoulder (with arm extended to the side and in front). The subjects (one female and two males) pressed for 5 sec against a load cell used to measure forces. Measurements showed a range of maximum forces of 16 to 102 N, with the smallest at the PIP joint and the largest force at the shoulder. Thus force exertion output grows from the most distal joint to the most proximal one. The degree of controllability over maximum force is expressed by the percentage of standard deviation of the load cell output. Good force controllability means small standard deviations (SDs). Results showed that controllability decreased from the shoulder (only 0.88% SD) to the PIP joint

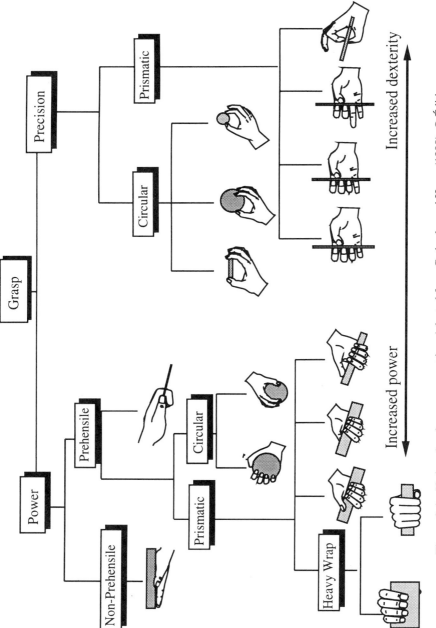

Figure 2.4 Various hand grasp geometries. Adapted from Cutkosky and Howe (1990). © Éditions Hermès. Reprinted by permission.

TABLE 2.4   Force Distribution among Hand Phalanges and Grasps

	Power Grasp (N)	Tip Pinch (N)	Pulp Pinch (N)	Key Pinch (N)
Male	400	65	61	109
Female	228	45	43	76

Reprinted by permission from An et al. [1986]. ©Éditions Hermès.

(force standard deviation of 3.32%). The female subject had a smaller force output and less control over it. These results are illustrated in Table 2.5. The small subject population of this study does not provide sufficient data for generalization, a fact acknowledged by the researchers.

Sustained Force Exertion. It is important to remember that humans can exert maximum force only for short periods of time, before the onset of fatigue. Muscle fatigue in turn adversely affects both sensing and motor control, and eventually leads

TABLE 2.5   Average Maximum Controllable Force in the Arm

Joint	Subjects		
	Female	Male #1	Male #2
PIP	16.5 N (3.99)	41.9 N (4.48)	50.9 N (4.24)
MCP	17.6 N (4.5)	45.1 N (4.47)	42.6 N (4.24)
Wrist	35.5 N (3.12)	64.3 N (5.02)	55.5 N (2.65)
Elbow	49.1 N (3.19)	98.4 N (2.47)	78.0 N (2.79)
Shoulder (side)	68.7 N (3.67)	101.5 N (0.51)	102.3 N (0.46)
Shoulder (front)	87.2 N (2.54)	101.6 N (0.46)	101.7 N (0.86)

Adapted with permission from Tan et al. [1994].
Force given in N. Percentage standard deviation shown in parentheses.

to discomfort and pain. It is therefore necessary to determine what forces can be sustained comfortably by subjects for long durations. These will probably be the forces that haptic interfaces need to produce during task simulations.

Wiker et al. [1989] performed a study of the relationship between fatigue during grasping, as a function of force magnitude, rest duration, and progression of the task. The subjects performed a series of 15-sec isometric pinch grasps, with forces of only 5%, 15%, and 25% of their maximum force or maximum voluntary contraction (MVC). The cyclic grasps were separated by rest intervals of 7.5 or 15 sec. After every 10-minute cyclic-grasp period, subjects were tested for fatigue and discomfort. Results are illustrated in Figure 2.5.

The tests showed a direct correlation between magnitude of discomfort (percentage of discomfort tolerance) and magnitude of pinch force. The higher the pinch force (% of MVC), the higher the discomfort, which also increased linearly as the task progressed. The work vs rest ratio was not important for low forces (below 15% MVC) but was effective in reducing fatigue for pinch forces of 25% of MVC. Wiker et al. state that:

> At higher level of grasp force (i.e. 25% MVC) significant levels of discomfort were encountered in as little as 10 minutes. Discomfort, regardless of initial exertion level, continued to build with progression of the task in a constant manner... The direct mechanical stress could be tolerated at 15% MVC with moderate reports of discomfort after 104 minutes. However, at 25% of MVC a few subjects were near their tolerance limit, and would probably have been unable to complete a two-hour task.
>
> —Wiker et al. [1989]

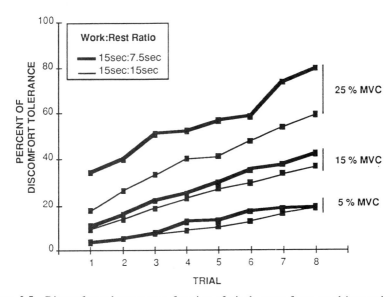

Figure 2.5 Discomfort tolerance as a function of pinch grasp force, work/rest ratio, and progression of the task. Reprinted by permission from Wiker et al. [1989].

Another negative effect of prolonged exertion of high forces was the shift in force perception that occurred above 15% MVC. This led to overexertion of forces when the task required low forces, and underexertion when the task called for large grasping forces. Signs of localized fatigue always preceded the shift in force perception.

2.2.2. Force Tracking Resolution

Force tracking represents the human ability to control contact forces in order to follow a given target force profile. This profile can be constant in time, or it can be time-varying. Experiments on force tracking usually use medium rather than maximum force to prevent subject fatigue.

Srinivasan and Chen [1993] studied the fingertip normal force control using a custom six-axis force sensor interfaced to a 486 personal computer. The experiments used both constant and time-varying target forces (ramp and sinusoids). The constant force was changed in the range 0.25 to 1.5 N in 0.22 N increments. The ramp target force was 0 to 1.5 N, whereas sinusoidal targets had amplitudes of 0.5, 1.0, and 1.5 N. The computer monitor served to display both the target and actual forces, thus providing visual feedback to help the subjects in the tracking task. Some constant force tracking trials were performed blindfolded to quantify the benefit of visual feedback.

These experiments also aimed at determining the specific roles played by tactile and kinesthetic sensors in contact force control. Therefore, the subjects performed tests under both normal conditions and under local (cutaneous) anesthesia administered to the middle phalanx. Anesthesia blocked tactile feedback and allowed only kinesthetic sensing. Figure 2.6 shows average tracking error rates for constant target forces. When no visual feedback was present, the absolute error rate increased with target magnitude and was between 11% and 15%. When subjects had visual feedback, the error rate was much smaller (as illustrated by curve 1) and did not change with target force magnitude. Finger anesthesia increased tracking error but did not affect the dependence on target force magnitude (curves 2 and 4).

Results on the tracking of time-varying target forces showed average errors increasing versus constant targets, the worst case being the tracking of sinusoidal forces. This was to be expected, however the surprising result was that for each experimental condition, the absolute tracking error did not vary with the target force magnitude. Furthermore, the rate of target force changes did not significantly affect tracking performance for the ramp and for sinusoids of 0.5-N amplitude. Based on their results, Srinivasan and Chen recommend that haptic interfaces have a force resolution of at least 0.01 N in order to take full advantage of human haptic capabilities.

2.2.3. Torque, Compliance, and Viscosity Resolution

Torque Resolution. Another important measure of human motor capabilities involves torque discrimination and control. Torque control involves both force and position sensing; therefore, errors are expected to be larger than those for force control alone. Jandura and Srinivasan [1994] studied the sensing and control of torques

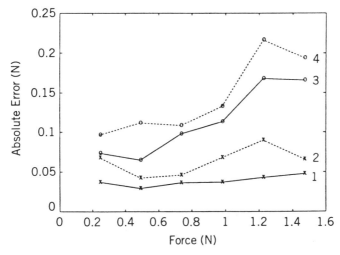

Figure 2.6 Absolute tracking error as a function of constant target force: (1) Normal fingerpad and visual feedback; (2) anesthetized finger and visual feedback; (3) normal fingerpad and no visual feedback; (4) anesthetized finger and no visual feedback. Reprinted by permission of the ASME from Srinivasan and Chen, [1993].

applied during pinch grasping (between thumb and index fingers). Their experiments used three subjects that applied torques on an "instrumented screwdriver" apparatus illustrated in Figure 2.7.

Subjects placed their fingers on a very smooth semicylindrical handle that was mounted coaxial with a torque sensor. Resistance to the handle motion was generated by an electrically controlled magnetic particle brake. An optical (noncontact) encoder installed on the same axis measured the handle position in real time. Data acquisition and control was done with a 486 PC through a pair of analog/digital/analog (A/D/A) boards.

The study was divided into two parts, namely a torque-discrimination test and a torque-control test. Both tests were done without any visual feedback. During torque discrimination, subjects turned the handle clockwise from 0 to 180° against constant resistive torque applied by the break. Subjects were asked to distinguish between a reference torque τ_0 of 60 mN-m, or a larger torque $\tau_o + \Delta\tau$. Here the increment $\Delta\tau$ represented 5%, 10%, 20%, 30%, and 50% of the reference torque. Results showed a torque JND of 12.7%, a value that is larger than previously presented force JND results.

During torque-control experiments subjects were asked to maintain constant angular velocity while turning the shaft clockwise 180° against constant torque. The torque was again changed for various trials as $\tau_o + \Delta\tau$. Under these conditions, the subject's ability to maintain a constant speed (equivalent to constant torque) was expressed by the standard deviation of the angular velocity. As seen from Table 2.6, there was no noticeable influence of resistive torque levels (60–90 mN-m) on torque-control performance. Over all trials, the standard deviation of angular velocity

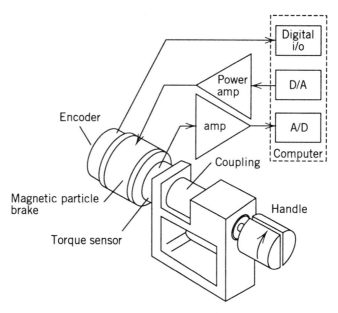

Figure 2.7 Block diagram of the "instrumented screwdriver" used for pinch torque control studies. Reprinted by permission of the ASME from Jandura and Srinivasan [1994].

TABLE 2.6 Pinch Torque-Control Measurements Using the "Instrumented Screwdriver"

Subject		Angular Velocity	Standard deviation, %
DSL	A	257.9 ± 43.7	17.4
	B	297 ± 38.5	17.6
JGD	A	293.3 ± 60.4	11.6
	B	483.2 ± 99.7	12.8
JG	A	411.71 ± 116.9	12.0
	B	586.4 ± 97.6	14.2

Source: Adapted from Jandura and Srinivasan [1994]. Reprinted by permission of the ASME.
A: Resistive torque of 60 mN-m.
B: Resistive torque of 90 mN-m.

was in the 9% to 17.6% range, with 10% to 14% being typical. Thus torque-control performance was similar to that measured for torque discrimination (expressed by %JND).

Compliance Resolution. Another variable that is important for designing the human–computer interface is the ability to judge compliance (or softness) of manipulated real or virtual objects. Compliance information is critical in many daily tasks. Tan et al. [1992] have used the sensorized apparatus shown in Figure 2.8 to study compliance discrimination of the two-finger grasp.

The experimental device consists of two parallel plates, one of which could move along a track perpendicular to the plates. The subjects grasped the two plates between the thumb and forefinger, squeezing the movable plate with the thumb. Position, velocity, and force transducers mounted on the plates were sampled by a PC using a digital signal processing (DSP) and A/D boards. Resistive force was applied on the movable plate through a power amplifier and a direct current (dc) linear actuator. The tests (which involved thousand of trials) used the single-interval forced-choice methodology similar to that used for the linear discrimination test described previously.

By squeezing the plates, subjects had to decide between randomly presented reference compliance C_0 and reference plus increment $C_0 + \Delta C$. The force F felt when squeezing a compliant object is inversely proportional with its compliance C ($F = d/C$). Squeezing a sponge requires less effort than necessary when squeezing

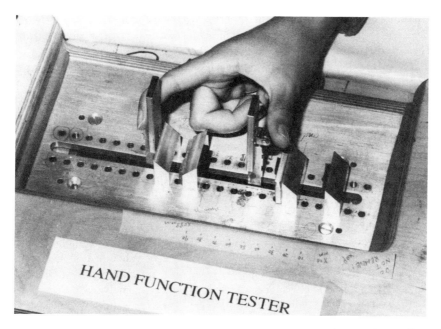

Figure 2.8 Electromechanical apparatus used to measure manual force and compliance resolution. Reprinted by permission of the ASME from Tan et al. [1992].

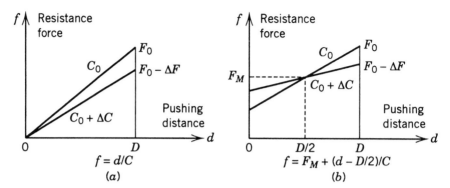

Figure 2.9 Force–distance profile for compliance discrimination tests (a) with work clues; (b) without work clues. Reprinted by permission of the ASME from Tan et al. [1993].

a less compliant tennis ball. Therefore, the slope of the force F for reference compliance C_0 is higher than the slope corresponding to increased compliance $C_0 + \Delta C$, as shown in Figure 2.9a.

When the total pushing distance D was kept constant during trials, the measured compliance JND was on average 8%. This is on the same order of magnitude with force JND presented earlier in this chapter. Previous results for the forearm showed a much larger compliance JND (23%) [Jones and Hunter, 1992]. Subsequent tests used a roving D to prevent subjects from discriminating compliance by merely discriminating the final force sensed during maximum squeeze. Using a roving D had a strong degrading effect such that the average compliance JND jumped to 22%. These results are illustrated in Figure 2.10 [Tan et al., 1992].

Researchers hypothesized that subjects based their compliance discrimination on the amount of work (force times displacement) performed when squeezing the plates. To verify this work hypothesis, Tan et al. [1993] repeated their 1992 tests, but using the force–distance profile shown in Figure 2.9b. It can easily be seen that the area under both curves is the same for compliances C_0 and $C_0 + \Delta C$. This area is in fact the work performed by subjects during squeezing. The final-force cue was also minimized by increasing the midpoint force F_M. Results showed that the compliance JND increased monotonically with F_M for a given (fixed) reference compliance C_0 and pushing distance D. When F_M and D were fixed, the compliance JND increased monotonically with C_0. Finally, for fixed C_0 and F_M, the compliance JND decreased monotonically with the pushing distance D. As can be seen in Figure 2.11 [Tan et al., 1993], the equal-work–force-displacement profile produced compliance JNDs between 15% and 99%! This represents a much larger value than the average 8% compliance JND measured when the work and force cues were present [Tan et al., 1992]. These results tend to validate the work hypothesis, namely that the compliance discrimination relies heavily on total work done during squeezing, as well as the final force value.

The above tests simulated a compliant object with a rigid surface (from the metal plates used in the experiments). Compliance perception is also influenced by the

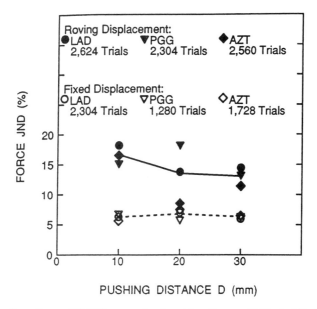

Figure 2.10   Compliance JND(%) versus fixed pushing distance D (dashed line) and roving D (solid line). Reprinted by permission of the ASME from Tan et al. [1992].

deformation of the surface of the squeezed object, as well as the deformation of the fingertip flesh. Srinivasan and LaMotte [1994] studied the perception of softness (a subjective measure of object compliance) looking at the roles played by cutaneous and kinesthetic receptors. Specifically, they wanted to know if the SA-I receptor sensitivity to skin curvature plays a major role in compliance discrimination.

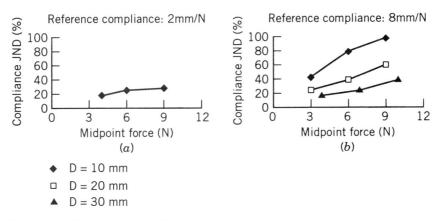

Figure 2.11   Compliance JND(%) versus midpoint force F_M, reference compliance C_0 and pushing distance D (equal-work–force-displacement profile). Reprinted by permission of the ASME from Tan et al. [1993].

The degree of fingertip deformation depends not only on the shape and compliance of the grasped object but also on the compliance (or stiffness) of the finger subcutaneous tissue. Srinivasan and Dandekar [1995] looked at various models of the fingertip compliance (from "semi-infinite plane," to "cylinder" and "cube"). They found that the best approximation of the fingertip deformation under indentation corresponds to that of a membrane enclosing an incompressible liquid (the so-called "waterbed model") [Srinivasan and Dandekar, 1995].

The researchers indented the fingertip skin with several rubber specimens and looked at the temporal variation of the corresponding sensorial coding. Tests showed that during normal conditions (with both cutaneous and kinesthetic cues) compliance perception was better when the compliant object had deformable (rather than rigid) surfaces. Discriminability was higher for higher forces.

When the object has deformable surface, the skin curvature (sensed by the SA-I receptors) depends on the object compliance and applied force. For a given force, it depends only on object compliance so that tactile information is able to encode softness. This is not the case for rigid surfaces, which set the fingertip skin curvature regardless of applied forces. Srinivasan and LaMotte [1994] state that:

> ... for compliant objects with rigid surfaces, the spatial distribution of a given force within the contact region, and hence the deformation of the fingerpad under that force are independent of object compliance. Therefore, tactile information alone is insufficient to determine object compliance; both tactile and kinesthetic information are necessary to discriminate the compliance of objects with rigid surfaces, which is likely to be based on purely temporal information.
>
> —Srinivasan and LaMotte [1994]

Tests were also performed with anesthetized fingers, when only kinesthetic information was available. Results showed that under these conditions subjects were unable to judge the softness of objects with deformable surfaces. Conversely, when the finger was fixed (passive touch), tactile information alone was sufficient to discriminate softness of an object with deformable surfaces. Later tests did confirm a strong correlation between the neural discharge rate of SA-I receptors and the degree of curvature during skin deformation under probe contact [Dandekar and Srinivasan, 1994].

Viscosity Resolution. Whereas compliance represents displacement/force, viscosity is obtained by dividing the applied force by the resulting velocity. The higher the force is for a given velocity, the higher is the perceived viscosity of the manipulated object.

Jones and Hunter [1992] studied the forearm sensitivity to stimulus stiffness (the inverse of compliance) and viscosity. Their experiments used two high-performance electromagnetic linear motors controlled by an IBM R6000 computer. The experimental protocol was a contralateral-limb matching procedure in which subjects had to adjust the amplitude of a matching stimulus until it was perceived to be the same as a reference stimulus. The matching viscosity was applied by one motor to one arm, and the reference viscosity was applied to the other arm. The study used eleven subjects who received stimuli of amplitudes ranging from 2 N-sec/m to 1,024 N-sec/m. Results showed that the subjects were very accurate in matching the two viscosities. However, the standard deviation of the matching viscosities was large (34%). At small viscosities, the standard deviation (or differential threshold) was even larger (83% for a reference viscosity of 2 N-sec/m). Jones and Hunter [1992] speculate that this loss of perceptual resolution is due to the subjects integration of both force *and* velocity cues in order to judge viscosity:

> These findings clearly indicate that in any situation in which subjects must respond to changes in stiffness or viscosity of a mechanical system connected to their limbs (e.g. in a master–slave system), their performance will be considerably inferior to that seen when changes in force or movement are being discriminated.
>
> —Jones and Hunter [1992]

2.2.4. Finger Mechanical Impedance

The relationship between the applied force and displacement of the hand is given by its impedance. The human arm–hand impedance plays a key role in the sensitivity and stability of human–machine interfaces. Hogan [1989] hypothesized that the impedance of the hand is indistinguishable from that of a "passive" system (even though the arm is clearly an active system). Moreover, the parameter adaptation in humans requires a significantly longer time than the sensorimotor response time. Hogan's initial experiments showed a response time for voluntarily changing the hand and arm impedance of approximately 1 sec and a natural frequency of a few Hz.

Hajian and Howe [1994] recently looked at the passive impedance of fingers. Their study was motivated by the need to better-model the haptic interfaces that they had developed to provide force feedback to the fingers. The researchers estimated that the relationship between transient forces $f(t)$ applied on the fingertip and the resultant displacements $x(t)$ is given by Eq. (2.1)

$$m\ddot{x}(t) + b\dot{x}(t) + kx(t) = f(t) \tag{2.1}$$

where m represents the equivalent finger mass (kg), b is the viscous damping of the MCP joint (N-sec/m), and k is the joint stiffness (N/m). The experimental apparatus used in the above study is illustrated in Figure 2.12.

It consists of a pneumatic piston with a small platform on which subjects placed their extended forefinger. The wrist was resting on an arm support while a handle was grasped to provide a mechanical ground. The piston displacement was only 5 mm, and took less than 50 msec to complete. This was necessary to prevent voluntary muscle reflex contraction which would increase the stiffness k. The fingertip force and acceleration were measured by a force sensor and an accelerometer installed on the moving platform. These sensors were in turn sampled by a computer through an A/D board.

A total of five subjects participated in the experiment. They had to press against the mobile platform past a randomly changed force threshold (in the range of 2 to 20 N). Once the threshold was exceeded, the piston was pressurized and pushed the finger

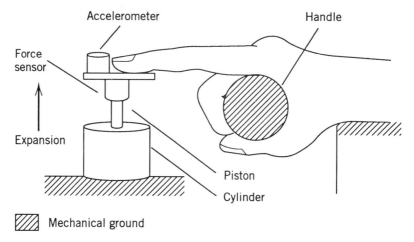

Figure 2.12 Experimental apparatus used in finger mechanical impedance evaluation. Reprinted by permission of the ASME from Hajian and Howe [1994].

upward (extension) while the computer read forces and accelerations. Subsequently, the three impedance parameters m, d, and k were obtained through fitting the least-squares data to the differential equation above. These parameters varied as a function of the applied fingertip force (see Figure 2.13).

Results showed that the equivalent mass remained almost unchanged with the applied force, whereas the damping and stiffness increased linearly. Over all subjects and all force thresholds the variations were 3.5 to 8.7 g for the mass, 4.02 to 7.40 N-sec/m for damping and 255 to 1,225 N/m for stiffness. Also of interest was the damping ratio $\xi = (b/2\sqrt{mk})$ which was approximately 1.4. This ratio was almost constant over the applied force range and is significantly larger than previous results obtained for the elbow. The overdamped ξ may be explained by the longer tendons actuating the MCP joint, with corresponding muscles located in the forearm. Further research is needed to investigate the impedance variation versus other parameters (besides fingertip force) such as joint angle or level of cocontraction of antagonist muscles.

2.3. SENSING AND CONTROL BANDWIDTH

We cannot end our discussion of human haptics without mentioning the very important sensing and motor-control bandwidth. Here sensing bandwidth refers to the frequency with which tactile, kinesthetic (or proprioceptive) stimuli are sensed, and control bandwidth refers to the rapidity with which humans can respond. The sensing and control loops are asymetric, meaning that input (or sensing) bandwidth is much larger than output (or control) bandwidth. We sense tactile and kinesthetic stimuli much faster than we can respond to them.

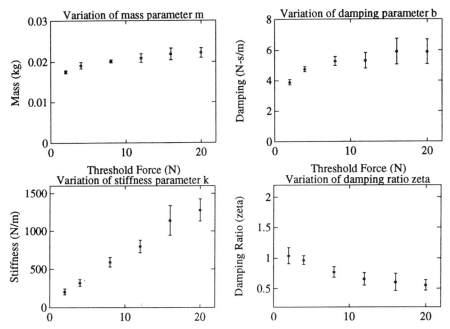

Figure 2.13   Mean and standard deviation of the fingertip mass, damping, stiffness, and damping ratio versus applied forces (for one subject). Reprinted by permission of the ASME from Hajian and Howe [1994].

In his review paper, Shimoga [1992] showed that the output loop, which represents the ability of the hand and fingers to exert forces, has a 5- to 10-Hz bandwidth. By comparison, the kinesthetic/proprioceptive sensing has a bandwidth of 20 to 30 Hz, and tactile sensing has 0- to 400-Hz bandwidth. Very fine feature recognition, such as surface textures with small rugosities, requires a much higher bandwidth (up to 5,000 to 10,000 Hz). Figure 2.14 summarizes the sensing-and-control bandwidth characteristics of the human finger [Shimoga, 1992].

2.4. DESIGN IMPLICATIONS

At the beginning of this chapter, we stated that human (sensing and control) characteristics have to serve as the basis for good haptic interface design. Our discussion outlined key quantitative characteristics such as maximum and sustained force exertion, tactile and proprioceptive sensitivity, control and sensing bandwidth, and so on. However, we do not attempt to extrapolate these parameters into an ideal haptic interface, because we view this endeavor as both impractical and risky.

The spectrum of tasks to be simulated calls for a large variety of interface types, so that a "boiler plate" model will not be adequate. Suffice to say that the whole area of haptic interfaces for VR is (still) new, and surely new interface types will

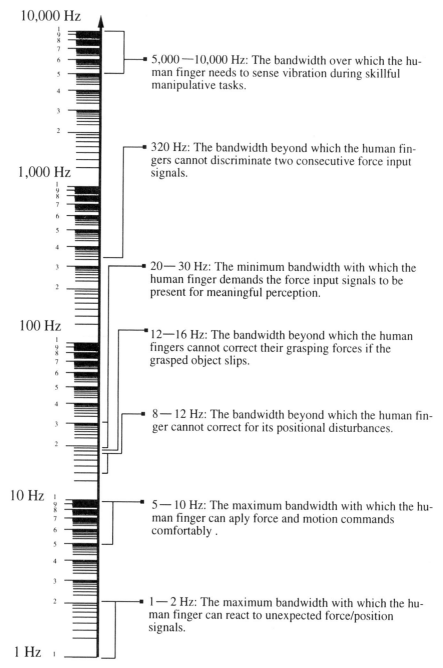

Figure 2.14 Human finger sensing and control bandwidth. Adapted from Shimoga [1992]. © Éditions Hermès. Reprinted by permission.

be developed. Furthermore, it is risky to base one's recommendation on the few studies that exist, especially when the results have been obtained using dissimilar experimental setups and methods and a small number of subjects.

Several aspects of sensing and control have competing requirements. Force exertion is a case in point; large feedback forces are required for simulating hard contact. This conflicts with the need to minimize user fatigue and therefore provide only small feedback forces. Another example is vibrotactile arrays used for fingertip tactile feedback. Here the need for good spatial resolution calls for inter-pin distances as small as the two-point limen, whereas lower vibration amplitudes require large sensitivity, which in turn means large contact areas. One cannot have both very large vibrator pins (large contact area) and high array density (small inter-pin distances) at the same time.

Simulation of hard contact also requires a stiff interface with very small compliance. This in turn requires a stiff mechanical interface design and stiff actuator servocontrol. Stiff mechanical design means using metal (which may be heavy) and tight tolerances (which may induce dead friction). A heavy master will tire the user easily, and friction may mask the smaller interaction forces. Servo-stiffness in turn requires sufficiently powerful actuators (which tend to be heavy) and a high control bandwidth. This, however, should not be confused with the overall interface bandwidth, which is determined by the ability of the computer to calculate forces in real time, plus a fast communication line (to have low latencies). Rosenberg [1995] recommends latencies as low as 1 msec. However, this seems to be too stringent in view of the recognized VR latencies, which can be as large as 100 msec [Burdea and Coiffet, 1994].

We showed before that the kinesthetic/proprioceptive input bandwidth is in the range of 20 to 30 Hz. Rosenberg [1995] recommends a force feedback bandwidth of at least 50 Hz. However studies by Howe and Kontarinis [1992] showed that even 8 Hz is sufficient. No significant advantages were observed when the force feedback bandwidth was increased to 32 Hz. Richard et al. [1996] used a 15-Hz force feedback loop with good results.

The joint space and Cartesian position resolution of the interface has to be superior to the corresponding human position resolution, to prevent sensing round-off errors. The best joint JND is the shoulder ($0.8°$) [Tan et al., 1994], and the best Cartesian JND was found to be 1 mm [Tan et al., 1992]. Hasser [1995a] suggests a four-times better resolution for the interface. This would require a 0.2 to $0.5°$ rotational resolution and 0.25-mm end-tip position resolution, similar to the recommendation made by Rosenberg [1995]. A summary of the tactile/force feedback interface requirements as seen by Ellis [1995] is given in Figure 2.15.

2.5. CONCLUSIONS

This chapter discussed the various aspects of human tactile, thermal, and proprioceptive/kinesthetic sensing. Subsequently we presented the human sensory–motor con-

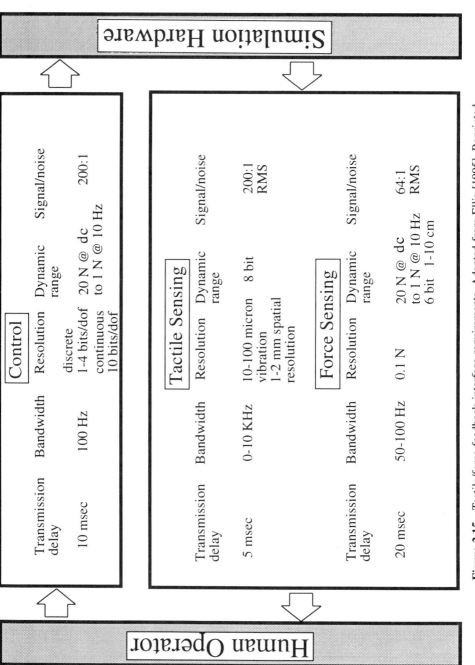

Figure 2.15 Tactile/force feedback interface requirements. Adapted from Ellis [1995]. Reprinted

trol in terms of maximum and sustained force exertion, force tracking resolution, torque-compliance-viscosity resolution, and the finger mechanical impedance. The human sensory–motor system is asymetrical, so that the tactile sensing bandwidth is (much) larger than the force output bandwidth. Optimal haptic interface designs have to take into account all the above characteristics in order to assure an efficient, comfortable, and realistic simulation.

CHAPTER 3

ACTUATORS

Haptic interfaces incorporate actuators that are used to feed back force or tactile sensations to the user. Without actuators, the interface can only function as an input device to the computer. The haptic feedback loop is broken, and the simulation realism suffers. We chose, therefore, to dedicate this chapter to the various classical actuator technologies used today, from electrical motors to hydraulic pistons and pneumatic muscles. Other technologies such as magnetostrictive [Brimhall and Hasser, 1994] and piezoelectric motors [NASA, 1994], polymeric gels [Brock, 1991; Shahinpoor, 1994], and metal hydrades [Shimizu et al., 1994], show promise for use in tomorrow's haptic interfaces. These novel actuators are discussed in the last chapter of this book.

The various actuator types mentioned here can be compared based on their functionality, control, and general performance parameters such as maximum force (or torque) output, sustained force or torque, power consumption, and bandwidth. There are, however, a number of *specific* performance parameters related to the actuator's integration in a haptic interface. Portable hand masters should be light to minimize fatigue but also powerful enough to apply significant forces. As discussed in the previous chapter, these forces should not be larger than 25% of maximum force-exertion capability to minimize user fatigue. The PHANToM Master [Massie and Salisbury, 1994], one of the more recent commercial haptic interfaces, produces realistic simulations with only 8.5 N (roughly 20% of hand maximum exertion force) [Sutter et al. 1989]. Thus haptic actuators need to maximize their *power-to-mass ratio* to be both powerful and light.

The large number of degrees of freedom of the hand requires a correspondingly large number of actuators in the interface. If these actuators are located at the finger joints, the system is simpler, cheaper, and exhibits better dynamics (since transmissions are eliminated). This means that only very compact actuators with large *power-to-volume ratios* should be used. Brimhall and Hasser [1994] calculated that the average joint colocated actuator should have approximately 4 to 10 W of power, which would correspond to a power-to-volume ratio of 0.3 to 0.8 W/cm^3. Their estimate is based on a sustained exertion at 50% of maximum force, which seems too high. However, Brimhall and Hasser do not account for transmission losses, which reduce the force actually felt by the user.

Ideally, the interface should be transparent, which means that no forces should be exerted on the user's hand (or other parts of the body) when no physical interactions exist in the VR simulation. That means that the actuators should be able to follow the user's hand motion rapidly, and without opposition, a quality called *backdrivability*. The user will feel any friction forces present in the actuator and gears or transmissions incorporated in the interface. Therefore, backdrivability requires minimal static friction and low actuator inertia. An additional negative effect of friction is the possible masking of small feedback forces, calculated by the computer but never felt by the user. The ratio of maximum actuator output versus its friction defines its *dynamic range*. High simulation fidelity requires actuators with high dynamic range and high bandwidth.

Finally, haptic feedback actuators are placed in close proximity to the user, therefore their intrinsic safety becomes a concern. This would preclude high pressure fluids, high voltages, or high currents from being used. Additional harm to the user can come from excessive noise, therefore noisy actuators should also be avoided.

This chapter contains a detailed description of "classical" actuator technology (electrical, hydraulic, or pneumatic). These actuators are available commercially today and have been extensively studied and tested for many years. They satisfy some, but not all, of the specific requirements outlined above for integration in haptic interfaces. Brimhall and Hasser [1994] state that

> The design of a dextrous force-reflecting hand master presents daunting challenges. . . . Power densities required from the actuators are not readily attainable with the available technology, and may be impossible without significant innovations. Furthermore, the sensitivity of the human hand and the demanding requirements of dextrous manipulation call for a high fidelity interface. . . The quality of actuation systems has been recognized as the bottleneck of control in dextrous telemanipulation where force feedback is required.
> —Brimhall and Hasser [1994]

The chapter ends with a comparative discussion of various actuators based on the previously mentioned performance parameters. This discussion uses as a "standard" for comparison the very efficient human muscle actuator (an approach taken also by Hollerbach et al. [1992]).

3.1. ELECTRICAL ACTUATORS

By far, the haptic actuators most used today are electrical direct-current (dc) motors. They are easy to install (no complex piping, wiring, or pump rooms needed), clean (no oil leaks), quiet (no noise-generating oscillations), and easy to control (solid-state electronics). Other types of electrical actuators discussed here are magnetic particle brakes and shape-memory metal (SMM) actuators.

3.1.1. Direct-Current Motors

Direct-current (dc) rotary motors consist of a fixed stator and a rotating rotor. The mechanical power that moves the rotor is due to the interaction between two (time-varying) magnetic fields. As shown in Figure 3.1 [Rizzoni, 1993], the magnetic field of the stator is produced by current through its "field winding" coils. The second magnetic field is produced by currents through conductors embedded in the cylindrical rotor, called *armature winding*. The ends of the armature winding are connected to a commutator (not shown) which assures electrical contact with the dc power supply through two sliding contacts called *brushes*.

Alternately, the field winding may be replaced by a permanent magnet (PM) for PM dc motors. These are of interest to haptic interface design, because they are smaller, lighter, and easier to control than wound motors of the same power rating. Conversely, the motor may have a PM instead of the armature winding, which obviates the need for brushes and commutators. Such motors are called *brushless* dc motors. It is not possible to have permanent magnets for both stator *and* rotor, because the corresponding magnetic fields would not be time-varying (resulting in a frozen rotor).

Brushed Direct-Current Motors. Motors that have armature winding can be further classified according to their field winding electrical connection, as shown in

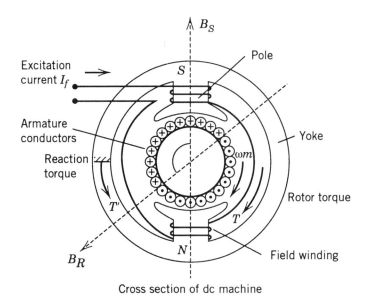

Cross section of dc machine

Figure 3.1   Cross section of a brushed dc motor. Reprinted from Rizzoni, *Principles and Applications of Electrical Engineering,* 1993, by permission of Richard D. Irwin.

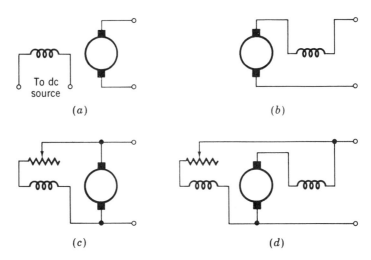

Figure 3.2 Field-circuit connections of dc motors: (a) separate excitation, (b) series, (c) shunt, (d) compound. Reprinted with permission from Fitzgerald et al., 1983, *Electric Machinery*, The McGraw-Hill Companies.

Figure 3.2. If the field and armature windings are connected to separate dc voltages, the motor is separately excited. A *series-connected* motor has the two windings connected in series, whereas a parallel connection corresponds to a *shunt* motor. This circuitry uses a variable resistor to change the voltage on the field winding. Finally, a *compound* motor has a combination of both series and parallel winding connections.

The field's magnetic flux $\phi(t)$ is proportional to the field current $i_f(t)$ as in

$$\phi(t) = k_f i_f(t) \tag{3.1}$$

where k_f is a proportionality coefficient. The motor torque τ_m is proportional to the field magnetic flux as well as to the armature current $i_a(t)$. Thus

$$\tau_m = k_m \phi(t) i_a(t) \tag{3.2}$$

$$\tau_m = k_m k_f i_f(t) i_a(t) \tag{3.3}$$

For series dc motors, the field current $i_f(t)$ is equal to the armature current $i_a(t)$. Thus Eq. (3.3) becomes

$$\tau_m = k_s i^2(t) \tag{3.4}$$

where k_s is called the *torque constant* of the motor. The above equations show that it is possible to control the torque τ_m produced by the motor by controlling the current through its windings. In general, the torque is also dependent on the rotational velocity $\omega_m(t)$, decreasing from zero velocity (or *stall torque*) to minimum torque at maximum rated velocity. Compared to other brushed dc motors, those that are series wound have very high starting torques and are useful in low-speed, high-torque applications (such as haptic interfaces).

Not all the electrical power absorbed by the motor is delivered as mechanical power to the load (in our case the haptic interface mechanical structure). The torque applied at the motor shaft τ_{load} is smaller than τ_m due to rotor inertia J_m and viscous damping b_m [Stadler, 1995]. Therefore τ_{load} is given by

$$\tau_{load} = \tau_m - J_m \frac{d\omega_m}{dt} - b_m \omega_m \tag{3.5}$$

Fasse et al. [1994] studied the possibility of producing a variable-impedance electromechanical actuator by connecting all stator windings and one rotor winding to external current sources. The remaining rotor windings were short-circuited. Results showed that it was possible to change the shaft stiffness and damping by changing the currents through the stator and rotor. They showed that such an actuator is posturally stable, without requiring feedback stabilization. Such an actuator is well behaved during impact with stiff environments (a difficult control problem), and can be used in low-bandwidth applications. According to Fasse et al., an additional advantage of postural stability is a safer system. They state that:

> A variable impedance actuated system is less susceptible to failures of sensory and control systems. For example, in the event of the crash of the computer control system the steering signals will be constant. A variable impedance actuator would respond by going into a sort of *rigor mortis*, that is, by assuming a stable posture. A DC servomotor would respond by generating a constant torque. A flow-controlled hydraulic actuator would move at constant velocity. The consequences of these responses depend on the application and other safety precautions, but for many applications, assuming a stable posture is a "safe" response.
>
> —Fasse et al. [1994]

Direct-current motors with miniature PM are also of interest because of their compactness and lightness. For such motors the torque-to-current relationship is simpler; because there is no field current

$$\tau_{mPM} = k_{sPM} i_a(t) \tag{3.6}$$

where k_{sPM} is the PM motor torque constant. The motor torque drops with increased speed, similar to the motors with field winding. It can be shown [Rizzoni, 1993] that there is a linear relationship between the torque of a PM dc motor and its velocity, as in

$$\tau_{mPM} = \frac{V_s}{R_a} k_{sPM} - \frac{\omega_m}{R_a} k_{sPM} k_{aPM} \tag{3.7}$$

where V_s is the voltage applied on the armature winding and R_a is the winding electrical resistance. The maximum torque corresponds to zero velocity (no negative term), so that the stall torque of a PM dc motor is

$$\tau_{mPM-stall} = \frac{V_s}{R_a} k_{sPM} \qquad (3.8)$$

This equation shows that we can increase the stall torque by increasing the voltage V_s, taking care not to overheat the motor. Excessive voltages (or temperatures) can demagnetize the stator, and render the motor useless. The torque constant k_s does depend on temperature due to the increase in winding electrical resistance with temperature. The thermal conductance R_{therm} represents the number of watts dissipated per degree Centigrade, and the torque constant k_s indicates how much torque is produced per dissipated watt. Therefore, Hollerbach et al. [1992] chose $\frac{k_s}{\sqrt{R_{therm}}}$ as a parameter that indicates how much torque can be continuously sustained for a given winding temperature.

An example of a miniature PM dc motor is the MicroMo Model 1331-012S, whose torque-to-velocity characteristic is shown in Figure 3.3 [MicroMo. Electronics Inc., 1995]. This motor uses a stator made of samarium cobalt, which reduces its external diameter to only 1.3 cm. Without gears, its length is 3.12 cm, its mass is (only) 20 grams (0.71 oz), and its volume 4.14 cm^3. Its power of 2 W continuously (2.7 W at peak) corresponds to a power-to-volume ratio of 0.48 W/cm^3 continuously (0.65

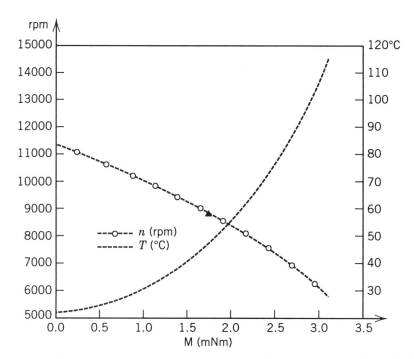

Figure 3.3 Torque and velocity characteristic of the MicroMo Model 1331-012S PM dc motor. Courtesy of MicroMo Electronics Inc.

W/cm^3 at peak). Unfortunately, the high motor velocity (up to 12,000 rotations per min or rpm) requires a gear transmission. A 43:1 gearhead increases the overall actuator package volume to 7.2 cm^3, and its mass is increased to 55 grams. Thus the power-to-volume ratio is reduced to 0.29 W/cm^3 continuously (0.38 W/cm^3 at peak), whereas the power-to-mass ratio drops to 36 W/kg continuously (49 W/kg at peak). This power density is at the lower limit of the interval specified by Hasser [1995a] for joint colocated actuators. The geared MicroMo motor has a continuous torque-to-mass ratio of 5.5 N-m/kg and a density of approximately 7,600 kg/m^3. Hollerbach et al. [1992] surveyed geared motors with densities of 3,000 to 5,000 kg/m^3 and found that the achievable torque-to-mass ratio was less than 6 N-m/kg. Table 3.1 summarizes the characteristics of the MicroMo PM dc motor as discussed above.

Brushless dc Motors. Brushless dc motors consist of coils in the stator and a rare earth (solarium cobalt) permanent magnet in the rotor. A position sensor on the rotor is read by the motor controller, which delivers current to the appropriate stator winding as a function of the rotor position and generates the motor torque. The overall motor size is smaller than that of corresponding brushed motors since the rotor has no windings. This results in lower motor inertia J_m and improved dynamic response. Heat is also better dissipated. The disadvantage when compared with brushed dc motors is the additional position sensor and complex controller required to produce a rotating magnetic field. Thus brushless dc motors tend to be more expensive. Table 3.2 [Moog Inc., 1984] compares brushed and brushless dc motors.

One example of miniature brushless dc motors is the artificial muscle actuator AM-20 [Wittenstein Motion Control GmbH, 1993]. This actuator was developed for

TABLE 3.1 Performance Specifications for the MicroMo 1331-012S Motor

Specification	Ungeared		Geared	
	Continuous	**Peak**	**Continuous**	**Peak**
Power/volume (W/cm^3)	0.48	0.65	0.29	0.38
Power/mass (W/kg)	99	134	36	49
Stall torque (N-m)	0.0025	0.0089	0.30	0.45
Torque/mass (N-m/kg)	0.12	0.44	5.5	8.2

Adapted from Hasser [1995a]. Reprinted by permission.

TABLE 3.2   Comparison of Brush and Brushless dc Motors

	Brush Motor	Brushless Motor
Advantages	Lower cost Simpler electronics Smaller controller	Smaller motor Improved dynamics Better heat dissipation
Disadvantages	EMG interference Brush wear (shorter life) Smaller maximum speed Poorer dynamic response	Electronic commutation required Position sensor required higher cost

Source: Adapted from Moog Inc. [1984]. Reprinted by permission.

the German Aerospace Research Establishment (DLR) and had to be both compact and powerful. It uses a three-winding stator and a ball-screw arrangement to produce a linear motion with a speed up to 30 mm/sec. Although the actuator volume is small (22.1 cm^3), its maximum force (tension) is an impressive 300 N, and its power is 9 W. This corresponds to a power density of 0.40 W/cm^3 and a power-to-mass ratio of 90 W/kg (for an actuator mass of 100 grams). These ratios are almost twice those of the geared MicroMo brushed dc motor (as seen in Table 3.1).

A more powerful brushless motor that is useful in single-person motion platforms is the Moog servoactuator Model 17E373 [Moog Inc., 1984] shown in Figure 3.4. A servoactuator is an actuator (electrical, hydraulic, or pneumatic motor) that incorporates sensors to measure its shaft position (and sometimes its velocity or acceleration). The sensor(s) data is then fed back to the actuator controller through a feedback loop and used for improved control.

The 17E373 actuator uses a ball-screw arrangement to produce linear motion, similar to the AM-20 actuator described previously. The maximum shaft speed (no load) is 205 mm/sec (8.1 in./sec). The shaft position is measured by a linear variable differential transformer (LVDT) transducer installed in parallel with the actuator. A tachometer is used to provide minor-loop speed feedback to improve performance. Tests showed that the tachometer feedback more than doubled the positional resolution and "stiffness" of the actuator. The servomotor maximum force (at stall) is 1,777 N (400 lb) and continuous force output is 826 N (186 lb). The actuator mass is 1.2 kg (excluding the controller box) and its peak and continuous power outputs are 186 W (0.25 hp) and 97 W (0.13 hp), respectively. This corresponds to a power density of 155 W/kg at peak and 80.8 W/kg continuously. Again, these power densities are more than double those of the geared MicroMo brushed actuator.

Figure 3.5 [Moog Inc., 1984] illustrates the control diagram of a Moog servoactuator. Operational amplifiers differentiate between the commanded and actual shaft positions (provided by the LVDT) and velocities (measured by the tachometer). This signal is used to drive a pulse-width modulator which energizes the three stator windings. A Hall-effect noncontact sensor measures the rotor shaft position and feeds it back to the pulse-width modulator logic circuitry. In pulse-width modulation, rotor

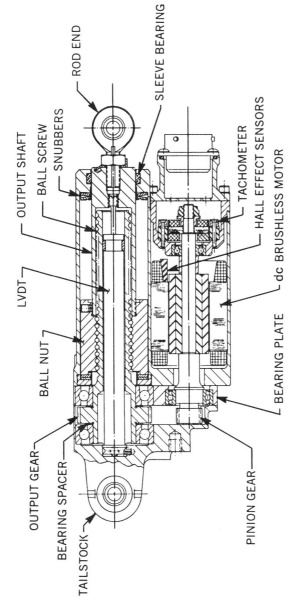

Figure 3.4 Construction of the Moog Model 17E373 servoactuator. Reprinted by permission from Moog Inc. [1984].

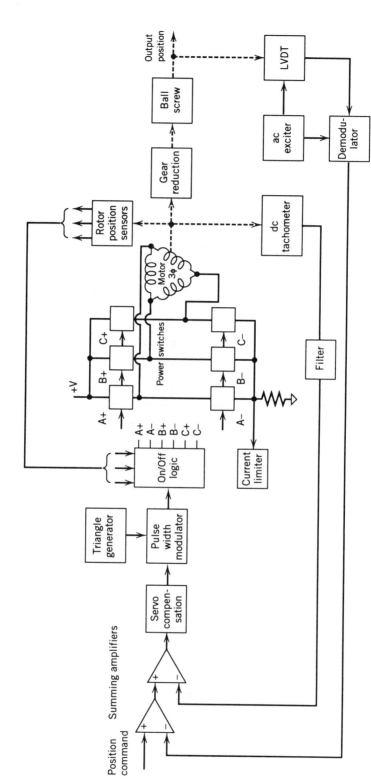

Figure 3.5 Control Diagram of the Moog Model 17E373 Servoactuator. Reprinted by permission from Moog Inc. [1984].

velocity ω_m is proportional with the on/off ratio of the periodic function used for control as in

$$\omega_m \sim \frac{T_{\text{on}}}{T_{\text{on}} + T_{\text{off}}} \qquad (3.9)$$

The sequence in which the power switches are triggered (clockwise or counterclockwise) determines the direction of rotor rotation.

3.1.2. Magnetic Particle Brakes

All the dc motors described above are active elements that apply power to the user. There is, however, a second class of *passive* electrical actuators that absorb, or dissipate, the power generated by the user. These are magnetic particle brakes (MPB) as illustrated in Figure 3.6 [Russo and Tadros, 1992].

The MPB structure consists of an axial shaft and disk enclosed in a chamber containing small iron particles (filings). The surrounding brake housing contains a toroidal coil located in the same plane with the disk. Current through the coil generates a magnetic field perpendicular to the coil and thus to the disk. The iron particles orient themselves along the magnetic field lines and attach themselves to the disk and to the chamber walls. The stronger the current, the more iron particles are attached, resulting in an increased resistance to the rotation of the brake shaft. The relationship between the coil current i_b and the resulting resistive torque τ_b is

$$\tau_b = k_b i_b \qquad (3.10)$$

where k_b is a proportionality constant.

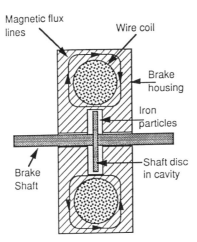

Figure 3.6 Cross section of a magnetic particle brake. Reprinted by permission of the ASME from Russo and Tadros [1992].

The MPB can be used to simulate dissipative devices but not energy-storing elements. The power into the brake is always positive:

$$P_{in} = \tau_b \omega_b > 0 \qquad (3.11)$$

where ω_b is the shaft velocity.

It is not possible with a simple MPB to simulate a spring decompression, since, unlike the spring, the brake does not accumulate energy. The simplest element to simulate using a brake is a viscous damper, with

$$\tau_b = k_b k_v \omega_b \qquad (3.12)$$

where k_v is the velocity feedback gain. Compressing a spring or moving an inertial element can be simulated by torques as

$$\tau_b = k_b k_p \theta P(\omega_b) \qquad (3.13)$$

$$\tau_b = k_b k_a \dot{\omega}_b P(\omega_b) P(\dot{\omega}_b) \qquad (3.14)$$

where k_p and k_a are, respectively, the position and acceleration feedback gains and $(\dot{\omega}_b)$ is the shaft acceleration. The one-directional characteristic of the brake is expressed by the coefficients $P(\omega_b)$ and $P(\dot{\omega}_b)$ as

$$P(x) = 0 \text{ for } x \le 0 \text{ and } P(x) = 1 \text{ for } x > 0 \qquad (3.15)$$

Probably the best use of MPBs are in simulating contact with hard objects (such as walls). An electrical motor simulates a hard wall with a very stiff spring model. The resulting high forces combined with system inertia can (and usually do) result in contact instabilities. The MPB can give a much "crisper" simulation of the hard contact as illustrated by the force versus position experimental graphs shown in Figure 3.7 [Russo and Tadros, 1992].

Unfortunately, MPBs have their drawbacks. A major problem is magnetic hysteresis, so that, when the power is removed from the brake coil, the iron particles maintain some alignment. Thus the resistive force does not drop to zero once the user moves away from the simulated hard wall. Tadros [1990] used a short voltage pulse to drive the current in the coil in the opposite direction and to free the iron particles. Another solution is to couple a MPB with an electrical motor acting coaxially with the brake. In this way, the simulation of energy-storing elements becomes possible, and contact instabilities are dampened by the MPB.

3.1.3. Shape Memory Metals

Shape memory metals (SMM) such as titanium-nickel (TiNi) are alloys that exhibit the so-called mechanical-memory effect. This is caused by a structural transition between a martensitic phase and a austenitic phase, characterized by higher crystalline

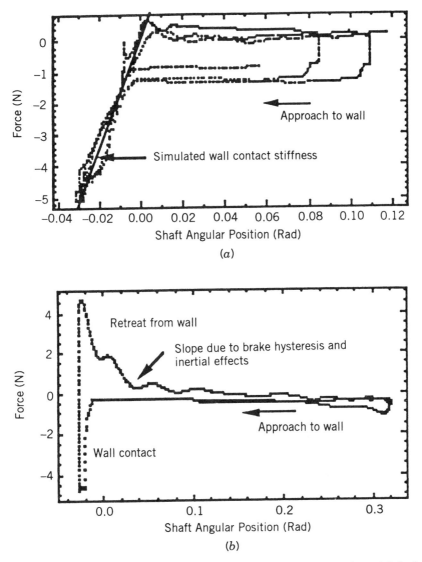

Figure 3.7 Contact simulation using (*a*) electrical motors, and (*b*) magnetic particle brakes. Reprinted by permission of the ASME from Russo and Tadros [1992].

symmetry [Hunter et al., 1993]. This transition starts when the alloy is heated past its austenitic start temperature (A_s) and ends upon reaching the austenitic finish (A_f) temperature. Typically the heating is done by passing a current through the alloy (using the Joule effect). If the alloy is mechanically deformed in its martensitic phase and then heated, it will reform to the memorized austenitic shape, producing large tensile forces.

Once the current is interrupted, the SMM alloy cools and returns to its martensitic phase, in which it can be again deformed by some external action. Cooling takes significantly longer than heating; therefore, it takes longer to return to the martensitic phase than it took to reach the austenitic phase. This longer cooling time in turn limits the bandwidth of SMM actuators with an adverse effect on actuator control and simulation quality.

Typical SMM actuators consist either of a simple wire of very small diameter or of a SMM spring. Unlike previously described actuators, these actuators have no gears or other moving parts. Shape-memory-actuator wires have large forces (stress), but their deformation is small (approximately 6%). Conversely, SMM springs have larger deformations, but generate smaller forces. Overall, SMM actuators have very large power-to-weight ratios, approximately 200 W/kg [Hirose et al., 1989], which is an order of magnitude larger than those of dc motors. Hollerbach et al. [1992] cite power-to-weight ratios for modified titanium-nickel fibers as large as 50 kW/kg! Such power density is significantly larger than for other actuators, as illustrated in Figure 3.8.

Their compactness, lightness, and excellent power-to-weight ratios make SMM actuators useful for haptic interfaces. We first discuss the use of SMM wires and subsequently describe actuators integrating SMM springs.

Shape-memory-actuator wires have been incorporated in tactile feedback arrays placed at the user's fingertip by Johnson [1992]. His tactile actuator, or tactor, consists

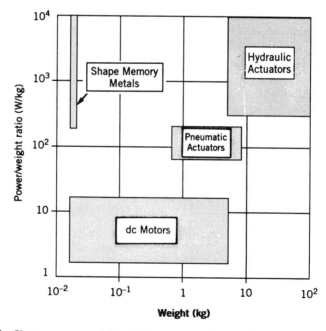

Figure 3.8 Shape memory metal (SMM) power density vs. other actuators. Adapted from Hirose et al. [1989] and Hollerbach et al. [1992]. Reprinted by permission of the MIT Press.

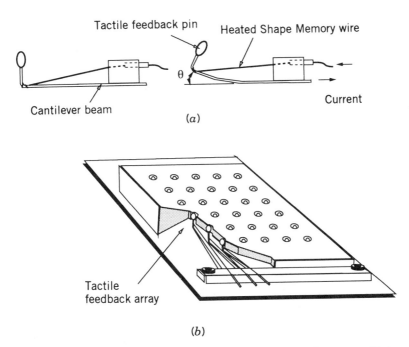

Figure 3.9 Shape memory metal (SMM) tactile stimulator. (*a*) Single actuator. (*b*) Actuator array. Adapted from Johnson [1992]. © Éditions Hermès. Reprinted by permission.

of a beryllium-copper SMM wire connected to a copper cantilever beam, as shown in Figure 3.9. One end of the cantilever beam is fixed to a base plate, whereas the other is bent upward and holds a plastic pin. When a current passes through the tactor, the SMM wire shrinks (shape memory effect) and pulls the plastic pin upward. The pin then protrudes through a hole in the tactile array housing and contacts the user's fingertip. When the current is interrupted, the SMM cools, and the pin is retracted. By temporal switching the same actuator on and off, it is possible to generate vibrations. Switching between several actuators produces spatial tactile patterns felt by the user. Typically the tactors are controlled through pulse-width modulation with a duty cycle of 50% in order to prevent overheating (which can damage the SMM actuator). Commercially available tactile arrays manufactured by Xtensory Inc. have at least 3 × 3 tactors, with other research prototypes reaching densities of 6 × 4 [Kontarinis et al., 1995] and 6 × 5 [Hasser and Weisenberger, 1993]. These actuator densities are still small compared with the fingertip two-point spatial discrimination mentioned in Chapter 2. The SMM array is controlled by a microprocessor-based interface, which stores a database of various tactile patterns. In this way, the host computer running the simulation is relieved of all the low-level array control, and the communication bandwidth requirements are reduced significantly.

From the description at the beginning of this section, it becomes clear that the SMM actuator has a unidirectional characteristic. If bidirectional actuation is desired, then two opposing actuators are needed. Additionally, when longer displacements are required, then springs are preferred to SMM wires. One bidirectional actuator using springs is the ξ-array illustrated in Figure 3.10 [Hirose et al., 1989]. It consists of two sets of springs installed mechanically in parallel and electrically in series. The mechanical parallelism helps increase the actuator force, whereas the series electrical connection increases the overall resistance. There are two advantages in a larger electrical resistance. The first is a faster Joule heating, and thus faster actuator motion (since heat is directly proportional with the SMM resistance). The second advantage is improved SMM servocontrol. During phase change, the SMM electrical resistance varies by as much as 20%. This means that a larger martensitic electrical resistance will produce a larger (absolute) change to the corresponding austenitic resistance. This change can be used as a feedback signal for the actuator control. The ξ-array actuator described above can produce active force feedback at the interface joints. The linear motion of the actuator is then transformed into rotary motion using a circular pulley.

Another actuator using SMM springs is the passive joint brake illustrated in Figure 3.11 [Gharaybeh and Burdea, 1995]. It consists of a titanium–nickel spring that pushes a sliding gear against a matching gear installed coaxially with the joint of an exoskeleton. When the two gears engage, the joint is prevented from rotating in the direction of grasping. Motion in the opposite direction is still possible. Once the brake current is cut, two bias springs retract the sliding gear toward the actuator cover, thus releasing the joint. The back cover of the actuator is metallic having the dual purpose of electrical connector and heat sink.

Gharaybeh [1992] used this SMM brake to block an index joint of an EXOS Dextrous Hand Master [Marcus et al., 1991]. Unfortunately, the brake took seconds to disengage, because of the slow air cooling. More efficient water cooling would have improved actuator bandwidth. However, this solution was impractical because of the associated increase in master weight and complexity.

The above example illustrates a major drawback of SMM actuators, namely their very low bandwidth. One interesting solution to this problem was proposed by Hollerbach et al. [1992]. The researchers modified titanium-nickel wires by treating them to large electromagnetic fields. The result was a doubling of the bandwidth compared to that of regular titanium-nickel wires.

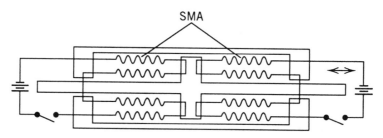

Figure 3.10 Shape memory metal (SMM) ξ-array actuator. Reprinted by permission from Hirose et al. [1989].

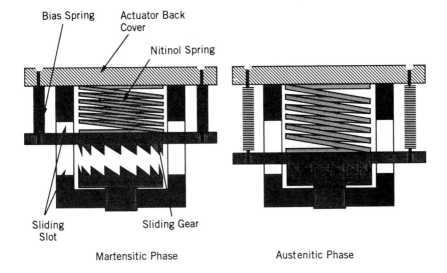

Figure 3.11   Cross section SMM passive brake. Adapted from Gharaybeh and Burdea [1995]. Reprinted by permission.

Another drawback of SMM actuators is their extremely low energy efficiency (on the order of 2% to 5%). Hasser [1995a] estimates that a nine degree-of-freedom hand master would have to dissipate approximately 500 W in order to provide 7 W of mechanical power at each joint. This very large power consumption is lost as heat, making such an SMM-based hand master both expensive and uncomfortable (if not dangerous) for the user to operate.

3.2. HYDRAULIC ACTUATORS

One class of actuators that does not suffer from low-bandwidth problems is hydraulic actuators. In fact, hydraulic pistons and rotary actuators exhibit the largest bandwidth of all actuators discussed in this chapter. This is from the incompressibility of the hydraulic fluid (oil) transmitting energy from the pump to the feedback interface. Additionally, the large oil pressure (2000 to 3000 psi) results in a very large force (torque) exertion capability. The actuators designed to withstand such pressures are necessarily heavier, but their resulting power-to-weight ratio is very high (as seen in Figure 3.8). Another advantage of hydraulic systems is their high positioning stiffness. The system responds very fast because disturbances propagate in oil about four times faster than in air. Furthermore, oil is self-lubricating, so that (unlike pneumatic systems) friction does not pose a problem.

These advantages of hydraulic actuation come at a price. First, using high-pressure oil requires a complex *hydraulic system* to presurize, transmit, and regulate oil flow. Secondly, large valve pressure losses result in low energy efficiency and systems that are costly to produce and operate. Thirdly, oil must be continuously filtered and cleaned because very small particles (on the order of 1/5000 of an inch) can cause the hydraulic system to lock up. Finally, despite careful fitting and piping design, oil leaks do occur. In the best case, these leaks result only in the contamination of the simulation site. This possibility makes hydraulically based haptic interfaces unusable in clean environments (such as hospital operating rooms). In the worst case, high-pressure oil leaks are a safety hazard.

> For the hydraulic system at 2,000 psi, even a pinhole leak can wreak havoc: Oil can quickly soil a large area, and the nearly invisible high-pressure stream can damage equipment and injure human operators. Also, oil is flammable, which requires extreme caution and necessitates continuous cooling to maintain proper operating temperatures, whereas pneumatic systems are relatively indifferent to temperature changes.
>
> —Stadler [1995]

3.2.1. The Hydraulic System

The energy delivery, control, and safety requirements outlined above result in a hydraulic system with a typical configuration illustrated in Figure 3.12 [Stadler, 1995]. This system consists of four essential elements, namely the hydraulic pump, the reservoir, the control valve(s), and the actuator(s). The *reservoir* holds a large amount of oil and serves to cool and clean the returning (low-pressure) oil. Additionally, it prevents the occurrence of damaging air bubbles (otherwise produced by pressure transients).

The *hydraulic pump* is typically a positive displacement motor that is sealed between outlet and inlet (to prevent backflow). The pump creates and maintains a constant oil flow Q (in.^{3}/sec) even when the outlet may be constricted. The oil passes a filter where contaminants are removed. A pilot-relief valve and an accumulator are designed to maintain proper system flow in the event of pressure transients. The

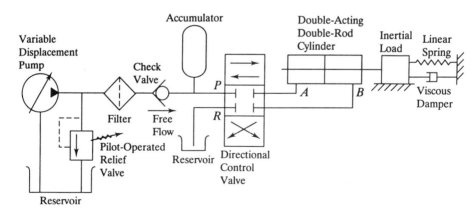

Figure 3.12 Typical structure of a hydraulic system. Reprinted with permission from Stadler, 1995, *Analytical Robotics and Mechatronics*, The McGraw-Hill Companies.

accumulator absorbs the flow that is forced back by a sudden increase in the actuator load, whereas the relief valve opens when the pressure becomes too great. Some of the fluid is thus rerouted back to the reservoir until the pressure transient passes. The *actuator* and *control valve* components of the hydraulic system are described in the following sections.

3.2.2. Actuators

Hydraulic actuators may be classified either as linear or rotary, depending on their output motion. Additionally, these actuators may have either single action or double action. A *single-action* actuator can exert forces (or torques) in only one direction. Return to the neutral (unenergized) shaft position is assured by a spring. Thus the force on the load (neglecting piston friction) is:

$$F_{single-action} = A_p p_A - k\Delta x \qquad (3.16)$$

where A_p is the piston area, p_a is the oil pressure in the cylinder, k in the spring stiffness, and Δx is the displacement from neutral position. For soft springs and large oil pressures, p_A the second term in the above equation can be neglected.

When the cylinder has two pressure ports, then its position can be actively controlled in both directions, and there is no need for spring return. Such a *double-acting* cylinder can be controlled by pumping oil into both inlet ports, as illustrated in Figure 3.13 [Stadler, 1995]. In this case, the force on the load becomes

$$F_{double-action} = A_p(p_A - p_B) \qquad (3.17)$$

where A_p is now the area of the cylinder less that of the double shaft. If the actuator is rotary, then the torque on the load is

$$\tau_h = V_0 (p_A - p_B) \qquad (3.18)$$

where V_0 is the volumetric displacement per radian of actuator shaft rotation. The speed of linear and rotary actuators is a function of their control flow Q_c and internal volume, so that

$$v_h = \frac{Q_c}{A_p} \qquad (3.19)$$

$$\omega_h = \frac{Q_c}{V_0} \qquad (3.20)$$

The actuator mechanical power is defined as force (or torque) times velocity, so that

$$P_{mech-linear} = F \cdot v_h = Q_c(p_A - p_B) \qquad (3.21)$$

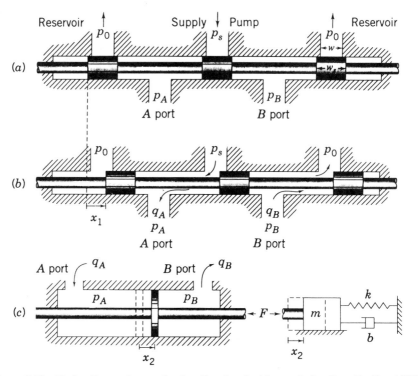

Figure 3.13 Hydraulic spool control valve. Reprinted with permission from Stadler, 1995, *Analytical Robotics and Mechatronics*, The McGraw-Hill Companies.

and

$$P_{mech-rotary} = \tau_h \cdot \omega_h = Q_c(p_A - p_B) \tag{3.22}$$

Table 3.3 summarizes the characteristics of the hydraulic actuators described above.

3.2.3. Hydraulic Control Valves

The control valve in a hydraulic system is used to set the actuator oil pressure as a function of the supply pressure p_s produced by the pump and the control signal received from the computer. In this section, we discuss two models of control valves, namely spool and suspension valves.

A *spool valve*, as illustrated in Figure 3.13, has a central shaft and spools that translate under servo control. This translation opens and closes ports from the supply tank (at pressure p_s) and return to the pump (at pressure p_0). Once the shaft is commanded to translate to the right, oil flow $Q_c = Q_A$ is directed to the actuator port A. At the same time, the oil flow Q_B returns from the actuator port B to the reservoir. This results in a pressure difference and a translation of the actuator shaft to the right. The reverse is true when the valve translates its spool shaft to the left.

TABLE 3.3 Comparison of Linear and Rotary Hydraulic Actuators

Output	Linear Actuator	Rotary Actuator
Force/torque	$A_p(p_A - p_B)$	$V_0(p_A - p_B)$
Velocity	Q_c/A_p	Q_c/V_0
Mechanical power	$Q_c(p_A - p_B)$	$Q_c(p_A - p_B)$

Source: Adapted from Hollerbach et al. [1992]. Reprinted by permission of the MIT Press.

The valve pressure drop Δp_{valve} depends on the valve oil flow and the pressure on the load p_{load} so that

$$\Delta p_{valve} = (p_s - p_0) - p_{load} \tag{3.23}$$

where p_{load} is the pressure difference in the actuator ($p_A - p_B$). Furthermore, if $\Delta p_{valve-rated}$ is the valve pressure drop at the rated flow Q_r, then the valve pressure drop at a given oil flow Q_c is

$$\Delta p_{valve} = \Delta p_{valve-rated} \sqrt{\frac{Q_c}{Q_r}} \tag{3.24}$$

Finally, the pressure that needs to be provided by the oil pump is

$$p_s = \Delta p_{valve} + p_{load} \tag{3.25}$$

Because Δp_{valve} may be a large percentage of the pump pressure p_s, the system has low mechanical efficiency. Thus, hydraulic systems are not only costly (because of expensive high-precision servo valves) but also expensive to operate. Moog [1994] compared operating costs for hydraulic and electromechanical motion platforms. They found that the hydraulic platform was an order of magnitude more expensive (resulting in a yearly difference of $3700 per motion platform). These costs become significant for multiple-platform applications, such as location-based entertainment (LBE) described in Chapter 10. Denne [1994] states that

> The real killer for hydraulic motion systems is their extreme inefficiency. Whenever a hydraulic ram is moved, oil at high pressure is transferred from the power unit into the system, and an identical volume of oil, at zero pressure, returns to the tank. There is a lot of energy in this oil, and it can be shown that 98 percent of it disappears as heat when the oil passes through the control valve. Hydraulic motion systems consume a lot of power for nothing.
>
> —Denne [1994]

Another type of hydraulic valve is the single-stage SARCOS *suspension valve* Model A3000H/50 shown in Figure 3.14 [Hollerbach et al., 1992]. Instead of a spool shaft, this valve uses a flexible pipe that is deflected to direct flow to one of two

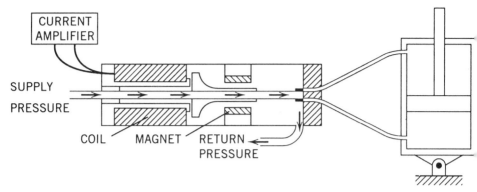

Figure 3.14 The SARCOS suspension valve Model A3000H/50. From Hollerbach et al. [1992]. Reprinted by permission of the MIT Press.

actuator ports on the front receiver plate. The central pipe deflection is accomplished by a magnetic field produced by a coil that is coaxial with the supply pipe. While still exhibiting large energy losses, the overall package of a suspension valve is much smaller than that of a spool valve, having a length of 1.84 in., a diameter of only 0.5 in. and a weight of less than 1 oz. The lighter moving element results in reduced inertia and faster dynamic response (and bandwidth) versus spool valves. The suspension valve rated flow Q_r is 0.5 gpm at a supply pressure p_s of 3000 psi.

The SARCOS suspension valve was integrated in a dextrous arm with seven degrees of freedom [Jacobsen et al., 1991a]. The small valve size allowed for colocation inside the dextrous arm, together with load cells and potentiometers (used for force and position feedback). The resulting overall actuator and valve power-to-mass ratio is 600 W/kg and the torque-to-mass ratio is 120 N-m/kg [Hollerbach et al., 1992].

3.3. PNEUMATIC ACTUATORS

The last class of actuators discussed in this chapter are the pneumatic actuators. Their force output is a function of the compressed air pressure used to transfer energy from the power source (compressor) to the haptic interface. Typically, air is compressed at 100 psi (7 atm), resulting in a smaller force (torque) exertion capability than with hydraulic actuators (which use oil at a pressure of 2000 to 3000 psi). Since pressures are significantly lower, the pneumatic actuators have a lighter construction than the hydraulic ones. This results in high power-to-weight ratios that are superior to those of electrical actuators. Secondly, air is not flammable and is clean; therefore pneumatic haptic interfaces may be used in clean environments. Thirdly, in pneumatic, unlike hydraulic, systems, there is no return piping to the compressor, because air is exhausted at the control valve. Furthermore, the technology is simpler and much cheaper than hydraulics, with systems that are easier to install and operate.

For all the above advantages, pneumatic actuators have their drawbacks. Air is compressible; therefore, the system stiffness response (and bandwidth) is much

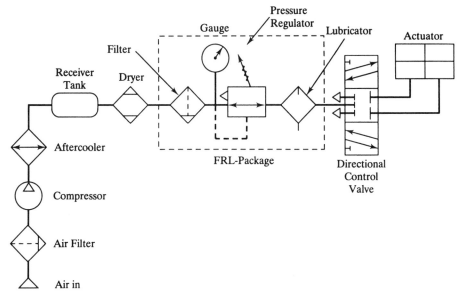

Figure 3.15 Pneumatic system components. Reprinted with permission from Stadler, 1995, *Analytical Robotics and Mechatronics*, The McGraw-Hill Companies.

lower than for hydraulic actuators.[1] Static friction becomes important, because dry air, which is used in pneumatic systems, is not self-lubricating. Large friction forces can mask small feedback forces produced during interaction with soft virtual objects [Richard et al., 1993]. Therefore additional lubrication must be provided. Noise can also become a problem if miniature mufflers are not used on the control valve exhaust. The above drawbacks have prompted research into higher bandwidth pneumatics, low-friction actuators, and some novel actuator configurations, which are discused later in this chapter.

3.3.1. The Pneumatic System

The pneumatic system is designed to provide pressurized air and to transport it to the actuator. Its main components are the compressor, the receiver tank, the pressure regulator, the control valve(s), and the actuator(s), as illustrated in Figure 3.15 [Stadler, 1995].

The *compressor* usually consists of a piston and chamber with an intake and outlet valve. The inlet port is connected to an air filter that traps impurities to prevent piston jam. The outlet valve releases air into an after-cooler designed to cool the hot compressor exhaust and remove water. This improves the system efficiency (owing

---

[1] In the context of this book, compressibility also has a good aspect because it increases the built-in safety of the haptic interface.

to the air pressure dependency on temperature) and reduces corrosion (owing to moisture removal).

The *receiver tank* serves as a buffer for the air flow variations in the system (similar to the accumulator tank used in hydraulic systems described previously). A pressure sensor turns on the compressor whenever the tank pressure is below a preset value and turns the compressor off when the tank pressure has reached the desired upper limit. A *pressure regulator* is used to provide a supply of different values to different actuators in the system. It maintains the set pressure despite pressure variations owing to load changes at the actuator. The regulator usually has a filter that removes the remaining water and oil droplets before reaching the control valve.

3.3.2. Pneumatic Control Valves

The *pneumatic control valve* operates similarly to the hydraulic valves previously described. It receives compressed air from the air regulator and sets the actuator direction and force. The valve may have a spool, or it may use spring-loaded solenoids. Earlier valves were analog and operated in an open loop. Later models, such as the Buzmatics SPCJr have integrated a pressure sensor, becoming essentially a servo valve pressure control system. As illustrated in Figure 3.16a [Buzmatics Inc., 1993], the SPCJr consists of a compact electronics board and two solenoid valves. An internal pressure sensor measures the output air pressure to the actuator. This pressure is continuously compared with the command input from the host computer. When the output pressure is lower than the commanded one, output from the operation amplifiers on the electronics board is used to open the intake valve. When the output pressure is greater than desired, the input valve is closed and the exhaust valve is opened, thus reducing the actuator pressure (and force).

The result is a very linear output pressure proportional with the input command voltage of 0 to 10 V direct current. The SPCJr bandwidth was measured using a square input signal, as illustrated in Figure 3.16b [Gomez, 1993]. The output signal is not the internal sensor pressure, but a force produced by a piston connected to the SPCJr. These tests showed a bandwidth of approximately 14 Hz before controller saturation occurred, with no feedback of force levels.

Another pneumatic valve configuration is the *jet pipe valve* used in the control of the Utah/MIT Dextrous Hand [Henri and Hollerbach, 1994]. The valve construction is very similar to the previously described hydraulic suspension valve manufactured by SARCOS Co. Tests done at McGill University Biorobotics Laboratory by Henri and Hollerbach [1994] were aimed at determining the static and dynamic characteristics of the jet valve and measure the actuator bandwidth under closed-loop force control. Tests showed good linearity of the deflection force to current ratio in the valve solenoid. Furthermore, a hysteresis of roughly 8% was measured and identified to be caused by nonlinear mechanical effects. When connecting the jet pipe valve to a low-friction actuator, the open-loop sinusoidal frequency response was measured at only 0.8 to 2.8 Hz. This bandwidth was raised dramatically to 80 Hz by adding a simple proportional feedback control loop. A nonlinear feed-forward component equivalent to the inverse of the actuator force-to-current characteristic was added to

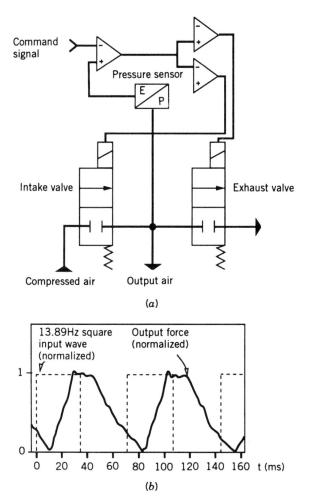

Figure 3.16 Pneumatic servovalve Model SPCJr: (*a*) construction [Buzmatics Inc., 1993]; (*b*) output signal for a square input voltage [Gomez, 1993]. Reprinted by permission.

eliminate offsets in the force output. Figure 3.17 shows the resulting actuator output measured when tracking a 5-Hz-square input signal [Henri and Hollerbach, 1994].

3.3.3. Actuators

Pneumatic actuators used in haptic interfaces have various configurations, such as micro bellows, linear pistons, rotary motors, or braided inflatable tubes. *Micro bellows* are miniature inflatable air pockets incorporated in double-layered sensing gloves. Their small dimension allows for several such bellows to be placed in a fingertip array. Larger bellows may be placed in the palmar area, as well as on the inner side of

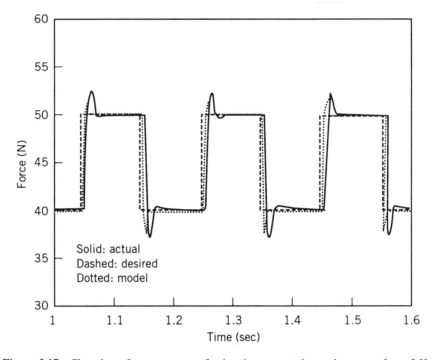

Figure 3.17   Close loop force response of a jet-pipe servo valve and actuator for a 5-Hz square input signal. Reprinted with permission from Henri and Hollerbach [1994]. © 1994 IEEE.

the fingers [Stone, 1991]. When inflated at low pressures (12 to 30 psi) these bellows are forced by the outer elastic glove to press against the user's hand and produce tactile sensations.

   Linear actuators are in many respects similar to the hydraulic ones previously described. They can be single-acting or double-acting, depending on whether a spring is used to return the actuator to its neutral position. Single-acting pistons used in haptic interfaces need to be modified by removing the internal spring [Burdea et al., 1992a]. In this way the user does not feel the spring resistance when grasping. Friction is important, especially for small feedback forces, and has to be taken into account in the actuator control equations:

$$F_{\text{single-action}} = \mu A_{\text{p}} p_{\text{A}} \tag{3.26}$$

$$F_{\text{double-action}} = \mu A_{\text{p}} (p_{\text{A}} - p_{\text{B}}) \tag{3.27}$$

where A_{p} is the cylinder area (with and without the double shaft), $p_{\text{A,B}}$ is the cylinder air pressures, and μ is a thrust coefficient, which depends on friction and air pressure [Hollerbach et al., 1992]. Typical metal pistons can have static friction as high as 10% of their output force. Pyrex glass–graphite linear actuators, such as the *airpot* [Airpot

Co., 1982] can considerably reduce friction. The drawback is a larger air leak, from larger tolerances between the glass cylinder and graphite piston.

We now illustrate linear pneumatic actuators with three examples. The first is a small custom-built RM-II actuator used in the Rutgers Master II haptic interface [Burdea and Gomez, 1994; Gomez et al., 1994]. The second is a much larger electropneumatic PemRAM actuator used in small motion platforms [Denne, 1994]. The third is a braided pneumatic muscle [Caldwell et al., 1994a].

The RM-II actuator is made of a small pyrex glass cylinder and a Lexan plastic piston, as illustrated in Figure 3.18. The novel feature of this actuator is an inner pair of infrared (IR) light-emitting diode (LED) and phototransistor. The phototransistor is fixed on the cylinder end, while the IR LED is embedded in the piston shaft, and thus is mobile. A graphite mesh at the exterior of the pyrex cylinder provides mechanical shielding and prevents external light from arriving at the phototransistor. Two additional rotary Hall-effect sensors placed at the cylinder base measure its orientation (yaw and pitch angles) versus the palm. As the user moves his fingers the IR light sensed by the phototransistor changes with the distance from the piston. This dependence is almost linear and through calibration it is possible to measure the fingertip position versus the cylinder base. No additional friction is produced during position measuring since both the rotary and linear sensors are noncontact.

The RM II actuator is very compact and light, weighing approximately 25 grams (excluding the control valve), and having a volume of $0.66 \, \text{cm}^3$. Yet it is both powerful and responsive, having a force output of 16.38 N (at 100 psi) and friction of only 0.05 N. This corresponds to an output of approximately 8.5 W of mechanical power.

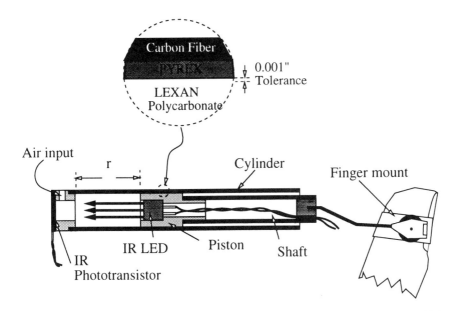

Figure 3.18 Rutgers Master II pneumatic actuator. Adapted from Gomez et al. [1994]. Reprinted by permission.

The resulting force and power densities are 655 N/kg, 340 W/kg, and 12.9 W/cm^3, respectively. This power density is an order of magnitude larger than that of the geared MicroMo electrical actuator described previously. Additionally, the dynamic range (maximum force divided by friction) is approximately 330, which indicates high haptic simulation fidelity.

The PemRAM actuator is a novel technology designed to replace hydraulic linear actuators with more efficient pneumatic rams [Denne, 1994]. The actuator consists of a cylinder embedding a series of coils and a piston housing a strong permanent magnet, as illustrated in Figure 3.19a. [Denne Developments Ltd., 1994a,b]. The cylinder is connected to a small air tank and is pressurized at the start of simulation. Subsequently the connection to the air tank is closed, and the actuator becomes a passive air spring. No energy is required when no current is passing through the cylinder coils. The magnetic field resulting from current passing through the coils interacts with the piston, resulting in a linear motion. On-board power electronics and microprocessors are used to cycle the cylinder coils to control both direction and speed. The fast dynamic response of the actuator (about 10 msec) results in an actuator bandwidth of 100 Hz. Vibrations with frequencies up to 30 Hz can be overimposed on the actuator linear motion (as required in certain simulation effects).

The PemRAM actuator presently has two configurations, namely Model 3300 and Model 5500 [Denne Developments Ltd., 1995]. The first model has a 0.3-m linear stroke, a weight of 40 kg, a peak thrust of 500 kgf (4.9 kN) and a volume of 0.011 m^3. The values for the larger Model 5500 are 0.5 m stroke, 900 kgf (8.8 kN) thrust, 90 kg weight and 0.025 m^3 volume. Table 3.4 illustrates the corresponding power-to-weight and power-to-volume ratios, assuming a peak thrust duration of 0.1 sec and peak velocity of 3 m/sec.

Figure 3.19b shows a 3-DOF motion platform integrating three PemRAM actuators. Such a system can carry a two-person simulation capsule, or a 4-seat open platform, and still provide motion ques at up to 50 Hz.

Braided *pneumatic muscle actuators* (PMA) are variations of an older actuator called the McKibben Muscle [Schulte, 1962] used in prosthetics applications. More recently Caldwell et al. [1994a] describe an application of PMAs to robotics and haptic interfaces [Caldwell et al., 1995a]. The actuator consists of an inner thin rubber layer and an outer flexible sheathing, as illustrated in Figure 3.20a [Caldwell et al., 1994a]. The inner layer has two plastic plugs and a threaded inlet pipe at one end. The outer sheathing is made of interwoven nylon fibers that limit the expansion of the inner rubber layers. The two layers (rubber and nylon fibers) are bonded only at the actuator end caps. Thus the actuator changes length and diameter as it compresses or expands (with an elongated-to-compressed length ratio of about 3:1). The external plastic shell and inner rubber form a series of pressurized trapezoids that are the driving surfaces of the muscle.

The PMA exhibits a minimum energy-to-force state when the nylon fibers form an angle of 54.5°. This corresponds to a minimum force $F_{\min}$ of

$$F_{\min} = p_{\text{internal}} \left(\pi D_{\min} L_{\min} + 2E_a \right) \quad (3.28)$$

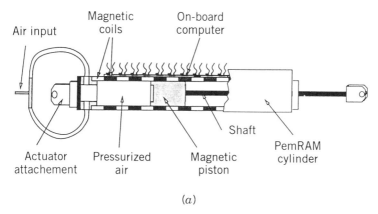

(a)

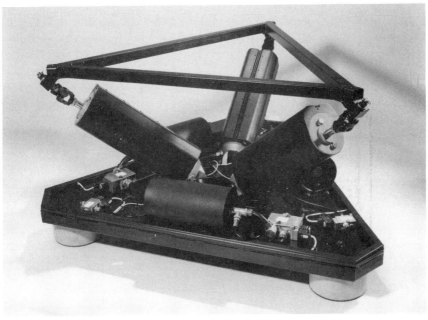

(b)

Figure 3.19 The PemRAM actuator: (a) components (adapted from Denne Developments Ltd. [1994a]). (b) three-actuator motion platform. Courtesy of Denne Developments Ltd. Reprinted by permission.

TABLE 3.4   Performance Specifications for the PemRAM Actuator

Actuator Type	Peak Power (kW)	Power/Weight (W/kg)	Power/Volume (W/cm^3)
3300	14.7	367	1.34
5500	26.5	294	1.06

Source: Adapted from Denne Developments Ltd. [1995]. Reprinted by permission.

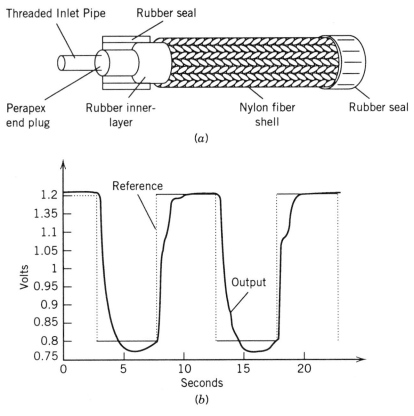

Threaded Inlet Pipe   Rubber seal

Perapex   Rubber inner-   Nylon fiber   Rubber seal
end plug   layer   shell

(*a*)

Reference

Output

Volts

(*b*)

Figure 3.20 Pneumatic muscle actuator: (*a*) construction; (*b*) square input tracking using a high-order adaptive controller. Reprinted by permission from Caldwell et al. [1994a]. © 1994 IEEE.

where D_{min} and L_{min} are the overall muscle diameter and length, and E_a is the area of the end plates. When the muscle is stretched (or compressed) it produces a very large restoring force F_{drive} equal to

$$F_{drive} = \varepsilon(F_{new} - F_{min}) \tag{3.29}$$

where ε is a conversion factor due to friction losses and the force F_{new} corresponds to the new internal pressure as in

$$F_{new} = p_{new} (\pi D_{new} L_{new} + 2E_a) \tag{3.30}$$

The researchers report forces of 50 to 75 N at air pressures of 29 psi (2 atm). Because the actuator (without control valves) weighs only 10 g, the resulting power-to-weight ratio is extremely large at 1 to 1.5 kW/kg. The Rubbertuator Model 5 made by Bridgstone Co. has a length of 0.15 m and weighs 28 g [Hollerbach et al., 1992].

When pressurized to 87 psi, it produces a force of 800 N, for a force-to-weight ratio of 28.6 kN/kg. The corresponding power-to-weight ratio is estimated at 10 kW/kg.

Subsequent tests by Caldwell et al. [1994a] integrated the PMA described above in a system using piezoelectric valves (with a switching bandwidth of 40 to 50 Hz) and an adaptive control feedback. This system showed good joint positional accuracy (on the order of 1°). The drawback was an extremely low bandwidth of only 0.3 Hz. Figure 3.20*b* shows the force tracking of a square input signal using a high-order adaptive controller [Caldwell et al., 1994a]. Another drawback of PMA actuators is the hysteresis of the tension-length relationship, as determined by Chou and Hannaford [1994]. Static and dynamic tests showed that the actuator hysteresis was independent of velocity (up to 10 Hz excitation signal) and was most likely from the Coulomb friction between the two layers of the pneumatic air muscle actuator. When lubricants were added on the braided shell and inner rubber bladder, the Coulomb friction was marginally reduced.

3.4. DISCUSSION

The previously described haptic actuators utilize traditional electrical, hydraulic, and pneumatic technologies. Whenever possible examples of haptic interfaces using such technologies were given. It is now time to put things in perspective and rank these actuators based on two important variables, namely their power-to-weight ratios and mechanical bandwidths.

The power-to-weight ratio is a measure of the strength *and* lightness of a given actuator. Therefore this criteria is important especially for portable haptic interfaces. Hasser [1995a] states

> Assuming a master glove structure could be built at about 28 grams (1 oz) per dof, and that the designer still wanted... 69 grams (2.4 oz) per dof on the hand, that would leave 41 grams (1.4 oz) for actuators, requiring a power-to-mass ratio of 170 W/kg in the actuators. Actuators with power capabilities ranging from 20–50% of the human maximum MCP joint power and mass of 41 grams (1.4 oz) would have power-to-mass ratios ranging from 100–250 W/kg.
>
> —Hasser [1995a]

In view of the fatigue effects described in Chapter 2, it would seem better to adopt the lower power-to-weight ratio recommended by Hasser, namely 100 W/kg. Figure 3.21 illustrates the power-to-weight ratio of the actuators discussed in this chapter. At the bottom of the graph is the geared MicroMo brushed dc motor, which has almost the same power-to-weight ratio as the human biceps muscle [Hollerbach et al., 1992]. Thus the MicroMo is inadequate to be used on a portable haptic interface. In the middle range are pneumatic actuators such as the RM II [Gomez et al., 1994], which has more than three times the ratio recommended here. At the top of the range are the SARCOS hydraulic actuator with 600 W/kg and the pneumatic air muscle [Caldwell et al., 1994a] with 1000 W/kg. Between the two, the air muscle has the advantage of cleaner operation.

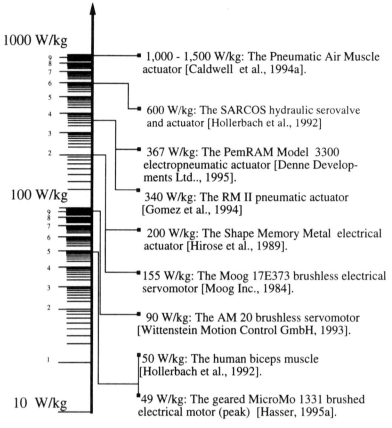

Figure 3.21 Haptic feedback actuator comparison based on power-to-weight ratio.

The actuators were subsequently ranked based on their mechanical (force-feedback) bandwidth. This criteria is important for overall haptic simulation fidelity, and needs to match the human sensorial requirements described in Chapter 2. Ellis [1995] recommends bandwidths of 50 to 100 Hz for force feedback and up to 10 kHz for tactile feedback. Hasser [1995a] suggests a lower actuator bandwidth range:

> The literature seems to suggest increasing usefulness of force-reflecting bandwidths from 2–30 Hz. with diminishing gains as 30 Hz is approached and surpassed. Systems with flat responses out to 30 Hz will likely be able to represent vibrations at higher tactile frequencies with lower magnitudes sufficient for the tactile sense. Such systems will require servo rates in excess of 300 Hz for good fidelity.
>
> —Hasser [1995a]

Figure 3.22 ranks the same actuators discussed previously but now ordered according to their mechanical bandwidth. The human hand force bandwidth of 5 to 10 Hz [Shimoga, 1992] would indicate a minimum actuator bandwidth of 10 Hz. This

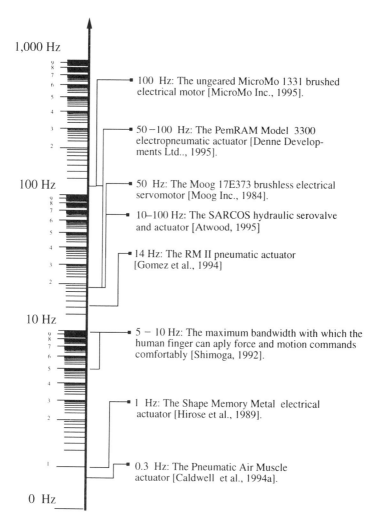

Figure 3.22   Haptic feedback actuator comparison based on mechanical bandwidth.

eliminates SMMs and the pneumatic air muscle from consideration in haptic interface design. At the top of the chart are the ungeared MicroMo electrical motor and the SARCOS hydraulic hand master actuator [Atwood, 1995]. The MicroMo, however, is not acceptable because of its lower power-to-weight ratio, and the SARCOS actuator is expensive and dirty. The PemRAM and Moog actuators have good bandwidth but are not usable in portable haptic interfaces. The RM II is at the low acceptable band-width range and has a sufficient power-to-weight ratio to be integrated in portable masters (this ratio does not count the servovalve and related electronics).

The above discussion left out several other performance criteria (such as force/torque vs. mass, or power-to-volume ratios). However, the point is made that traditional actuator technologies cannot fulfill *all* requirements of power, compact-ness, responsiveness, lightness, cleanliness, safety, and low cost. Thus compromises have to be made depending on the specific application and available budget.

3.5. CONCLUSIONS

In this chapter, we reviewed various classical actuator technologies used in present haptic interfaces. These actuators were compared based on specific performance cri-teria (such as power-to-weight ratio and bandwidth) which are crucial for good haptic interface design. This discussion provides the necessary foundation for subsequent chapters describing actuator integration in various haptic feedback systems.

CHAPTER 4

NONPORTABLE FORCE FEEDBACK

After having reviewed the underlying actuator technology, we are now ready to proceed to an analysis of various haptic feedback hardware architectures. Our discussion starts with force feedback systems, followed by a discussion of tactile-feedback hardware in Chapter 6.

Force feedback is designed to apply forces that are related to (or equal with) those generated by the computer running the Virtual Reality simulation. As such, the feedback hardware represents a more sophisticated form of input/output device, complementing others such as keyboards, mice, or trackers. Input from the user is in the form of hand (or other body segment) position or exerted force, whereas feedback from the computer is in the form of force or position (respectively). These systems are also called *masters* because they are similar to hardware used in master–slave teleoperations.

Force-feedback masters, can be classified based on the type of control or communication loop (as described in more detail in Chapter 8), or based on the type of actuator used. We can thus distinguish between hydraulic, electric, or pneumatic force-feedback systems. Each have advantages and disadvantages, as described in detail in the previous chapter. Another classification relates to the distribution or grounding of feedback forces. As explained by Salisbury and Srinivasan [1992], *force grounding* through mechanical attachments is necessary to assure the equilibrium and mechanical stability of the haptic interface:

> ... For example, exploration or manipulation of a virtual object requires that force vectors be imposed on the user at multiple regions of contact with the object. Consequently, equal and opposite reaction forces are imposed on the interface.... if the forces are

unbalanced, as in pressing a virtual object with a single fingerpad, the equilibrium of the interface requires that it be grounded."

—Salisbury and Srinivasan [1992]

Several mechanical grounding locations exist, as illustrated in Figure 4.1 [Bergamasco, 1993b].

Most of today's force-feedback systems are grounded on the desk, which supports their weight and prevents the master from sliding or toppling. Such systems are feedback joysticks or track balls, pen-based masters, or more complex hand masters. Other masters are exoskeletons or robot arms that have their base frame fixed on the walls or ceiling. The user only grabs the end of the master arm, as illustrated in Figure 4.1b. The next step is to ground the master arm not only at its extremities, but also at several intermediate locations on the user's arm, forearm, and wrist. This provides a more natural interaction, as well as the possibility of simulating contact with virtual objects at various locations on the arm. Another class of force-feedback systems that are grounded to the floor and apply forces at various locations on the body are single or multiuser motion platforms. Finally, as shown in Figure 4.1d, the interface can be grounded on the user's back or torso, which provides the most natural interaction and largest work space. The drawback is that the user perceives the weight of the entire exoskeleton structure, which can lead to false sensations, fatigue, or loss of equilibrium. A subclass of these exoskeletons (not shown in the figure) are hand masters which are grounded at the wrist and forearm.

Portability is another way of classifying force-feedback hardware. Those systems that are desk, wall, ceiling, or floor grounded are *nonportable*, as they limit the user's freedom of motion. Conversely, hand or full-body exoskeletons are *portable*, thus allowing the most natural type of interaction. Nonportable systems are more prevalent today, because of the poor power-to-weight and power-to-volume ratios of current feedback actuator technology. Portable systems are less developed at the time of this writing, and are the subject of active research at various sites worldwide. Nonportable force-feedback hardware is the subject of this chapter; the next chapter discusses portable force-feedback systems. The various systems will be compared based on force output capability, feedback bandwidth, number of degrees of freedom, and user work envelope.

4.1. DESK-GROUNDED MASTERS

Desk-grounded masters are the most prevalent form of force feedback interface in use today. They tend to be more compact, easier to install, and less expensive than other types of force feedback systems. Within desk-grounded masters we distinguish various types of joysticks [Schmult and Jebens, 1993a; Millman et al., 1993; Ellis et al., 1993], newer pen-based interfaces, such as the PHANToM Master [Massie and Salisbury, 1994], as well as the SPIDAR [Ishii and Sato, 1994a] and the "Sensor Glove" [Hashimoto et al., 1994] systems developed in Japan. The latter example should not be confused with portable sensing gloves described in Chapter 5.

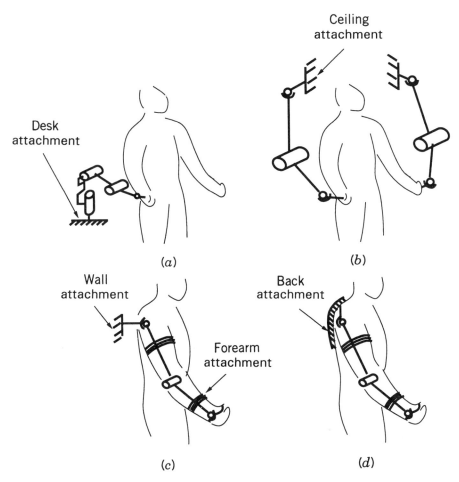

Figure 4.1   Possible force-feedback mechanical-grounding locations. Adapted from Berga-masco [1993b]. Reprinted by permission.

4.1.1. Joysticks

Joysticks have been used for many years as a simple and intuitive input device for computer graphics, industrial control, and entertainment (video games) applications. These general-purpose joysticks typically have a two-degrees-of-freedom swing arm with a handle that is positioned by the user, as illustrated in Figure 4.2 [Adelstein and Rosen, 1992]. The handle is supported at one end by a spherical joint, and at the other by two sliding contacts on slotted swing arms. Rotary potentiometers located at the base measure the handle shaft orientation versus the axis 1 and 2. Geometrical transformations then determine the absolute position of the handle versus a fixed coordinate system at the base. Typically a spring returns the handle to vertical "neutral" orientation upon release by the user.

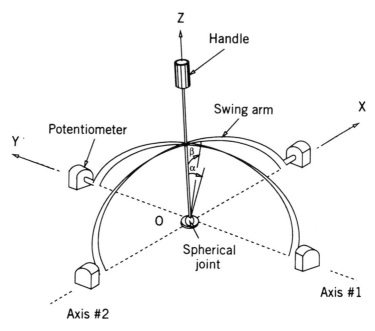

Figure 4.2 Slotted swing arm joystick with two degrees of freedom. Adapted from Adelstein and Rosen [1992]. Reprinted by permission of the ASME.

The simple joystick construction described above provides only position information to the computer, with no force feedback to the user. Certain modifications are necessary to close the control loop and exert forces on the user's hand. First, the return spring needs to be removed to prevent the spring force from confusing the user. Secondly, actuators need to be integrated to provide active forces during the simulation. Typically, these actuators are dc motors because of ease of installation and control. The number of actuators needed is at least equal to the number of degrees of freedom of the joystick, whereas their size is dictated by the force that is required at the handle attachment. Thirdly, the number of degrees of freedom and the joystick work envelope typically need to be increased compared to those of open-loop joysticks.

Our discussion of haptic joysticks starts with simpler two-degree-of-freedom spherical configurations similar to the open-loop case described above. Subsequently we describe Cartesian configurations that allow translation of the handle (in addition to rotation) and thus have larger work envelopes than spherical joysticks. A newer class of haptic joystick are small "Stewart platforms" using parallel actuator structures. These have large force exertion capability and are more compact than Cartesian joysticks. Finally, we describe a magnetically levitated force-feedback joystick prototype that has no static friction, thus providing more accurate force-feedback sensation for the user.

Spherical Configuration Haptic Joysticks. An example of spherical configuration haptic joystick is the device developed by Adelstein and Rosen [1992] for
the study of hand tremor. They developed a novel closed-chain linkage arrangement
that provides high structural bandwidth and simplifies control computations for end-
point impedance. The actuators used are two permanent magnet dc motors that have
minimal torque ripple and no cogging. The motors are driven by pulse-width modulation through analog servo amplifiers enabling a 5 N-m stall torque at the actuator
shaft and 20 N continuous force for each handgrip degree of freedom. The joystick
displacements are sensed by incremental optical encoders coupled with each motor
shaft with a resolution of 0.044 degree (or 176 μm at the handgrip). Additional sensing is provided by analog tachometers mounted on each motor, which sense handle
velocities and piezoresistive accelerometers that monitor shaft accelerations. Since
the joint velocities and accelerations are sensed directly, there is no need for differ-
entiation of joint position, which reduces real-time computation load, and improves
overall control quality. The resulting feedback bandwidth is approximately 48 Hz,
with minimal lag. The forces $\mathbf{F}_x$, $\mathbf{F}_y$ at the joystick handle are related to the actuator
torques τ_α, τ_β by the following relation:

$$\mathbf{F}_x = \left[\frac{\cos \beta \sqrt{1 - \sin^2 \alpha \sin^2 \beta}}{R_0 \cos \alpha} \right] \tau_\beta \tag{4.1}$$

$$\mathbf{F}_y = - \left[\frac{\cos \alpha \sqrt{1 - \sin^2 \alpha \sin^2 \beta}}{R_0 \cos \beta} \right] \tau_\alpha \tag{4.2}$$

where R_0 is the handle length from the handgrip to the origin of the (x, y, z) system
of coordinates, and α and β are the handle orientation angles versus the two rotation
axes (x and y). Thus the actuator torques τ_α, τ_β are decoupled in the x/y plane, each
contributing to either $\mathbf{F}_x$ or $\mathbf{F}_y$.

Another spherical force-feedback joystick was developed by Schmult and Jebens
at AT&T Bell Laboratories [Schmult and Jebens, 1993a,b]. This is also a two-degree-
of-freedom device, but its dimensions are almost as small as those of an open-loop
joystick (namely $20 \times 11 \times 5$ cm). The overall appearance and internal mechanism of
the AT&T force-feedback joystick are illustrated in Figure 4.3 [Schmult and Jebens,
1993a].

It uses two custom actuators with axes normal to each other, and a right-angle shaft
that attaches to the joystick handle. The connection between the actuator shaft and
joystick handle is done by adjustable bearings that compensate for the imperfect right-
angle intersection of the two motor shafts. Each shaft houses a four-pole permanent
magnet rotor and a potentiometer that measures the joystick handle position. The
joystick handle has a motion of approximately 55 mm, measured with a resolution of
approximately 35 μm. The use of custom actuators together with the reduced joystick
inertia results in high control bandwidth, with resonance occurring at approximately
220 Hz. The drawback to this compact device is small feedback force, which for
each handle axis is up to 0.73 N (75 grams force). The joystick can function either
in servo mode or in position input mode (absolute or relative). Its high bandwidth

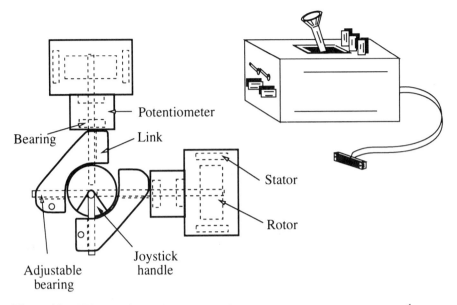

Figure 4.3 AT&T haptic joystick. Adapted from Schmult and Jebens [1993a]. © Éditions Hermès. Reprinted by permission.

allows the joystick to be used for several types of haptic feedback, such as direct forces, vibrations, impulses, or variable-stiffness simulation.

Cartesian Joysticks. Cartesian joysticks differ from spherical ones in that they have two (sometimes three) orthogonal axes allowing the whole base of the handle to translate. This results in a much larger work volume and increased mobility for the user. The drawback is increased use of desk space to support the device.

Ellis et al. [1993] at Queen's University (Kingston, Canada) developed the three-degree-of-freedom joystick illustrated in Figure 4.4. It has a moving platform that translates in the x/y plane using rails and sliding blocks. The base dimensions are 65×65 cm, with a workspace of 15×15 cm. Each translation axis is actuated by an electrical dc motor through a pulley and cable transmission. The Teflon-coated cable drivers used for x/y translation were chosen because of low friction, low inertia, high bandwidth, and high backdrivability. The translating handle block supports another rotary motor, which actuates a third degree of freedom (rotation about the z axis). Position sensing is assured by resolvers with 0.006-rad resolution and LVDT linear sensors installed on the side blocks. The overall position accuracy and repeatability is 0.03 mm. Additionally, a force sensor mounted on the moving platform is used to determine the differential force between the mechanism and the human operator. It is thus possible to compensate for unmodeled device dynamics.

The actuators are brushed dc motors powered by linear current amplifiers. Tests conducted on the x/y force-feedback platform (with the rotary actuator removed) showed a maximum open-loop force of 56 N, with passive friction accounting for

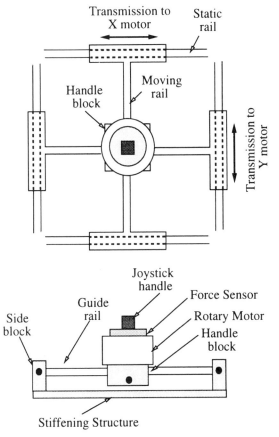

Figure 4.4 Three-degree-of-freedom Cartesian joystick. Adapted from Ellis et al. [1993]. Reprinted by permission of the ASME.

1.7 N. During closed loop tests the maximum force felt was 8.4 N, with a force bandwidth of up to 80 Hz.

A Cartesian joystick which has six degrees of freedom is the "Programmable Environment Reality through Force" (PER-Force) hand controller illustrated in Figure 4.5. This device produced by Cybernet Systems Co. has a $x/y/z$ translating platform on which are installed three actuators for handle orientation. The joystick dimensions are 37.1 × 37.1 × 27.1 cm (nominal). The three linear axes have 10 cm translation range, while the rotational axes have 90 degree for yaw and pitch and 180 degree for roll. These can be increased optionally up to 60 cm of translation, 180 degree yaw, and 270 degree roll. The position measurement resolution is 7.5 μm for translation and 1/90th of a degree for rotation. An aircraft-type control stick incorporates three cuing buttons, an analog trigger, and a palm-actuated deadman safety switch [Cybernet Systems Co., 1995].

The PER-Force joystick has six dc brushless actuators that produce up to 53 N of translational force and 300 oz-in. torque. The static friction is approximately 0.5 N,

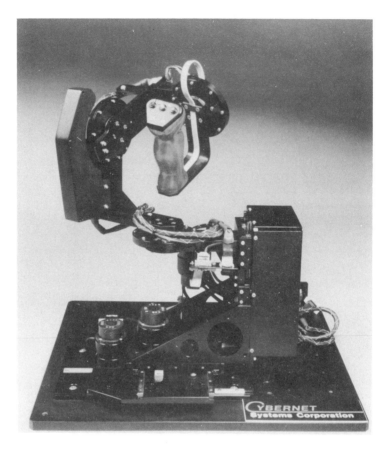

Figure 4.5 The PER-Force (programmable environment reality through force) Cartesian joystick. Courtesy of Cybernet Systems Co.

and the control bandwidth is approximately 100 Hz. Several control modes (force, position, or rate) as well as scaling and position/orientation/axis locking are available using the Motion Controller Software provided by the manufacturer. The complete system (including hand controller, 486 DX processor, and C software library) retails for approximately $60,000 [Cybernet Systems Co., 1995]. Systems with two, three, four and five degrees of freedom are also available at a lower cost.

Stewart Platform Joysticks. Stewart [1965] developed a six-degree-of-freedom mechanism used as a motion platform for flight simulators. It consisted of a fixed base and a mobile platform interconnected by six actuator arms arranged kinematically in parallel. Compared with the more common serial kinematic manipulators, parallel link manipulators have higher load capacity, better positioning accuracy, better durability, faster inverse kinematics computations and better dynamic characteristics

[Arai et al., 1990]. The drawbacks are a smaller work envelope, difficult force control, difficult direct kinematics computations, and kinematic singularities from the interference of the actuator arms.

The high force output of Stewart platforms has attracted the attention of telerobotic system developers and lately of researchers designing haptic interfaces for Virtual Reality. The kinematic singularity problem was solved by various methods, such as reducing the number of arms (and thus degrees of freedom), or providing actuator redundancy (a larger number of actuators than that of the arms connecting the stationary and mobile platforms). An example is the haptic joystick developed by Millman and his colleagues [1993] at Northwestern University, which is illustrated in Figure 4.6.

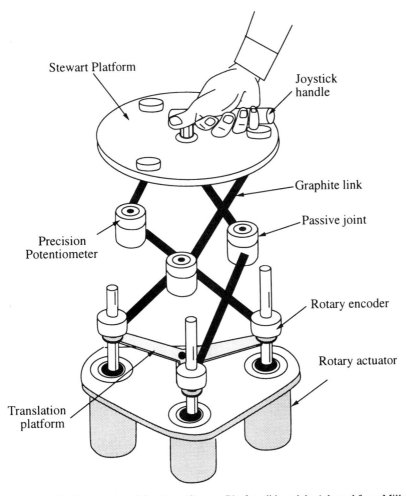

Figure 4.6 The four-degree-of-freedom "Stewart Platform" joystick. Adapted from Millman et al. [1993]. © 1993 IEEE. Reprinted by permission.

It consists of a fixed platform and a mobile one holding the joystick handle. A closed-chain parallel kinematic mechanism allows the handle to move in three translational degrees of freedom and one rotation about the vertical axis. The structure is made of composite graphite beams that have low inertia and high structural strength. Three revolute joints at the base are actuated through low-friction zero-backlash ball splines that transmit torque from three brushless dc motors. A prismatic joint in the base allows translation in the vertical direction using a Y-shaped triad construction that pushes the three spline nuts simultaneously. The triad is actuated by a fourth motor in the base through a pulley and steel belt transmission.

Each graphite arm has two additional revolute joints that are passive and hold potentiometers for angular position sensing. The potentiometers are supplemented by optical encoders on the motor shafts allowing for measurements of all nine joint angles. This sensorial redundancy in turn simplifies and speeds up computations. Each optical encoder has a very high resolution of 9×10^5 counts/revolution, which dramatically reduces control instabilities during hard-contact simulation. The potentiometers installed on the passive links have a resolution of 10^{-3} radians.

The length of the graphite links was kept small to further improve accuracy (which is inversely proportional to the link length). The resulting work space allows for horizontal translations in a 20-cm circle, vertical translation of 8.5 cm, and rotations of $\pm 45°$. The static output is 45 N (10 lb) translational force and 135 N-cm (12 lb-in.) torque throughout the workspace. Update rates are given by Millman et al. [1993] as over 1000 Hz, whereas the lowest natural frequency of the device is approximately 100 Hz.

Another Stewart Platform-type joystick is the Haptic Master illustrated in Figure 4.7. This device, produced recently by Nissho Electronics Co. [1995] of Japan, is based on an earlier prototype developed by Iwata [1990] at the University of Tsukuba. It consists of a six-degree-of-freedom triangular platform and a base platform connected by three actuated arms. These arms attach at the mobile platform through spherical joints, allowing for both translation and rotation of a spherical joystick handle. At the other extremity the parallelogram (pantograph) links connect to dc motors installed in the base. Each pantograph has two dc motors connected to it through reduction gears, for a total of nine actuators. Actuator redundancy is needed to eliminate kinematic singularities in the workspace.

The Haptic Master workspace is a 40-cm-diam sphere centered on the mobile platform. The dc motors are controlled by a controller using pulse width modulation. The controller has analog–digital converters for position sensing and parallel i/o for the dc motors. An RS232 assures communication with a host computer running the simulation. The Haptic Master can thus produce a maximum output force of 69 N (7 kgf). The force-control bandwidth is 50 Hz [Iwata, 1994], which is higher than the 10 Hz of the Iwata's earlier prototype.

Magnetically Levitated Joystick. The last type of force-feedback joystick to be discussed here is the magnetically levitated device developed by Salcudean and Vlaar [1994] at the University of British Columbia (Canada). Whereas all previously mentioned joysticks had some static friction (approximately 5% of output), the mag-

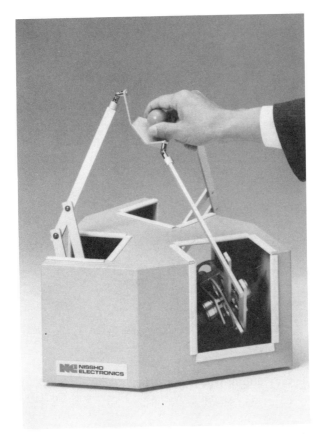

Figure 4.7   The Haptic Master six-degree-of-freedom joystick. Courtesy of Nissho Electronics Co.

netically levitated prototype has no friction at all. This in turn greatly increases the interface dynamic range as well as sensitivity for small feedback forces.

The joystick assembly is illustrated in Figure 4.8 [Salcudean and Vlaar, 1994]. It consists of a six-degree-of-freedom "flotor" housed inside a vertical magnetic assembly. It has six Lorenz actuators arranged in a star configuration (with 120° symmetry). The actuator flat coils are immersed in a magnetic field produced by four rectangular magnets attached to permeable plates. The location of the joystick handle (or flotor) with respect to the stator is detected by three pairs of narrow-beam LED and two-dimensional position sensing diodes located within the vertical magnet assembly. The forces and torques on the joystick handle are proportional to the currents producing the magnetic fields resulting in a maximum vertical force of 60 N. Continuous output force is 20 N on the vertical axis.

Heating by the electrical currents through the Lorenz actuators (Joule effect) prevents operation over extended periods of time. Additionally, the BSC Joystick, like other magnetically levitated devices, needs to have small distances between flotor

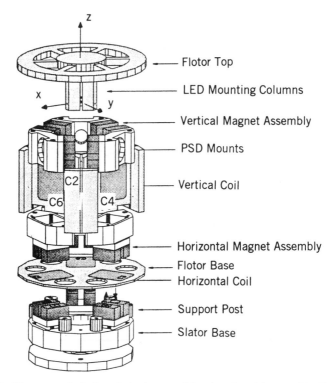

Figure 4.8 The magnetic levitated six-degree-of-freedom joystick assembly. Reprinted by permission of the ASME from Salcudean and Vlaar [1994].

and stator (to capture the magnetic fields effectively). This results in a very small work envelope when compared with the other joysticks described previously. The translation range is ±4.5 mm and rotation range is ±6° about each axis. The position sensing resolution is very good, namely 5-μm translation and 10-μrad. rotation. The control bandwidth is also extremely high, with a force and torque frequency response of more than 3 kHz. Position control is the limiting factor, being more than 30 Hz translation and 15 Hz for rotations.

4.1.2. Pen-based Masters

Pen-based masters allow interaction with the virtual environment through familiar tools such as a pen (or pointer) or a scalpel (in the case of surgical simulators). These desk-top devices are compact, typically have a workspace larger than spherical and magnetically levitated haptic joysticks and have between three and six degrees of freedom. Since the tool (pen) is geometrically constant, regardless of the user's hand size, there is no need for complex calibrations associated with sensing gloves.

University of Washington Pen-based Force Display. Buttolo and Hannaford [1995] at the Biorobotics Laboratory of the University of Washington have recently developed the three-degree-of-freedom haptic prototype shown in Figure 4.9. It has a serial-parallel kinematic configuration that moves a feedback arm below a circular platform. The design has a redundant actuator arrangement with three actuators for translation in the plane of the platform, and two more actuators for platform tilting. The actuators are direct-drive electrical motors, which assures backdrivability, responsiveness, and lack of backlash.

The head of the feedback arm protrudes through a platform cutout allowing for the placement of a pen tip or the user's fingertip. The peak force applied by the end effector is 13.5 N, whereas continuous force is reported at 4.5 N. The work envelope of the device is given at 1.5 cm^2 planar and 1 cm vertical, which is relatively small. No data is given on the force-feedback bandwidth.

The PHANToM Master. The Personal Haptic Interface Mechanism (PHANToM) is another desk-grounded pen-based mechanism designed for virtual force feedback [Massie and Salisbury, 1994]. As illustrated in Figure 4.10, the interface main component is a serial-feedback arm that ends with a fingertip thimble-gimbal support. Alternately the thimble can be replaced by a stylus. Of the six degrees of freedom of the arm, three translational ones are active, and the gimbal orientation is passive. It is thus possible to simulate single frictionless fingertip contact with virtual objects. Thus only translational forces (no torques) can be applied at the stylus (or fingertip). The arm design has certain very clever features. For example, two of the three feedback

Figure 4.9   The University of Washington pen-based force display.

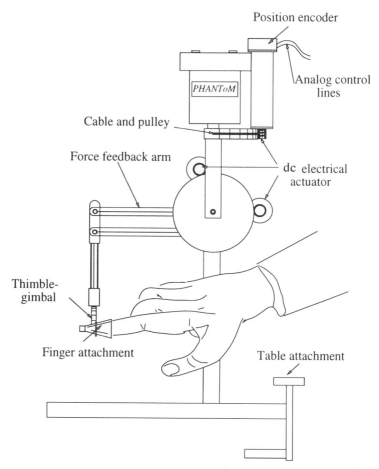

Figure 4.10 The PHANToM Master. Adapted from Massie and Salisbury [1994]. Reprinted by permission of the ASME.

actuators are installed so that their weight counterbalances the arm weight. Since the PHANToM is statically balanced, there is no need for active gravity compensation through biased motor torques. The first rotation axis of the arm is located directly above the user's wrist, allowing for the alignment of the spherical workspaces of the interface and user's wrist. The workspace is approximately $8 \times 17 \times 25$ cm.

The PHANToM uses three dc brushed motors with optical encoders placed at the actuator shafts. Transmissions are done with cables and pulleys, with a simplified reduction mechanism that meshes two motor capstans with a single cable. Additionally, the transformation matrix between motor axis rotation and arm endpoint translation is nearly diagonal, so that the three actuators are nearly decoupled. Thus the interface is perceived as having the same inertia and backdrivability (friction) in all directions. Inertia at the tip is perceived as 0.1 Kg, whereas static friction is 0.1 N.

The peak output force of the PHANToM is 10 N, and continuous force (without actuator overheating) is only 1.5 N.

The PHANToM is controlled by a PC through a three-channel, 12-bit D/A/D card and separate power amplifier and conditioning interface box [SensAble Devices Co., 1994]. A safety switch is also connected to the power amplifier box to instantly disable the feedback arm. The actuator control loop runs at 800 Hz, which allows for the superposition of vibrations on the force-feedback signal. No data is provided on the mechanical arm bandwidth. When tried by the author, the system seemed responsive and hapticly convincing even with these low feedback-force levels. Surface textures were also easily perceived and discriminated. The lack of torques at the fingertip did limit, however, the kinds of simulations demonstrated to mostly two-dimensional ones.

The PHANToM is now sold by SensAble Devices Co. for approximately $20,000 (which includes the haptic mechanism, the interface card, and power electronics, as well as a small software library). The company is working to increase the PHANToM range of motion and number of actuators, with prices expected to drop in 1996.

Six-degree-of-freedom Pen-based Force Display. Simulation of forces and torques about a point in space requires six actuators integrated in a six-degree-of-freedom device. Such a pen-based haptic interface developed at the University of Tsukuba [Iwata, 1993] is illustrated in Figure 4.11a. It replaces the single serial arm of the PHANToM with two three-degree-of-freedom arms connected to a stylus. The first three joints of each arm (MA1...MA3; MB1...MB3) are active, whereas the stylus attachment joints are passive. Depending on the direction of forces F_A and F_B the device can apply both forces and torques on the user's hand. If both forces are equal in magnitude and direction, then pure translational forces are fed back to the user. If the two forces are equal in magnitude but opposite in direction, then pure torques are applied. For example, torques about the roll (stylus) axis are produced by F_A and F_B acting in opposition along that axis. A push button on the stylus allows for user actions on the environment, such as grasping or releasing a virtual object. The maximum force generated by Iwata's pen-based force display is reported as 5 N within a spherical work envelope of 44 cm diam.

The force display was integrated with an Indigo graphics workstation through an RS232 line communicating to an interface electronics box. This houses a 8086 microprocessor performing low-level control of the actuators through pulse-width modulation. The sensors on the two feedback arm joints are read through an A/D card with an overall stylus point positional accuracy of 2 mm. The force feedback and graphics display are integrated in a high-level loop with a rate of 10 frames/sec. Color Plate 1 shows the user moving the pen-based haptic display to control a virtual tool. This tool deforms a two-dimensional mesh with resultant forces being felt by the user. Chapter 7 will present a more detailed discussion on the underlying surface deformation algorithm.

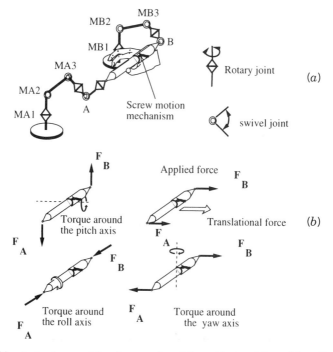

Figure 4.11   A six-degree-of-freedom pen-based force display. Adapted from Iwata [1993]. © Éditions Hermès. Reprinted by permission.

4.1.3. Stringed Force-Feedback Interfaces

Stringed force-feedback displays differ from other desk-grounded haptic interfaces in that they use thin steel cables (or strings) to apply forces on the user's hand. Actuators are placed remotely from the hand, being attached to a (typically) cubic supporting structure. Stringed haptic interfaces have therefore very low weight, small inertia, and substantially larger workspace than joysticks, owing to the long cables used. The drawback for stringed interfaces is their unidirectional (tensile) force exertion capability. To be able to exert three-dimensional forces (and torques), it is necessary to use a large number of strings and actuators. Depending on the particular design, the large number of strings may interfere with each other and with the user's hand.

The Texas 9-String Force Display.   One of the early string haptic interfaces was the Texas 9-string kinesthetic joystick developed by Lindemann and Tesar [1989] at the University of Texas at Austin. It was originally designed as a generalized master for space telerobotics applications. As shown in Figure 4.12, this six-degrees-of-freedom interface had nine strings and three air cylinders supporting a T-shaped handle in the middle of a cubic enclosure.

The pneumatic actuators were supported by an adjustable bracket in the center of a two-degree-of-freedom gimbal. These pistons applied compressive forces to

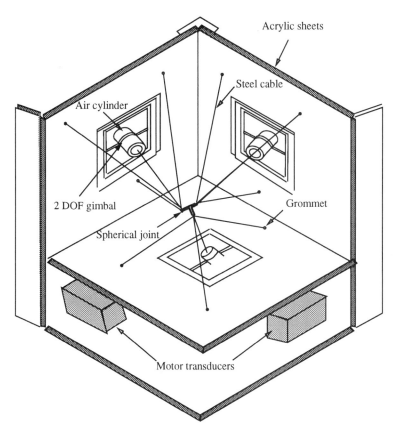

Figure 4.12 The Texas 9-string force display. Adapted from Lindemann and Tesar [1989]. Reprinted by permission.

compensate for the tensile ones produced by the nine rotary actuators and strings. Each group of three strings and one cylinder shaft attached to one end on the T-shaped handle through spherical joints. The 45-cm stroke of the air cylinders resulted in a 45-cm-diam spherical workspace.

The string lengths (and thus the handle three-dimensional position) were measured by custom rotary potentiometers attached to a winding spool. Permanent-magnet brushless dc servo motors were used to control string tension. The motors were controlled in current regulation mode by servo controllers commanded by a host (Microvax) computer through a D/A converter. When all actuators were energized, it was possible to apply a triad of arbitrary forces on the T-shaped handgrip (limited by the maximum achievable string tension). The three force vectors sum up to produce the desired force and torque at the center of the handgrip. Tests showed that the prototype had a pure force maximum output of 43.4 N (9.75 lbf) in any direction and maximum torque of 4.8 N-m (43 lb-in.). Unfortunately, the large Coulomb friction in the actuator mechanism masked the smaller feedback forces and made precise (small) motions difficult. Additionally, the computation load needed for real-time kinematics was not matched by the computing power available at the time of the experiments, resulting in a low update rate of 9 to 10 Hz. This produced large time delays and jerky motion of the haptic interface.

The SPace Interface Device for Artificial Reality (SPIDAR). Another stringed haptic interface is the SPace Interface Device for Artificial Reality (SPIDAR) developed by Ishii and Sato [1993, 1994a] at the Tokyo Institute of Technology. Compared with the Texas 9-string interface, the SPIDAR system has a simpler, more compact construction.

The initial prototype shown in Figure 4.13a had four strings attached to a cap worn on the user's pointer finger. Each string passed through fulcrums at the vertices of a cubic metallic support frame placed on the user's desk. The length of each cable is measured by rotary encoders coaxial with dc actuators. The encoders have a resolution of 100 pulses/revolution, or 0.503 mm (for a 16 mm pulley). Considering that the length of each string is $l_0 \dots l_3$, and a cube structure of volume $a \times a \times a$, the

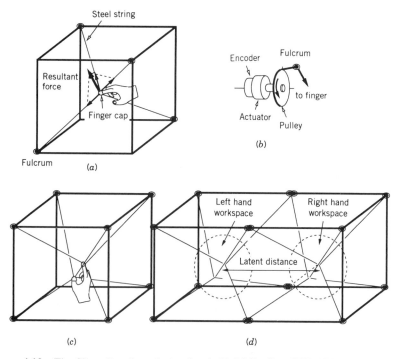

Figure 4.13 The SPace Interface device for Artificial Reality (SPIDAR): (*a*) SPIDAR I; (*b*) motor-encoder assembly; (*c*) SPIDAR II; (*d*) string setting for two-hand manipulation. Adapted from Ishii and Sato 1994a,b; Ishii et al. [1994]. Reprinted by permission from the MIT Press.

Cartesian fingertip position is given by

$$x = \frac{l_0^2 + l_1^2 - l_2^2 - l_3^2}{8a} \tag{4.3}$$

$$y = \frac{l_0^2 - l_1^2 + l_2^2 - l_3^2}{8a} \tag{4.4}$$

$$z = \frac{l_0^2 - l_1^2 - l_2^2 + l_3^2}{8a} \tag{4.5}$$

Considering the encoder resolution δl of 0.503 mm, the fingertip position uncertainty is given by the volume:

$$\Delta V_{\text{finger}} = \left[\frac{(\sum_{i=0}^{3} l_i)\delta l}{4a} \right]^3 \tag{4.6}$$

The resultant force vector **F** felt by the user is a function of the values of the tension in each string a_i $(0 - 4 \text{ N})$ and the tension unit vectors $\mathbf{u}_i$ so that

$$\mathbf{F} = \sum_{i=0}^{3} a_i \mathbf{u}_i \qquad (a_i \geq 0) \tag{4.7}$$

When controlled by a PC through A/D/A boards the overall position and force feedback bandwidth of SPIDAR was measured at 20 Hz.

Subsequently the SPIDAR system was modified to allow feedback to both thumb and pointer fingers as shown in Figure 4.13c. With both fingers requiring four strings, the system now had eight strings. Occasional kinematic interference was reported by the researchers for extreme abduction/adduction angles. The SPIDAR II system made possible the simulation of grasping forces and of the virtual object weight. The workspace was now a sphere of 30 cm diameter and virtual objects such as 5-cm cubes were comfortably grasped.

Another modification to the original design was the addition of a second hand in the simulation, as shown in Figure 4.13d [Ishii et al., 1994]. To add the second hand the researchers "merged" two SPIDAR II systems on a single support frame. In this way, each hand had a spherical workspace, 30 cm in diameter within a planar 120×60 cm structure. The distance between the two spheres called "latent distance" expresses the mapping between the user's real and virtual hands. When the user's hands are separated by the latent distance the corresponding virtual hands are touching in the virtual scene. Human factors studies showed that a 30 to 40 cm latent distance was the most comfortable for the user.

The SPIDAR II with a two-hand configuration was subsequently integrated with a graphics workstation, as shown in Figure 4.14. The display was placed in front of the user at a distance of 75 cm. The graphics show a pick-and-place task involving solid cubes. The measured force-feedback bandwidth was 30 Hz, and the graphics update rate was 10 frames/sec.

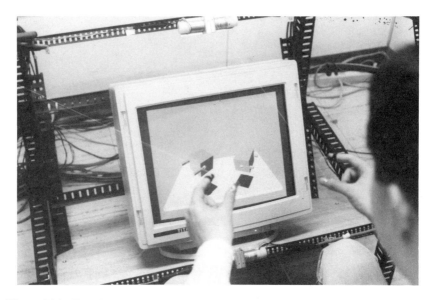

Figure 4.14   Experimental setup using the SPIDAR II configured for two-hand manipulation. Courtesy of Tokyo Institute of Technology.

4.1.4. The University of Tokyo Sensing Glove

The last type of desk-grounded haptic interface is the "Sensing Glove" developed by Hashimoto and his colleagues [1994] at the University of Tokyo. The interface, which is shown in Figure 4.15, consists of a mechanical exoskeleton supported by the desk. It has a large three-degree-of-freedom wrist through which the user places his hand. Thus the wrist can be rotated but not translated, which limits the user's mobility and natural interaction. The hand fingers receive independent force feedback through mechanical attachments. The thumb has two degrees of freedom, the index has three, and the other three fingers are grouped together with a support having two degrees of freedom. Thus the sensing glove has a total of 10 degrees of freedom, which allows for more dextrous tasks to be simulated. However, the glove's 10 degrees of freedom represent less than half of the human hand's 26 degrees of freedom (including wrist).

The Sensing Glove was integrated in a distributed simulation environment using a Sun Sparcstation 2 for glove calibration and a PC for low-level actuator control. The glove calibration, which relates exoskeleton angles to fingertip Cartesian positions, was done using a standard three-layer neural network through a custom transputer system. The force control loop is parallel to the graphics and modeling loop. Graphics is displayed at 30 frames/sec by a Silicon Graphics IRIS Indigo, and force feedback is done at 6 to 8 Hz. A separate Hewlett Packard 710 workstation was used for dynamic force simulation and modeling. It communicates with the other two computers participating in the graphics loop (SGI and Sun) over an ethernet. The Sun workstation, in turn, communicates with the PC low-level controller over a serial RS232 line.

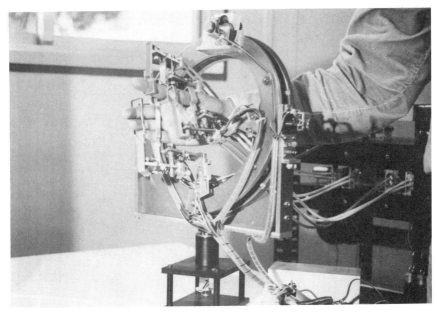

Figure 4.15   The University of Tokyo Sensing Glove. Courtesy of the University of Tokyo.

Our discussion of desk-grounded haptic interfaces concludes with Table 4.1, which summarizes the characteristics of all force-feedback devices discussed above.

4.2. FLOOR- AND CEILING-GROUNDED MASTERS

Having reviewed various desk-grounded haptic interfaces, we now start our discussion on floor- and ceiling-grounded ones. Within this category, we distinguish generalized masters (originally developed for telerobotics), robot arms of various configurations, individual motion platforms, and floor-grounded exoskeletons. In comparing various systems, we again use objective parameters such as number of degrees of freedom, output force capability, work space, and control bandwidth.

Generally speaking, floor- and ceiling-grounded force-feedback interfaces are larger, more complex, and more expensive than the desk-grounded ones. Owing to their large force output, user safety becomes more critical. This is especially true for exoskeletons, where the user is inside the workspace of the interface at all times. High costs and increased user safety concerns account for the limited use of today's floor- and ceiling-grounded haptic interfaces outside research laboratories.

4.2.1. Generalized Masters

Early telerobotic systems used kinematically identical master and slave devices. Users positioned the master arm, which had sensors and actuators. The sensors read master

TABLE 4.1 Comparison of Desk-Grounded Haptic Interface Performance

Interface Type	Degrees of Freedom	Output Force/Torque	Work Space	Band-width
Joysticks				
Spherical	2	20 N	17.6 cm	48 Hz
AT&T	2	0.7 N	5.5 cm	220 Hz
Cartesian	3	8.4 N	15 × 15 cm	80 Hz
PER-Force	6	53 N	10 cm; 90–180°	100 Hz
Stewart platform	4	45 N 135 N-cm	20 × 8 cm	100 Hz
Haptic master	6	69 N	40 cm	≥10 Hz
Magnetic levitated	6	60 N (peak) 20 N (sustained)	0.9 cm; 12°	3,000 Hz
Pen-based Masters				
University of Washington	3	13.5 (peak) 4.5 (sustained)	1.5×1.5×1 cm	N/A
PHANToM master	6/3	10 N (peak) 1.5 (sustained)	8×17×25 cm	≤800 Hz
University of Tsukuba	6	5 N (peak)	44 cm-diam sphere	≥ 10 Hz
Stringed Haptic Interfaces				
Texas 9-string	6	43.4 N (peak) 4.8 N-m (peak)	45 cm-diam sphere	9–10 Hz
SPIDAR	3	4 N/string	N/A	20 Hz
SPIDAR II	6–12	4 N/string (peak)	30 cm-diam sphere	30 Hz
Sensing Glove				
University of Tokyo Glove	10	N/A	hand-dependent	6–8 Hz

arm joint values, which were then replicated by the remote slave [Vertut and Coiffet, 1986]. Contact forces at the remote site were subsequently sent to the master and felt by the user. The master–slave kinematic equivalency was necessary because computer power did not allow for real-time complex kinematic transformations required by dissimilar master–slave pairs. Bejczy and Salisbury, who pioneered the generalized master concept, explain its advantages:

"A limiting factor for broadening the application of force-reflecting master–slave manipulator control technology is the nature of the master arm. The master arm in normally a one-to-one size kinematic replica of the slave arm, and each slave arm must have its own master arm. . . . the universal force-reflecting hand controller concept can be viewed as a generalization of the force-reflecting bilateral master–slave manipulator control technique.

—Bejczy and Salisbury [1980]

The subsequent increase in computer power allowed for generalized or universal master arms (also called hand controllers) that could command any number of slave configurations. Initially, the slaves were real, but subsequently virtual slaves were used for training and programming applications. Eventually, generalized masters were used to control other types of virtual objects (hand, tool, furniture, etc) and to provide force feedback to the user immersed in the simulation. Force feedback is applied at the wrist level, without independent finger output. A generalized master typically has, depending on the specific design, between four [Tanie and Kotoku, 1993] and six degrees of freedom [Yokoi et al., 1994; Adachi, 1994].

The JPL Universal Master. One of the first generalized masters was developed at NASA's Jet Propulsion Laboratory (JPL) by Bejczy and Salisbury [1980]. This six-degree-of-freedom interface, illustrated in Figure 4.16a, has a three-axis handgrip that slides and rotates around a fixed support attached to the floor.

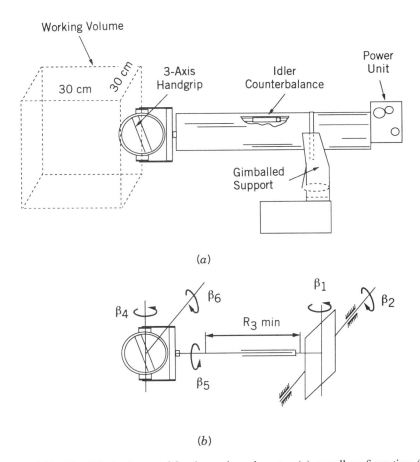

Figure 4.16   The JPL six-degree-of-freedom universal master: (*a*) overall configuration; (*b*) master kinematics. Adapted from Bejczy and Salisbury [1980]. Reprinted by permission of the ASME.

The handgrip has three intersecting axes $\beta_4, \beta_5, \beta_6$ and is supported by a gimbal. The hand gimbal is connected to a shoulder gimbal by a translating axis R_3. The shoulder gimbal has two rotation axes β_1, β_2. The joint range of motion is $\pm 180°$ for $\beta_4, \beta_5, \beta_6$, 0 to 30 cm for R_3 and $\pm 20°$ for β_1 and β_2. This results in a cubic workspace of $30 \times 30 \times 30$ cm.

The motors for the hand gimbal axes and for R_3 are mounted on a drive unit that is stationary with respect to the motion of the hand gimbal. Transmission is done by cables, with large curvatures to reduce friction and increase backdrivability. The power unit is thus placed remote from the handgrip, which minimizes the weight of the handgrip assembly as well as the counterbalance weight. An idler mechanism translates in the opposite direction to R_3 to maintain the center of gravity of the controller fixed and to preserve tension in the cables to the hand gimbal.

The hand master kinematics is shown in Figure 4.16b. The handgrip Cartesian position ($x_{hand}, y_{hand}, z_{hand}$) can be found as a function of joint values $\beta_1, \beta_2, R_3, \beta_4, \beta_5, \beta_6$:

$$x_{hand} = R_3 \cos \beta_1 \sin \beta_2 \tag{4.8}$$

$$y_{hand} = R_3 \sin \beta_1 \sin \beta_2 - \frac{1}{2}(R_{3,max} - R_{3,min}) \tag{4.9}$$

$$z_{hand} = -R_3 \cos \beta_2 \tag{4.10}$$

Similarly, the handgrip orientation angles as a function of rotation joint values are

$$yaw_{hand} = \beta_1 - \beta_4 \tag{4.11}$$

$$pitch_{hand} = \beta_5 \tag{4.12}$$

$$roll_{hand} = \beta_2 - \beta_6 \tag{4.13}$$

Finally, the relationship between the Cartesian forces $\mathbf{F}_x, \mathbf{F}_y, \mathbf{F}_z$ acting on the virtual object and the forces and torques that need to be applied along the axes β_1, β_2, R_3 are

$$\tau_{\beta_1} = -n R_3 [\mathbf{F}_x(\cos \beta_4 \cos \beta_5 \cos \beta_6 + \sin \beta_4 \sin \beta_6)$$
$$+ \mathbf{F}_y(\sin \beta_4 \cos \beta_6 - \cos \beta_4 \cos \beta_5 \sin \beta_6)$$
$$+ \mathbf{F}_z(\cos \beta_4 \sin \beta_5)] \tag{4.14}$$

$$\tau_{\beta_2} = n R_3 [\mathbf{F}_x(\sin \beta_5 \cos \beta_6) - \mathbf{F}_x(\sin \beta_5 \sin \beta_6) - \mathbf{F}_z(\cos \beta_5)] \tag{4.15}$$

$$\mathbf{F}_{R_3} = n [\mathbf{F}_x(\sin \beta_4 \cos \beta_5 \cos \beta_6 - \cos \beta_4 \sin \beta_6)$$
$$- \mathbf{F}_y(\sin \beta_4 \cos \beta_5 \sin \beta_6 + \cos \beta_4 \cos \beta_6)$$
$$+ \mathbf{F}_z(\sin \beta_4 \sin \beta_5)] \tag{4.16}$$

where n is a scaling factor.

The handgrip was designed to apply arbitrary forces up to 9.8 N (35 oz) and torques up to 0.5 N-m (70 oz-in.), with friction accounting for only 5% of the output. This low friction combined with low effective inertia at the handgrip (less than 1 kg/cm^2) increased the interface force fidelity. The simple position-to-force transformations coupled with the natural counterbalancing mechanism mentioned above reduced real-time computation load. This allowed for a high control bandwidth of approximately 40 to 50 Hz [Bejczy and Salisbury, 1980].

In recent years the JPL generalized master was retrofitted with a dextrous hand controller to allow the teleoperation of multifinger robotic hands [Jau, 1992; Jau et al., 1994]. The hand master has 16 degrees-of-freedom (four each for the thumb, index, middle, and ring fingers). Each finger exoskeleton structure integrates position sensing, force sensing (through strain gages), and flex cables that transmit torques from a separate actuator box.

Since the actuators are not placed on the back of the hand the total weight of the exoskeleton is about 1 kg. A quick snap-on connection outside the palm attaches to the circular ring of the JPL generalized master (replacing the grip handle).

The MEL Master Arm. The interface described here was intended for telerobotic applications, and its usage was subsequently extended to VR simulations. Researchers at the Mechanical Engineering Laboratory (MITI, Japan) developed a master arm specifically designed for VR applications [Kotoku et al., 1989, 1992, 1994]. As opposed to the JPL universal master that has six degrees-of-freedom, the MEL arm has only four (x-y-z translations plus roll). As illustrated in Figure 4.17a, this haptic interface has a special design that uses a parallelogram link that includes the second

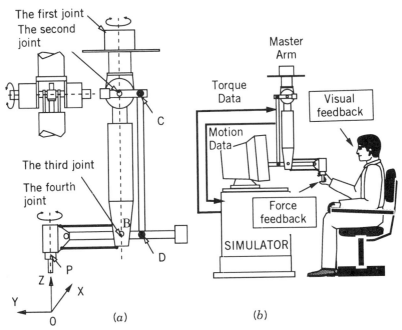

Figure 4.17 The four-degree-of-freedom direct-drive MEL Master Arm: (a) overall arm configuration; (b) simulation system. Adapted from Tanie and Kotoku [1993]. © Éditions Hermès. Reprinted by permission.

and third joints. This assures a decoupling of the arm dynamics and configuration-invariant inertia, without the need for computation-intensive active compensation torques.

The first three revolute joints have a range of $\pm 70°$, $\pm 25°$, and $\pm 30°$, respectively. This results in the arm tip moving in a work envelope approximatley $40 \times 42 \times 30$ cm. Joint angles are measured by high-resolution optical encoders (50,000 pulses/rev). By measuring the joint angles and using direct kinematics equations it is possible to find the arm hand grip Cartesian position:

$$x_{hand} = (L_1 \sin \theta_2 + L_2 \cos \theta_3 + L_3) \sin \theta_1 \qquad (4.17)$$

$$y_{hand} = -(L_1 \sin \theta_2 + L_2 \cos \theta_3 + L_3) \cos \theta_1 + L_2 + L_3 \qquad (4.18)$$

$$z_{hand} = -L_1 \cos \theta_2 - L_2 \sin \theta_3 + L_1 \qquad (4.19)$$

The handle orientation versus the z axis is:

$$\varphi_{hand} = \theta_1 + \theta_4 \qquad (4.20)$$

where $L_1 \ldots L_4$ are the arm link lengths, and $\theta_1 \ldots \theta_4$ are the joint angles. The orientation of the fixed (x-y-z) system of coordinates is shown in Figure 4.17a and its origin corresponds to the handle position when all joints have zero values. It is thus possible to determine the handle position with a translational accuracy of 2 mm.

An additional design improvement over the JPL master is the use of direct-drive actuators placed at the arm joints (without the need for cables and pulleys). The actuators used are frameless ac brushless motors capable of up to 70 N-m torques. This results in a translational force at the tip of the arm of up to 20 N, and 0.4 N-m torque about the arm handle.

To generate the same force vector **F** at the tip of the master arm, it is necessary to create a torque vector τ at the master joints given by

$$\tau = \mathbf{J}(\theta)^T \mathbf{F} + \tau_c(\theta) \qquad (4.21)$$

where $\mathbf{J}(\theta)^T$ is the transpose of the master arm Jacobian matrix, and $\tau_c(\theta)$ is the compensation torque for arm inertia and weight. Force control accuracy tests were performed using a six-axis force sensor integrated in the arm wrist. These tests showed a force control error of approximately 2 N (10% of output).

Figure 4.17b shows the MEL direct-drive arm integrated in a VR simulation system using a Sun 25-MHz Sparc for graphics display. Computations are distributed on a parallel computing scheme using three T800 CPUs. The T800 32-bit processors are used for arm position computation (based on joint sensor data) and for computation of virtual world collisions and feedback forces. These forces are written to a D/A board and then to actuator motor controllers. These direct-drive controllers are servoing the actuators at approximately 1000 Hz, whereas the high-level graphics (and force-feedback) loop is closed at approximately 16 frames/sec. (or 16 Hz) [Kotoku et al., 1992].

The SPICE Haptic Interface. Another floor-grounded haptic interface that uses direct-drive actuators is the SPace Interface deviCE (SPICE) [Adachi, 1994; Adachi et al., 1995] illustrated in Figure 4.18.

This six-degree-of-freedom interface uses brushless dc motors placed at the arm joints coupled with optical encoders for position measurement. The actuator maximum torques drop from 227 N-m at the first (base) joint to 1.6 N-m for the handgrip

Figure 4.18   The SPICE haptic interface. Courtesy of Suzuki Motor Co.

roll. The encoder resolution is high for the first three joints (324,000 pulses/rev) and low (10,000 pulses/rev) for the handle joints. Similar to the MEL master design, a parallelogram mechanism is used to assure invariant and decoupled arm inertia [Adachi, 1994].

The SPICE arm was integrated into a VR system using an IRIS 420 VGX for graphics display and a VME-distributed multiprocessor computation architecture [Adachi, 1993]. Two 68030 CPUs are used for simulation of the virtual environment and for the control of the feedback arm. The high real-time computation load required the addition of three 50 MHz, 32 bit vector processors. The vector processors are very effective in homogeneous matrix computations (products, Jacobians, etc.) which are needed for kinematics and force control. Researchers report a 1000-Hz sampling rate for low-level control and 10 Hz for high-level graphics and force-feedback computations [Adachi et al., 1995]. No information is provided on the overall arm workspace or on its output forces and torques.

The Six-Degree-of-Freedom Cartesian Manipulator. The last generalized master arm to be discussed here is the six-degree-of-freedom interface developed at the National Institute of Bioscience and Human Technology in Japan [Yokoi et al., 1994]. As illustrated in Figure 4.19, the device resembles a Cartesian joystick, similar to the PerForce interface discussed earlier in this chapter. The kinematic construction has three orthogonal Cartesian axes using linear actuators and three orthogonal revolute axes with actuators used to orient a handle. The X-Y-Z axes

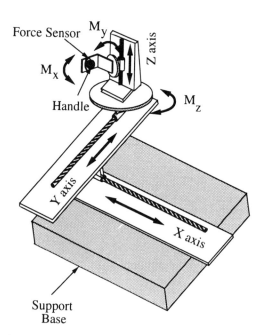

Figure 4.19 The six-degree-of-freedom Cartesian manipulator. Adapted from Yokoi et al. [1994]. Reprinted by permission of the SICE.

have a range of motion of 40 cm, 40 cm, and 20 cm, respectively [Fukui, 1995]. The roll-pitch-yaw axes each rotate 230°.

There are however, major differences in the control of the two devices. The six-degree-of-freedom Cartesian manipulator uses a force sensor in the arm wrist to read user force inputs. Feedback from the simulation moves the arm to minimize these input forces (when simulating free-space motion), or to oppose the user (for hard contact simulation). Thus the arm is controlled in a force-feedforward–position feedback mode. All joysticks discussed previously had position feedforward–force-feedback control.

The Cartesian manipulator has six servo actuators (dc for the X and Y axes and AC for the other four axes). Force sensor data from the arm handle is read by a PC9801 controller and used to drive the positioning actuators. The reported force-feedback electromechanical bandwidth is 4 Hz. The force sensor resolution is approximately 9.8×10^{-3} N and 4.9×10^{-4} N-m for torques.

The researchers acknowledge control difficulties with the device (shaky movement and resonance). Large vibrations occurred whenever the handle (and force sensor) was grasped tightly by the user. Recent tests showed improved control when gains were changed dynamically (reducing them for high grasping forces) [Fukui, 1995].

4.2.2. Robot Arms

Robots have been used since the early 1980s in industry to perform simple tasks with high speed and repeatability. Most of today's industrial robots have serial kinematics and remote actuator transmission, and they operate in position control [Fu et al., 1987]. They are controlled in real time by dedicated computers called robot controllers, which may or may not communicate with more powerful host computers.

Robots can also be teleoperated, typically when the task is remote or the environment is dangerous for direct human involvement (undersea, nuclear facilities, etc.). Telerobotics allows increased task flexibility, since users are part of the control loop. They input commands through master manipulators similar to the ones described in the previous section.

A more recent use of industrial robots is in providing haptic feedback for VR simulations. One approach is to use a small six-degree-of-freedom robot manipulator with a wrist force sensor and a handlegrip [Sayers and Paul, 1994]. Forces applied by the user on the manipulator wrist (force feedforward) are sent over serial lines to a host computer running the VR simulation. These forces are mapped into virtual object velocities (rate control) or contact forces (force control) depending on the particular simulation event. Feedback from the host computer is then sent to the robot controller in the form of robot position commands (position feedback).

Magnetic Robot Interface. Another application of industrial robots to VR haptic feedback is in providing mechanical grounding and support for the haptic interface. One example is the magnetic interface being developed by Luecke and Winkler [1994] at Iowa State University. As shown in Figure 4.20*a*, the robot manipulator supports

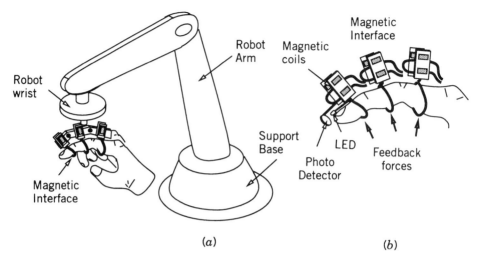

(a)   (b)

Figure 4.20   The robot-supported magnetic haptic interface: (*a*) robot manipulator support; (*b*) finger attachment. Adapted from Luecke and Winkler [1994]. Reprinted by permission of the ASME.

the heavy weight of a hand exoskeleton with multiple coils. These coils provide the magnetic field necessary to levitate a feedback structure worn on the user's fingers.

As shown in Figure 4.20*b* the system is being designed to provide feedback forces on each finger link. The placement of finger attachments and thus force exertion in its sagital plane is sufficient to generate effective grasping forces [Bergamasco, 1993a]. Each sagital plane structure consists of a pair of permanent magnets supported by the robot and light coils attached to the user's finger. The force applied on each finger link is then proportional with the current through the corresponding coil. The robot wrist then provides additional feedback necessary to simulate virtual object weight and inertia, which cannot be done by hand-grounded interfaces alone. Fingertip tracking is assured with pairs of photoemitters and photodetectors. These track the fingertip position so that the robot and its part of the magnetic structure follows the hand grasping motion. No currents are applied when there is no need for force feedback, and, because no contact exists, friction is essentially zero. As long as the coil remains within the constant magnetic field zone the force felt by the user is also constant (for a given current). Therefore small tracking lags from the robot point-to-point motion control are automatically compensated by the system. As explained by the researchers:

> This lurching motion of the robot drew attention to one advantage of using the electromagnetic coupling for the application of forces to the operator. Because there is no mechanical connection, relative motion between the manipulator and the operator does not change the level of force perception.... This is an important quality, because the robot trajectory disturbances caused by nonlinear dynamic effects are not perceived by the operator.

—Luecke and Winkler [1994]

An additional advantage of the above system is its large workspace (compared with desk-grounded haptic interfaces) with increased user's freedom of motion. Tests on a first single-coil prototype showed forces up to 4 N for a 4-amp current and a 70-turn coil. Joule-effect heating became a problem due to the close proximity to the user's skin. It was then necessary to limit the coil current to 2 amps, which reduced feedback forces to 3 N.

The Shape Approximation Device. Yet another robotic application for VR haptic feedback is the "Shape Approximation Device" developed by Tachi and his colleagues [Tachi et al., 1994] at the University of Tokyo. The system is intended to provide force feedback during large space interaction with surfaces of various shapes and impedances. User's wear a passive seven-degree-of-freedom exoskeleton that measures the position and orientation of a single fingertip. A six-degree-of-freedom manipulator called "Active Environment Display" moves to anticipate and if necessary counter the user's actions to display contact with virtual surfaces. The robot manipulator is a pantograph with range of motion of 60 × 60 × 60 cm for translations and 360°, 180°, and 135° for yaw, roll, and pitch, respectively.

The wrist of the manipulator carries a device with a complex surface geometry grouping vertices, as well as convex and concave edges and flat surfaces. It is thus possible to simulate contact with continuous surfaces by moving the Shape Approximation Device in the tangential plane to the contact point (fingertip brace). Contiguous surfaces are displayed by reorienting the corresponding facet of the Shape Approximation Device. Users wear a head-mounted display which immerses them in the virtual world and prevents them from seeing the manipulator arm. This significantly increases the simulation realism, at the cost of only allowing single-point contact with the virtual environment.

4.2.3. Personal Motion Platforms

Another type of floor- and ceiling-grounded haptic interfaces are motion platforms, which distribute feedback forces over the user's body. Although originally intended for defense and aerospace training applications, motion platforms are today part of sophisticated entertainment theaters. These include game arcades, Disney parks, or newer interactive movie theaters where entire rows of chairs move and vibrate to enhance the viewer's experience [Bizio, 1994]. Single-user, or personal motion platforms have recently become technically and economically feasible due to advances in actuator technology, coupled with increased user interest. The requirement for compactness, large carrying capacity, and good motion range and acceleration led to Stewart platform configurations being used by many designers.

The University of British Columbia Hydraulic Platform. Researchers at the University of British Columbia have developed a single-user, six-degree-of-freedom hydraulic motion platform [Salcudean et al., 1994]. As shown in Figure 4.21, this simulator uses a reversed-Stewart-platform configuration, with the 1-m-diam circular base being mounted on the ceiling.

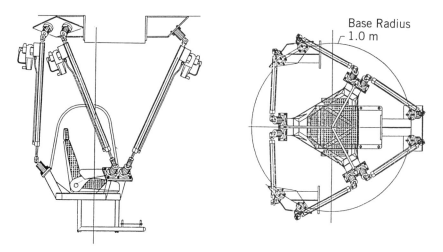

Base Radius
1.0 m

Figure 4.21 The University of British Columbia hydraulic single-user motion platform: (*a*) overall configuration; (*b*) ceiling support. Adapted from Salcudean et al. [1994]. © 1994 IEEE. Reprinted by permission.

Thus the user's chair is placed on a smaller (0.65-m-diam) platform suspended from the ceiling by six actuators. Because the actuators are in tension and not compression as in traditional designs, they are narrower without being subject to buckling. The disadvantage, of course, was difficulty in maintenance of ceiling-mounted actuators.

The prototype platform was designed to have ±1 m-translations and ±45° rotations, with linear and rotational velocities of ±1 m/sec and ±30°/sec, respectively. Accelerations are expected to reach ±9.8 m/sec² and ±400°/sec². To satisfy the above design requirements, the platform uses long actuators with 1.5-m stroke low-friction Teflon seals. They use oil at 2000 psi to produce 4000 N force and velocities of 1.5 m/sec.

Special three-stage proportional valves are used to control the substantial oil flow required. For safety reasons, the installation also includes homing valves that are placed in parallel with the proportional valves. These normally closed isolation valves can gradually return the platform to the floor in the event of a malfunction or when the user presses a panic button.

Computations are performed by a SPARCengine, with a lag-type prefilter control at 200 Hz and trajectory points generated at 20 Hz. Further tests are needed to ascertain the overall feedback control bandwidth.

The PemRAM Six-Axis Platform. The lower payload required by single-user motion platforms makes possible the use of other actuator types besides hydraulics. This results in easier installation, reduced costs, vastly improved energy efficiency, and lower operating expenses. One such actuator is the PemRAM electropneumatic cylinder discussed in Chapter 3. Figure 4.22 [Denne Developments Ltd., 1994b]

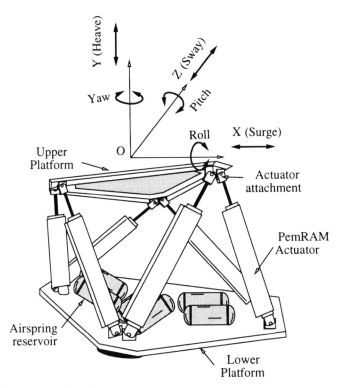

Figure 4.22   The PemRAM six-axis platform. Adapted from Denne Developments Ltd. [1994b]. Reprinted by permission.

shows the PemRAM 306 motion platform that uses six such actuators in a Stewart platform arrangement.

Each actuator is pressurized at the start of each simulation using air stored at 2 bars in an 5-liter air tank placed on the base platform. The upper platform translates in x (surge), y (sway), and z (heave) with a range of motion of ± 20 cm. Rotation range about these axes is $\pm 20°$ for roll and pitch and $\pm 25°$ for yaw, as shown in the figure. Control is handled by a central interface and power unit that coordinates position controllers integrated in each actuator. The central unit in turn communicates with the host computer running the simulation over a serial line. The excellent actuator response (small latencies) and good thrust combine to produce accelerations up to 4.9 m/sec^2 and a control bandwidth of 50 Hz. Vibrations up to 30 Hz can be superimposed on the platform motion. The PemRAM 306 platform is sold by Denne Developments Ltd. for $50,000.

The Flogiston Chair.   Another single-user motion platform is the Flogiston chair illustrated in Figure 4.23. It integrates a special shape chair frame with a three-degree-of-freedom motion platform PemRAM 303. The shape of the chair aims at placing

Figure 4.23 The Flogiston chair with Denne motion platform. Courtesy of the Flogiston Co.

the user in a biomechanical equilibrium. Its design combines a neutral body posture experienced in outerspace with a Yoga relaxation posture.

The Flogiston chair is made of aluminum covered with long-memory foam and leather and attaches through a small triangular base to the underside PemRAM platform. Its payload is 500 kg and the range of motion is ±18 cm Z (heave), −24° to +18° pitch, and ±20° roll. The platform is controlled similarly to the model 306 described previously, with a bandwidth of up to 20 Hz [Flogiston Co., 1994].

When the Flogiston is in static equilibrium, it provides body relaxation, thus increasing the user's simulation immersion. Of course, this immersion is further increased once the motion platform is energized and the user receives haptic feedback cues. The chair manufacturer (Flogiston Co.) hopes to reduce its price to approximately $5,000 once market demand increases.

4.2.4. Floor-Grounded Exoskeletons

Exoskeletons are the last type of floor-grounded haptic interface to be discussed in this chapter. They differ from previously described desk or floor- and ceiling-grounded interfaces in that contact forces may be applied at the wrist and other user's arm segments. Because exoskeleton masters are worn, the user's freedom of motion is increased, together with the number of degrees of freedom where forces are applied. Thus, floor-grounded exoskeletons are the most complex and expensive nonportable haptic interfaces. They are related to, but differ from, portable exoskeletons discussed in the next chapter. For now we describe two nonportable systems. The first is the Dextrous Arm Master produced by SARCOS Co. for $250,000 [Jacobsen et al., 1991*b*]. The second is a recent prototype called FREFLEX, developed by Odetics Co. for the Air Force [Burke, 1992; Hasser, 1995*b*].

The SARCOS Dextrous Arm Master. The Dextrous Arm Master was originally developed by SARCOS Co. for underwater telerobotic applications, where it controlled a dextrous slave robot. Subsequently the master arm was configured as a stand-alone system and is presently being adapted as haptic interface for VR simulations. The master arm kinematics was designed to resemble that of the user's arm wearing it. It has three shoulder/humeral degrees of freedom (flexion/extension, abduction/adduction, and rotation), one at the elbow for flexion/extension and three at the wrist (flexion/extension, abduction/adduction, and rotation). The wrist supports a modular hand unit where the user places his hand. The hand unit has fewer degrees of freedom than the user's hand, allowing control by the thumb (anteposition/retroposition and abduction/adduction) and another finger (abduction/adduction). Thus the Dextrous Arm Master has a total of ten degrees of freedom as illustrated in Figure 4.24 [Jacobsen et al., 1991a].

Each master exoskeleton joint groups a specially designed load cell, a hydraulic actuator/servovalve, and a high-precision potentiometer. The arm load cells are of a proprietary "twist" design, whereas the ones in the hand are cantilever beam strain gauges. They are used to measure the user's input force for the simulation. The potentiometers measure joint positions that are needed for low-level joint servo control. The servo valves are also an invention of SARCOS and are extremely compact and sturdy, with a bandwidth of approximately 500 to 650 Hz. The arm feedback bandwidth depends on the joint location and configuration and varies between 10 Hz (shoulder) and 100 Hz (wrist) [Atwood, 1995]. The actuators use high-pressure oil at 3000 psi and provide the feedback positioning to oppose the user's motion. Their maximum torque decreases from the shoulder (97.7 N-m) to elbow (50 N-m), wrist (22 N-m) and hand (5.5 N-m). All the wiring and hydraulic piping is routed inside the exoskeleton, which prevents accidental rupture and reduces injury risks. There are three hydraulic hose routes, namely supply (high pressure), return (low pressure), and drain. The manifolds in the back of the master support are routed to an oil pump

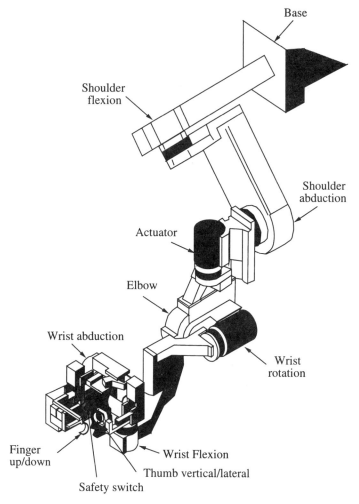

Figure 4.24 The SARCOS Dextrous Arm Master. Adapted from Jacobsen et al. [1991a]. Reprinted by permission.

that provides the energy needed by the arm. The drain system is intended by the manufacturer to catch all oil leaks at the servo valves. In the author's experience, these leaks can still soil clothes.

Apart from the exoskeleton arm and oil pump, the system also includes a controller interface and host computer that runs the simulation. The controller groups the joint controller boards, power supply, fan unit, and i/o communication board. Communication with the host computer is done over a 16-line parallel bidirectional i/o bus. Each joint controller board is responsible for a single exoskeleton joint. Gains can be set locally on the board, or can be digitally downloaded from the program running the

TABLE 4.2   Comparison of Floor- and Ceiling-Grounded Haptic Interfaces

Interface Type	Degree of Freedom	Output Force/torque	Work space	Bandwidth
Generalized Masters				
JPL master	6	9.8 N 0.5 N-m	30×30×30 cm cube	40–50 Hz
MEL master	4	20 N-m 0.4 N-m	40×42×30 cm	16 Hz
SPICE arm	6	N/A	N/A	10 Hz
Cartesian arm	6	N/A	40×40×20 cm	4 Hz
Robot Arms				
Magnetic interface	6 + finger	3 N	N/A	4 Hz
Shape approximation	6	N/A	60×60×60 cm	N/A
Personal Motion Patforms				
Hydraulic (UBC)	6	2,000 N/act. 250 kg payload	±100 cm X, Y, Z ±45° roll, pitch, yaw	≤20 Hz
PemRAM 303	3	500 kg payload	±18 cm Z −24° to +18° pitch, ±20° roll	50 Hz
PemRAM 306	6	1000 kg payload ±25° yaw	±20 cm X, Y, Z ±20° pitch, roll	50 Hz
Flogiston (PemRAM 303)	3	≤500 kg payload	±18 cm Z −24° to +18° pitch, ±20° roll	20 Hz
Exoskeletons				
SARCOS Dextrous Arm Master	10	97 N-m shoulder 50 N-m elbow 50 N-m wrist 5.5 N-m hand	180° shoulder 105° elbow 105°×180°×100° wrist 80° thumb	10 Hz 100 Hz
FREFLEX (Odetics Inc.)	7	25 N (at handgrip)	125×100×75 cm (at handgrip)	20 Hz

simulation. The joint controller boards have variable-intensity LED status indicators that are very useful in case of trouble shooting.

Since the user is in close proximity to the exoskeleton, and since this is a very powerful system, the user's safety is of major concern. Each joint controller board monitors the difference between commanded and actual joint positions. Whenever this value exceeds a preset threshold, a position error is detected and the arm is powered down. The same is true for forces measured by the load cells placed in the arm. The assumption is that either there is a software glitch that sets unreasonable joint position/force values, or something blocks the arm from reaching its commanded configuration. The arm may also be shut down by "watch dog timer" routines, by joint mechanical limit switches, or by a "dead-man switch" held by the user. High forces that occur during simulation of hard contact may also inadvertently trigger a safety shutdown. Unfortunately, there may not be an easy solution to this problem.

The FREFLEX Master. The Force REFLecting EXoskeleton (FREFLEX) Master is an electrical exoskeleton prototype developed for research at the Wright-Patterson Air Force Base. The master arm has seven degrees of freedom (similar to the SARCOS master) but no additional degrees of freedom at the hand. The system uses electrical dc actuators and cables to transmit forces to the user's hand, as illustrated in Color Plate 2. These actuators are located on a vertical console attached to the floor. Force sensing is done by a six-degree-of-freedom wrist sensor installed under the user's handgrip and a separate one-degree-of-freedom sensor at the elbow. This is used by the exoskeleton to track the user's elbow in order to improve performance.

When wearing the exoskeleton in the neutral position (shown in Color Plate 2) the user can reach 125 cm vertically, 100 cm laterally, and 75 cm front to back. This ovoidal workspace is approximately 80% of that of a person with fixed shoulders, but who is not wearing an exoskeleton. The actuators produce at least 25 N force at the handgrip. Whereas the control bandwidth is approximately 200 Hz, the exoskeleton force feedback bandwidth is only approximately 20 Hz because of the large arm inertia, gear friction, and backlash. Table 4.2 summarizes the performance characteristics of this and previously discussed floor- and ceiling-grounded haptic interfaces.

4.3. CONCLUSIONS

This chapter discussed various desk-grounded and floor- and ceiling-grounded force-feedback interfaces, comparing their degrees of freedom, force output, workspace, and bandwidth. Although these nonportable systems limit the user's freedom of motion, they do provide some haptic feedback capability and (in the case of desk-top systems) compactness and ease of use. Our discussion here leads to the next chapter, which describes research on portable force feedback for maximum user freedom of motion in the simulation.

CHAPTER 5

PORTABLE FORCE FEEDBACK

The previous chapter described nonportable force-feedback interfaces that were mechanically grounded to a desk, ceiling, or floor. The advantage of nonportable haptic interfaces lies in their ability to off-load the actuator weight from the user. The disadvantage is a reduction in the user's freedom of motion, and thus in the simulation naturalness. To allow maximum freedom of motion for the user receiving haptic feedback from the simulation, it is necessary to use a portable force-feedback interface. By *portable* interface, we mean an actuating or sensing structure that is grounded on the user's body (either on the back, chest, arm, or palm). Such portable masters are more difficult to design because there are limitations in overall weight and volume, dictated by the need to avoid user fatigue during prolonged simulations. This in turn implies high power-to-weight and power-to-volume ratios for the actuating system. Although several nonportable force-feedback interfaces are commercially available, most portable systems are under active research, reflecting the state of transition in haptic feedback hardware.

Portable force-feedback interfaces can be classified according to their mechanical grounding as either arm exoskeletons, or hand masters. *Arm exoskeletons*, sometimes called external force feedback (EFF) systems [Bergamasco, 1993a], are usually grounded to a back plate of the type used in rehabilitation therapy and to the forearm. Conversely, *hand masters*, also called hand force feedback (HFF) systems are grounded to the user's wrist, or to the palm, depending on their particular design. Their functionality within the VR simulation complements that of EFF systems, because

> The role of the HFF system is that of replicating mid-intensity forces on the fingers of the hand, as those recorded during common manipulation tasks of small–middle size objects. In the other situations (when the object is heavy or high collision forces have high

intensities, or conversely, when it is required the replication of very fine microindentation cues) the HFF can work in conjunction with complementary components of the whole force feedback system, such as the EFF and tactile feedback systems.

—Bergamasco [1993a]

Thus arm exoskeletons are able to replicate the weight of virtual objects, and collisions with the environment at other locations besides the hand. Hand masters, depending on their complexity, are more suitable for dextrous manipulation as well as exploration of the virtual environment. Our discussion in this chapter starts with arm exoskeletons, followed by hand masters. Tactile feedback systems which are incorporated in some hand masters will be discussed in detail in the following chapter of this book.

5.1. ARM EXOSKELETONS

Portable arm exoskeletons are structures that measure the user's arm motion and apply forces as required by the simulation. The human arm has seven degrees of freedom, as illustrated in Figure 5.1 [Caldwell et al., 1995a]. The shoulder has

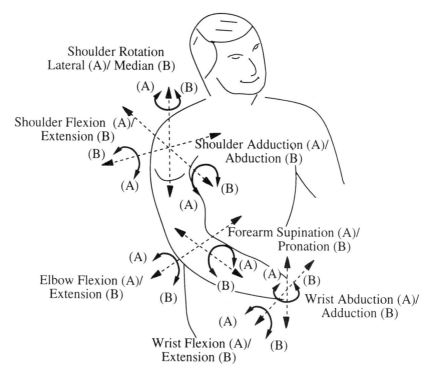

Figure 5.1 Terminology of the human arm degrees of freedom. Adapted from Caldwell et al. [1995a]. © 1995 IEEE. Reprinted by permission.

three degrees of freedom, namely adduction/abduction, flexion/extension, and rotation (medial/lateral). The elbow has two degrees of freedom that allow for forearm rotation and supination/pronation. Finally, the wrist has adduction/abduction and flexion/extension. Thus, to apply three-dimensional feedback forces, an arm exoskeleton would need seven degrees of freedom [Caldwell, 1995c]. Some systems, such as the GLAD-IN-ART EFF master [Bergamasco et al., 1994a] and the EXOS Force ArmMaster [EXOS Co., 1993a; Marcus, 1993], have only five actuated degrees of freedom, because wrist feedback is provided by a separate hand master.

5.1.1. The GLAD-IN-ART Arm Exoskeleton

The Glove-like Advanced Interface for the Control of Manipulative and Exploratory Procedures in Artificial Realities (GLAD-IN-ART) is a collaborative European ESPRIT project between Italy, the United Kingdom, and Ireland. This multiyear, multimillion dollar effort centered at the Scuola Superiore Santa Anna in Pisa is probably the largest European investment in the development of virtual haptic feedback technology. The project, which started in 1992, has resulted in an arm exoskeleton as well as a glove-based hand master called the "ARTS Hand Force Feedback System" [ARTS Lab., 1994].

The GLAD-IN-ART arm exoskeleton uses dc servo motors that provide torques to five joints through a tendon-based transmission system. As shown in Figure 5.2 [Bergamasco, 1993a], the three degrees of freedom at the shoulder do not use any idle pulleys, whereas the transmission to the elbow and forearm joints presents complex cable routing [Bergamasco et al., 1994a]. The user controls the exoskeleton through a handle attached to the end of the last rigid link. Each joint has position sensors and torque sensors that measure the differential tension in the actuation cables. The total structure weight (including actuators and transmissions) is approximately 10 kg, which is significant. To alleviate user fatigue, active gravity compensation was necessary.

The torques, applied by the dc actuators is 20 N-m for the shoulder abduction/adduction and flexion extension, 10 N-m for the shoulder and elbow rotations, and 2 N-m for the forearm pronation/supination. These torques form a vector τ, which relates to the vector of three-dimensional forces **F** applied at the handle. In static equilibrium, this relationship is [Bergamasco et al., 1994a]

$$\tau = J^T(q) \ \mathbf{F} \tag{5.1}$$

where $J(q)$ is the exoskeleton Jacobian matrix that depends on the joint position values (q). To provide for active gravity compensation, it is necessary to add to the above torques an amount proportional to the vector of gravity effects **G**. Additionally, the large exoskeleton inertia (due to its mass) and cable friction need to be accounted for to improve the feedback control. This was realized by integrating a three-dimensional force sensor at the handle to measure the error between the desired feedback forces

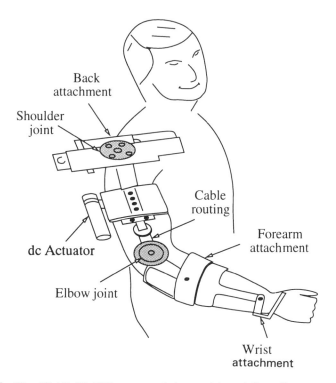

Figure 5.2 The GLAD-IN-ART arm exoskeleton. Adapted from Bergamasco [1993a]. Reprinted by permission of Springer-Verlag.

$\mathbf{F}_{\text{des}}$ and the actual forces $\mathbf{F}$ applied at the wrist [Bergamasco et al., 1994a]. Thus Eq. (5.1) becomes

$$\tau = \mathbf{G} + J^T(q)(\mathbf{F}_{\text{des}} + K(\mathbf{F}_{des} - \mathbf{F})) \tag{5.2}$$

where K is the 6×6 diagonal matrix of constant gains.

The above control algorithm was implemented on a distributed, transputer-based architecture. Two T800 transputers share the proportional-integrative-derivative (PID) joint control, and two other T800s perform gravity compensation and host communication with a Silicon Graphics Inc. (SGI) graphics workstation. Finally, two T222 transputers read the force sensor at the exoskeleton handle and drive the dc actuators. Data is shared by the transputers through synchronous communication, while communication with the host is done asynchronously. The control bandwidth is 1 kHz for the joint servo loop and lower for the less critical gravity compensation stage [Bergamasco et al., 1994a]. The quality of the feedback sensation is reported to be high [Rosenblum, 1994], despite the fact that adverse dynamics (such as coriolis and centrifugal forces) are not accounted for in Eq. (5.2).

5.1.2. The EXOS Force ArmMaster

Another five-degree-of-freedom arm exoskeleton is the "Force ArmMaster" produced by EXOS Co. [EXOS Co., 1993a] and shown in Color Plate 3. This haptic interface uses three dc actuators for the shoulder, one for the elbow, and one for the forearm, similar to the GLAD-IN-ART exoskeleton described previously. The ArmMaster compact design allows good freedom of motion so that the shoulder rotates 120°, respectively for flexion/extension and abduction/adduction and 90° for internal/external rotation. The elbow flexion/extension is 130°, and the forearm supination/pronation is 150°.

Each active joint has an encoder that measures its position and a torque sensor to measure actuator output. Torques are 6.3 N-m (56.6 lb-in.) at the shoulder joints, 1.6 N-m (14 lb-in.) at the elbow, and 0.38 N-m at the forearm. Static friction is approximately 4% of output. The total exoskeleton weight is approximately 10 kg (22 lb) which represents a 30% reduction in the 15 kg (33 lb) weight of the 1993 prototype. Most of the interface weight is distributed on the back attachment. Still, the 1.8 kg of the arm structure represents a significant weight for prolonged simulations and may lead to user fatigue and discomfort (even pain). More human-factor studies are needed to validate these concerns.

The ArmMaster control interface is illustrated in Figure 5.3 [Marcus, 1993]. A VME card cage contains counters that sample the joint position encoders at 1 kHz. Dual TI C40 DSP processors perform the exoskeleton control by calculating contact forces and corresponding exoskeleton torques. These torque values are then sent to the dc motors through a six-channel D/A board and servo amplifiers. A separate SGI host computer performs the VR simulation at a graphics update rate of 30 frames/sec. It receives master position information and sends corresponding action commands to the DSP controllers over an ethernet port connected to the VME bus. The 1995 list price for the Force ArmMaster is $78,000 (including the VME controller).

5.1.3. The University of Salford Arm Master

The arm exoskeletons described above all use dc actuators that have low power-to-weight ratios. This results in a heavy interface structure that weighs in excess of 10 kg. Researchers at the University of Salford (United Kingdom) are currently working on a lightweight arm master. In their view,

> For any tele-operated/virtual reality system prolonged use is a definite possibility and indeed for economic viability a necessity. It is therefore essential that in addition to simply performing the assignments outlined above, the exoskeleton structure should be comfortable, natural to use and lightweight. These requirements form the specification for the system design.
>
> —Caldwell et al. [1995a]

The significant reduction in exoskeleton weight is due to the use of very light pneumatic muscle actuators of the type described in Chapter 3. These compact actuators are 15 cm long and weigh only 15 grams; however their contractile force

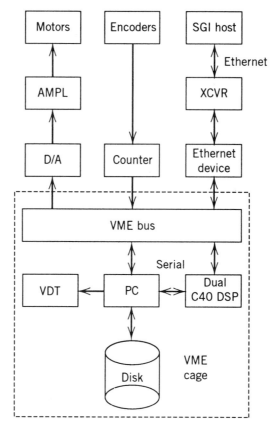

Figure 5.3 The EXOS ArmMaster control diagram. Adapted from Marcus [1993]. © Éditions Hermès. Reprinted by permission.

can exceed 150 N (at 7 bar or 100 psi). Recently, Caldwell [1995b] has reported very large forces of 1000 N (at 8 bar). As shown in Figure 5.4 [Caldwell et al., 1995a], the design uses actuators acting in opposition for each exoskeleton joint. The overall structure has seven degrees of freedom (three at the shoulder, two at the elbow, and two at the wrist) and attaches to the user through a body brace. Each joint position is measured by high-linearity potentiometers. The exoskeleton is constructed of a combination of steel (for load-bearing sections) and aluminum and weighs only 2 kg. Its geometry allows the user to reach over 90% of his normal work volume. The exoskeleton does limit shoulder extension (behind the back), but this is considered unimportant for the intended use in a VR simulation.

The compact actuator structure allows for integration close to their respective powered joints. Thus the forearm houses the wrist and forearm actuators, the upper arm integrates the elbow flexion/extension actuators, and the shoulder actuators are placed on the body brace. Low-stretch Kevlar tendons and pulleys are used to transform the pneumatic muscle linear contraction into a rotation needed for the exoskeleton rotary

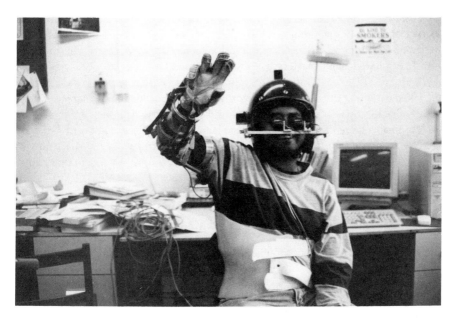

Figure 5.4   The University of Salford ArmMaster. Caldwell et al. [1995a]. © 1995 IEEE. Reprinted by permission.

joints. Wrist and forearm actuators can generate up to 200 N (at 8 bar), and upper arm and shoulder actuators produce up to 1000 N (also at 8 bar)! Control is done using piezoelectric valves placed remotely from the exoskeleton to control the actuators at 40 to 50 Hz. The intrinsic pneumatic muscle friction and hysteresis reduce the force-feedback bandwidth to only 1 to 2 Hz. Researchers are presently attempting to overcome the low-bandwidth problem through several approaches. One involves the use of newer 500 to 1000 Hz control valves, while another approach is a hybrid adaptive control/fixed operating point algorithm for the opposing muscles operating each joint. Researchers hope that these improvements will result in increased force-feedback bandwidth up to 10 Hz [Caldwell, 1995b].

5.2. HAND MASTERS

Hand masters are haptic interfaces that apply forces to the user's hand (and sometimes wrist) during the simulation of exploratory and manipulation tasks. Portable hand masters differ from the nonportable ones described in Chapter 4, because they are grounded on the user's forearm or palm. Therefore, the entire weight is sustained by the user remote from the body and may easily lead to user fatigue if the interface is heavy. Most of today's designs therefore place actuators remote from the hand (either on the forearm, or on the user's back). From there, cables and pulleys transmit motion and torques to the hand. Another motivation for remote actuation is the small "real estate" available on the fingers and palm for placing these actuators. The more degrees of freedom that are active (up to 20 for the hand alone) the more actuators are needed, and more surface is required for them. Therefore our discussion starts with string-based hand masters using exoskeletons [Iwata et al., 1992; Bouzit et al., 1993; EXOS Co., 1993b; ARTS Lab, 1994] or sensing gloves [Andrenucci et al., 1989; Kramer, 1993]. The drawback with remote actuation is increased static friction, backlash, and therefore reduced backdriveability. A newer design solution that eliminates these drawbacks is to place hand master microactuators on the hand, in a direct-drive configuration [Burdea et al., 1992a; Gomez et al., 1995]. Finally, we will present the IBM V-Flexor, which uses force sensors for independent finger input to the simulation [IBM, 1995].

5.2.1. The University of Tsukuba Hand Master

One of the first string-based portable hand masters for virtual haptic feedback was developed by Iwata at the University of Tsukuba [Iwata et al., 1992]. To keep the structure light (only 0.25 kg) the device provides feedback to only two fingers (thumb and pointer). As illustrated in Figure 5.5a, this haptic interface uses a string and pulley transmission to actuators placed on the dorsal side of the hand. This design permits maximum freedom of motion for the fingers and allows the grasping of real objects while the user is wearing the interface, because the palm area is free. A beam attachment on the back of the hand holds a rotary encoder that measures string displacement, a dc motor that provides up to 7-N feedback force, and a solenoid-actuated crutch. The crutch is used to simulate very hard objects by providing up to 20 N resistive force at the fingertip. The controller driving the actuators has a bandwidth of 350 Hz; however, no data is available on the electromechanical feedback bandwidth at the fingertip.

The placement of the pulley at a distance L_p of 10 cm from the actuator shaft allows for a joint angle θ of up to 60°. This permits the simulation of grasping (and feeling) virtual objects up to 9 cm in diameter. The fingertip position (P_{3x}, P_{3y}) is obtained based on the string length S using a table established during user calibration.

5.2.2. The LRP Hand Master

Another string-based hand master is the "LRP Hand Master" developed at the Laboratoire de Robotique de Paris (LRP) [Bouzit et al., 1993; Coiffet et al., 1993]. As illustrated in Figure 5.6a, this haptic interface provides feedback to all fingers at 14 hand locations.

Similar to the hand master developed by Iwata, the LRP Hand Master places all the feedback structure on the back of the hand, leaving the palm free. This exoskeleton transmits forces from remote actuators using a combination of micro cables (0.45 mm in diameter), pulleys, and flexible links. The cable translation inside transmission sheaths is measured by potentiometers placed at the motor shafts with an accuracy of 1°. This data is then used to estimate hand configurations during the simulation.

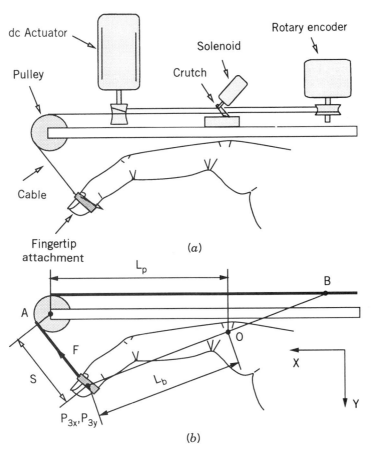

dc Actuator

Pulley

Solenoid

Crutch

Rotary encoder

Cable

Fingertip
attachment

(a)

L_p

B

A

F

S

O

X

L_b

P_{3x}, P_{3y}

Y

(b)

Figure 5.5 The University of Tsukuba Hand Master: (*a*) components; (*b*) geometry. Adapted from Iwata et al. [1992]. Reprinted by permission.

The plastic–aluminum exoskeleton incorporates force sensors that measure cable strain. This clever design allows for improved control despite cable friction and backlash. The feedback forces, which are normal to the finger segments during most of the grasping motion, are produced by dc disk motors. These actuators produce a continuous torque of 1.07 N-m and up to 11.48 N-m peak. All motors, power supply, and VME bus interface are placed in a separate control box that communicates with the host computer running the graphics simulation over an ethernet. No data is available on the control or feedback bandwidth of this system.

5.2.3. The ARTS Hand Force Feedback System

The ARTS Hand Force Feedback System [ARTS Lab., 1994] is a portable hand master developed by the GLAD-IN-ART European consortium. The hand master consists of a metacarpal plate and a glove-attached exoskeleton. The metacarpal plate has two

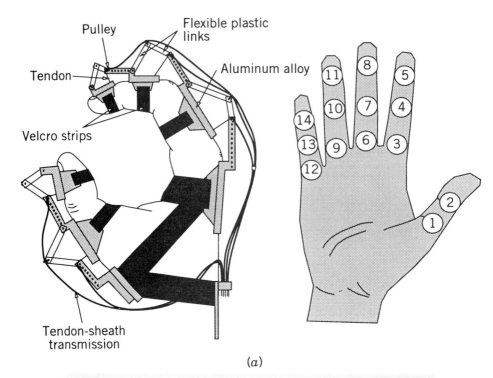

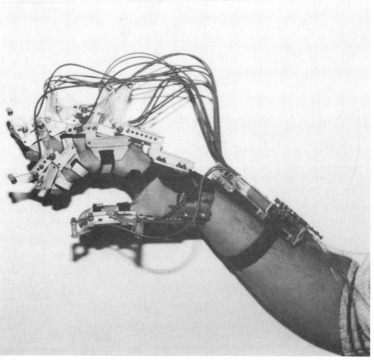

Figure 5.6 The LRP Hand Master: (*a*) construction; (*b*) the prototype. Adapted from Bouzit et al. [1993]; photograph courtesy of the Laboratoire de Robotique de Paris. © Éditions Hermès. Reprinted by permission.

degrees of freedom providing force feedback at the user's wrist. The plate functions as an attachment that allows the Hand Force Feedback System to connect to the distal end of the GLAD-IN-ART Arm Master described previously. The hand exoskeleton attaches to the back of the user's hand wearing a glove, as shown in Figure 5.7. The exoskeleton mechanical attachments allow for the exertion of normal forces to each phalanx of the thumb, index, middle, and ring fingers. The palm area is left free, which allows for totally unencumbered motion (joint flexions of 80° to 90° and abduction/adductions of ±15°). Position-sensing resolution for all degrees of freedom is very good (0.1°).

Feedback forces are exerted on each phalanx in the direction opposing grasping, up to a value of 1 N/phalanx. No force feedback is provided for abduction/adduction motion.

5.2.4. The EXOS SAFIRE Master

The Sensing and Force Reflecting Exoskeleton (SAFIRE) introduced in 1994 by EXOS Co. is the first commercially available portable hand master. Similar to the ARTS hand master, the SAFIRE uses dc motors and cables to apply forces on the thumb, index, and middle fingers. As shown in Figure 5.8, the actuators are placed on a structure on the back of the hand, thus leaving the palm area free. The master has two versions, namely SAFIRE I with five degrees of freedom and the SAFIRE II with eight degrees of freedom. Of these, the thumb and the index fingers have three degrees of freedom each, and the middle finger has two [EXOS Co., 1995a].

The SAFIRE allows a range of motion in flexion of 90°, whereas abduction/adduction and thumb anteposition is 45°. Each actuator has its own position

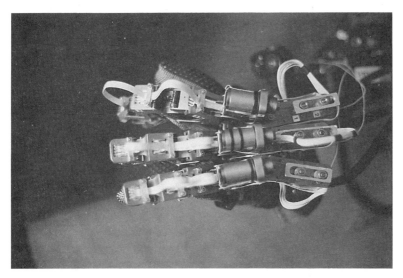

Figure 5.7 The GLAD-IN-ART Hand Master. Photograph courtesy of Scuola Superiore Santa Anna.

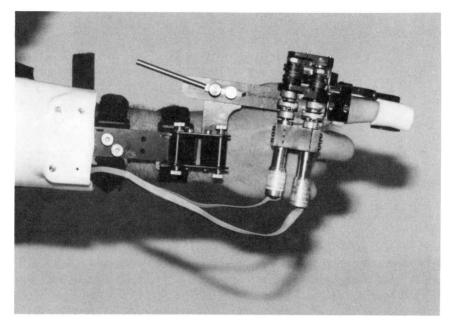

Figure 5.8   The EXOS SAFIRE Hand Master. Photograph courtesy of EXOS Co.

encoder and torque sensor for improved force-feedback control. The torques applied by the SAFIRE at the fingertips are 0.2 N-m. Static friction from the cables is approximately 4% of the output (or less) and backlash is less than 0.05°. The total weight of the hand master is 1.5 kg for the SAFIRE II (which is a significant reduction over the 2.5 kg or 5.5 lb of the 1993 prototype). Still, the weight of the master raises concerns on user comfort for extended simulation time. This is probably why the manufacturer offers an optional counterbalance mechanism (boom) and a six-degrees-of-freedom tracker. The current price of the SAFIRE I is $75,000 and the SAFIRE II costs $99,000 (including the VME controller and A/D/A boards).

5.2.5. The Virtex CyberForce Glove

All these hand masters use metallic exoskeletons and cables to transmit forces and torques from remotely placed actuators. Andrenucci et al. [1989] proposed a glove-based hand master with force feedback. Their design uses a double-layered glove with Kevlar tendons routed on the back of the hand. By eliminating the metallic exoskeleton, the master is significantly lighter and therefore more comfortable to use. The drawbacks are increased friction and more difficult control from the compliance of the glove support.

Later on, Kramer [1993] patented a similar design using a glove and Kevlar tendons, as illustrated in Figure 5.9. In addition to providing force feedback, Kramer's design also includes tactile feedback to the user's fingertips. A 3 × 3 micropin

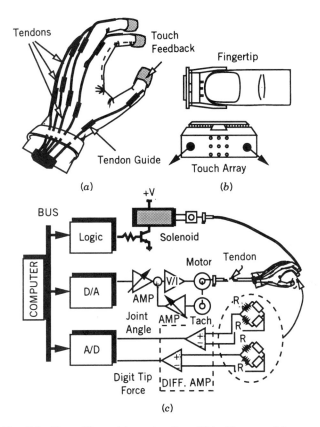

Figure 5.9 The CyberForce Glove: (*a*) construction; (*b*) tactile array; (*c*) computer control. Adapted from Kramer [1993]. © Éditions Hermès. Reprinted by permission.

array is attached to each fingertip using a metallic support. These pins are actuated by remotely located solenoids to produce various tactile feedback patterns. Force feedback is produced by pushing the array metal support back against the finger. The tendons are actuated by dc motors under computer control through a D/A board and power amplifiers. Hand position information, necessary to close the control loop is provided by position sensors integrated in the supporting glove. Virtex Co. which is manufacturing the open-loop CyberGlove, announced in 1994 the CyberForce Glove based on Kramer's patent. A year later this product is still not available, probably owing to difficulties in producing stable force feedback. However, in December 1995 the company announced the CyberTouch Glove which is a CyberGlove retrofitted with tactile feedback actuators [Virtual Technologies Inc., 1995]. The glove uses six electromechanical actuators distributed on the back of each finger and in the palm, and costs $14,000.

5.2.6. The Rutgers Master I

All the hand masters presented above use remote actuators and transmission of forces with cables, tendons, and pulleys. This results in increased master complexity, weight, and cost. Burdea and his colleagues at Rutgers University [Burdea et al., 1992a] developed a direct-drive design that eliminates the need for cable transmission, by placing the actuators directly in the user's palm. This hand master called "Rutgers Master I" was designed to retrofit open-loop sensing gloves such as the DataGlove [VPL, 1987] or the CyberGlove [Kramer et al., 1991]. As illustrated in Figure 5.10a, the force-feedback structure consists of four metallic microcylinders placed on a small L-shaped platform. The base of the pistons is coaxial with small spherical joints that allow the passage of small air tubes. Thus, each actuator has a conical work envelope that allows both finger flexion and adduction/abduction. The presence of the actuators in the palm does limit the hand mobility somewhat, and finger flexion is in the range of 40° to 50° (depending on the particular finger joint). Abduction/adduction angles are not affected. At the same time the piston dimension is such that fingers cannot be pushed backward past their straight ("zero") posture. This mechanical fail-safe design prevents accidents in case of computer failure. Velcro attachments at the fingertip and the palm platform allow for adjustments for different user hand sizes.

The actuators are off-the-shelf single-action pneumatic pistons modified by removing the inner return spring. These microcylinders have a very good power-to-weight ratio, producing a force of 4 N at the fingertip (for air at 90 psi). The total weight of the feedback structure in the palm is less than 100 g, which is the lightest of all hand masters discussed here. The actuator control is performed by proportional pressure regulators located in a separate control interface. This box also includes a dc power supply, main pressure indicator, and LED bar-graphs to visualize output pressures (i.e., forces) for each finger. A D/A cable connected to the interface box transmits output voltages from a D/A board installed in the host computer.

The Rutgers Master I has been integrated in a distributed ethernet-based simulation environment. A Sun 4 server is the host computer reading a DataGlove for position feedforward and driving the feedback actuators. Virtual world state information is sent to a dedicated graphics workstation (HP 755-CRX) that updates the virtual scene at 28 fps. The force-feedback loop has a bandwidth of 11 to 14 Hz (depending on the type of proportional controller used) and closes asynchronously with the graphics loop. The air pressure P_{cyl} for each finger is calculated based on the corresponding feedback force as

$$P_{cyl} = \frac{1.1\mathbf{F}_n}{A_{cyl}\ \cos(\gamma)} \tag{5.3}$$

where $\mathbf{F}_n$ is the feedback force normal to the user's fingertip and γ is the angle between the actuator shaft and the normal vector at the fingertip.

The Rutgers Master I, like any other portable hand master that has no wrist feedback, cannot simulate the virtual object's weight, or large collision forces with the environment. Burdea [1989] proposed to enhance the Rutgers Master I by integrating it with a wrist haptic interface such as the JPL Master [Bejczy and Salisbury, 1980;

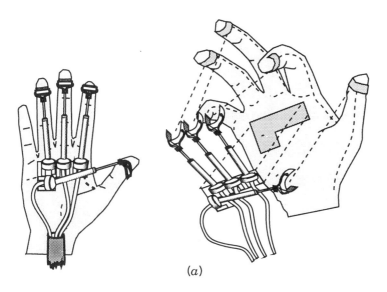

(a)

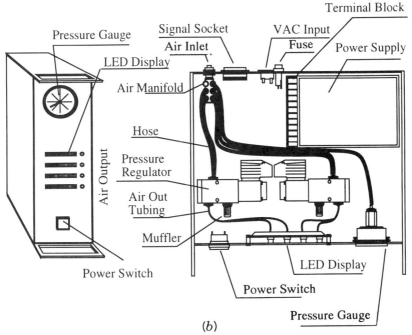

(b)

Figure 5.10 The Rutgers Master I (a) feedback structure; (b) control interface. Adapted from Burdea et al. [1992a]. © Éditions Hermès. Reprinted by permission.

also presented in Chapter 4 of this book]. The two haptic interfaces could be joined by simply replacing the JPL master handle with a connection to the Rutgers Master at the back of the hand. In this way, it is possible to track wrist motions in three dimensions using the JPL sensors, instead of using the DataGlove Isotrack three-dimensional sensor. Forces and moments can be applied at the wrist for gravity and collision simulation and at the fingertips for dextrous manipulation tasks. Several years later, NASA started experimenting with the same concept [Bejczy, 1993] but using its own force-feedback master to replace the handle of the JPL master (see also Chapter 4).

5.2.7. The Rutgers Master II

One of the difficulties with the Rutgers Master I was increased friction with the actuator wear, up to 10% of the output, as shown in Eq. (5.3). Another drawback was the hand master reliance on a commercial sensing glove for position sensing. This increased system costs and introduced unwanted sensing nonlinearities and coupling effects owing to the glove sensors. These problems have been addressed in the design of the Rutgers Master II [Burdea and Gomez, 1994; Gomez et al., 1994, 1995] which is shown in Figure 5.11.

The outward appearance of the Rutgers Master II looks similar to the first model, however the glove shown here is only used for support. All sensing had been inte-

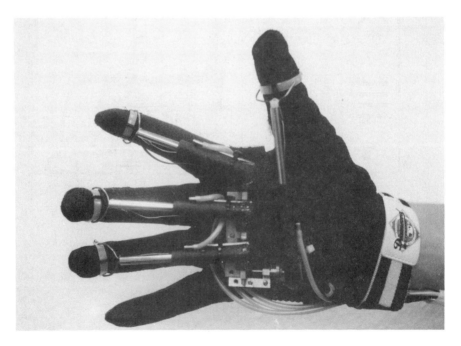

Figure 5.11   The Rutgers Master II prototype. Photograph courtesy of the CAIP Center, Rutgers University.

grated in the force-feedback structure, and the actuators were custom designed. When providing force feedback, it is important that sensing not introduce friction, therefore all the position sensors incorporated in the Rutgers Master II are noncontact.

Each cylinder attaches to the palm platform through two revolute joints with Hall-effect position sensors. The translation of the pistons in and out is detected by a pair of LED-phototransistor (as illustrated in Figure 3.18). Thus, the fingertip position and orientation is sensed directly in Cartesian space and not in joint space, as done by other hand exoskeleton devices. Therefore position errors in each sensor are not additive, and the overall sensing accuracy increases. The actuator glass-graphite construction reduces friction, whereas the larger diameter increased the force feedback at the fingertip. It is thus possible to produce fingertip forces up to 16.4 N (for 100 psi air pressure), four times more than the Rutgers Master I. Static friction in the cylinder accounts for only 0.05 N, which corresponds to a high dynamic range of 330. To date, the Rutgers Master II has been successfully integrated in the same single-user distributed environment described previously for the Rutgers Master I [Gomez et al., 1995]. Work is under way to create a Pentium-based system using the same control interface, but porting the software to a WorldToolKit commercial library [Sense8 Co., 1995].

5.2.8. The IBM V-Flexor

The last portable hand master to be discussed here is the V-Flexor control device developed by IBM-UK for the Project Elysium VR environment [IBM, 1995]. As opposed to the hand masters discussed previously, the V-Flexor, which is illustrated in Figure 5.12, does not have any actuators. Users feel "passive" force feedback by squeezing a sensorized handle in the palm. The handle has five air chambers and corresponding pressure sensors that measure the grasping force. The 8-bit analog output from these pressure sensors is input into an A/D coverter that is part of an Intel 80C198 microcontroller. Digital values are then sent to the host computer. The V-Flexor also includes a triple thumb and a three-dimensional tracker. The switch is used for navigating in the environment (forward, backward, reset), whereas the three-dimensional Polhemus tracker measures the palm position and orientation. During simulation, users command the grasping and releasing postures of a virtual hand by squeezing and releasing the V-Flexor. The advantage of the V-Flexor is its simple and robust construction, which eliminates the need for complex calibration required by glove and exoskeletons. Table 5.1 summarizes all the portable haptic interfaces discussed in this chapter.

5.3. CONCLUSIONS

Portable force-feedback interfaces allow a significant increase in the user's freedom of motion during the VR simulation. Arm exoskeletons provide force feedback at the wrist and forearm and allow the simulation of gravity and collision forces. Conversely, portable hand masters provide feedback to independent fingers and, thus, are suited

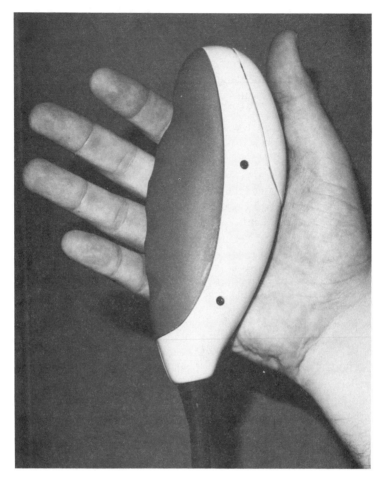

Figure 5.12   The IBM V-Flexor controller.

for the simulation of dextrous manipulation tasks. Prototype systems that couple arm exoskeletons and hand masters increase simulation realism at the expense of overall system complexity and cost. The vast majority of the interfaces described in this chapter place actuators remotely from the desired force application point. This is because of the poor power-to-weight and power-to-volume ratios of today's actuator technology. At least one hand master uses direct-drive actuators placed in the palm, resulting is a simple and extremely light design. Other force-feedback interfaces (such as the CyberForce) complement force feedback with tactile feedback. This feedback modality allows the simulation of contact geometry, surface texture, temperature, slippage, and so on, which supplements force-feedback information. Tactile feedback systems will be the subject of our next chapter.

TABLE 5.1   Comparison of Portable Haptic Interfaces

Interface Type	Degree of Freedom	Output Force/Torque	Work Space	Band-width
ARM MASTERS				
GLAD-IN-ART Arm Master	5	20 N-m shoulder, 10 N-m elbow, 2 N-m forearm	N/A	N/A
EXOS Force ArmMaster	5	40 N-m shoulder 13.4 N-m elbow	120° shoulder, 130° elbow, 150° forearm	30 Hz
University of Salford Arm Master	7	200 N wrist 1,000 N shoulder (at 8 bar)	90% of normal work volume	1–2 Hz
HAND MASTERS				
Univerity of Tsukuba	2/finger	7 N 20 N (crutch)	normal	N/A
LRP Hand Master	15	11 N-m peak	normal	N/A
ARTS Lab. Hand Master	12 (four fingers)	1 N/phalanx	normal	N/A
EXOS SAFIRE I SAFIRE II Master	5 (two fingers) 8 (three fingers)	0.2 N-m 0.2 N-m at fingertip	90° flexion 45° abduction 45° antepos.	30 Hz
CyberForce Glove	five fingers	N/A	normal	N/A
Rutgers Master I	4 active (four fingers)	4 N at fingertip	40–90° flexion 30° adduction	11 Hz
Rutgers Master II	4 active (four fingers)	16.4 N at fingertip	50–90° flexion full adduction	15 Hz

CHAPTER 6

TACTILE FEEDBACK INTERFACES

The preceding two chapters described various force-feedback interfaces used in virtual reality and (sometimes) telepresence applications. Whether portable or not, these haptic interfaces apply forces on the user's hand, wrist, or other body locations, in response to actions in the simulated world. Simulation tasks involving active exploration or delicate manipulation of the virtual environment make necessary the augmentation of feedback data with local information on the contact surface geometry or mechanical texture (smooth or rough surface). Such feedback is provided by tactile-feedback systems that are the subject of this chapter.

In general, tactile-feedback interfaces are simpler in design, lighter, and more compact than force-feedback interfaces. Within the haptic feedback category, tactile-feedback interfaces can function as stand-alone, or they can be integrated with force-feedback systems. Our chapter coverage starts with a description of tactile sensors used to realistically model the interaction task [Hutchings et al., 1994; Son et al., 1994; Burdea et al., 1995b]. Subsequently, we describe surface texture and geometry feedback [Stone, 1992; Patrick, 1990] followed by surface slip [Chen and Marcus, 1994] and temperature feedback [Ino et al., 1993b].

6.1. TACTILE SENSORS

Tactile sensors are used to measure simulation variables such as local or distributed forces, pressure, or deformation (surface shear). Within the scope of this book, we are interested in sensors that transduce the mechanical input into an electrical output. This electrical signal (voltage) is easily digitized and read by the host computer running the VR simulation. Additionally, tactile sensors used in VR applications need to be compact and light so not to encumber or tire the user. Moreover, tactile sensors need to have a range of measurement compatible with the user's exertion capability and need to be rugged and durable.

Among the various mechanoelectrical transducers available commercially, we discuss force-sensitive resistors (FSRs), miniature pressure transducers (MPTs) and ultrasonic force sensors (UFSs). We will also present a prototype piezoelectric stress rate sensor developed for the detection of surface slip. In comparing various tactile sensing technologies, we refer to sensor characteristics such as signal linearity, hysteresis, repeatability, and range. *Linearity* is the ability of the sensor to output a signal that is directly proportional with the input, and the output is expressed as a first-order equation of the input. Linear sensors are preferred, because they are easily calibrated and have a constant sensitivity over the measurement range. *Hysteresis* is apparent when a sensor is gradually cycled between no load and full load. Hysteresis represents the difference in output corresponding to the same sensor input for the loading and unloading curves. Sensors with large hysteresis are a poor choice for dynamic measurements because it is not possible to anticipate whether the sensor is under-loading or unloading input. Finally, *repeatability* represents the ability of the sensor to produce the same output for repeated measurements of a single input value. The higher the sensor repeatability (and accuracy), the more confidence we have in the measured value.

6.1.1. Force-Sensitive Resistor

Force-sensitive resistors are probably the first tactile sensors to be used in a VR application [Stone, 1991]. As illustrated in Figure 6.1*a*, they have of a thin layered structure consisting of an active area, a spacer, and a flexible substrate. The active area consists of a pattern of conductors that are connected to the output pins through an elongated tail. Any force applied on the flexible substrate will push a thick polymer film against the active area and change the sensor electrical resistance. The relationship between applied force and output resistance is dependent on the particular active area design (shape, number of conductors, etc). However, all FSRs exhibit a switchlike response, requiring a break force to decrease the 1-$M\Omega$ rest resistance to approximately 100 $k\Omega$, which is the beginning of the measurement range [Force Imaging Technologies, 1994]. As the force increases, the electrical resistance decreases over an initial linear way. Eventually the response becomes nonlinear from sensor saturation, as shown in Figure 6.1*b*. Any further increase in the applied force will not significantly change the electrical resistance.

The change in resistance is best measured when the active area of the FSR is attached to a flat, firm, and smooth surface. Unfortunately, when mounting the FSRs on a sensing glove, the sensors must be bent to conform to the finger and palm curvatures and the compliant underlying surface. Thus the two opposed layers are pushed together by the bending tension, resulting in reduced measurement range and resistance drift. The smaller the active area, the less effect a given curvature will have on the FSR's output. Additional problems relate to the sensors poor accuracy (errors up to 25% of output), which make FSRs unsuitable for precision measurements.

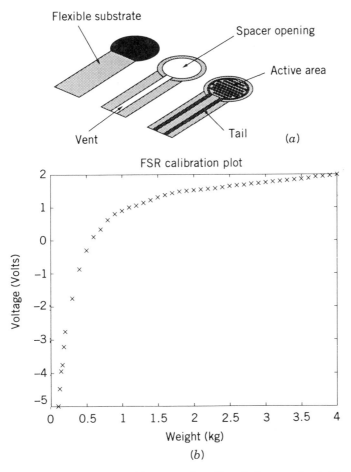

Figure 6.1 Force-sensitive resistor: (*a*) construction; (*b*) typical output signal. Adapted from Burdea and Goratowski [1994], Burdea et al., [1995b].

The sensor illustrated in Figure 6.1 can measure only one force over its active area. In tactile feedback, it is often necessary to measure a pattern of microforces distributed over the contact area. In such cases the FSR design is modified so that the two external pliable sheets contain electrical conductors sandwiching an internal polymer sheet. The conductors are oriented normally to each other to form the rows and columns of a sensing matrix. Such pads of 16×16 conductors have been used in robotics applications [Allen and Michelman, 1990]. No data is available on VR applications of such matrix pads, probably because of the large number of wires and the large pad dimension.

6.1.2. Miniature Pressure Transducer

Another tactile sensor is the miniature pressure transducer (Precision Measurement Co.) illustrated in Figure 6.2*a* [Burdea et al., 1995b]. It consists of a very small strain gauge that is installed on a flat support plate and protected by a cover. A small extension of the cover allows for the soldering of wire connections to the control and sensing circuit. The sensor dimensions are very small (approximately 2.6 mm diam and 0.28 mm thick), which makes installation easy on sensing or support gloves [Tan, 1988].

When force is applied on the MPT, its diaphragm is deformed, resulting in an elongation of the inner strain gauge. This increased length in turn results in an increase in the gauge electrical resistance. The change in resistance produces an imbalance on a Wheatstone bridge circuit to which the MPT is connected, and voltage is measured by an operation amplifier. By loading and unloading the MPT, it is possible to determine its hysteresis, as shown in Figure 6.2*b* [Burdea and Goratowski,

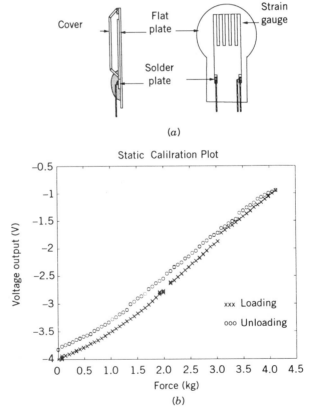

Figure 6.2 Miniature pressure transducer: (*a*) construction; (*b*) hysteresis curve. Adapted from Burdea and Goratowski [1994] and Burdea et al. [1995b].

1994]. This calibration plot shows that the MPT is relatively linear, with hysteresis of approximately 6% of its output. However, Tan [1988] and Burdea et al. [1995b] report problems with fragile wire connections from the small sensor size. A larger sensor may alleviate this problem at the expense of lower sensitivity in the range of forces humans can exert. Thus MPTs are considered less suitable for VR applications.

6.1.3. Ultrasonic Force Sensor

The previous discussion underscored the conflicting requirements for both mechanical ruggedness and electrical sensitivity and resolution. This problem has been recognized in the research community looking for the right balance of mechanical and electrical attributes. Hutchings and his colleagues state that

> The main problem with coupled mechanical–electrical transduction schemes is that it is impossible to optimize one form of transduction without compromising the other. For example, elastomer materials with excellent electrical characteristics have poor mechanical transduction, i.e., high hysteresis and fragility. When the mechanical characteristics are improved, the electrical transduction suffers.
>
> —Hutchings et al. [1994]

Hutchings and his colleagues reasoned that if the coupling problem could be solved then *both* mechanical and electrical sensor characteristics could be optimized. They developed a new type of sensor, called the ultrasonic force sensor (UFS), which measures forces through pulse-echo ranging. As illustrated in Figure 6.3a, the sensor consists of a deformable elastomer pad and an underlying two-dimensional array of ultrasonic transmitters and receivers. The thickness of the pad is measured by sending a high-frequency pulse and measuring the time taken by the reflected echo pulse to reach the same sensing element in the array. Since propagation speed is constant, time is proportional with the elastomer thickness and thus to the applied force. The echo time t_2 corresponding to the deformed pad (distance d_2) is smaller than the propagation time t_1 when the pad was undeformed (distance d_1). Thus the measured force is given by

$$\mathbf{F} = k(d_1 - d_2) = \frac{1}{2}kc(t_1 - t_2) \tag{6.1}$$

where c is the speed of sound in the elastomer pad and k is the rubber mechanical stiffness.

Typical pulse transmission times are on the order of 5 μsec so that pad deformation of a few microns can be detected. The amplitude of the reflected signal depends on the type of surface with which the sensor makes contact. Hard surfaces reflect well, whereas liquids or biological soft tissue produce very small echo amplitudes that may be undetectable. In such cases, a thin and rugged sheet of urethane foam can be bonded on the elastomer surface to produce a surface of known reflectivity.

Figure 6.3b shows a typical calibration curve for a UFS produced by Bonneville Scientific Inc. Over the low force range of 0 to 4 kg, the UFS linearity is better than

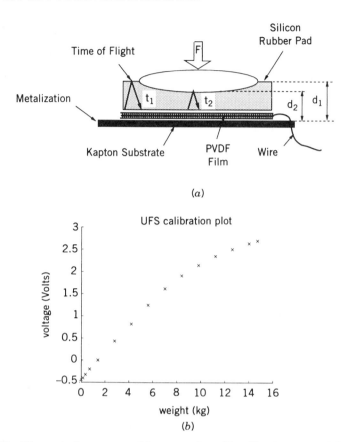

Figure 6.3 Ultrasonic force sensor: (*a*) construction; (*b*) calibration curve. Adapted from Hutchings et al. [1994] and Burdea and Goratowski [1994]. © 1994 IEEE. Reprinted with permission.

those of either FSRs or MPTs. Furthermore, there is no turn-on effect associated with FSRs, so that the sensor can measure very minute forces. Its range of measurement (up to 14 kg) and repeatability (less than 1%) are superior to either FSRs or MPTs. Burdea and his colleagues [1995b] did extensive testing of the three tactile sensors described above to develop a tactile sensing glove for hand rehabilitation applications. The results of these tests are summarized in Table 6.1.

6.1.4. Piezoelectric Stress Rate Sensor

All the tactile sensors described above measure forces (or pressures) providing information that is useful in determining when contact occurs and what the contact forces are. Once an object is grasped, it is necessary to have information on its motion in contact or slip. Thus it is necessary to measure the rate of change of forces in contact. Son et al. [1994] have developed such a sensor for teleoperation applications in

TABLE 6.1   Comparison of Commercially Available Tactile Sensors

Parameter	FSR	UFS	MPT
Electrical			
Excitation	None	5 V	1.5 V
Power supply	± 5 VD @ 0.4 mA	± 12 VD @ 200 mA	± 12 VD @ 200 mA
Output	−5 V to +3.5 V	−0.5 V to +2.5 V	−4 V to -0.5 V
Impedance	2 KΩ–MΩ	450 Ω @ 3.5 MHZ	350 Ω
Capacitance	0	100 pF	0
Response time	0.2 sec	0.1 sec	0.1 sec
Steady state drift	1 mV/sec (5 g/sec)	2.2 mV/sec (9 g/sec)	13 mV/sec (16 g/sec)
Mechanical			
Thickness	0.2 mm to 1.25 mm	3.5 mm	1.25 mm
Turn-on force	100 g	10 g	10 g
Range	0.1–4 kg	0.01–14 kg	0.01–4 kg
Hysteresis (static)	Not tested	1%	6%
Repeatability	Poor	Good	Good
Lifetime	10 million actuations	Not reported	Not reported

Source: Burdea et al. [1995b].

conjunction with the haptic feedback research at Harvard University. As illustrated in Figure 6.4, this stress-rate sensor consists of multi-element piezoelectric film strips molded on a curved silicon rubber contact surface. This external skin has a multitude of nibs that make contact with the grasped object surface. To improve the sensor response, these nibs are designed to generate large curvature and stress changes at the base, when they are compressed by the grasped object. At the opposite end, the piezoelectric film passes through a polyester foam support and attaches to connectors S_1 to S_4. The overall prototype dimensions are reported as 25 mm diam and 45 mm long.

The piezoelectric film in the stress rate sensor produces an electrical charge in proportion with its deformation (strain). A thin layer of silver ink deposed on the film surface collects and transmits this electrical signal. The sensor has no dc response, so it has no saturation from drift. Its output is amplified by an operation amplifier and then low-pass filtered, with a resultant 30-Hz bandwidth. Figure 6.4*b* shows the

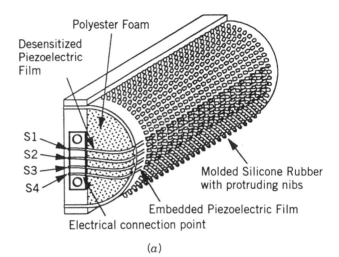

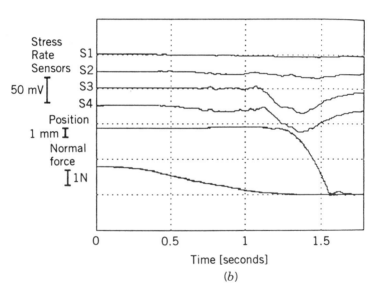

Figure 6.4 The multi-element stress rate sensor: (a) construction; (b) output signal. Reprinted by permission from Son et al. [1994]. © 1994 IEEE.

sensor output for the four piezo films (S_1. . . S_4) when slip occurs. As can be seen, the output voltage of S_3 and S_4 drops just prior to the occurrence of slip (expressed by a change in position).

6.2. SURFACE TEXTURE AND GEOMETRY FEEDBACK

The tactile sensors described above measure interaction forces and slippage at the contact surface with the (real) environment. This data is then used by the host computer for telepresence or for improved modeling of VR simulations. In certain cases, the simulated interaction has no equivalent in reality, and needs to be modeled purely mathematically. Such tasks are grasping and feeling a radar wave or a wind vortex [Appino et al., 1992]. Eventually the modeled haptic sensations involved in the interaction need to be fed back to the user. We present here tactile interfaces that replicate the feeling of the contact surface texture and geometry (tactile feedback); systems that provide surface slippage and temperature feedback are discussed subsequently.

Shimoga [1993], in his review article on tactile feedback technology for telemanipulation tasks, distinguishes five possible approaches: (a) visual display, (b) pneumatic stimulation, (c) vibrotactile stimulation, (d) electrotactile stimulation, and (e) functional neuromuscular stimulation. *Visual display* of tactile data represents a form of sensorial substitution where tactile data is presented to the user visually as part of the graphic image. Visual tactile display has been used by Patrick [1990] to augment his vibrotactile feedback (see Section 6.2.2) by showing the relative position of thumb and index fingertips versus the object to be grasped. An alternate use of visual tactile feedback involves the interaction once the virtual object has been grasped. For example, it is possible to color the fingers of a virtual hand to visualize the contact location and force intensity during grasping. Such an approach was used by Burdea and his colleagues for the tactile glove used in hand diagnostics and rehabilitation [Burdea et al. 1996]. The advantages of visual tactile display is that it has low complexity, does not encumber the user, does not introduce numbness or pain, and is noninvasive. Its disadvantages are a lack of direct haptic sensation and a need to preserve an unobstructed line of sight to the user, which may not be possible when interacting with a crowded virtual world.

Another approach to tactile feedback is *functional neuromuscular stimulation* (FNS), which involves placing electrodes in the muscles and even in the nervous system. By stimulating the primary cortex electrically, the user feels as if he grasped or touched an object. Unfortunately, unlike visual tactile display, the FNS approach is highly invasive and risky for the user. It has high complexity, can produce pain, and has high liability. Therefore, FNS is considered inappropriate for use in virtual haptic feedback and will not be discussed further here. The following sections detail the pneumatic, vibrotactile, and electrotactile stimulation approaches to tactile feedback.

6.2.1. Pneumatic Stimulation

Tactile feedback through pneumatic stimulation uses compressed air to press against the skin, typically at the fingers. The pneumatic stimulation can be accomplished using air jets, air rings, or air bellows (pockets). Pneumatic stimulation has the advantage of simplicity, cleanliness, and lower cost than vibrotactile or electrotactile approaches.

Air jets have been used initially to help visually impaired persons to read. By placing a small 12 × 12 array of micro air jets on the skin it was possible to display various letter patterns. Air jets are noninvasive and do not produce pain. However, they can lead to discomfort when used for extended periods of time, and the device is heavy, therefore less suitable for portable haptic interfaces.

Air rings (or cuffs) are circular inflatable devices that squeeze the user's finger when pressurized. Sato and his colleagues have developed such a pneumatic actuator to retrofit a DataGlove. As illustrated in Figure 6.5 [Sato et al., 1991], the actuator consists of a small rubber balloon (8 mm diam) which is pressed against the user's fingertip by a small plastic cuff. A strain gauge interposed between the inflatable balloon and the fingertip measures the actual force exerted on the finger. The air is pressurized at 3 kg/cm^2 by a compressor and regulated by a custom electric–pneumatic converter. Hand position information from the DataGlove is read by a controller that issues electric signals to provide either proportional feedback or amplitude- and frequency-modulated vibrations. Tests showed that the fingertip compliance reduced actual feedback bandwidth to 5 Hz (compared to 10 Hz on a rigid surface).

Another approach to provide pneumatic stimulation is to pressurize small air pockets or *bellows* in a double-layered glove worn by the user. Modulating a given bellow pressure simulates the corresponding grasping force, while spatial sequencing of bellows in the palm conveys the sensation of object exploration and manipulation. Jones and Thousand [1966] at Northrop Corporation were the first to propose such an approach in their patent of a "Remote Handling Device" (see Figure 1.4). Here a large

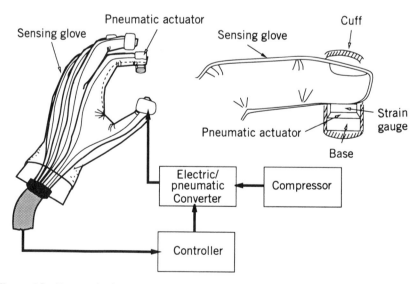

Figure 6.5 Pneumatic ring actuator system. Adapted from Sato et al. [1991]. © 1991 IEEE. Reprinted with permission.

bellow spanning the length of the index finger was pressurized by feedback signals from a remote robotic gripper. Subsequently Stone and Henequin [1992] patented a layered "Teletact Glove" incorporating 20 small air pockets. This double-layered glove consisted of an external DataGlove used for hand position information and an inner lycra glove sandwiching the small air pockets on the palmar side. Each air pocket is inflated up to 12 psi through two capillary tubes from a control interface with solenoid valves, as illustrated in Figure 6.6a. Thus a total of 40 tubes are grouped together in a single tether and connected to the control interface housing a small compressor. Command signals from the host computer running the simulation are sent to a pressure control board in the interface. Actual pressures are measured by small transducers in the air bellows and sent to the board for closed-loop control. The Teletact glove was subsequently improved by Advanced Robotics Research Ltd. and Airmuscle Ltd. and became the Teletact II (illustrated in Figure 6.6b). This version had a larger number of air pockets (29 small ones and one large) including four on the index fingertip. This fingertip bellow array allows the simulation of object slippage (through spatial sequencing) while the large palm pocket provides force feedback when pressurized to 30 psi. The same group of researchers at Advanced Robotics Research Ltd. (UK) also developed the Commander haptic interface shown in Figure 6.7 [Stone, 1992]. This device eliminates the need for a glove by housing the air pockets inside a handle grasped by the user. The Commander handle has four push-buttons, which are pressed against the user's fingers when pressurized up to 12 psi. Capillary tubes inside the handle are fed to a control box housing simple soleniod-actuated pistons. These pistons make a separate compressor unnecessary, thus reducing the overall system cost. A Polhemus tracker inside the Commander is used to measure three-dimensional hand position and a thumb switch is used for navigation in the virtual environment, similar to the V-Flexor interface described in the previous chapter.

6.2.2. Vibrotactile Stimulation

Another approach to providing tactile feedback during VR simulations is to use vibrotactile stimulation. The vibration stimulus can be applied locally, or spatially over the user's fingertip, depending on the type of human receptors that need to be triggered. Referring to these tactile receptors, Kontarinis and Howe [1994] state that

> . . . the FA II units are the most important receptors for vibratory information above about 64 Hz. Since these receptors do not exhibit a localized response, we can provide high frequency vibration information with a single vibration display for each fingertip. For lower frequencies, an array-type display may be needed to provide spatially resolved stimuli for the FAI and SA receptors.
>
> —Kontarinis and Howe [1994]

Thus for contact detection at the fingertip, or for simulating the compliance of the contact surface, we can use a single actuator vibrating at frequencies above 64 Hz. Such actuators are voice coils [Patrick, 1990] or miniature loudspeakers [Kontarinis

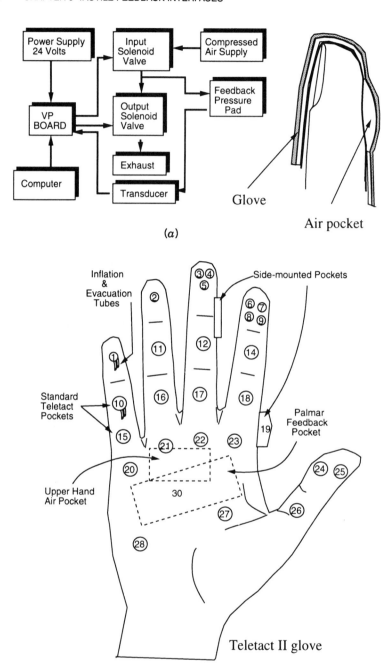

(a)

(b)

Figure 6.6 Pneumatic bellows: (a)Teletact glove; (b) Teletact II. Adapted from Stone [1992]. © Éditions Hermès. Reprinted by permission.

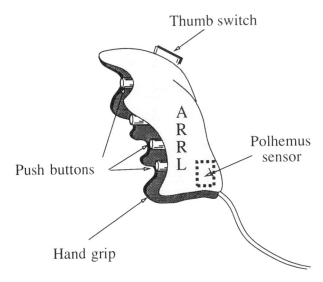

Thumb switch

A
R
R
L

Polhemus
sensor

Push buttons

Hand grip

Figure 6.7 The Commander tactile interface. Adapted from Stone [1992]. © Éditions Hermès. Reprinted by permission.

and Howe, 1994]. Conversely, when providing information on the geometry of the contacted surface, array-type actuators are more appropriate, since they provide spatial discretization. These actuators are typically SMM micropin arrays [Hasser and Weisenberger, 1993; Kontarinis et al., 1995] that are vibrated at low frequencies.

Voice Coils and Miniature Loudspeakers. Voice coils are small and light disklike vibrators compact enough to fit on the user's fingertip. Their high-frequency vibration capability (above 200 Hz) and their small size make them ideal for use in tactile feedback for VR simulations. Additional advantages involve user comfort, low power requirement, lack of pain, and sensorial substitution. Disadvantages involve relatively noisy operation, higher complexity than pneumatic stimulation, and higher cost.

Patrick [1990] placed a pair of voice coils made by Audiological Engineering on the thumb and index of an user wearing the EXOS Dextrous Hand Master [Marcus and Churchill, 1989]. Vibrotactile stimulation was provided by driving the voice coils at a fixed frequency of 250 Hz and using real-time amplitude modulation. The analog-signal control circuitry illustrated in Figure 6.8 uses a function generator to produce a sinusoidal base signal C, which is then transmitted to a two-channel amplifier.

The amplifier gain is adjusted independently for the two fingers by the analog signals A and B coming from the host computer running the simulation. Thus the sine signal C is modulated to produce two variable amplitude signals E and D. A pair of power amplifiers are used to strengthen the signal to the level required to drive the two voice coils (G and F). In tests performed by Patrick using the above system, it was found that the voice coils improved performance by 30% when the visual display was corrupted (to simulate a low-visibility task).

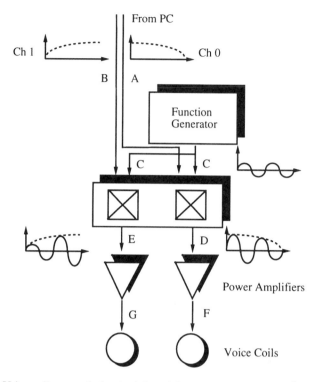

Figure 6.8   Voice coils control circuit. Adapted from Patrick [1990]. © Éditions Hermès. Reprinted by permission.

Later, EXOS Company introduced a commercial version of the above system called the "Touch Master" [EXOS Co., 1993b], which is shown in Figure 6.9. This system allows the use of up to 10 voice coils that are excited at a fixed frequency of 210 Hz. All the electronics are located in a separate control box that includes the amplifier as well as A/D and digital i/o cards for communication with the host computer. The current price for the Touch Master is $7000, which includes the control interface. Optional variable-frequency circuitry is also available.

Miniature loudspeakers are another type of actuator that may be used in vibrotactile stimulation. The relatively large weight of the loudspeakers (from their magnets and coils) makes installation directly on the fingertip difficult. An alternative solution is to incorporate the miniature loudspeaker in a master arm (preferably with force feedback) and transmit vibrations through the interface structure grasped by the user. This approach was taken by Howe and his colleagues at Harvard University in the development of an advanced telerobotics system. As illustrated in Figure 6.10*a* [Kontarinis and Howe, 1995], a small 0.2-W loudspeaker was stripped of its outer cone and metal frame and mounted upside-down on the master hand grip. This inverted mounting was chosen to provide a higher moving mass and thus inertial force for the loudspeaker magnet. When driven by an audio amplifier the moving mass had a 3-mm range of motion, and produced up to 0.25-N force at 250 Hz. These

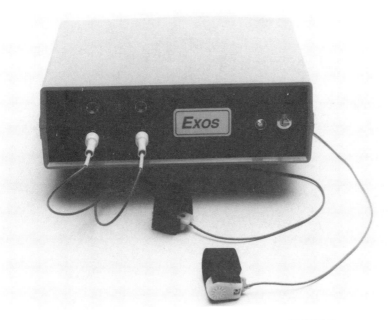

Figure 6.9   The Touch Master. Photograph courtesy of EXOS Co.

vibrations were felt by the operator through the aluminum bracket handle mounted at the end of the master arm. The audio amplifier gain was adjusted to determine the overall system sensitivity.

Figure 6.10*b* shows the vibrotactile display integrated with the telemanipulation master arm developed by Howe. This nonportable hand master consists of a two-degree-of-freedom, direct-drive, parallel linkage mechanism. Force feedback is produced in the vertical plane and measured by a strain gauge sensor at the handle (for improved control). The angles of the master joints are read by a force reflection controller that transmits position information to a slave arm. Forces sensed at the slave gripper are then fed back to the user with a bandwidth greater than 80 Hz. Vibration information from the slave is overimposed on the force feedback using the miniature loudspeakers. When tried by the author, this haptic interface proved reliable and responsive, and felt natural to use. Tactile feedback felt realistic and was a useful complement to force feedback alone.

Micro-Pin Actuators   An alternative to voice coils for vibrotactile stimulation is the use of micro-pin actuators, either individually or in an array configuration. Compared to voice coils, micro-pin actuators have higher power requirements, have higher noise-to-signal ratios and may produce some pain to the user if used inappropriately. Advantages include the ability to produce highly localized forces and contact geometry information (for micro-pin arrays).

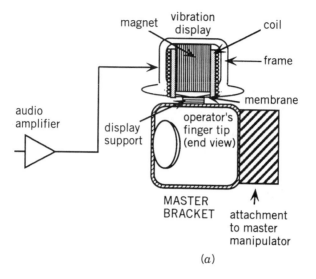

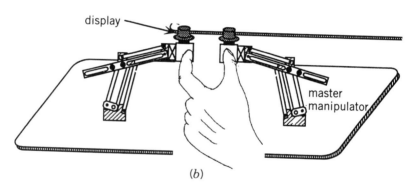

Figure 6.10 Telemanipulation system with force and tactile feedback: (*a*) tactile display; (*b*) master manipulator. From Kontarinis and Howe [1995]. Reprinted by permission of The MIT Press.

A single micro-pin tactile actuator has been integrated by Akamatsu et al. [1994] in a multimodal mouse designed to improve graphic–user interaction. A regular mouse was modified by adding a solenoid-actuated aluminum pin that protrudes through a hole in one of the buttons, as illustrated in Figure 6.11*a*. The pin movement is only 1 mm with a frequency up to 80 Hz. A rubber film fixed on the backside of the mouse button returns the pin to its zero position once the solenoid is deenergized. Additionally, the mouse incorporates a small force-feedback actuator consisting of an electromagnet and an iron pad. Whenever the magnet is energized, there is up to a 20% increase in moving friction over the pad. By synchronizing the haptic feedback with the image on the screen, it is possible to give the user a feel of "touching" a graphics window or button. As long as the cursor is in the target area, resistive

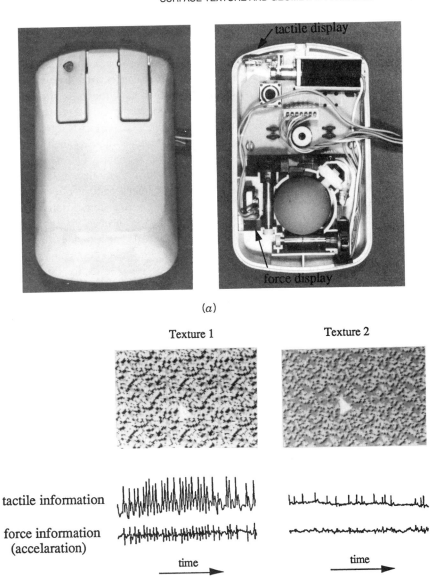

Figure 6.11   The multimodal mouse: (*a*) construction; (*b*) surface texture feedback. From Akamatsu et al. [1994]. Reprinted by permission of The MIT Press.

force feedback is applied. Once the user has clicked over the target area (the usual menu-based selection process), or the cursor has left that area, tactile feedback is discontinued.

Such tactile stimulation may be useful for users with a sight impairment, or in tasks involving complex window-based graphics and menus. An additional capability of the multimodal mouse is surface texture feedback, as illustrated in Figure 6.11*b* [Akamatsu et al., 1994]. By modulating the micro-pin vibration amplitude and frequency, it is possible to convey information on the surface smoothness. Texture 1 on the left is a rougher surface than Texture 2, and produces vibrations with higher amplitude and frequency. Additionally, force feedback can be added to simulate large ridges on the surface being explored. The researchers report 100% correct answers when five subjects were asked to compare the roughness of the two textures using the multimodal mouse. Logitech Inc. developed a multimodal mouse called Cyberman. Its marketing status is unclear at the moment.

An alternative to using a single micro-pin actuator for vibrotactile stimulation is to use actuator arrays, particularly when contact geometry information is desired. Figure 6.12 [Burdea and Coiffet, 1994] illustrates a virtual finger translating over the edge of a virtual object. The corresponding tactile feedback is applied to the user's hand by a micro-pin array placed at the fingertip. The array has several rows of micro-pins that are activated in sequence (row 1, then row 2, etc.) in synchronism with the translation of the virtual finger. Alternately, it is possible to vibrate a single or group of actuators to convey surface texture information, similar to the example given previously for the multimodal mouse.

A micro-pin array has to be sufficiently dense to convey useful geometry information and be able to vibrate in the bandwidth range that is optimum for the fingertip cutaneous receptors. This is a challenging design task, because portability, lightness, and compactness also need to be maintained. For example, it is not practical to use solenoids as array actuators, because they are both bulky and heavy. If the actuator array is integrated with a (portable) force-feedback master, then additional requirements are placed on the design. As explained by Kontarinis,

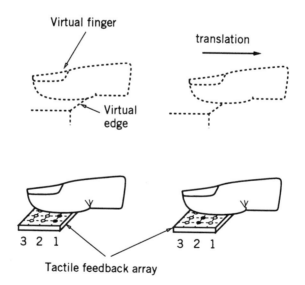

Figure 6.12 Conveying touch-area geometry information using micro-pin arrays. Burdea and Coiffet [1994]. © Éditions Hermès. Reprinted by permission.

First, the display must be small enough that it fits between the fingers when manipulating an object, and light enough to avoid overloading the master and limiting force reflection range and responsiveness. In addition, because it is located at the point of contact between the manipulator and the operator's fingertip, it must be strong enough that the entire reflected force can be supported by the display while maintaining the desired shape.

—Kontarinis et al. [1995]

An electromagnetically based array has been recently demonstrated at Sandia National Laboratories [Garcia, 1995], but it had only six actuators per fingertip (two rows of three elements). Until recently, there were no actuators that had sufficient power-to-weight and power-to-volume ratios to satisfy the above requirements for use in micro-pin arrays. Johnson [1992] patented the use of shape memory metal (SMM) actuator arrays of the type described in Chapter 3 (see Fig. 3.9). These very light and compact actuators satisfy the weight and volume requirements for portability, while at the same time having a very simple construction. The micro-pins are actuated by passing a dc current through a very thin SMM wire, which then shrinks under heating. The control circuitry proposed by Johnson involves the use of pulse-width modulation (PWM), as illustrated in Figure 6.13 [Johnson, 1992].

Each SMM actuator is controlled independently through a separate circuit block like the one shown in the dashed line in Figure 6.13. The actuators are connected electrically in parallel, with one end tied to the 5 V distribution line and the other to their respective control block. A solid-state latch chip serves as interface between a PC host and the SMM controllers. When the computer cycles the input lines to the latch, its output lines are "ON" and 5 V is applied to the SMM controller. This

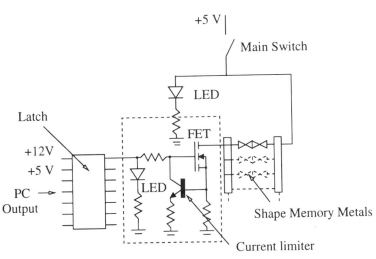

Figure 6.13 SMM micro-pin array control circuitry. Adapted from Johnson [1992]. © Éditions Hermès. Reprinted by permission.

turns the FET transistor into conduction state and current passes through the actuator. A parallel circuit inside the dashed block contains another transistor and a current limiting resistance. These are used to set the particular value of the current through the SMM actuator. Light emitting diodes (LEDs) are used to provide visual feedback when the array or a particular actuator are turned on. An improvement upon Johnson's design is to use a local microprocessor to store a library of tactile patterns, instead of relying entirely on the PC host for actuator control. This frees the host for other high-level tasks, and reduces its computation and communication loads substantially. Such a solution was adopted by Xtensory Inc., in their 3×3 "tactools" array which costs about $3000 [Cutt, 1993].

Hasser and Weisenberger [1993] at the Armstrong Laboratory of the Wright-Patterson Air Force Base used Johnson's L-shaped cantilever SMM actuators in a dense 30-pin array, as shown in Figure 6.14. The actuators are arranged in six rows of five micro-pins each, in a rectangle 1.2 cm wide and 1.5 cm long. The tips of the SMM actuators are evenly spaced 3 mm apart in both directions. This distance is larger than the two-point spatial resolution of the fingertip cutaneous receptors, as discussed in Chapter 2. Each L-shaped cantilever is actuated by a 1.5-cm-long SMM wire with a diameter of only 0.1 mm. This small diameter was necessary to shorten the actuator cooling time once current is cut off. To accommodate so many actuators in the small space available, it was necessary to use cantilevers with three lengths (short, medium, and long). This produced an unwanted geometric variability in the actuator response, since the longer cantilevers extend further up when actuated. The force exerted against each fingertip by an individual micro-pin was approximately 0.2 N.

Hasser and Weisenberger subsequently performed a series of studies of the above prototype under PWM control, by applying a series of rectangular voltages of varying periods and duty cycles. Here duty cycle represents the percentage of the time period

Figure 6.14   Prototype of micro-pin SMM array with 30 actuators. Courtesy of Capt. Christopher Hasser, Armstrong Laboratory, Wright-Patterson AFB.

when the binary pulse is on. They used a sophisticated laser Dopler velocimeter to measure the displacement of the tactile actuators as a function of signal duty cycle and time period. Results illustrated in Figure 6.15a [Hasser and Weisenberger, 1993] show that for all actuator lengths (short, medium, or long), there is an increase in the micro-pin travel with increased duty cycle. Higher duty cycles deliver more energy to the SMM actuator causing more contraction of the thin wire. The longest actuator has the largest travel increase, as expected. Figure 6.15b shows that increasing the period of the vibrating signal produced a linear increase in the actuator travel, for duty cycles of 30% to 70%. Subsequent human-factor studies were performed to determine the

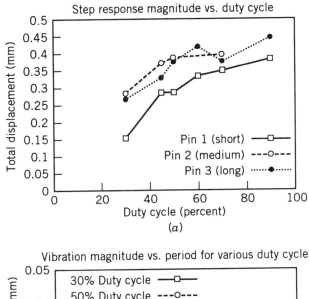

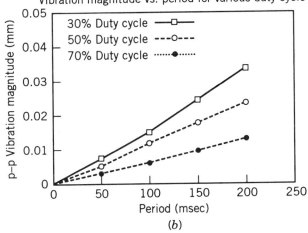

Figure 6.15 SMM actuator array displacement as a function of (a) duty cycle; (b) PWM time period. From Hasser and Weisenberger [1993]. Reprinted by permission of the ASME.

effectiveness of such an actuator array in presenting both static and dynamic tactile patterns to the user. These studies will be discussed in more detail in Chapter 9.

Research on SMM micro-pin arrays was also performed by Kontarinis and his colleagues in connection with the telerobotic system developed at Harvard University. The actuator used is a 30-mm-long straight SMM wire of 0.075 mm diameter, arranged between a fixed attachment and a lever, as illustrated in Figure 6.16a [Kontarinis et al., 1995]. When current passes through the SMM wire, it shrinks and makes the lever pivot about its shaft. The other end of the lever then pushes a micro-pin upward through the array cover and toward the user's fingertip. The lever produces a threefold increase in pin displacement, and a threefold reduction in applied force, resulting in a vertical pin translation of 3 mm and a contact force of 1 N. A spring installed at the other end of the actuator helps pull the pin down once the current is cut off and the SMM wire cools down. To have a compact actuator array, the vertically translating pins have four lengths, corresponding to four actuator groups that are

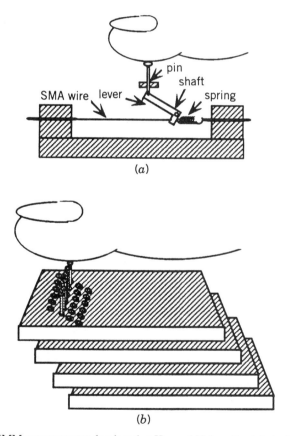

Figure 6.16 SMM actuator array developed at Harvard University: (a) single actuator construction; (b) 6×4 array configuration. From Kontarinis et al. [1995]. © 1995 IEEE. Reprinted by permission.

stacked vertically, as illustrated in Figure 6.16*b*. The resultant inter-pin spacing is 2.1 mm, matching the fingertip spatial resolution.

Earlier tests with the same actuator showed difficulty in obtaining control bandwidths above 1 Hz, due to the thermal mass of the SMM wire and its pronounced hysteresis between applied current and output force [Kontarinis and Howe, 1993]. Significant control delays were observed as explained by Kontarinis:

> There is a significant delay between an increase in input current and the appearance of a force increase at the pin due to the integrating effect of the thermal mass of the wire. On the descending phase, the delay is due to the slow cooling rate, so that the temperature drops more slowly than the current. Thus proportional control results in a bandwidth less than a tenth of the desired value of 10 Hz.
>
> —Kontarinis et al. [1995]

To solve the above problems, the research team replaced the proportional controller with a proportional-derivative (PD) one with a large phase lead. This feed-forward scheme introduces large current peaks to heat the SMM wire more quickly. Thus the array control law is

$$I_{out}(t) \; = \; K_p \cdot \mathbf{F}_d \; + \; K_v \cdot \dot{\mathbf{F}}_d \; + \; K_{old} \cdot I_{out}(t \, - \, \Delta t) \tag{6.2}$$

where $I_{out}(t)$ is the current to the SMM wire at time t, $I_{out}(t - \Delta t)$ is the previous current value, $\mathbf{F}_d$ is the desired force, K_p and K_v are proportional and velocity gains, and K_{old} is the weight that averages the present and previous input [Kontarinis and Howe, 1993]. The cooling time was also shortened by providing forced-air cooling of the actuators. Additionally, pairs of emitter–detector noncontact microoptical sensors were integrated on each array element to provide closed-loop control of the actuator position [Kontarinis, 1995]. Although the above improvements did bring the control bandwidth close to the desired 10-Hz value, they also increased the system complexity and made the array nonportable.

6.2.3. Electrotactile Stimulation

The last approach discussed here for providing contact surface geometry and texture feedback is electrotactile stimulation. Electrotactile (or electrocutaneous) stimulation uses very small currents passing through specially designed electrodes placed on the skin to excite the local cutaneous receptors. It should not be confused with electromyography (EMG) [Farry and Walker, 1993; Iberall et al., 1994] which uses electrodes to measure small myoelectric signals or voltages produced by the user's muscle contraction.

Research on electrotactile stimulation originated in the medical community looking for sensorial aids for the visually or hearing impaired [Kaczmarek and Bach-y-Rita, 1995]. Such a device is, for example, the Tacticon 1600 which is used to detect sounds for deaf people. Sounds sampled by a microphone are divided into 16 frequency bands and delivered to the skin through an array of 16 electrodes placed on the abdomen. Zhu [1988] describes experiments in which the microphone was substituted by input from 16 tactile sensors placed on an astronaut's space suit glove. Here the Tacticon 1600 output signal is used as a sensory enhancement for diminished tactile sensation due to the thick space suit glove. Another, more recent, device intended for the visually impaired is the Videotact Display abdominal array manufactured by Unitech Research Inc.. This 768-electrode (32 × 24) tactile array measures approximately 6 × 8 inches. Each electrode signal (waveform stimulus) is controlled independently from a host computer.

Researchers in virtual reality are also interested in electrotactile stimulation because of its advantages versus other forms of tactile feedback. Compared to vibrotactile stimulation described previously, electrotactile feedback has lower power consumption and weight (a plus for portable systems), has no moving parts, and maintains constant contact with the skin. Its drawbacks involve increased risk of user discomfort and even pain when using improper electrodes or driving current. It has the highest invasiveness of all tactile-feedback approaches discussed thus far, due to the use of electrical currents applied to the skin.

The electrodes used in electrotactile stimulation must not react chemically with the skin, because this leads to irritation and produces an insulating layer between the electrode and skin. Nonreactive metallic electrodes use titanium, gold, platinum, silver, or stainless steel [Kaczmarek and Bach-y-Rita, 1995]. The electrodes typically have a concentric configuration, as shown in Figure 6.17a [Kaczmarek et al., 1994]. The inner electrode is active and is used to apply the control signal (current), whereas the surrounding annular electrode is used to ground the skin currents. The smaller the inner electrode, the more spatially localized the tactile sensation is. However, if the active electrode has too small a contact area with the skin (about 1 mm^2), the local current density (expressed as mA/mm^2) is too large and can produce discomfort or pain. Larger electrodes produce a comfortable touch or vibration sensation, at the expense of less spatial localization. The insulator between the two concentric electrodes prevents unwanted discharges, so that the current must close through the skin to travel from the center to the grounding electrodes. The design developed by Kaczmarek and his colleagues has added a small air gap to the insulator. This was necessary because of the tight spatial distribution of the electrodes in a feedback array and to minimize arcing, tracking, and shunting problems when the scanning fingertip is wet. An air gap does, however, allow the accumulation of debris in the cavity around the active electrode, a fact acknowledged by the researchers.

A problem related to electrotactile stimulation is the variability of skin electrical resistance and of the contact area with the applied electrode. The skin resistance is high (150–300 kΩ) when dry, but drops significantly when the skin is wet. When single electrodes are used, it is possible to improve the electrical contact with the skin by applying an electrolytic paste. This paste eliminates high concentrations of current flowing through the skin. Alternately, one can apply warm water and a perspiration-retaining material [Zhu, 1988]. Hairless skin is better than hairy skin for electrotactile stimulation. Figure 6.17b [Kaczmarek and Bach-y-Rita, 1995] shows a model for the electrical characteristics of the electrode–skin interface, where R_p is a variable resistance that decreases in value with increasing stimulation current.

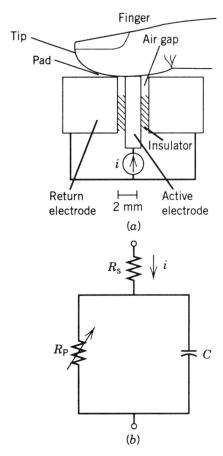

Figure 6.17   Electrotactile stimulation: (*a*) electrode configuration [From Kaczmarek et al. 1994]. © 1994 IEEE. Reprinted with permission. (*b*) electrode–skin contact model [Kaczmarek and Bach-y-Rita, 1995]. Reprinted by permission of the Oxford University Press.

Another important aspect of electrotactile stimulation is the type of current signal sent to the electrode. The most frequently used signal is a rectangular pulse where the current pulse width, amplitude, duration, and frequency can all be altered to produce the desired tactile feedback sensation. Pulses that are all positive are called "monophasic" and produce skin reddening (from accumulated charges at the electrode–skin interface). A better signal is one that alternates positive and negative pulses, and produces a more comfortable sensation. Such signals are called *balanced-charge biphasic*, since the negative pulse reverses (or balances) the electrochemical processes produced during the positive pulse. A typical balanced-charge biphasic current signal is illustrated in Figure 6.18*a* [Kaczmarek and Bach-y-Rita, 1995]. Here *W* is the width of the positive (or negative) pulse, whereas the interphase time delay (*IPI*) prevents the negative pulse from masking the response produced by the positive

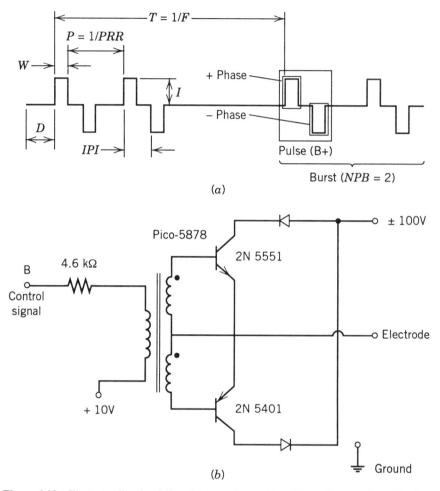

Figure 6.18   Electrotactile stimulation: (*a*) current wave form [From Kaczmarek and Bach-y-Rita, 1995]. Reprinted by permission of the Oxford University Press; (*b*) driving circuit [Zhu, 1988]. © John Wiley & Sons, Inc. Reprinted by permission.

pulse. The pulses are grouped in bursts (two biphasic pulses make up a burst). Bursts are in turn separated by a time T required to minimize sensorial adaptation, which would otherwise occur. The pulse amplitude (or current intensity I) determines the intensity of the tactile feedback signal. Typical currents vary in intensity from 1 to 10 mA [Kaczmarek et al., 1994], whereas active electrode-to-ground voltages are relatively high (100 to 500 V) [Zhu, 1988]. Figure 6.18*b* shows a control circuit that produces a balanced-biphasic current. It consists of a center-tapped transformer with the output connected to the electrode and to two transistors. The control signal is applied on the transformer primary, whereas the electrode supply voltage of ±100 V is connected to the output transistors. The positive pulse corresponds with the power supply being positive and the top transistor being in conduction. The negative pulse occurs when the power supply is negative and the bottom transistor conducts. The time delay between positive and negative pulses occurs when both transistors are off. The amplitude of the stimulation signal can be adjusted by changing the voltage of the power supply, whereas the frequency relates to the control signal applied on the transformer primary coil.

Table 6.2 compares all the tactile feedback approaches discussed so far to present the user with contact surface geometry and texture. Other surface characteristics such as slippage or temperature will be discussed next.

6.3. SURFACE SLIP FEEDBACK

Surface slip feedback together with force feedback are required whenever the grasping of a virtual object must be modeled realistically. When no slippage feedback is present in the simulation, users are required to apply large normal forces to maintain stable grasp, resulting in fatigue and discomfort. When slippage feedback is present users reduce the grasping force to much smaller levels. Edin and his colleagues [1993] studied the best physiological methods to present incipient slippage to the user. They concluded that sensory substitution (through visual or audio feedback) is undesirable because it requires conscious attention, thus increasing response latencies. In Edin's opinion, electrotactile stimulation is not useful either for conveying surface slip information, because

> ...humans adapt to such stimulations and cease to respond after just 2 to 3 trials. Thus, electrical skin stimulation is not useful for relaying information about slips... A preferred approach is to present mechanical stimuli to the human operator that trigger the same physiological responses as when an object is directly manipulated by the human hand.
>
> —Edin et al. [1993]

TABLE 6.2   Subjective Comparison of Tactile Displays

Display	Visual	Pneumatic			Vibrotactile			Electro-	FNS
Feature	Feedback	Jets	Bellows	Rings	Pins	Coils	Piezo	tactile	
Weight	med	high	high	high	high	med	med	low	low
Comfort	good	fair	fair	fair	good	good	good	fair	poor
Numbness	none	low	low	low	med	med	med	high	?
Pain	none	none	none	none	some	none	none	some	some
Liability	none	low	low	low	med	med	med	med	high
Invasiveness	none	low	low	low	med	med	med	high	v. high

Source: Shimoga [1993]. © 1993 IEEE.

The researchers used an instrumented block with a mass of 350 g and two contact plates covered with sandpaper. The user grasped the contact plates between the thumb and index fingers. Two solenoids were activated in sequence to move the plates in the vertical plane and thus change the center of gravity of the grasped object. Edin and his colleagues showed that 90 msec following the slip the users increased the normal forces followed by a sustained increase in the normal-to-tangential force ratio. Thus, it was possible to simulate early slippage and to produce the required user's response.

Later Chen and Marcus [1994] developed a mechanical actuator for the simulation of continuous slippage and skin stretch. As illustrated in Figure 6.19, the actuator consists of a small motor with a 64:1 gear reduction rotating a small derlin cylinder against the user's fingertip. A velcro strip attaches the feedback actuator to the finger, allowing only a small portion of the cylinder to make contact with the finger. The maximum rotating speed of the actuator is 2.54 cm/sec (1 in./sec) and the torque can overcome up to 17.8 N (4 lb) of force applied normally to the direction of rotation. The overall actuator weight is small (0.28 N or 1 oz), which makes it useful in prolonged simulations. Since the slip display is positioned in front of the finger, it does not reduce range of motion so that the thumb and index can be brought together in a pinch grasp.

Chen and Marcus performed constant force tracking experiments to determine the optimum actuator control method. They found that open-loop, constant force control was worse than simple visual control, due to difficulties in user calibration. Instead they chose a speed servoing with a constant offset which does not require calibration. The motor torque **T** is then given by

$$\mathbf{T} = T_{\text{offset}} + K_v(v_{\text{belt}} - v_{\text{slip motor}}) \tag{6.3}$$

where T_{offset} is the calibrated stall torque for the corresponding target normal force, K_v is the velocity gain, v_{belt} is the belt calculated speed, and $v_{\text{slip motor}}$ is the actual

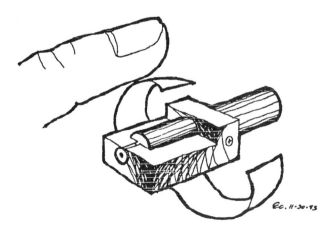

Figure 6.19 One degree-of-freedom slip feedback actuator. From Chen and Marcus [1994]. Reprinted by permission of the ASME.

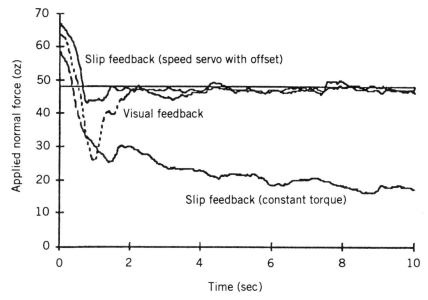

Figure 6.20   Constant force tracking using visual feedback or slip feedback. Reprinted by permission of the ASME from Chen and Marcus [1994].

speed of the motor. The torque offset component produces a continuous shear force at the fingertip. However, initiation of movement of the slip display happens only when the user's normal force is too low (regardless of the frictional characteristics of the finger-display contact surface). This resulted in improved force target tracking, when compared with open-loop (constant torque) control, as illustrated in Figure 6.20 [Chen and Marcus, 1994].

EXOS Co. has integrated the slip feedback actuator described above into the newly announced Hand Exoskeleton Haptic Display (HEHD). This force-feedback exoskeleton has four-degrees-of-freedom force feedback and two slip actuators at the thumb and index fingers. Its weight is supported by a table mounted boom, which makes it a nonportable force/slip feedback master. Its current price is $40,000.

6.4. SURFACE TEMPERATURE FEEDBACK

The last type of tactile feedback discussed in this chapter is surface temperature feedback. Anybody can understand that thermal feedback is required when navigating in very cold (or very warm) virtual worlds, or when grasping cold or hot virtual objects. Additionally, thermal feedback helps identify objects based on their "thermal signature." This is especially true when direct tactile exploration is impossible. Ino and his colleagues [1993b] performed human-factor studies in which subjects were asked to identify five materials (aluminum, glass, rubber, polyacrylate, and wood) through static touch. Thus the subjects could not trace the material surface and had no surface texture data to help in the recognition of the grasped material. Results showed that subjects could reliably recognize aluminum (91%) and wood (82%) based on force and temperature information alone. However, glass, rubber, and polyacrylate were recognized less than half of the time, their contact temperature signature being less characteristic.

As one may observe when touching objects with the fingertips, temperature is also an integral part of the human overall tactile sensing strategy. Thermal effects also help determine the "feel" or texture of a surface. . . . What the fingers detect thermally is not the absolute temperature of a material alone, but also its thermal conductivity and diffusivity. This is because the human finger is a source of heat, which at approximately 34°C is slightly above the ambient temperature of most objects we encounter. What the nerves in the finger detect is the outflow of heat from this source.
—Monkman and Taylor [1993]

If we could actively control the user's skin temperature through a thermal-feedback actuator, then we could recreate virtual thermal signatures to add realism to the simulation. A thermal actuator used for this purpose needs to be light and compact, so that the user's freedom of motion is not diminished. It needs to be clean and fast, so that rapid temperature changes can be produced. Such actuators are thermoelectric pumps that function on the principle discovered back in 1834 by Peltier, a French watchmaker. He observed that by applying dc current to two dissimilar materials placed in contact with each other a temperature differential is created and maintained. Today Peltier pumps use solid-state N and P-type semiconductors sandwiched between ceramic electrical insulators. As shown in Figure 6.21 [Levine, 1989], a dc source is connected to the semiconductors through copper electrodes so that the two junctions are electrically in series and thermally in parallel. Ceramic plates placed between the heat pump and the cold or hot end plates serve as thermal conductors and provide high mechanical strength. When current is applied, the P or N charges in the semiconductors are accelerated to the copper connectors, and transfer heat to the heat sink. The more current is applied, the more charges are attracted and the more heat is removed from the heat source. The net result is a drop in temperature at one end plate and a raise in temperature at the heat sink. Single thermoelectric pumps can produce temperature differentials up to 65°C, whereas four-stage devices (such as the ones produced by Melcor) can attain up to 125°C difference between the end plates.

Such large temperature differentials are not required in VR applications, in view of the user's thermal comfort zone, which is 13° to 46°C. Temperatures above or below these limits produce discomfort or pain. Several researchers have adapted single-stage Peltier heat pumps as thermal/tactile feedback actuators for VR. Zerkus and his colleagues at C&M Research Co. developed the Displaced Temperature Sensing System (DTSS) consisting of eight thermodes and a control interface unit. The thermode shown in Figure 6.22a [Zerkus et al., 1993] has a thin Peltier pump placed on a large heat sink. A fast thermocouple is attached to the top plate and is used to read the user's fingertip temperature in real time. This temperature is then sent to the control interface where it is compared with the programmed temperature. Temperature values can be set locally on the front of the interface unit or remotely

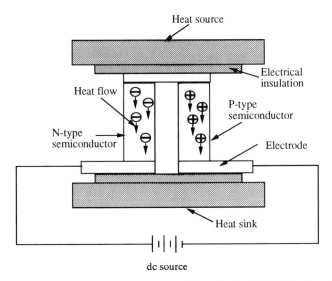

Figure 6.21 Thermoelectric heat pump. Adapted from Levine [1989]. Reprinted by permission.

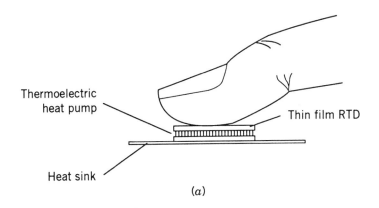

(a)

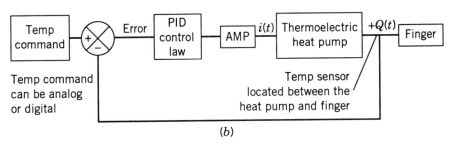

(b)

Figure 6.22 Temperature feedback for VR: (a) thermode construction; (b) control diagram. From Zerkus et al. [1993]. Reprinted by permission of C&M Research Co.

by the host computer through an RS232 serial line. As shown in Figure 6.22b, the difference between the actual and commanded fingertip temperatures is used as input to a software-implemented PID controller. The controller output is then sent to current amplifiers that drive the thermoelectric heat pump and the control loop is closed. The host computer can also change the gains of the PID controller to implement different control laws as required by the simulation. Software and hardware safety measures prevent the thermode from operating outside the user's comfort zone. Otherwise, if the pump has been operating for a long time and it fails, all the heat from the heat sink will travel back through the pump and burn the user's fingertip.

Later Caldwell and his colleagues [1995c] incorporated a Peltier heat pump in a multimodal sensing and feedback glove used in telerobotics and VR applications. As illustrated in Figure 6.23, the glove support is a smooth and strong leather cycling glove, which makes attachment of sensors and actuators easy. The user's position input is read by Hall-effect sensors placed at the thumb and finger joints, with an accuracy of 2°. Multimodal feedback from the simulation provides information on grasping force, tactile smoothness, surface temperature (and conductivity), and danger (pain). Thermal feedback is provided to the index finger by a small Peltier heat pump placed on the back surface of the first joint. This location was chosen for its high thermal sensor density and for not reducing the grasping range of motion. The heat pump weighs only 10 g and has overall dimensions of 15 × 15 × 3 mm. Its 15-W power output allows rapid (20°C/sec) cooling or heating, within the interval of

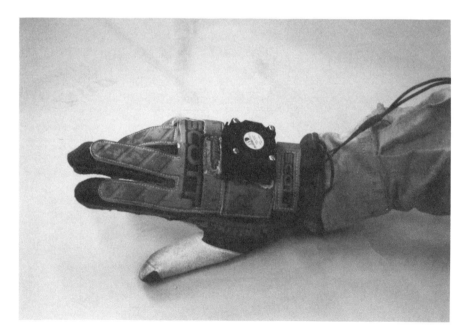

Figure 6.23 The Salford University force/tactile/thermal feedback glove. Photograph courtesy of Professor Darwin Caldwell, Department of Electronic Engineering.

−5°C to 50°C [Caldwell et al., 1994b]. This larger temperature interval was chosen so that grasping and manipulation of frozen virtual objects is possible. Additionally, pain feedback was provided by raising the temperature very rapidly to 50°C. It was reported that users responded to this overload condition in under 1 sec!

Besides the Peltier heat pump, the glove developed at Salford University incorporates miniature piezoelectric disks of lead zircon titanate placed at the user's fingertips. These disks have a metal support of 15 mm diam and weigh less than 2 g. When driven by high voltages (160 to 300 V) they vibrate to produce tactile texture feedback. Force feedback is produced by the same actuator but using a series of increasing amplitude vibrations. The electromechanical behavior of the piezoelectric actuators [Tiersten, 1969] is given by

$$\mathbf{D} = [\epsilon^T]\mathbf{E} + [\mathbf{d}]\mathbf{T} \tag{6.4}$$

where $\mathbf{D}$ is the electric displacement vector, $\mathbf{E}$ is the electric field vector, $[\mathbf{d}]$ is the piezoelectric constant matrix, $\mathbf{T}$ is the stress vector and $[\epsilon^T]$ is the dielectric matrix evaluated at constant strain.

Thermal recognition tests using the glove showed rates over 80% even for the confusing no change condition. Operators reported that the thermal feedback felt realistic, but slower than in reality (due to the finite power of the heat pump). In graded force recognition tests between 2 N (0.5 Hz) and 60 N (10 Hz) users had over 90% recognition rates. This is encouraging in view of the fact that force feedback was subject to sensorial substitution and was felt through cutaneous receptors as vibrations. Surface texture recognition rates using the glove were also above 90% [Caldwell and Gosney, 1993].

6.5. CONCLUSIONS

This chapter was the last in a series of three to discuss haptic feedback hardware. Here we presented various tactile feedback actuators needed to convey information on the contact surface geometry, texture, slippage, and temperature. We reviewed tactile feedback approaches from simple visual displays to pneumatic, vibrotactile, and electrotactile stimulation. To these, we added surface slip feedback for both incipient and continuous slip. Our discussion concluded with temperature-feedback actuators (heat pumps) that help in the recognition of the grasped object and enhance simulation realism. With this knowledge, we are now ready to proceed with various physical modeling techniques that are used to generate input to the haptic interface.

CHAPTER 7

PHYSICAL MODELING

The interface devices presented in the preceding chapters provide computer-generated haptic feedback to the user interacting with the virtual world. Another key part of the VR simulation is the input to the haptic interface, which depends on both simulation modeling and control algorithms. Because today's haptic interfaces do not have imbedded intelligence, they rely entirely on real-time computer input. Without such input, the most sophisticated haptic feedback interface would be useless. Thus, it is necessary to take a closer look at *physical modeling*, which generates the variables (forces, accelerations, vibrations, temperatures, etc.) necessary for haptic interface control.

Physical modeling has the challenging task of determining the dynamic behavior of virtual objects in the simulation based (primarily) on Newtonian physical laws. First, it is necessary to determine if objects (such as a virtual hand, a wall, or a ball) collide, and program the appropriate response. *Collision detection* assures that objects do not traverse each other if they are not supposed to. One particular collision is the *grasping* of virtual objects, a necessary first step in any manipulation task. If grasping is not properly modeled, then a virtual hand can visually pass through virtual objects (an unfortunate feature in some of today's VR commercial packages). *Surface deformation* is a result of grasping compliant virtual objects. Especially important is the deformation in the region of contact of two objects, whether this deformation is plastic or elastic. Sometimes objects are rigid. *Hard-contact* simulation is a daunting task, but nevertheless necessary when objects collide with a very stiff environment. *Physical constraints* such as gravity and friction are other aspects of physical modeling that add to the simulation realism. Figure 7.1 summarizes the various components of physical modeling that are the subject of this chapter. Chapter 8 details the computer control of haptic interfaces.

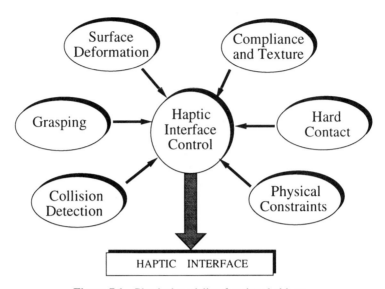

Figure 7.1 Physical modeling for virtual objects.

7.1. COLLISION DETECTION

Collision detection is a first step in the physical modeling of the virtual world. It involves the automatic detection of an imminent interaction of two objects and of the location where this interaction takes place. At the moment of impact, the simulation produces a *collision response* as objects bounce, deform, crash, explode, fall to the ground, and so on. If the user is mapped to one of the interacting objects (through a virtual hand, for example), then collision response may also produce forces, vibrations, or other haptic feedback to the user. Without collision detection, the simulation realism suffers, as explained by Moore and Wilhelms:

> When no special attention is paid to object interactions, the objects will sail majestically through each other, which is usually not physically reasonable and produces a disconcerting visual effect. Whenever two objects attempt to interpenetrate each other, we call it a collision.
>
> —Moore and Wilhelms [1988]

Collision detection for static objects has been known for a number of years. Cyrus and Beck [1978] developed an algorithm that detects the interaction of two- and three-dimensional lines against arbitrary convex polyhedrons. If the dot product between the normal to an edge and the vector from one of the vertices of that edge and the point of interest is negative, then penetration has occurred. For n polyhedra with m vertices each, the algorithm complexity is $O(n^2m^2)$.

Moore and Wilhelms [1988] later extended the Cyrus-Beck algorithm to collision detection for computer animation. Here, the trajectory of the object of interest is known *a priori* and parameterized as a function of time. The algorithm performs the collision, checking at fixed time intervals mapping the corresponding intermediate object positions over the trajectory. If the time interval is small, then collision detection is accurate, but, if it is large, then collision may be undetected and the objects pass through each other without triggering a collision response.

Unfortunately, in a VR simulation, it is impossible to know *a priori* the trajectory of every object as the user's actions (and the resultant sequence of events) are random. For these reasons, it is not possible to apply off-line collision detection algorithms:

> ...in a walkthrough environment, we usually do not have any information regarding the maximum velocity or acceleration, because the user may move with abrupt changes in direction and speed. Due to these unconstrained variables, collision detection is currently considered to be one of the major bottlenecks in building interactive simulated environments.
>
> —Cohen et al. [1995]

What is needed is a sufficiently simple algorithm that can detect collisions in real time, corresponding to graphics refresh rates of 25 to 30 frames/sec. At the same time, and especially for physical modeling, we need to know not only when a collision occurs, but also where, and to determine the extent of interpenetration between the two objects. Thus much higher rates are needed in order to prevent instabilities when detecting contact with rigid environments. The need for both speed and accuracy in the face of limited computing power clearly calls for a compromise.

7.1.1. Approximate Collision Detection

One solution is to use *bounding boxes* to enclose all virtual objects of interest. In Figure 7.2, we see two virtual objects, each with its own system of coordinates. Additionally, there is a third system of coordinates, called a world system of coordinates that is a reference for the motion of the two objects. A bounding box for Object 2 is the prism (shown in dashed lines) that encloses the whole object. The bounding box edges are parallel with the world system of coordinates, whereas its opposite corners are $(x_{min}, y_{min} z_{min})$ and $(x_{max}, y_{max} z_{max})$ [Foley et al., 1990].

Bounding boxes in turn can be subdivided into static and dynamic ones. *Static* bounding boxes have a constant dimension, regardless of the orientation of the object they enclose. Thus they have to be large enough to accommodate any possible orientation of the enclosed object versus the world system of coordinates. *Dynamic* bounding boxes change dimensions as a function of enclosed object orientation in space, while remaining aligned with the world system of coordinates [Cohen et al., 1995]. Dynamic bounding boxes better track the volume in space occupied by the enclosed object, at the expense of increased computational load. This is especially true for objects with high rotation velocities.

Bounding box collision detection involves determining whether the two prisms (rather than the two objects) overlap. Cohen et al. [1995] use three orthogonal projections of the bounding boxes in the xy, yz, and zx planes. If there is overlapping in all three projections, then the two bounding boxes are in collision. Using bounding boxes, it is possible to replace the slow testing of every vertex of one object versus

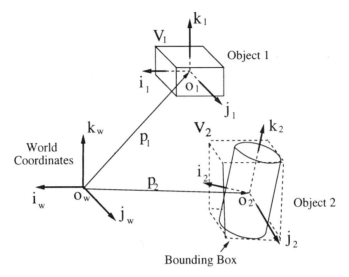

Figure 7.2   Bounding boxes for collision detection. Reprinted by permission from Burdea and Coiffet [1994]. © Éditions Hermès.

those of the second object with a much faster algorithm at the expense of reduced positional accuracy.

7.1.2. Exact Collision Detection

When positional accuracy of the collision and interpenetration locations is desired, an exact collision detection algorithm is needed. The performance of such algorithms usually degrades with the complexity of the virtual scene. Lin [1993], in her doctoral dissertation on mobile robot path planning, developed a fast algorithm that has almost constant performance versus the number of object vertices. For most objects including spherical ones the running time is roughly $O(\sqrt{n})$ where n is the number of vertices in each object. The algorithm uses *local* features (such as vertices, edges, or facets) of convex polyhedra, and is extendable to concave ones. Figure 7.3 illustrates the local vertex-facet collision test developed by Lin. The facet is separating external and internal "Voronoi" volumes. The external one is defined by planes extending the facets adjacent to the one of interest towards Object A. The internal Voronoi volume is defined by the prism having the facet as base and the apex at the centroid of Object B. The collision test is then performed for the closest features of the two objects, provided that the vertice falls in the external Voronoi volume. Once the vertex is inside the internal Voronoi volume, a collision has occurred. When any facet has more than five edges a preprocessing stage is added to divide its external Voronoi volume into subvolumes (each resting on a facet with less than five edges). This is needed to decouple the collision detection computation time from the number of vertices.

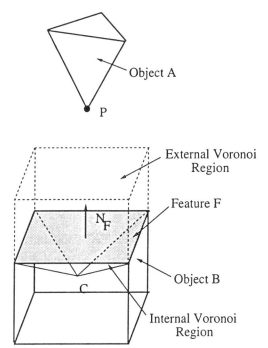

Figure 7.3   Local collision detection using Voronoi Volumes. Adapted from Lin [1993] and Ponamgi et al. [1995]. Reprinted by permission of the Association for Computing Machinery.

Later on Cohen and his colleagues at the University of North Carolina at Chapel Hill [Cohen et al., 1995], extended Lin's local collision detection algorithm to multibody collision detection for VR simulations. To have both speed and accuracy, the researchers took a two-step approach consisting of an approximate (gross) collision detection followed by an exact collision detection where needed. As illustrated in Figure 7.4, the simulation loop starts with a pruning of multibody pairs where overlapping bounding boxes are detected. These are then subject to pairwise exact collision detection. In this way the number of possible interactions is trimmed from $O(n^2)$ to $O(n + m)$, where n are the simultaneously moving objects and m are the objects that are very close to each other.

Not all overlapping boxes will correspond to a collision, due to their larger volume. If the exact collision detection does confirm a collision, then an analysis is performed involving object dynamics, interpenetration forces, and so on, and an appropriate collision response is generated. This closes the simulation loop, and the process is started from scratch. Tests performed by Cohen on a HP-9000-750 graphics workstation showed that it took less than 50 msec to determine all the collisions in an environment consisting of 1000 moving convex polyhedra each with 50 facets. Thus the simulation ran at 23 frames/sec when static bounding cubes were used! Dynamic bounding boxes brought a slight performance degradation, especially when the poly-

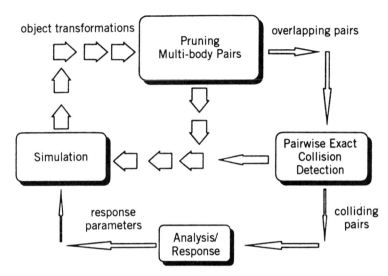

object transformations

overlapping pairs

Figure 7.4 Multiple body collision detection algorithm. Cohen et al. [1995]. Reprinted by permission of the Association for Computing Machinery.

hedra were rotating at high speed. Ponamgi et al. [1995] subsequently extended this algorithm to objects of general shape (concave, curved, etc).

Another exact collision detection method was proposed by Schlaroff and Pentland [1991] at MIT Media Laboratory. Instead of using a polygon representation for an object shape they use *implicit functions* that algebraically define the object's surface. These superquadrics of the form $f(\mathbf{x}) = 0$ have an "inside-outside" feature which can detect whether a point is inside or outside of the volume bounded by the implicit function. All points $\mathbf{x} = (x, y, z)$ for which $f(\mathbf{x}) < 0$ are inside this volume, while points outside the volume correspond to $f(\mathbf{x}) > 0$. Thus, when a vertex $\mathbf{P}$ satisfies $f(\mathbf{P}) < 0$, collision has occurred. The resulting algorithm has a complexity of $O(m)$ where m is the number of collision checks (points).

7.2. GRASPING

The previous section showed that collision detection is a key part of virtual object interactions. One such interaction is grasping, in which the object to be manipulated is captured by a virtual hand responding to the user's input. In this case, the collision between the hand and object must be detected by the simulation. The majority of commercial software contents itself with very coarse collision detection as explained by Bergamasco:

> At present, grasping operations of virtual objects are performed according to a very simple procedure: usually when the virtual hand enters in contact with the virtual object, the virtual object is considered *captured* and graphically connected with the

virtual hand. The collision detection is usually performed testing the distance between one characteristic point of the virtual hand (usually the center of metacarpus) and the sphere or the bounding box enveloping the virtual object.

—Bergamasco et al. [1994b]

Visually the hand appears to stab through the object, due to Z-buffering in the graphics hardware which overides distant pixels with ones closer to the viewer.

Within the context of this book, our interest is not how "nice" the graphics look, but the haptic feedback *associated* with grasping. It is clear that bounding box collision detection is not the answer here, as it does not provide local information on collision location and interpenetration. What is needed is an exact algorithm verifying collision between finger segments, the palm, and the object of interest. Figure 7.5 shows how Lin's algorithm was extended to perform exact collision detection between the hand and objects in the environment. The distal segments of the ring and pinkie fingers are colored to signify collisions.

Bergamasco and his colleagues at Scola Superiore Santa Anna developed an integrated approach to grasping using the HFF master (see Section 5.2.3). Accordingly, the three stages of virtual object grasping are collision detection, contact force generation, and determination of grasp stability subject to external forces. Collision detection starts with a preliminary test based on a "gross control point," located at the wrist, and the center of mass of the virtual object. If this distance is less than a given threshold then an exact collision detection is executed. This test uses a large

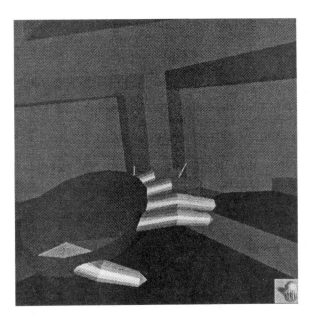

Figure 7.5   Hand collision detection. Courtesy of Department of Computer Science, University of North Carolina at Chapel Hill.

array of control points located on the palmar side of the virtual hand. The model developed by Bergamasco [1994b,c] uses an orthogonal grid of 5×7 points on each phalanx and two such groups in the palm. These control point groups form a set $\mathbf{G} = \{G_1 \ldots G_{17}\}$, each consisting of a set of control points $\mathbf{P}_i = \{P_{i1} \ldots P_{i35}\}$.

When collision does occur the virtual hand and object interpenetrate at several locations on the palm and fingers, as shown in Color Plate 4 and Figure 7.6. Due to real-time constraints Bergamasco treats the hand and grasped object as indeformable. For each contact group $\mathbf{G}_i^*$ (a subset of $\mathbf{G}_i$) the interpenetration volume V_i has its center of mass given by

$$\hat{\mathbf{P}}_i = \frac{\sum_{j=1}^{35} \mathbf{P}_{ij} \Downarrow \mathbf{h}_{ij}}{\sum_{j=1}^{35} \mathbf{h}_{ij}} \tag{7.1}$$

where $\mathbf{h}_{ij}$ are segments normal to the surface for all the interpenetrating points within group $\mathbf{G}_i$. The point $\hat{\mathbf{P}}_i$ is the point of application of the contact force at each contact group. Figure 7.6 shows the contact groups in the palm shaded, whereas contact forces are represented by vectors pointing outward from the grasped object.

7.2.1. Grasping Forces

Once contact has occurred, the virtual hand applies forces on the grasped object. The applied force usually has both tangential and normal components to the object surface. Normal contact forces $\mathbf{F}_{Ni}$ are proportional with the interpenetration volumes, such

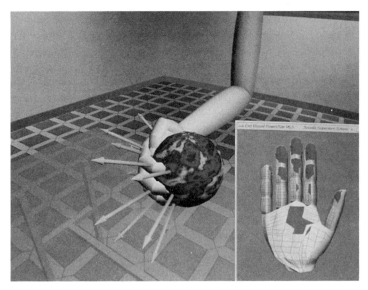

Figure 7.6 Collision detection and contact forces during grasping. Courtesy of Professor M. Bergamasco, Scuola Superiore Santa Anna, Italy.

that $|\mathbf{F}_{Ni}| = KV_i$. Their direction passes through $\hat{\mathbf{P}}_i$. Tangential forces are opposed by static friction forces $\mathbf{F}_{Si}$, which depend on the surface static friction coefficient μ_s. If the surface is smooth (small μ_s) or the tangential force is large (contact force outside the friction cone [Kuni and Hashimoto, 1994]), then there is a relative motion between the virtual hand and the grasped object. This motion is opposed by dynamic friction forces $\mathbf{F}_{Di}$ which depend on the surface dynamic friction coefficient μ_d. Finally, the grasped object is also subject to gravity forces and external forces trying to destabilize the grasp. Such forces are termed by Bergamasco "external forces" $\mathbf{F}_{Eobj}$. Thus the generalized force vector applied on the grasped object is given by

$$\mathbf{F} = \mathbf{F}_{Eobj} + \sum \mathbf{F}_{Ni} + \sum \mathbf{F}_{Si} + \sum \mathbf{F}_{Di} \qquad (7.2)$$

where $\sum \mathbf{F}_{Si}$ is done over all contact regions G_i, where there is no relative motion, and $\sum \mathbf{F}_{Di}$ over all contact regions where the palm or fingers are moving relative to the grasped object surface.

7.2.2. Grasp Stability

Grasp stability reflects the ability of a given virtual hand grasp configuration to withstand external forces (or moments) without losing the grasped object. Intuitively one realizes that a delicate, dextrous grasp, where contact with the object is only at the fingertips, has much less chance to resist external destabilizing forces than a power grasp where contact is with the full hand. But even for power grasps, there still are combinations of hand postures and grasping forces where the object may be lost. Modeling grasp stability is important, not just for VR but for other fields as well. In robotics, for example, motions are performed at high speeds, and a lost object (workpiece) may become a dangerous projectile. Ismaeil and Ellis [1994] in their article on robot grasping state that a stable grasp needs to satisfy certain conditions:

> . . . the object must be in equilibrium; all the tangential forces at the contact points must be within the cones of static friction; all the normal forces must be finite and less than some maximum value, which depends on the properties of the workpiece and the system constraints; and no displacement of the workpiece occurs when it is subjected to small forces.
>
> —Ismaeil and Ellis [1994]

These conditions still leave a wide range of forces and moments that can be applied on the object while keeping the finger forces within some bounds. Among these possibilities, one needs to find an *optimum grasp* which preserves stability using finger forces as small as possible. Small finger forces are needed to avoid user fatigue and overload of the haptic-feedback system. Mirtich and Canny [1994] looked at optimum grasps of three-dimensional objects using three fingers. They visualized the space of possible stable grasps with an equilateral triangular circumscribing prism. As shown in Figure 7.7, the grasped object is circumscribed in a prism that has an equilateral triangular cross section with three infinite planes. These touch the enclosed object in one point each. Depending on the prism rotation angle θ about its longitudinal axis, the area of the equilateral triangle may grow or shrink. The optimum grasp of a smooth three-dimensional object is the one corresponding to the *maximum* circumscribing prism.

7.2.3. Grasp Invariants

Once a virtual object has been grasped, the need arises to describe its motion together with the user-controlled virtual hand. Haptic masters and open-loop sensing gloves have position sensors that provide real-time information on the hand position. A Polhemus tracker, for example, has a fixed source and a mobile receiver attached to the hand. The tracker receiver position and orientation versus the world coordinate system is typically expressed as a 4×4 homogeneous transformation matrix [Denavit and Hartenberg, 1955; Foley et al., 1990] of the form:

$$\mathbf{T}_{\text{world}\leftarrow\text{tracker}}(t) = \begin{bmatrix} \mathbf{R}_{3\times3}(t) & \mathbf{P}_{3\times1}(t) \\ 0 \quad 0 \quad 0 & 1 \end{bmatrix} \tag{7.3}$$

where $\mathbf{R}_{3\times3}$ is the rotation submatrix expressing the orientation of the tracker receiver system of coordinates versus the world, and $\mathbf{P}_{3\times1}$ is the vector expressing the position of the origin of the tracker receiver system versus the origin of the world system of coordinates.

Similarly, the object position and orientation is expressed by $\mathbf{T}_{\text{world}\leftarrow\text{object}}(t)$. Robinett and Holloway [1992] observed that, as long as the object is in a stable grasp, its position and orientation versus the hand do not change. In other words $\mathbf{T}_{\text{hand}\leftarrow\text{object}}$ is invariant, regardless of the hand motion in space. Other invariant transformations

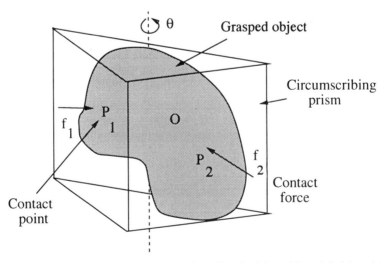

Figure 7.7 Circumscribing triangular prism for object O. Adapted from Mirtich and Canny [1994]. © 1994 IEEE. Reprinted by permission.

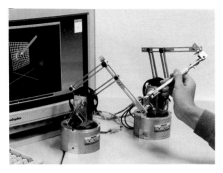

Color Plate 1. Surface deformation using a pen-based haptic interface developed by Professor H. Iwata, University of Tsukuba, Japan.

Color Plate 2. The FREFLEX nonportable force feedback exoskeleton. Photograph courtesy of Captain C. Hasser, Wright-Patterson AFB.

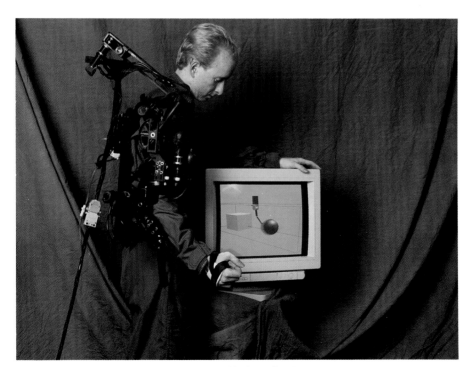

Color Plate 3. The Force ArmMaster portable force feedback exoskeleton. Photograph courtesy of EXOS Co.

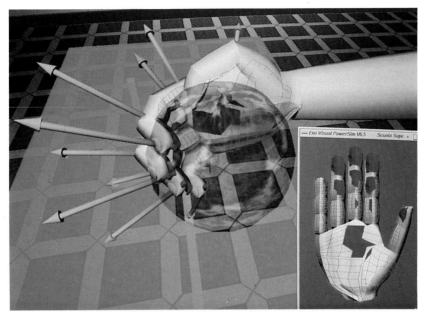

Color Plate 4. Physical modeling of contact forces during the grasping of a non-deformable virtual ball. Reprinted with permission from Bergamasco et al., 1994c. © 1994 IEEE.

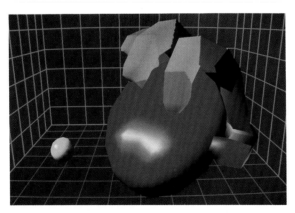

Color Plate 5. Surface deformation during the grasping of a compliant virtual ball. Photograph courtesy of the CAIP Center, Rutgers University.

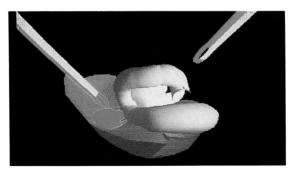

Color Plate 6. Tissue deformation during the simulation of gall bladder removal surgery. Photograph courtesy of Professor N. Ezquerra, Georgia Institute of Technology.

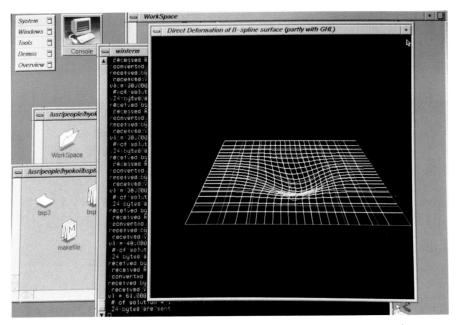

Color Plate 7. Direct free-form deformation of a β-spline surface using a trowel-type tool. Reprinted with permission from Yamashita et al., 1994, © Society of Instrumentation and Control Engineers of Japan.

Color Plate 8. Grasping forces displayed by the Rutgers Master I interface LED bar graphs for a plastically deformed soda can. From Burdea et al., 1995. Reprinted with permission of Ablex Publishing Corporation.

Color Plate 9. Muscle tissue deformation during the palpation of a virtual knee model. Reprinted with permission from Langrana et al., 1994, Elsevier Science BV.

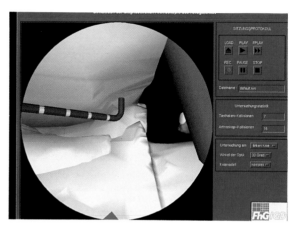

Color Plate 10. Arthroscopy training simulator with two-dimensional display of a virtual camera inside the knee joint. Photograph courtesy of Dr. W. Muller, Fraunhofer Institute for Computer Graphics, Germany.

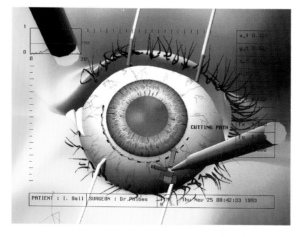

Color Plate 11. Eye surgery simulator developed for a telerobotic system with bilateral force feedback. Reprinted with permission from Hunter et al., 1993. © The MIT Press.

Color Plate 12. Hand rehabilitation exercise using a virtual Digi-Key instrument mapped to the Rutgers Master I. Photograph courtesy of the CAIP Center, Rutgers University.

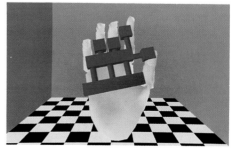

Color Plate 13. Virtua Racing simulator used in location-based entertainment. The steering wheel provides force feedback to the player. Photograph courtesy of SEGA of America, Inc.

Color Plate 14. Virtual Motion three-dimensional platform using PemRAM actuators. Photograph courtesy of Denne Developments Ltd., UK.

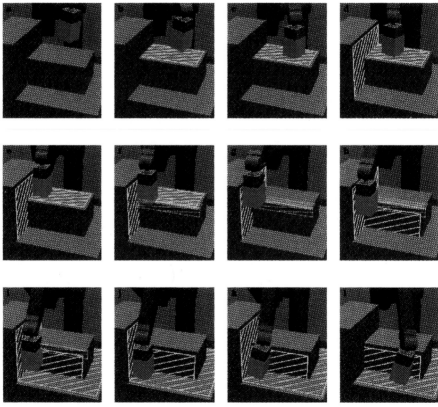

Color Plate 15. Virtual fixtures used as haptic guides during robot teleprogramming. Photograph courtesy of P. Sayers, GRASP Laboratory, University of Pennsylvania.

Color Plate 16. Teleoperation of a scanning tunneling microscope using the Argonne Arm III with force feedback. Photograph courtesy of the Computer Science Department, University of North Carolina at Chapel Hill.

Color Plate 17. Direct tactile feedback for the RAVECTA flight simulator with see-through, head-mounted display. Photograph courtesy of British Aerospace, UK.

Color Plate 18. The individual soldier "I-Port" combat simulator with resistive forces provided by a mobility platform. Photograph courtesy of Professor M. Zyda, Naval Postgraduate School.

are those between the world coordinates and the room and between the room and the tracker source. Therefore, the motion of the grasped object can be expressed as

$$\mathbf{T}_{\text{world}\leftarrow\text{object}}(t) = \mathbf{T}_{\text{world}\leftarrow\text{tracker}}\mathbf{T}_{\text{tracker}\leftarrow\text{hand}}(t)\mathbf{T}_{\text{hand}\leftarrow\text{object}} \tag{7.4}$$

where $\mathbf{T}_{\text{world}\leftarrow\text{tracker}}$ relates the tracker source and world system of coordinates, and $\mathbf{T}_{\text{tracker}\leftarrow\text{hand}}(t)$ is the time-dependent transformation between the tracker receiver (on the hand) and the tracker source. Using transformation invariants saves time, because many of these kinematic transformations may be precomputed off-line. Grasping invariants will, however, not apply if the user manipulates (rotates or translates) the grasped object versus his palm. Interested readers may also consult Sturman's Ph.D. Thesis [1992] for further discussion on manual control in VR (which he calls whole-hand input).

7.3. SURFACE DEFORMATION

In our grasping force calculation example, the assumption was made that both the virtual hand and grasped object are undeformable. Bergamasco and his colleagues [1994b] used this simplification because of real-time computation constraints. In reality, surfaces are (usually) deformable, so that a grasped virtual object will change shape in response to the user-applied forces. If the object regains its shape once released, then the deformation is elastic, otherwise the object remains deformed (dented), in which case the deformation is plastic. It is thus necessary to take a closer look at surface deformation models that are interactive and satisfy the real-time requirement of VR simulations. These methods can be largely classified as *vertex-based* and *spline-based*, depending on whether the object surface is represented by polygonal meshes or parametric equations.

7.3.1. Vertex-Based Methods

Most VR models are represented by polygon meshes, containing a number of polygons that depends on the desired level of geometrical detail [Viewpoint Datalabs, 1993]. These polygons are formed by vertices $\mathbf{V}_i = (x_i, y_i, z_i)$ defined in the world system of coordinates, and by edges E_j. Most of the time, both vertices and edges are shared by several (adjacent) polygons. It is thus wasteful to save the mesh as vertices, since each vertex would have to be stored several times. Instead, most graphics languages save the mesh as a look-up table with pointers to edges, and subsequently to vertices [Foley et al., 1994]. Thus a polygon may be defined as

$$\mathbf{P} = (E_1, \dots, E_n) \quad \text{with} \quad E_j = (\mathbf{V}_i, \mathbf{V}_{i+1}, P_k, P_l) \tag{7.5}$$

where E_j are the edges making up the polygon, $\mathbf{V}_i, \mathbf{V}_{i+1}$ are the vertices describing the edges E_j, and P_k, P_l are the polygons sharing the edge E_j.

Direct Vertex Manipulation. Some commercial toolkits such as WorldToolKit [Sense8 Co., 1995] allow direct vertex manipulation. The user can interactively change the location of a vertex in the look-up table, thus redefining the shape of the polygons sharing it during image rendering. General graphics libraries such as Starbase [Hewlett-Packard, 1991] provide connectivity information in the look-up table. The user can thus modify a vertex and its neighbors according to some application-dependent deformation propagation law. An example is the virtual hand squeezing a virtual rubber ball as illustrated in Color Plate 5. The graphics-rendering algorithm uses data sent by the collision detection process that determines the point of contact and the degree of deformation between the fingertips and the ball. This information is then used to map affected vertices to smaller spheres concentric with the ball [Burdea et al., 1995a]. To make the ball deformation appear more realistic a "bulging" effect is introduced, as illustrated in Figure 7.8. The bulging effect is created by modifying the z component of each vertex as a function of $\cos(\theta)$ for the ball mesh. Since the x and y vertex coordinates are unchanged, the bulging is more noticeable at the poles than at the equator. Users wearing a dextrous force-feedback interface such as the Rutgers Master [Burdea et al., 1992a] can feel forces proportional to the ball deformation. When the ball is released it regains its spherical shape.

Active Surfaces. In the previous example the object to be deformed had a fairly regular surface (sphere) which made modeling easy. There are, however, surfaces of much more complex shape, an example being body organs (gall bladder, liver, kidney, etc.). Cover and his colleagues at Georgia Institute of Technology and the Medical College of Georgia [1993] proposed the concept of active surfaces to model tissue deformation and cutting in VR surgical training. An *active surface* is an

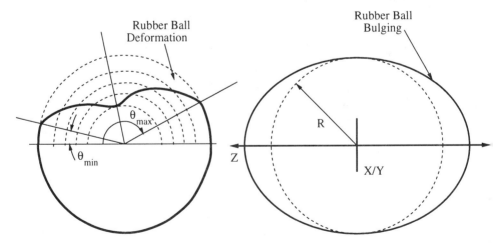

Figure 7.8 Rubber ball deformation and bulging. From Burdea et al. [1995a]. Reprinted by permission of Ablex Publishing Corporation.

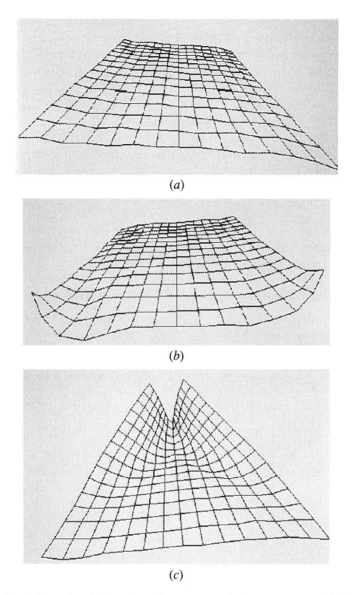

(a)

(b)

(c)

Figure 7.9   Active surface deformation: (a) zero-energy; (b) low-energy state; (c) high-energy state. Photographs courtesy of Professor N. Ezquerra, Georgia Institute of Technology.

energy-minimizing polygonal mesh which, when deformed, will seek to return to a low-energy state. Figure 7.9 [Cover et al., 1993] illustrates an active surface in zero-, low-, and high-energy states.

Currently, the energy-minimization process is modeled with ideal springs attached at each mesh vertex. The springs are located between each vertex and its neighbors, and between the vertex current and rest (home) positions. As points are pulled away from their rest position the surface springs determine the amount of deformation energy and its effect on the whole surface. The deformation of one vertex will impact its neighbors, and therefore the object mesh look-up table needs supplemental information. This includes the total force applied to that vertex, a flag telling whether the vertex is "frozen" in place, and what is its home position. Thus each vertex is stored as

$$\mathbf{V}_i = \{\mathbf{V}_i^{\text{location}}, \mathbf{V}_i^{\text{frozen}}, \mathbf{V}_i^{\text{neighbors}}, \mathbf{V}_i^{\text{force}}, \mathbf{V}_i^{\text{home}}\} \tag{7.6}$$

Color Plate 6 shows a gall bladder model developed by Cover et al. being deformed in a surgery simulation. A haptic feedback tool is being integrated to provide force feedback to the user deforming the active surface of the bladder. The research team is also working to extend this three-dimensional deformation by adding tissue cutting, tearing, and ripping.

Surface Cutting. Modeling tissue-cutting during surgery requires an algorithm that allows topological changes in the surface being manipulated. Song and Reddy [1995] at the University of Akron are developing a tissue-cutting simulation with haptic feedback. The cutting tool is simulated by an instrumented wand measuring

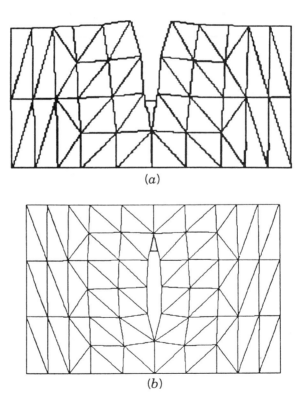

(a)

(b)

Figure 7.10   Virtual tissue surface cutting: (*a*) vertical plane; (*b*) horizontal plane. Reprinted by permission from Song and Reddy [1995].

the user's hand position and applied forces. A finite element model is formulated in the vicinity of the virtual cutting tool once it touches the surface of the virtual object. This model uses a template of nodes that moves beneath the surface of the object as the cutting tool moves in space. Actual cutting takes place if the force exerted by the user on the instrumented wand exceeds the shearing resistance of the virtual object.

Figure 7.10 [Song and Reddy, 1995] illustrates the surface mesh being cut in (a) a vertical plane and (b) a horizontal one. The node being cut is released and replaced by two duplicate nodes. A spring model is added to retract the two newly created nodes to a more stable configuration, thus enlarging the cut. During real-time simulation the finite-element template is made transparent, resulting in increased visual realism. Eventually a haptic feedback tool will be integrated in the system to provide tissue turgidity information to the user.

7.3.2. Spline-based Methods

Another way of representing virtual objects is through parametric bicubic surfaces. These use functions that are of a higher degree than the linear functions describing a polygonal plane, use less storage, and provide increased surface smoothness compared to polygonal meshes. We first describe briefly parametric surfaces, their underlying geometry, and local deformation procedures. Then we discuss free-form deformation methods that allow the user to indirectly change the shape of virtual objects enclosed in a lattice of control points. Finally, we present research to improve free-form deformation by allowing direct, real-time manipulation of the object surface.

Parametric Surfaces. A parametric three-dimensional curve segment is generally described by points $x(t)$, $y(t)$, and $z(t)$, where the parameter $t = [0, 1]$. Typically these are cubic polynomials of the form [Foley et al., 1994]:

$$x(t) = a_x t^3 + b_x t^2 + c_x t + d_x, \tag{7.7}$$

$$y(t) = a_y t^3 + b_y t^2 + c_y t + d_y, \tag{7.8}$$

$$z(t) = a_z t^3 + b_z t^2 + c_z t + d_z, \tag{7.9}$$

where a, b, and c are constant coefficients. A particular point location on the curve segment depends on the particular parameter t value ($t = 0$ and $t = 1$ correspond to the end points). Several such segments can be joined or splined smoothly at knot points by assuring continuity of the first and second derivatives. There are several kinds of *splines*, depending on the constraints (or control points) that determine the values of the constant coefficients. *Hermite splines* are defined by two end points and two end-point tangent vectors. *Bezier splines* are defined by two end points and two other points that control the end-point tangent vectors. Finally, β-*splines* have four control points, none of which are the curve segment end points. In our discussion, here we will emphasize β-*splines* since they are smoother than the Hermite or Bezier ones and have a local control behavior. Moving a control point in space affects only a small portion of a β-spline, namely four adjacent curve segments. Thus the time needed to recompute the polynomial coefficients is greatly reduced.

Parametric *surfaces* are an extension of parametric three-dimensional curves, with point coordinates $x(s,t)$, $y(s,t)$, and $z(s,t)$ being a function of two parameters s and t. Figure 7.11 [Foley et al., 1994] shows a three-dimensional parametric surface patch overlaid with a grid of constant-parameter curves. The bottom edge corresponds to points $x(s,0)$, $y(s,0)$, and $z(s,0)$ while the left edge has points with $x(0,t)$, $y(0,t)$, and $z(0,t)$. Intermediate points correspond to parameters $s \in (0,1)$ and $t \in (0,1)$. Deforming such a surface patch means interactively moving the lattice of three-dimensional control points that surrounds the surface. It is thus an *indirect* deformation method.

In the previous discussion, we assumed that the user can deform the parametric surface in any way he desires. However, there may be applications where this deformation is limited by certain geometrical constraints. Celinker and Welch at Carnegie-Mellon University [1992] looked at the deformation of β-spline surfaces subject to linear constraints. The researchers modeled the behavior of the β-spline surfaces using an energy-minimization approach, since:

> Energy minimizing surfaces mimic the behavior of everyday physical objects providing the user with a familiar metaphor for modifying the shape with forces in an intuitive manner. Surfaces can be pushed, pulled, and inflated to get desired shapes. The form of energy functional determines the properties of the shape being sculpted. We use a functional that causes the surface to minimize its area while distributing curvature over large areas to form very smooth and graceful shapes.
>
> —Celinker and Welch [1992]

This interactive modeling environment used sculpting tools (such as pressure, springs, and gravity), and geometric constraints to specify analytic conditions that the surface must satisfy while being deformed. Frozen geometrical constraints are added to the surface by freezing some geometric property of the surface while allowing the rest of the surface to vary. Tracked constraints vary in value over time, thus causing

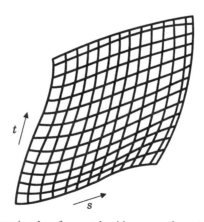

Figure 7.11   Three-dimensional surface patch with curves of constant s and t. From Foley et al. [1994]. Reprinted by permission of Addison-Wesley, Inc.

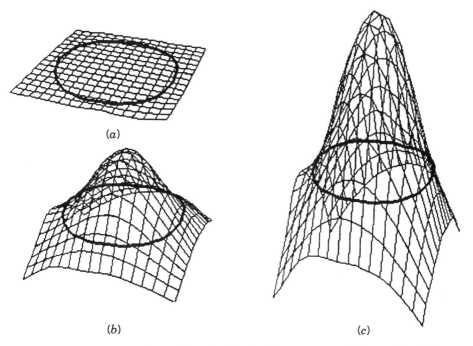

(a)

(b)   (c)

Figure 7.12 β-spline surface deformed with closed-curve geometrical constraint: (a) no pressure; (b) medium pressure; (c) high pressure. From Celinker and Welch [1992]. Reprinted by permission of the Association for Computing Machinery.

the surface to deform. Figure 7.12 shows a parametric curve being deformed subject to a frozen closed-curve constraint. A pressure sculpting load was applied to the surface patch inside the constraining curve producing a deformation proportional to the pressure magnitude. The user interacts with the simulation by increasing the value of the sculpting force using a slider bar GUI on an SGI workstation.

The above deformation method is indirect, since the user moves a slider bar to change the surface shape. Increased interactivity was achieved by Fowler [1992] who replaced the slider bar with a DataGlove. The finger flex angle was used to apply tension along one axis, while the thumb angle was used for tension applied along an orthogonal axis. The axes orientation was commanded by the glove tracker, while the keyboard was used to control the coupling and decoupling of the virtual hand with the surface being deformed. An SGI Iris 4D340/VGX rendered this interactive simulation at several frames per second.

Free-Form Deformation Methods. The previous examples described the deformation of parametric surface patches, with or without geometric constraints. Several such patches form an object, and several objects may need to be deformed simultaneously. In such cases, local deformation techniques described above do not suffice. Sederberg and Parry [1986] describe a procedure in which several objects lying within a bounded volume of space can be deformed at the same time. They call this mapping from $\mathbf{R}^3$ to $\mathbf{R}^3$ "free-form deformation" (FFD). The FFD method involves a parallelipipedic region of space subdivided by a lattice of evenly spaced control points. A local system of coordinates relates the surface points to the control points. This mapping can then be used to deform the surfaces of all enclosed objects by moving the enclosing lattice control points. Parametric surfaces remain parametric after the deformation. If the surface is given by $x = f(r,s)$, $y = g(r,s)$, and $z = h(r,s)$, and the FFD is given by the mapping $\mathbf{X}_{FFD} = \mathbf{X}(x,y,z)$, then the deformed parametric surface patch is given by

$$\mathbf{X}_{FFD}(r,s) \;=\; \mathbf{X}(f(r,s), g(r,s), h(r,s)) \tag{7.10}$$

Subsequently Coquillart and Jancene [1991] at Institut National De Recherche En Informatique Et En Automatique (France) developed a technique to allow animated sequences of FFD objects. The Animated Free-Form Deformation (AFFD) sets up two three-dimensional lattices corresponding to the user-defined initial and final lattice. Then a key-frame technique is used to specify parameters such as position, orientation, and scaling at some key position and to interpolate the key parameters. Figure 7.13 [Coquillart and Jancene, 1991] shows AFFD being applied to a swollen cylinder segment. The first column shows the FFD lattice at various intermediate positions, whereas the second column shows the corresponding FFD deformation

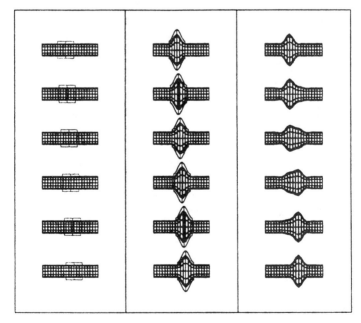

Figure 7.13   Animated free-form deformation sequence for a swollen cylinder: (*a*) lattice interpolation; (*b*) corresponding AFFD sequence; (*c*) morphing being added to AFFD. From Coquilart and Jancene [1991]. Reprinted by permission of the Association for Computing Machinery.

of the cylinder. The third column shows a metamorphic deformation where the deformation changes over time, not just in location but also in shape.

Both FFD or AFFD allow only indirect manipulation of the object surface. This presents a number of problems to the user as observed by Hsu and his colleagues:

1) Exact shape is difficult to achieve;
2) Exact placement of object points is difficult to achieve;
3) Users unfamiliar with splines do not understand the purpose of the control points and the results of their movement;
4) The control points become difficult to manipulate when occluded by the object being deformed, or when there are so many they clutter the screen.

—Hsu et al. [1992]

In view of these limitations it is much easier to deform surfaces if the surface points could be moved directly. Hsu and his colleagues developed a Direct Free-Form Deformation (DFFD) approach, which allows the user to select a point on the object's surface and then move the pointer to where the new location of that point should be. The algorithm then calculates the necessary change to the *control-point* lattice that would induce the desired change in the surface shape. The problem is under-determined, because there are many lattice configurations that would yield the same deformation location for the selected surface point. Thus a least-squares solution is used to select among possible control lattice candidates. Overall, the DFFD method offers increased interactivity and better deformation control (compared to the FFD method) at the expense of a larger computation load.

Yamashita and his colleagues [1994] report on an adaptation of the DFFD methodology to real-time VR simulations. Their simulation environment called "ViSurf" allows local direct deformation using a multitude of tools. These user-selected tools act on several surface points simultaneously. Color Plate 7 shows a trowel-type tool used to obtain a small flattening on the object surface in the area where the user pushes. The external control points were made transparent to achieve increased visual realism. Haptic feedback is being integrated to the simulation so that the user can feel the surface compliance while it is being deformed. Force feedback is produced by a six-degree-of-freedom haptic feedback interface (previously illustrated in Figure 4.19) interconnected to an SGI Iris workstation.

7.4. SURFACE MECHANICAL COMPLIANCE

The previous description of surface deformation methods was purely geometric in nature. It is now time to see how to model the forces associated with surface deformation. Intuitively we know that a given object deformation may correspond to small forces if the object is soft, or to large forces if it is hard. This softness or hardness felt during static interactions is expressed in terms of the object mechanical *compliance*. A more general variable that takes into account dynamic effects (that grow with the object mass, velocity, and acceleration) is the mechanical *impedance* [Colgate and Hannaford, 1993] of the modeled object.

Another property, which clearly influences the force variation during surface deformation, is the *elasticity* of the virtual object [Burdea et al., 1995a]. Nonelastic objects that remain deformed behave differently from elastic objects that regain their initial shape once the interaction ends. A special category is that of undeformable (very stiff) objects that generate large interaction forces without surface deformation.

7.4.1. Elastic Deformation

Most researchers working on VR haptic feedback model elastic deformations using the (simple) Hooke's law:

$$\mathbf{F} = K_{object}\Delta x \tag{7.11}$$

where K_{object} is a constant expressing stiffness of the virtual object and Δx is the surface deformation along a specified direction. This linear equation is well suited for fast real-time force computation while at the same time allowing the modeling of object stiffness. Figure 7.14 illustrates the feedback forces during the deformation of hard and soft elastic objects [Burdea et al., 1993]. The object elasticity explains why feedback forces are present during both compression and relaxation. The same object deformation Δx corresponds to a larger force for the hard object with stiffness $K_1 > K_2$ of the soft object. There is a limit to the achievable object deformation (and force) dictated by the maximum haptic interface output.

Burdea and his colleagues [1993, 1995a] applied Hooke's law for modeling the interaction between an elastic rubber ball and a virtual hand, as shown in Color Plate 5. The feedback forces produced by the Rutgers Master were modeled as:

$$\mathbf{F}_i = K_b\Delta x_i \quad \text{for } i = 1 \ldots 4 \tag{7.12}$$

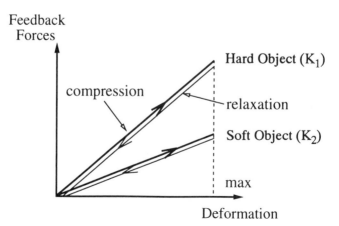

Figure 7.14   Elastic deformation using Hooke's law. Adapted from Burdea et al., [1993]. © Éditions Hermès. Reprinted by permission.

where $\mathbf{F}_i$ is the feedback force at finger i and Δx_i is the ball deformation at fingertip i. This model is a simplified one since fingertip contact was considered at a single point, and no friction forces were included. Furthermore, there was no influence of forces applied at one finger on those felt at the other fingers.

A more complex elastic deformation model based on Hooke's law was developed by Kotoku and his colleagues at Ministry of International Trade and Industry (Japan) for interactions between frictionless convex virtual objects [Kotoku et al., 1992]. As shown in Figure 7.15, the researchers considered two basic contact models, a face–vertex contact and an edge–edge contact.

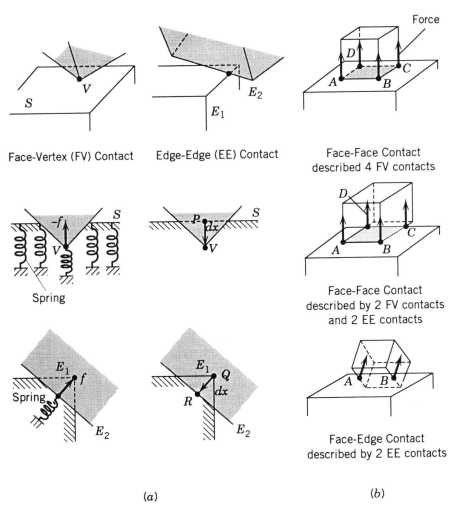

Figure 7.15 Contact forces during convex objects interaction: (*a*) basic contact models (face–vertex and edge–edge); (*b*) complex contact models (face–face and face–edge). Reprinted by permission. From Kotoku et al., [1992]. © 1992 IEEE.

Contact forces for the face–vertex case are proportional with the distance dx, which is the penetration of the edge V past the surface S. The contact force $\mathbf{f}$ is also proportional with the average stiffness K_{av} which is:

$$K_{av} = \frac{K_1 K_2}{K_1 + K_2} \tag{7.13}$$

where K_1 and K_2 represent the stiffnesses of the two objects. In the edge–edge contact model the force $\mathbf{f}$ is proportional with the same K_{av} and the interpenetration of the edge E_2 inside E_1. Kotoku and his colleagues use these basic contact configurations to model more complex face–face and face–edge contacts, as illustrated in Figure 7.15b. These various contact forces are then compounded and expressed in relation to an object-based system of coordinates located at its center of gravity. It is thus possible to obtain the resultant force and moment $\mathbf{f}_{total}$ and τ_{total} as in:

$$\mathbf{f}_{total} = \sum_{i=1}^{n} \mathbf{f}_i \tag{7.14}$$

and

$$\tau_{total} = \sum_{i=1}^{n} r_i \times \mathbf{f}_i \tag{7.15}$$

where $\mathbf{f}_i$ is the force vector at the contact model point P_i and r_i is the vector from the center of gravity of the object to the contact point P_i.

In the above example, the compliance of the two objects was considered constant throughout their volume. There are cases, however, when a given object has a dual-stiffness characteristic. Such objects may have, for example, a hard interior kernel surrounded by a softer exterior. This is the case when modeling a virtual peach or a malignant nodule inside the breast. Dinsmore [1995] performed compression tests on a 2.8-in. Avira foam ball with an 1-in. hard rubber interior ball. As illustrated in Figure 7.16, the compression force has an intial linear increase with a small slope expressing the elastic deformation of the softer exterior ball. This is followed by a steeper exponential increase once the compression approaches the hard interior ball. The contact force for this dual-compliance object can be approximated by a two-segment linear law, as in

$$\mathbf{F} = \begin{cases} K_1 \Delta x, & \text{if} \quad 0 \le \Delta x \le x_t \\ K_1 x_t + K_2 (x - x_t), & \text{if} \quad x_t < x \end{cases} \tag{7.16}$$

where x_t corresponds to the point of slope discontinuity in Figure 7.16. A more accurate model for this linear-to-exponential force profile is given by Rosenberg [1994]:

$$\mathbf{F} = (K x_t) 10^{\frac{\log(W_f)}{D_s}(x - x_t)} \quad \text{for} \quad x_t \le x \tag{7.17}$$

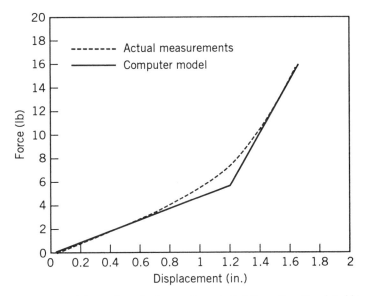

Figure 7.16 Feedback forces for a dual-compliance ball deformation. Reprinted by permission from Dinsmore [1995].

where W_f is the Webber fraction related to the human force just-noticeable difference (as discussed in Chapter 2) and D_s is the position resolution of the haptic interface (in this case a force-feedback joystick).

Elastic deformation models are also applicable to new three-dimensional graphic user interfaces enhanced with haptic feedback. Such graphic interfaces are extremely useful in VR simulations, allowing users to select from various menus while immersed in the simulation. One example is virtual buttons, which model the tactile feel of their real counterparts. Figure 7.17 illustrates a virtual hand pressing one of two virtual buttons included in a virtual control panel. At the beginning, the user feels an increasing resistance that models the compression of a return spring inside the button. When the displacement of the button reaches a given value m the spring is disengaged and the force drops to a very small value $\mathbf{F}_r$ due to static friction. If the user continues to press against the virtual button past the threshold n, the feedback force grows very quickly to the maximum value allowed by the haptic interface output. This signifies that the button has reached its linear travel limit and is now pushing against the supporting back plane. The force profile shown in Figure 7.17b is expressed as:

$$\mathbf{F} = K_1 x(1 - u_m) + \mathbf{F}_r u_m + K_2(x - n)u_n \qquad (7.18)$$

where u_m and u_n are unit step functions that have zero value for $x < m$ and $x < n$, respectively. This force profile is designed to give the user a characteristic haptic click [SensAble Devices Inc., 1994] that confirms the user's action.

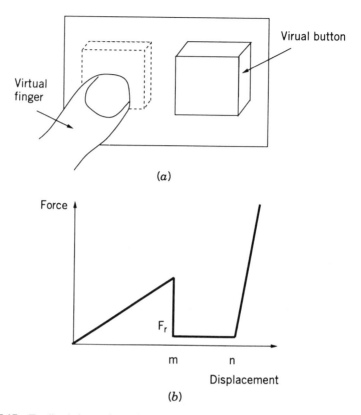

Figure 7.17 Feedback forces for a virtual button with haptic click. Adapted from SensAble Devices Inc. [1994]. Reprinted by permission.

7.4.2. Plastic Deformation

Plastically deformed objects differ from elastic ones owing to their shape hysteresis property. Plasticity precludes the object from regaining its original (undeformed) shape once the interaction ends. Figure 7.18 [Burdea et al., 1993] illustrates the contact forces when grasping and deforming a virtual soda can. Initially the undeformed can has a small elastic deformation zone in which forces grow linearly with the deformation. Once this initial zone is passed, forces grow further, but the deformation becomes permanent. When the virtual hand relaxes its grip, contact with the can is lost at the fingertips and forces drop to zero. At subsequent grasps, forces remain zero until the fingertips press against the deformed surface. Color Plate 8 shows a virtual hand deforming the can and the interface box for the Rutgers Master used in the simulation. As can be seen from the LED bar graphs on the interface front panel, only the user's middle finger receives force feedback. The other fingers of the virtual hand are not in contact with the deformed can.

Another example of plastic object deformation is the carving algorithm developed by Yamamoto and his colleagues at Nagoya University [Yamamoto et al., 1993]. Their

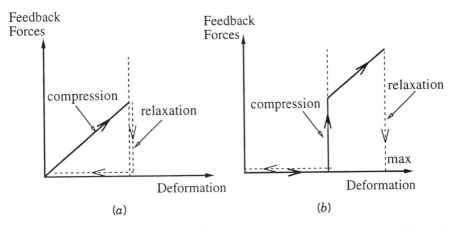

Figure 7.18 Plastic deformation: (*a*) initially undeformed object; (*b*) initially deformed object. Adapted from Burdea et al. [1993]. © Éditions Hermès. Reprinted by permission.

approach differs from previously described surface deformation methods, because vertices are replaced by voxels. These voxels are nodes in a regular lattice spanning the volume of the virtual object being carved. The researchers used as a carving tool a virtual finger of paraboloidal shape. Surface deformation is then implemented by eliminating the voxels that fall inside the volume of the fingertip, as illustrated in Figure 7.19*a*.

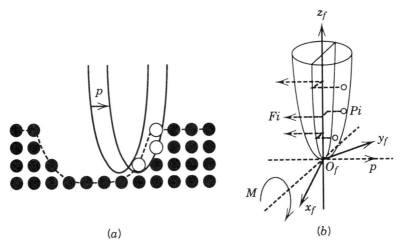

Figure 7.19 Plastic deformation during virtual wood carving: (*a*) volume deformation through voxel decimation; (*b*) contact forces and moments. From Yamamoto et al. [1993]. © 1993 IEEE. Reprinted by permission.

The carving simulation is realized by coupling the voxel elimination with the translation of the fingertip in the direction given by vector $\mathbf{P}$. Each voxel resists the finger motion by a small force $\mathbf{F}_i$ which depends on the object stiffness. Thus the total interaction force $\mathbf{F}(t)$ and moment $\mathbf{M}(t)$ depend on the number of voxels n inside the fingertip at the time t:

$$\mathbf{F}(t) = \sum_{i=1}^{n} \mathbf{F}_i = K_{\text{object}} \; n \cdot \frac{\mathbf{P}}{|\mathbf{P}|} \tag{7.19}$$

$$\mathbf{M}(t) = \sum_{i=1}^{n} \mathbf{z}_i \times \mathbf{F}_i \tag{7.20}$$

where K_{object} is the object stiffness coefficient, and $\mathbf{z}_i$ represents the position of voxel $\mathbf{P}_i$ inside the finger along its z axis, as seen in Figure 7.19b.

7.4.3. Virtual Walls

We set aside walls as a class of very stiff virtual objects that are neither elastic nor plastic. A real wall does not deform under impact (except for very high forces) and produces an instantaneous and very large increase in the contact force. Creating such large feedback forces is problematic given the current state of haptic interface technology. If a simple Hooke's law (spring) model is used then present achievable stiffnesses of 2000–8000 N/m cannot reproduce metal on metal or other hard-contact sensation [Colgate et al., 1993]. Commercial haptic interfaces, such as the PHANToM [Massie and Salisbury, 1994], have much smaller stiffnesses (tens of N/m).

There is, however, another, more subtle problem with simulating virtual walls, owing to the difference between ideal springs and virtual ones. This is an unfortunate result of the digital computer control of the haptic interface, which introduces sample-and-hold artifacts. Colgate and his colleagues note that:

> Because it is implemented in discrete time, the force provided by the spring will not increase smoothly with deflection. Instead, the force will be repeatedly held at a constant value until updated. Because of this, the average force during squeezing will be slightly less than for a physical spring of identical stiffness, and the average force during release will be slightly greater.
>
> —Colgate et al. [1993]

The net result of this energy imbalance between squeezing and releasing is that a virtual spring *generates* energy. Thus, unlike real walls, which are passive, virtual walls modeled as a stiff spring are active, which may induce unwanted oscillations in the haptic interface. Thus a dissipative term has to be added to the Hooke's law model to increase passivity. Therefore,

$$\mathbf{F} = \begin{cases} K_{\text{wall}}\Delta x + B\dot{x}, & \text{for} \quad \dot{x} < 0 \\ K_{\text{wall}}\Delta x, & \text{for} \quad \dot{x} \geq 0 \end{cases} \tag{7.21}$$

where B is a directional damper and $\dot{x}$ is the velocity of the object hitting the wall. Here a negative velocity means moving into the wall and a positive velocity means moving away from the wall.

Adding a dissipative damper is beneficial not just for system stability (discussed in greater detail in Chapter 8) but also for improving the user's perception of wallness. Rosenberg and Adelstein [1993] describe three perceptual qualities of rigid surface contact, namely *crispness* of initial contact, the *hardness* of rigid surface, and the *cleanliness* of the final release. They performed human-factor studies modeling virtual walls as either a spring or a pure damper. Results showed that

> A virtual model of a pure linear damper ... produced a very crisp, abrupt force upon initial contact which could be described as being more of a thud than a bounce. Inter-action with this model proved a very realistic sensation of a rigid surface for the first instant of contact. Of course, after the first instant the pure damper could not maintain the illusion because it lacks static rigidity and allows the joystick to sink slowly into the wall model.
>
> —Rosenberg and Adelstein [1993]

Thus the best approach to insure both crispness of initial contact and surface hardness is to combine the pure damper with the spring model. Cleanliness of final release is helped by replacing the pure damper with a directional one, which, as shown in Equation 7.21, provides no resistance when moving away from the wall.

Salcudean and Vlaar [1994] studied the simulation of virtual walls using the UBC Maglev Joystick (see Fig. 4.8). They argued that a major limitation of this joystick and of other direct-drive haptic interfaces with colocated sensors and actuators is due to the time delays in data acquisition and control. These delays reduce the perceived wall stiffness produced by the interface. The solution proposed by the researchers is to add a third term to the proportional-derivative control law given by Eq. (7.21). This term is a short breaking force "pulse" applied when crossing into the wall. Experimental results obtained by Salcudean and Vlaar showed a reduction of the joystick flotor penetration (and associated oscillations) when a braking pulse was applied.

7.5. SURFACE SMOOTHNESS

Surface smoothness (or mechanical texture) is another important part of VR physical modeling, which allows virtual objects to be characterized as smooth, rough, or bumpy. This surface texture information is then presented to the user through a tactile feedback interface having high control bandwidth. Within the context of this chapter, we are interested in how to model the small feedback forces felt by the user.

One approach to smoothness modeling is the use of local surface gradients in the direction of the surface normal (z axis). Figure 7.20 [Minsky et al., 1990] illustrates a cross section of the surface-depth map modeled as a sequence of micro hills and valleys. Forces fed back to the user are proportional to the height of these hills, so that the valleys represent local minima. Minsky and her colleagues at the MIT and at

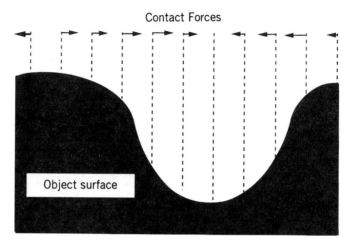

Figure 7.20 Enlarged surface cross section used for surface smoothness modeling. Adapted from Minsky et al. [1990]. © Éditions Hermès. Reprinted by permission.

the University of North Carolina used a force-feedback joystick to allow the user to explore various sandpaper patches. The forces opposing the user's translation motion were calculated as

$$\mathbf{F}_x = A \frac{\Delta h}{\Delta x} \tag{7.22}$$

where x is the translation direction, A is a proportionality constant, and h is the surface height above the x − y plane. $\Delta h/\Delta x$ is thus the local gradient used to compute the feedback resistive forces.

Another approach to smoothness modeling is the use of sinusoidal functions. Massie, in his demonstration of the PHANToM Haptic Interface, uses high-frequency vibrations [SensAble Devices, Inc., 1994] superimposed on the force-feedback signal felt at the user's fingertip. Here surface texture in the z direction is modeled as

$$z = A \sin(mx) \sin(ny) \tag{7.23}$$

7.6. PHYSICAL CONSTRAINTS

The last topic in our chapter on physical modeling is the integration of physical constraints in the VR simulation. These constraints limit the behavior of virtual objects by assuring compliance with the laws of mechanics. The resulting increase in simulation realism and user productivity comes at the price of increased computational load. The requirement of maintaining real-time simulation updates dictates a compromise in selecting the number of physical constraints.

Papper and Gigante [1993] chose a *simplified set* of four physical constraints: gravity, friction, pushing, and anchor in connection with a space planning application.

Such applications are, for example, office furniture placement in a new office or road design for urban planning. Simplified *gravity* ensures that objects rest on other objects or on the ground. Simplified *friction* causes objects resting on top of a manipulated object to move with it. *Pushing* enforces object solidity such as an object can push and move another object. Finally, *anchor* disables pushing by making an object (such as a wall partition) immobile. The researchers performed comparative human-factor tests, with and without physical constraints being present in the simulation. Results showed a significant reduction in task completion time when constraints were enabled. Furthermore,

> ... users have expressed the opinion that constraints are strongly preferred. Without use of constraints, the resultant designs had physical inconsistencies such as objects which interpenetrated and objects which floated in space.
>
> —Papper and Gigante [1993]

In the above study, the tests were performed by grasping the manipulated objects with an open-loop DataGlove. Thus the users had no haptic feedback to feel the gravity or frictional forces. Iwata [1990] developed a gravity (weight) simulation for a virtual photo camera using his prototype six-degrees-of-freedom haptic interface. As illustrated in Figure 7.21, users felt a force **F** and moment **M**, which in static equilibrium are

$$\mathbf{F} = \mathbf{G} \qquad\qquad (7.24)$$

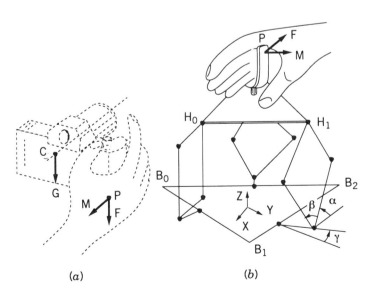

(a)   (b)

Figure 7.21   Weight simulation for a virtual photo camera: (*a*) forces and moments;(*b*) haptic feedback interface. Adapted from Iwata [1990]. © Éditious Hermès. Reprinted by permission.

and

$$\mathbf{M} = \mathbf{G}(\mathbf{c} - \mathbf{p}) \tag{7.25}$$

where **p** is the position vector of the palm center, **c** is the position vector of the center of gravity of the camera, and **G** is the camera weight. When fed back to the user, the force and moment become

$$\mathbf{F} = \sum_{i=0}^{i=2} \mathbf{F}_i \tag{7.26}$$

and

$$\mathbf{M} = \sum_{i=0}^{i=2} [(\mathbf{h}_i - \mathbf{p})\,\mathbf{F}_i] \tag{7.27}$$

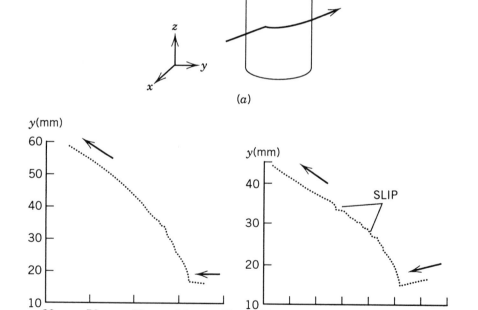

(a)

(b)

(c)

Figure 7.22 Friction feedback for a surface tracing task: (a) virtual cylinder to be traced; (b) tracing plot when friction feedback was present; (c) tracing plot with no friction feedback. Reprinted by permission from Adachi et al. [1995]. © 1995 IEEE.

where $\mathbf{F}_i$ is the force applied by actuator i, and $\mathbf{h}_i$ is the position vector for the corner H_i of the feedback horizontal platform.

Later Adachi and his colleagues at Suzuki Motor Co. studied the influence of friction forces in a task of tracing the surface of a stiff virtual object [Adachi et al., 1995]. The object to be traced was a cylinder with stiffness of 10000 N/m oriented as shown in Figure 7.22a. Users received force feedback through the SPICE interface (see also Figure 4.18) at a 10 Hz update rate. The component of the contact force normal to the surface was calculated using a proportional-derivative formula similar to Eq. (7.21). The component of the contact force tangential to the surface was calculated using the dynamic friction formula:

$$\mathbf{F}_d = u \, \mathbf{v}_t \tag{7.28}$$

where u is the surface viscous coefficient (in this case 600 N-sec/m) and $\mathbf{v}_t$ is the tracing velocity vector. Figure 7.22b shows the position the user's virtual finger measured at an update rate of 500 Hz (every 20 msec.). It can be seen that users had no difficulty tracing the surface of the virtual cylinder smoothly. However, when friction forces were removed, the surface felt slippery, and users had more difficulty tracing it. This resulted in a less smooth trajectory as shown in Figure 7.22c. Other tests showed that friction feedback was also able to compensate for low positional update rates (down to 3.3 Hz). Further reduction of the positional update rate to 2.5 Hz induced contact vibrations and the trace became wavy.

TABLE 7.1   Summary of Physical Modeling Approaches

Physical Model	Approach
Collision detection	Approximate or Exact
Grasping	Grasping forces, Stability, Grasping invariants.
Surface deformation	Vertex-based or Spline-based
Surface mechanical compliance	Elastic deformation, Plastic deformation, Virtual walls.
Surface smoothness	Local gradient or Sinusoidal functions
Physical constraints	Gravity forces, Friction forces.

7.7. CONCLUSIONS

This chapter detailed various physical modeling approaches for collision detection, grasping, surface deformation, mechanical compliance, surface smoothness, friction, and gravity. These are summarized in Table 7.1. The various modeling techniques presented here add significantly to the simulation realism and allow the computation of forces and moments necessary in haptic feedback. Certain simplifications were necessary due to the real-time constraints and limited computational power of today's VR systems. Once interaction forces and moments are determined, they are downloaded by the computer to the interface control hardware. The way in which the controller drives the haptic interface is the subject of the next chapter.

CHAPTER 8

CONTROL OF HAPTIC INTERFACES

The preceding chapter introduced several physical modeling techniques used to determine the forces associated with real-time VR interactions. These forces are calculated by the computer and subsequently sent to the controller unit driving the haptic interface. In this way, the user receives force feedback, and the haptic part of the simulation loop is closed. Alternately, the user can input forces into the simulation and receive position feedback through the interface. The choice of a particular control method depends on the hardware and software available, as well as on the particular application being developed [Salisbury and Srinivasan, 1992]. The overall system configuration integrating the user, haptic interface, control unit, and computing platform is illustrated in Figure 8.1.

The interaction between the user and the virtual environment is a bidirectional transfer of energy, since force multiplied by position represents mechanical work. Furthermore, the rate of change of this energy flow (or mechanical power) is determined by the instantaneous product of contact force and velocity [Hannaford and Venema, 1995]. This represents a fundamental difference from other feedback modalities (visual or auditory), which represent one-way information flow with minute energy exchange.

Energy transfer, if not properly controlled may have a detrimental, destabilizing effect, rather than a useful one, on the simulation. Thus another important issue related to interface control is the "quality" of the haptic feedback and especially the stability of the simulation system. This incorporates as an intrinsic component the user, who plays an important part in the overall system stability. Unfortunately, a rigorous analysis of haptic feedback quality is complicated by the lack of consensus among researchers and by the oversimplified cases presented in the related literature. However, it is agreed that low control bandwidth and poor interface design can make

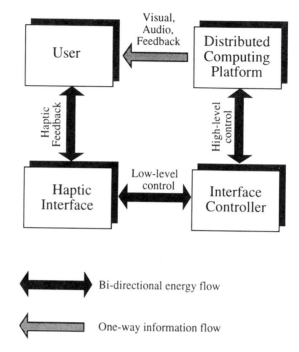

Figure 8.1 System architecture for VR simulations with haptic feedback.

the system unstable. Even the best haptic interface will not suffice if the control bandwidth is too low and simulation latencies are too large.

In a computer-controlled loop, high bandwidth and low simulation latencies require large computing power and fast communication links. The more complex the virtual world becomes, the higher the computation load requirements. It is thus necessary to replace traditional single-CPU machines with distributed computing on multiprocessor or multiworkstation architectures. The computers themselves need to be programmed (either using general-purpose programming languages, or more recent toolkits) to provide interactive haptic feedback during the simulation. In view of the above discussion, this chapter will detail four topics, namely control methodology, quality of haptic feedback (especially system stability), distributed computing, and VR programming with haptic feedback.

8.1. CONTROL METHODOLOGY

Several haptic control methods exist owing to the large variety of today's haptic interface designs and their specific application functionality. We discuss two fundamental and several derived modalities for controlling haptic interfaces integrated in a VR environment. The present discussion does not pretend to be exhaustive, rather it is intended as a guide to the interested reader.

8.1.1. Fundamental Control Methods

Haptic interfaces have two basic functions [Salisbury and Srinivasan, 1992]. The first is to measure positions and forces (and their time derivatives) at the user's hand or other body locations. The second function is to display forces and positions back to the user under the control of the computer running the VR simulation. Most often the position (or velocity) is input to the control loop and forces are fed back to the user, in a *force-feedback control* arrangement. Alternately, the simulation can use *position-feedback control*, in which forces applied by the user are sensed and positions (or velocities) are fed back through the haptic interface. Hannaford [1989] and later Hannaford and Venema [1995] extended network analysis theory to obtain a unified model for the two basic modes of user–haptic interaction. Their approach uses an analogy between mechanical and electrical variables, specifically between electrical voltage and mechanical force and between currents and velocities. Using this analogy the user interface system is reduced to the one-port equivalent model shown in Figure 8.2.

By applying the well-known Kirchhoff's voltage law the feedback force can be expressed as

$$\mathbf{f}_1 - z_1(v_p) = \mathbf{f}_2 - z_2(v_p) = \mathbf{f}_p \qquad (8.1)$$

where $\mathbf{f}_1$ is the force sensed (or applied) by the user, $\mathbf{f}_2$ is the force produced by the interface, z_1 and z_2 are generalized mechanical impedances of the user and haptic interface, respectively, and v_p is the velocity of the interface motion.

Some similarities exist between force feedback and position (or displacement) feedback displays. Both must allow free motion of the user's hand when no contact occurs in the virtual environment, thus they have to be backdriveable. They must be capable of sufficient force output (in the case of force feedback) and be sufficiently stiff (for position feedback) so that contact with rigid virtual objects can be adequately simulated. Furthermore, the displays must have sufficient bandwidth to reproduce contact transients and have good force (or position) fidelity. Comparing the two types of display Hannaford and Venema [1995] recommend the force-feedback modality.

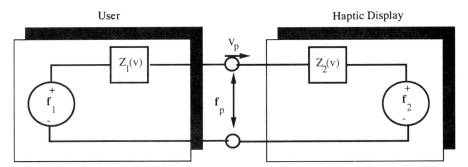

Figure 8.2 One-port model of the user–haptic interface system. Adapted from Hannaford and Venema [1995]. Reprinted by permission of the Oxford University Press.

Displacement feedback display mechanisms tend to be more expensive for a given level of performance than force feedback designs. This is because 1) Force/Torque sensors are more expensive than position sensors, and 2) true position actuators are not available. In practice, very stiff actuators are used with position feedback control. Thus, in addition to force sensors, position sensors and a servo control system for position is required. These systems also tend to be heavier due to the required stiff structure.

—Hannaford and Venema [1995]

Force-feedback control is thus the choice in haptic displays and is used, among others, by the JPL Generalized Master [Bejczy and Salisbury, 1980], the Rutgers Master [Burdea et al., 1992a], the EXOS Force ArmMaster [EXOS Co., 1993a], and the PHANToM Master [Massie and Salisbury, 1994]. Examples of position feedback controlled interfaces are the SARCOS Dextrous Arm Master [Jacobsen et al., 1991a] and the Cartesian Manipulator [Yokoi et al., 1994].

However, position-feedback control has the advantage of reduced modeling computation load, because forces are sensed rather than computed in real time. Therefore a given computing platform will have an increase in the high-level feedback loop bandwidth when position feedback is implemented. This feature was exploited by Kotoku and his colleagues [1994] in connection with their generalized force-feedback master (see Section 4.2.1). The researchers observed that modeling complex contact forces necessary for force-feedback control produced large computation delays. Therefore, they replaced the earlier force-feedback control [Kotoku et al., 1992] with a clever position–force-control *switching* mode. In free motion, there is no interaction with the virtual objects and zero feedback force is maintained through force control. Once the motion is constrained by obstacles in the virtual world, the system switches to position-control mode, and the master arm maintains the position corresponding to the contact geometry. In this way, the environment modeling loop is decoupled from the position-feedback loop and the two can be processed independently. Thus the complexity of the virtual world does not affect the servo rate of the position display, and the interface maintains a stiff position. Kotoku reports that experimental results proved positive, and that users felt the simulation was realistic and similar to teleoperation in a real world.

8.1.2. Derived Control Methods

In the force-feedback control examples described above there was no sensing of the feedback forces applied on the user. Such a scheme is called "open-loop" force control. In reality, forces do differ from the computed ones owing to several factors such as system noise, as well as friction and inertia in the interface mechanism. To compensate for the above effects and improve control accuracy, the interface needs to incorporate both position and force sensors. In this case, the force control becomes "closed loop" [Salisbury and Srinivasan, 1992].

An example of closed-loop force-controlled interface is the GLAD-IN-ART Arm Exoskeleton [Bergamasco, 1993a] (see also Section 5.1.1). The exoskeleton incorporates a six-axes force–torque sensor installed below the handle grasped by the user. This sensor measures the wrench of actual forces and torques $\mathbf{F}$ at the wrist. These feedback forces are different from the desired values $\mathbf{F}_{desired}$ owing to joint friction, arm dynamics effects (inertia and Coriolis forces), or errors in the exoskeleton kinematic model [Bergamasco et al., 1994a]. Partial compensation for the above effects is accomplished by controlling the vector of joint torques τ according to Eq. (5.2) (repeated here for clarity):

$$\tau = \mathbf{G} + J^T(q)(\mathbf{F}_{des} + K(\mathbf{F}_{des} - \mathbf{F})) \tag{8.2}$$

where K is the 6×6 diagonal matrix of constant gains, $\mathbf{G}$ is the vector of gravity compensation, and $J^T(q)$ is the transpose of the exoskeleton Jacobian matrix, which depends on the instantaneous joint position values. Figure 8.3 [Bergamasco et al., 1994a] illustrates a control block diagram that implements the above control law. The torques τ applied by the interface actuators produce a change in exoskeleton joint positions q. These are used by the direct kinematics block to obtain the Cartesian handle position and orientation X_e. This value is then changed by the user to X_0 which deflects the handle according to the arm–exoskeleton stiffness. The resulting wrist forces $\mathbf{F}$ are read by the force sensor and the control loop is closed.

Another control method that has been recently extended to haptic interfaces is *rate control* with force feedback. Rate control has been extensively used in other fields such as aeronautics, but it is less common in VR simulation applications. Rate control has as input the displacement of an input device (usually a joystick) from its neutral or home position. This input is used to control the speed (rather than position) of an aircraft. The further away the joystick is moved from its home position the higher the velocity of the plane. Force feedback is added in the form of a PD (spring–damper) controller which generates restoring forces that move the interface back to its home position. Das and his colleagues [Das et al., 1992] have extended this control method to telerobotics using the JPL Generalized Master. The PD controller was supplemented by feedback from a force–torque sensor measuring

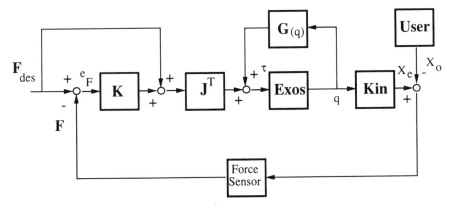

Figure 8.3   Closed-loop force control used by the GLAD-IN-ART Arm Exoskeleton. Adapted from Bergamasco et al. [1994a]. © 1994 IEEE. Reprinted with permission.

interactions in a (remote) real environment, as illustrated in Figure 8.4. When the Generalized Master was close to its home position the user felt only feedback forces from the remote site. However, as the interface was moved away from its home position to move the remote robot, the restoring spring forces produced by the PD controller became significant and could mask the remote force feedback. Das and his colleagues performed human-factor tests to compare rate control versus other modes of control based on position input. The tests used objective criteria such as task error rates, task completion time, average and cumulative force–torques, as well as user subjective ratings. Results showed that rate control was inferior to position input modes with force feedback.

In the above examples of fundamental and derived haptic interface control modes, the assumption was made that there is a one-to-one relationship between the forces (or positions) modeled by the simulation and those sent to the haptic interface. Similarly, we assumed that the position (or force) change measured at the interface is replicated by the corresponding change in the virtual object mapped to the haptic device. A 1-cm translation of the JPL Generalized Master, for example, would correspond to a 1-cm translation of a virtual hand controlled by the user. There are, however, cases when the virtual world is either too small (molecular level) or extremely large (outer space), so that the interface positions need to be scaled. Additionally, molecular forces are too small to be felt by the user and need to be scaled up, while simulation of heavy load lifting needs downward force scaling to avoid user fatigue. Thus micro–macro or macro–micro manipulation using a haptic interface requires both position and force scaling. There is, however, an additional mapping in the time domain, since micro objects have high-frequency oscillations that cannot be replicated by today's haptic interfaces. Kobayashi and Tatsuno [1994] have studied a micro–macro manipulation using a position display device. They showed that the force at the master is given by

$$\mathbf{f}_{\text{master}} = (m_t g^2) \frac{d^2}{dt^2} d_m + (\mu_t g) \frac{d}{dt} d_m + k_t d_m \qquad (8.3)$$

where m_t, μ_t, and k_t are the mass, coefficient of friction and spring constant at the slave (or virtual) site (micro world), d_m is the master displacement, and g is a scaling factor. Furthermore, the scaling of the slave force and displacement is given by

$$\mathbf{f}_{\text{master}} = g \, \mathbf{f}_s \left(\frac{t}{g} \right) \qquad (8.4)$$

$$d_m = g \, d_s \left(\frac{t}{g} \right) \qquad (8.5)$$

The above equations implement a time-scaling filter, because time in the virtual world is divided by a factor g. Such filtering may be beneficial when mapping the haptic interface to a dynamically changing mass–spring–damper virtual environment.

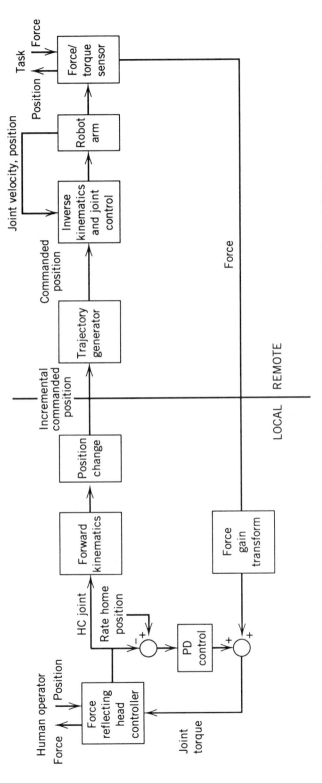

Figure 8.4 Rate control with force reflection used by the JPL Generalized Master. Adapted from Das et al. [1992]. Reprinted by permission of The MIT Press.

8.2. HAPTIC FEEDBACK "QUALITY"

The preceding discussion detailed several options on controlling haptic interfaces in a VR simulation environment. It is now time to look at the end result, namely the "quality" of the haptic feedback sensation perceived by the user. This should not be confused with the quality of the visual simulation in which the user is immersed.

Jex [1988] describes four tests that a good haptic interface should pass. First, it should be able to simulate a piece of light balsa wood, with negligible inertia, friction, or vibrations being perceived by the operator. Second, the interface should be able to simulate a crisp hard stop. Third, it should simulate Coulomb friction without sponginess or jitter, and, fourth, it should simulate a mechanical centering detent with crisp transitions and no lag. These tests define qualitatively the behavior of an ideal interface that is able to convey a very wide range of haptic sensations. In reality, interfaces are nonideal. The fidelity and rapidity with which a given interface is able to reproduce simulated haptic sensations depends on a number of factors, such as the quality of the interface mechanics, the controller capabilities (bandwidth, stability, etc.) and the user's actions (hand grip, muscle tone).

8.2.1. Impedance Dynamic Range

The relationship between the user's motion (position change or velocity) and the resulting forces he feels is given by the force-feedback interface apparent impedance. The larger the spectrum of forces the interface has to produce, the larger the range of its impedances. Conversely, the larger the range of velocities a given position-controlled interface can achieve, the larger its apparent admittance range. We use only impedances in our present discussion, since the majority of haptic interfaces are force-controlled, however results are extendable to admittances as well.

The majority of haptic feedback researchers believes that the interface needs to appear as "transparent" to the user as possible. That means that it should transmit as faithful as possible the actuator forces to the user when there is interaction in the virtual environment and be otherwise not felt by the user when the virtual object mapped to the interface moves in free space. Unfortunately, the forces felt by the user are smaller than those produced by the feedback actuators owing to friction and inertia losses in the interface mechanics. *Friction* occurs as surface contact motion in the transmission and actuator mechanisms and consists of static, Coulomb and viscous components [Hannaford and Venema, 1995]. Static and Coulomb friction components are nonlinear terms, whereas viscous friction is linearly proportional to the contact surface velocity. When the interface velocity is almost zero (such as when grasping rigid objects) viscous friction is small, but static and Coulomb friction components are very detrimental. *Inertia* is proportional with the interface mass, which in turn depends on factors such as gravity-compensating counter balances, or the mass of the transmission and actuators. A very light interface would have low inertia, but at the same time it may not have the required stiffness to withstand the load. Otherwise, the interface would at best bend and at worst break. Inertia effects are most detrimental when sudden velocity changes occur, such as during contact with hard surfaces.

Friction, inertia, and other dynamic effects (coriolis and centripetal forces) prevent a haptic interface from behaving like an ideal one. Fortunately, the human sensori-motor limitations prevent the user from distinguishing an ideal haptic interface from one that *appears* to be ideal. Lawrence and Chapel [1994] point out that

> ...an operator will not be able to distinguish the feel of a remote task presented by two different hand controllers, provided they are both of "sufficient quality," or are "equivalent" to an ideal hand controller in typical operation scenarios.
> —Lawrence and Chapel [1994]

They define an "ideal-equivalent" hand controller as one that can produce impedances smaller than the free motion impedance $\overline{Z}_f(\omega)$ and higher than a constrained motion impedance $\overline{Z}_c(\omega)$. For the specific case of a pencil grip, Lawrence and Chapel define the impedance bounds as

$$\overline{Z}_f(\omega) = \frac{\mathbf{F}_0(\omega^2 + {\omega_0}^2)}{A_0{\omega_0}^2} \tag{8.6}$$

$$\overline{Z}_c(\omega) = \frac{\omega^2 + (\mathbf{F}_m/\delta X)A_0\omega^2}{A_0{\omega_0}^2} \tag{8.7}$$

where $\mathbf{F}_0$ is the human force sensing threshold, A_0 and ω_0 are the amplitude and maximum frequency of the pencil tip sinusoidal trajectory, $\mathbf{F}_m$ is the maximum force, and δX is the kinesthetic sensing resolution.

A given haptic interface may be powerful enough so that it exceeds the $\overline{Z}_c(\omega)$ bound, but also have a free-motion impedance that is larger than $\overline{Z}_f(\omega)$. In that case, the force-feedback controller can be used to compensate, provided the force loop is not destabilized by the larger gains necessary and that the resulting reduced-constraint motion impedance is still above the $\overline{Z}_c(\omega)$ bound. Otherwise the free-motion impedance needs to be reduced through mechanical redesign of the interface, which reduces its friction, damping and mass.

Colgate and Hannaford [1993] and later Colgate and Schenkel [1994] argue that the traditional approach of minimizing the physical contribution of a haptic interface is misdirected. Instead they formulate the *midpoint impedance principle*, which states that to maintain passivity (prevent unstable oscillations) of a sample-data system such as a haptic interface, it is necessary to have some mechanical impedance, and this interface impedance needs to be mainly dissipative. The greater the interface internal damping b, the greater the range of virtual stiffness K and damping B it can reproduce. For the particular case of a virtual wall simulation, b is given by

$$b > \frac{KT}{2} + B \tag{8.8}$$

where T is the sampling time period.

Equation 8.8 shows the well-known principle that, for a given interface physical damping b, the faster the sampling is (smaller T) the higher the achievable virtual stiffness K. However, fast sampling can degrade the velocity estimation through derivation of position sensor data, especially when interface sensors have poor resolution. Colgate and Brown [1994] recommend the use of either analog velocity sensors (tachometers) or the implementation of low-pass filtering of velocity estimates. The researchers performed experimental studies to determine the "Z-width," or range of achievable impedances without destabilizing oscillations, of a one-degree-of-freedom haptic interface. The interface was a dc brushless motor, equipped with either low-resolution (8000 cpr) or high-resolution (900,000 cpr) encoders. The motor shaft was coupled through a steel tape to a viscous damper with b = 0.22 N-m·sec/rad. The encoder sampling rate was either low (100 Hz) or high (1000 Hz), and the controller had the option of using velocity filtering. Figure 8.5 [Colgate and Brown, 1994] shows experimental plots of maximum achievable virtual stiffness and damping under the above conditions. As can be seen in Figure 8.5a, the use of low-resolution encoders and no velocity filtering reduced the Z range when compared to that achievable through velocity filtering of high-resolution encoder data (Figure 8.5b). Furthermore, the addition of physical damping had a clear beneficial influence in the range of achievable virtual stiffnesses (thick line). The poorest performance (smallest Z width) was obtained when using a low sampling rate and no physical damping.

8.2.2. System Bandwidth

The above discussion clearly shows how various components of the haptic interface (such as sensors, dampers, etc.) influence the range of achievable haptic sensations expressed through the Z width. It was also apparent that low sampling rates (100 Hz in this particular case) had a detrimental effect on the ability to reproduce high stiffnesses. Another experiment that proves this point was conducted by Adachi and his colleagues [Adachi et al., 1995] at the Suzuki Motor Co. They used a SPICE haptic interface (Figure 4.18) to simulate a virtual wall under impedance control. The wall was modeled with high stiffness K = 1000 N/m and damping B = 1000 N-sec/m, and had to be traced by the user under high (500 Hz), medium (250 Hz), and low (167 Hz) sampling rates. Figure 8.6a shows a plot of the user's motion for a wall placed at x = -100 mm, and for a 500-Hz sampling rate. After a small initial penetration, the user has no difficulty tracing the wall. However, once the sampling rate was reduced to 167 Hz (Figure 8.6b) the plot becomes scattered reflecting the presence of unwanted vibrations. The wall boundaries become much less clear and the quality of the haptic sensation in terms of fidelity and stability suffers.

These examples underscore the necessity to take a closer look at the role of bandwidth in haptic feedback quality. What is important, however, is the overall or system bandwidth, not that of individual components.

The system's overall performance is summarized by its *bandwidth*, which is a measure of the highest frequency of motion that can travel all the way through the system. Haptic

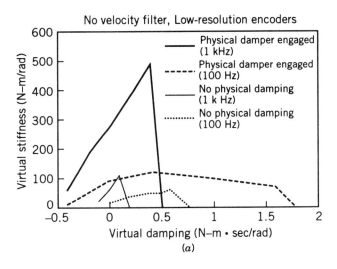

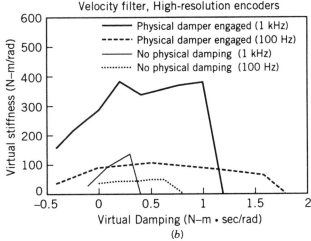

Figure 8.5 The influence of physical damping, encoder resolution, sampling rate, and velocity filtering on the Z width of a one-degree-of-freedom haptic interface: (a) no velocity filter, low encoder resolution; (b) velocity filter and high encoder resolution. Reprinted by permission from Colgate and Brown [1994]. © 1994 IEEE.

sensations that feel "sharp" or "crisp" require high bandwidth, whereas those that are more gradual, or "mushy" do not require much bandwidth.

—Jackson and Rosenberg [1995]

The system bandwidth depends on the characteristics of the haptic interface and on computational delays from the ratio of computational power and virtual model complexity. The system bandwidth is further influenced by transmission delays, which depend on the quantity of data exchange and the communication lines used. Lawrence

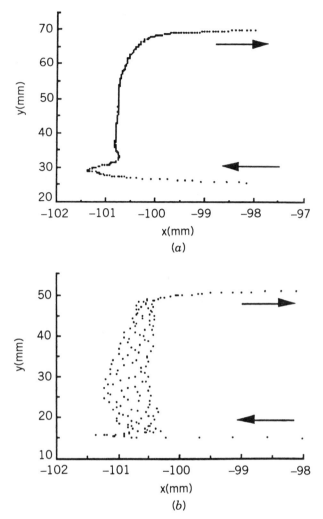

Figure 8.6 Tracing a stiff virtual wall with: (*a*) high sampling rate and (*b*) low sampling rate. Reprinted by permission from Adachi et al. [1995]. © 1995 IEEE.

[1988] shows that for an impedance-controlled manipulator the introduction of time delays above 30 msec led to system instabilities. For a stable system, the range of achievable damping and stiffness is reduced with the increase of the time delay. Kazerooni [1993] later conducted experiments with a position-controlled haptic interface showing that large computation delays led to limit cycle instabilities. He suggested the use of a fast computer so that the sampling time would be less than 3 msec. To reduce communication delays, Jackson and Rosenberg [1995] recommended the use of parallel interfaces or even direct motherboard interface whenever high-volume data needed to be transferred.

Brooks [1990] in his review article on teleoperation systems showed that band-width is affected by a number of factors such as the stiffness, inertia, and damping of the hand master, drive-train backlash, and friction. He recommended colocation of sensors and actuators, a sampling rate of 10 to 20 times that of the feedback signal being replicated, and a feedback bandwidth of 20 to 320 Hz. Brooks further points out that bandwidth is also influenced by the user's impedance, which needs to be taken into account when modeling a master–slave system.

The user's arm impedance increases with the simultaneous activation of opposing muscles and can vary over a wide range [Hogan, 1989]. Kazerooni [1993] showed that the force **f** applied by the user on a position-controlled haptic interface is a function of both the muscle force **m** and the interface position x, as in

$$\mathbf{f} = \mathbf{m} - Hx \qquad (8.9)$$

where H is the human arm impedance. Figure 8.7 [Kazerooni, 1993] illustrates the dynamic interaction of the user and haptic interface. Here S is a sensitivity function mapping external forces to hand controller positions, while G is a transfer function that maps the error function e to the hand controller end-point position x. K is a compliance compensator that is helpful whenever the interface has little or no back-driveability (when S is small).

The effective sensitivity of the interface with this compensator becomes equal to the sum of S and GK. Whereas G and S are fixed by the interface mechanical design, K can be varied, thus changing the feel of the hand controller. System stability imposes limits on the range of K. Kazerooni used Nyquist stability criteria to show that the following condition needs to be satisfied to assure system stability

$$|GK| < \left| S + \frac{1}{H} \right| \qquad (8.10)$$

Inequality 8.10 gives bounds for K so that system stability is maintained, for *a given value* of H. Users can easily increase their arm impedance through muscle co-contraction. They can destabilize a system if the arm becomes too stiff. Conversely, users have the ability to adapt to, and compensate for, small interface instabilities.

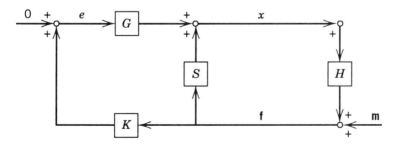

Figure 8.7 Position-feedback hand controller with force compensator. Adapted from Kazerooni [1993]. Reprinted by permission of the ASME.

Milner [1993] conducted experiments with a wrist interface consisting of a torque motor with position, velocity, and force sensors. Users holding a handle connected to the motor shaft were required to move a cursor on a computer screen by flexing their wrist. Muscle EMG activity was measured through electrodes placed on the wrist muscles. The haptic interface, when not grasped by the user, was purposely destabilized through positive position and velocity feedback. This mechanical instability was characterized by negative stiffness and negative damping (viscosity), respectively. Results showed that, for slow movements (approximately 550 msec for an 18° wrist rotation) and for small negative stiffness and damping, the human–machine system was stable. Thus, users were able to compensate for small instabilities, because of their intrinsic positive wrist viscosity. The higher the negative interface viscosity became, the harder it was for users to compensate, eventually leading to uncontrolled oscillations. Figure 8.8 [Milner, 1993] shows the resultant unstable human–machine system, when the steady increase in the interface oscillation amplitude led to system shut-down.

Chapel [1989] performed experiments on a teleoperation system with force feedback to determine the workload of the user (operator) to stabilize the system. He showed that time delays and environment stiffness increase the stiffness and damping required by the user to stabilize the system. Furthermore, the stiffness and damping are linearly related, and thus cannot be provided independently by the user. One cannot be increased (through muscle tension) without increasing the other. Underscoring the limited human ability for stabilizing the system, Chapel states that

> In the direction forward from the body, system designs requiring more than 10 lb/in stiffness or more than 0.7 lb-sec/in damping would be unacceptable for prolonged operation. Systems requiring more than 15 lb/in stiffness or more than 1.1 lb-sec/in damping could not be stabilized by human operators in this direction.
>
> —Chapel [1989]

8.3. DISTRIBUTED COMPUTATION

The above discussion of system bandwidth influence on the quality of haptic feedback stressed the importance of small computation and communication delays. This requirement in turn points to the need for faster communication lines and computers to handle the added computations associated with physical modeling.

Dinsmore and his colleagues at Rutgers University [Dinsmore et al., 1994] modeled the palpation of a virtual knee with haptic feedback, looking at graphics refresh rates as a function of model complexity. Figure 8.9 illustrates the increase in the simulation refresh rate (fps) with the reduction of model polygon count. Monoscopic rendering was faster than stereo rendering, since the workstation had only one graphics accelerator. The interesting detail, however, was the apparent plateau for lower polygon counts. Further reduction in model complexity (below 2500–3500 polygons/scene) did not produce an increase in graphics refresh rate. Clearly data was not transmitted to the graphics accelerator as fast as it could render it. The above result

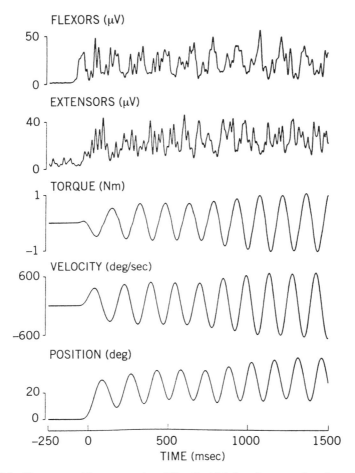

Figure 8.8 Human–machine system instability for high interface negative viscosity. From Milner [1993]. Reprinted by permission of ASME.

points to the need to offload the CPU and distribute the physical modeling computations. Computation distribution has been known for many years in VR systems, with dedicated hardware for graphics and three-dimensional audio rendering. It is now time to see how a haptic renderer (a term proposed recently by Salisbury [1995]) can be added to the VR architecture.

8.3.1. Multiprocessor Architectures

The first type of haptic computation distribution to be discussed here involves *parallelism on a single computer*. Such an approach was proposed by Stanley and Colgate [1993] at Northwestern University, based on the use of Inmos T805 transputers. These 32-bit processors are specifically designed for parallel computations and have

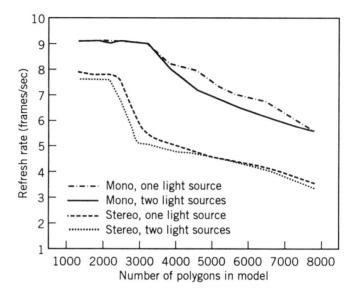

Figure 8.9   Graphics refresh rates vs. model geometrical complexity. From Dinsmore et al. [1994]. Reprinted by permission.

four built-in high-speed serial communication lines. Each communication line allows direct interprocessor data transfer at rates up to 2.4 Mbytes/sec! The approach taken by Stanley and Colgate was to configure the transputer array to mirror the topology of the virtual world. Specifically, this involves the assignment of one transputer to each object in the virtual environment. Multiobject structures are then built by connecting their respective transputers and passing the states of the connected objects over the transputer serial links. Each object in the simulation may have up to three others connected to it, owing to the use of the fourth serial link for collision detection data. At each time step in the simulation, a given transputer calculates the forces and torques acting on its object and the resultant object accelerations. The researchers estimate that this distributed architecture will allow extremely high simulation update rates (about 1 kHz) even for interactions with complex virtual environments.

Another example of transputer-based parallel architecture is that used by the Provision 100 VRX VR workstation produced by Division Ltd. (UK). The workstation has T425 transputers for graphics processing and T805 transputers for serial and programmable i/o communications. Additional transputers may be added on separate boards that communicate with the motherboard on an EISA bus [Division Ltd., 1992]. These transputers are assigned separate processes called *Actors* in the distributed Virtual Environment System (dVS) programming environment [Grimsdale, 1991a, b; Division Ltd., 1993b]. More details on haptic programming using dVS will be given later in this chapter.

8.3.2. Multicomputer Architectures

Distributing VR modeling and i/o load on a single multiprocessor computer imposes certain limitations on overall simulation performance. The number of processors (or transputers) that can be used is limited by the available physical space of the machine as well as the limits of the operating system. Furthermore, tight mapping of transputers to individual virtual objects does limit interaction capabilities as explained previously. Last, but not least, custom architectures, such as the one proposed by Stanley and Colgate [1993] do not exploit the existing general-purpose computation base of PCs and workstations.

General purpose computers have certain advantages that can be used in VR simulations. They are easily programmable through standard languages, and have familiar window-based graphical user interfaces (GUIs). They are networkable, allowing multiple (remotely located) users to participate in a given simulation. Finally, the existing tens of millions of PCs and workstations provide an easily accessible computation base. It is not surprising that many researchers have opted for computation parallelism on network-distributed multicomputer architectures. A case in point is the system developed by Bergamasco and his colleagues [1994c] for the control of the GLAD-IN-ART Arm Exoskeleton System (see also Section 5.1.1). As illustrated in Figure 8.10, the architecture consists of two PCs and an SGI 440-VGX multiprocessor workstation communicating over the ethernet.

The two PCs read the ARTS Glove and the exoskeleton position sensors using custom transputer boards. The 486 PC sends glove data to a *message router* process, which also receives exoskeleton data from the 386 PC. The Message Router runs on one of the workstation processors and relays the glove and exoskeleton position information to a *grasping simulation* process. The grasping simulation process calculates interaction forces, which are then transmitted to the 386 PC via the message router. Interaction information received by the message router is also transmitted to another process called *virtual workspace visualization*, which handles the graphics computations. Interprocess communication, which is done using Unix sockets, is synchronous between the message router and the grasping simulation. All other communications are done asynchronously, so that each task is done in parallel and as fast as possible. Overall, the system implements a four-stage pipeline in which data is acquired at time t, grasping simulation is done on data acquired at $t - 1$, force feedback is done on data at $t - 2$, and graphics maps data acquired at time $t - 3$. The resulting rates are 30 fps for graphics and 15 Hz for exoskeleton force feedback. Bergamasco and his colleagues acknowledge the existence of pipeline- and network-induced delays in the force-feedback loop. One solution proposed by the researchers is the installation of the transputer boards directly on the workstation VME bus.

Another example of single-user network-distributed architecture is the system developed by Burdea and colleagues [1993, 1995a] for the Rutgers Master I (see also Section 5.2.6). As illustrated in Figure 8.11, the architecture consists of four workstations communicating over the ethernet. A Sun 4/380 maintains virtual-object state information, performing collision detection, collision response, and physical modeling (surface deformation and contact forces). The same workstation is in charge of all user input and output, reading the DataGlove and sending force-feedback in-

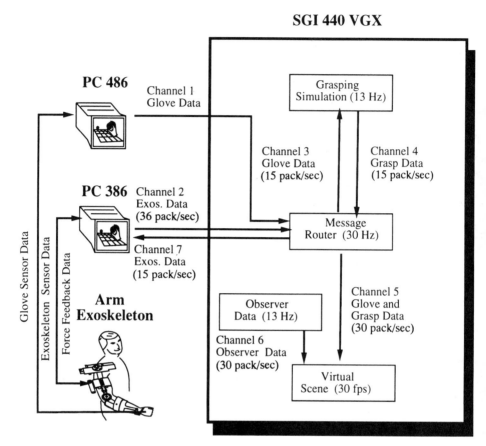

Figure 8.10 Distributed architecture for the GLAD-IN-ART Arm Exoskeleton System. Adapted from Bergamasco et al. [1994c]. © 1994 IEEE. Reprinted by permission.

formation to the Rutgers Master I control interface (through a D/A board). Object state information is also sent over the network to an HP 755 CRX graphics workstation, which renders and displays the corresponding virtual scene. A third workstation (namely a Sun ELC) is responsible for interactive sound. It receives sound ID data from the Sun 4 and uses a look-up table to a sound library to generate the corresponding sound. Finally, a Sun SLC allows the user to change the VR world perspective through a trackball connected to its serial port. Thus, the Rutgers distributed simulation consists of two main loops that execute asynchronously based on server–client communication. The main loop on the Sun 4/380 server cycles at about 28 Hz and sends information to a graphics loop on the HP workstation. The main loop also calculates forces and applies corresponding voltages on the D/A board, assuring a force feedback bandwidth of approximately 15 Hz. The graphics loop reads information from the Sun 4 as well as viewpoint information from the Sun SLC. It then renders the scene at approximately 28 fps.

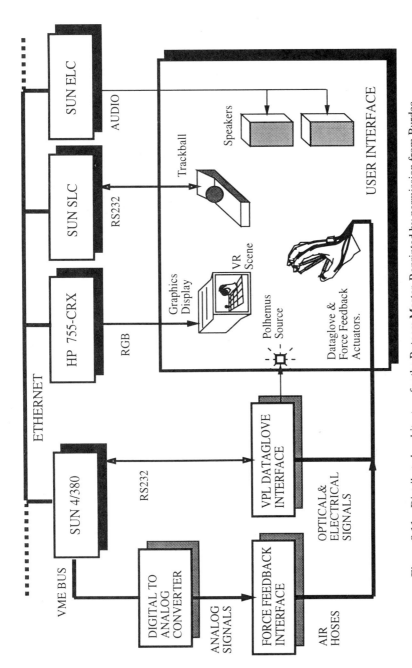

Figure 8.11 Distributed architecture for the Rutgers Master. Reprinted by permission from Burdea and Coiffet [1994]. © Éditions Hermès.

217

8.3.3. Multi-User Systems

In the preceding examples computations were distributed over the network among several computers while allowing only single-user interactions. Network distributed environments could also support multiuser interactions, provided that a number of conditions were met. First, communication delays have to be kept small to have quality haptic interactions. Small communication delays in turn require fast (even dedicated) communication lines, data encoding to reduce network throughput, and reasonable distances between users. Furthermore, provisions need to be made for the limit case of zero throughput (network breakdown) allowing for graceful and *safe* simulation shutdown.

The more users are connected to the same simulation the greater the chance that several dissimilar classes of haptic interfaces are used. Some users may have simple joysticks, whereas others may use arm exoskeletons or portable masters. Thus any multiuser simulation has to allow haptic interface device independence. Although complete device independence may not be feasible for now, at least a library of commercially available devices needs to be supported by the system. Such an approach was taken by Mark and colleagues [1996] at the University of North Carolina at Chapel Hill in the ongoing development of a multi-user force-feedback environment. The system, which is illustrated in Figure 8.12, currently supports several haptic interfaces such as the SARCOS Arm, the Argone Arm, and the PHANToM Master. Device independence is assured by Application Programmer Interface (API) "armlib" library designed on a client–server model. A simulation application runs as a client on a given computer, while the computers controlling the haptic interfaces connected to the same ethernet are the servers. Communication between the client and a particular server can be set by the API to synchronous or asynchronous mode. In a synchronous mode, the client sends position-read requests to the server and waits for the position data to be sent by the server. Conversely, the client can send force-write commands to the server, which then applies these forces to the user through the interface controller and sends an acknowledgment to the client. In asynchronous communication, position data is sent continuously to the client who reads when needed. Similarly, force-feedback commands are sent to the server without waiting for an acknowledgment. In cases when the users are at distant locations, the client application may run on two computers (rather than one). Thus, each client communicates with its server locally and with the other client over the network. This approach allows the two users to be losely coupled through two slightly different, but consistent, virtual worlds [Mark, 1994].

8.4. HAPTIC FEEDBACK PROGRAMMING

The previous discussion explained the physical modeling and haptic interface control aspects of virtual environments. No details were given, however, on the very important programming part of the development of a VR haptic simulation. Within the context of this book, the focus is on high-level modeling and control programming through

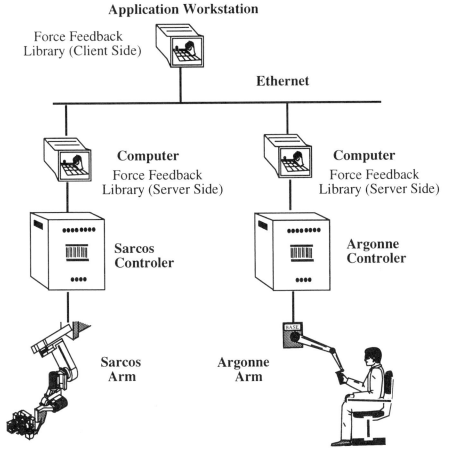

Figure 8.12   The University of North Carolina distributed architecture for multiuser force-feedback simulations. Adapted from Mark et al. [1996]. Reprinted by permission.

C and C++ languages. Readers interested in low-level assembly programming for microprocessor-based actuator control may consult Stone [1982] and Holland [1989], or other similar books.

General-purpose graphics libraries such as PHIGS [American National Standards Institute, 1988], GL [Silicon Graphics Inc., 1991], or Starbase [Hewlett-Packard, 1991] have been used for many years to create three-dimensional graphics for VR and other applications. One way to develop VR simulations with haptic feedback is to write a higher level program that executes in real time and calls lower level modeling, graphics, and i/o routines when needed. Writing such programs from scratch requires good programming skills and substantial debugging time. An alternative is to use newer toolkits such as WorldToolKit (WTK) [Sense8 Co., 1995], VCToolkit (VCT) [Division Ltd., 1993a] or Cyberspace Developer Kit (CDK) [Autodesk Inc., 1993]. These are extendable libraries of object-oriented functions designed specifically for

VR modeling, graphics, and real-time i/o. What follows is a short illustration of how toolkits can be used for physical modeling, real-time i/o, and distributed simulations.

8.4.1. Physical Modeling with the Cyberspace Developer Kit

The Cyberspace Developer Kit (CDK) is a library of over 1200 functions organized in 140 C++ classes. These classes are organized hierarchically with subclasses inheriting the attributes of their base class. Within the 12 categories of C++ classes, we are interested here in Geometry and Physics.

The Geometry class has a solid-body class called CySolid and a rigid-body class called CyRBESet. Objects in the CySolid class are undeformable, whereas deformable objects can be modeled by the CyNonRigidBody subclass of CyRBESet. Deformable objects have their surface modeled by polygonal meshes (CyPolymesh) or rectangular ones (CyRectmesh).

The other important class for haptic feedback simulations is the Physics category, which deals with collision detection and object dynamics. Collision detection is handled by CyCollisionServer which creates objects of the CyCollisionEvent type to monitor for collisions between objects. Bounding-box collision detection is implemented by the subclasses CyCollisionBoxBox, CyCollisionSphereSphere, and CyCollisionBoxSphere.

Object dynamics is provided by the CyDynamics and CyPhysical classes. Specifically, spring, friction, and gravity forces are simulated by CySpring, CyFriction, and CyGravity, respectively. These forces are then resolved by CyResolve into object positions and accelerations.

8.4.2. Real-Time Input/Output with WorldToolKit

Another task involved in VR programming is the ordering or scheduling of simulation events, so that overall latencies are minimized. By events we mean reading the sensors mapped to the simulation (such as a DataGlove, a trackball, or a PHANToM master), updating the status of the virtual objects mapped to these sensors (position, velocity, etc.), adding object intelligent behavior in response to sensor input, rendering the virtual scene, and displaying the associated audio and haptic feedback. Some toolkits, such as the "WorldToolKit" (WTK) have built-in event scheduling capabilities, as illustrated in Figure 8.13 [Sense8 Co., 1992].

The process starts with universe_new() to initialize and universe_load() function to load the particular virtual world to be simulated. New objects are created with myobject=WTobject_new() and their status updated during the simulation whenever WTobject_addresor(myobject) is executed. This call needs to exist in the real-time simulation loop following the universe_go(). Sensors can be mapped to virtual objects with calls to WTsensor_new(), WTpolhemus_new(), geoball_new(), etc. Collision detection can be performed with WTobject_intersect(object1, object2). If, for example, one object is a virtual hand and the second is a ball and they intersect, the ball can be attached to the hand by calling WTobject_attach(hand, ball). Force feedback is not directly supported by WTK. However, haptic feedback can be integrated by adding in

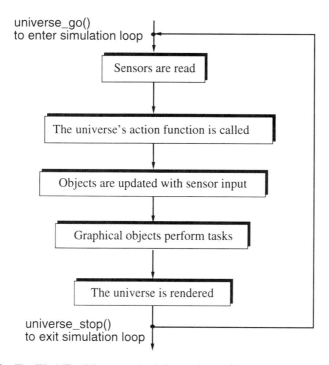

universe_go()
to enter simulation loop

Sensors are read

The universe's action function is called

Objects are updated with sensor input

Graphical objects perform tasks

The universe is rendered

universe_stop()
to exit simulation loop

Figure 8.13   The WorldToolKit event scheduling. Adapted from Sense8 Co. [1992]. © Éditions Hermès. Reprinted by permission.

the main program calls for other classes that provide serial or D/A driver communication (as needed by the particular haptic interface used). Once the graphics scene is rendered, the simulation loop is reinitialized and the above events repeated. Exiting the simulation requires a call to universe_stop(), which can be done, for example, by pressing a mouse button or a key. This in turn calls universe_delete(), which cleans up and frees the allocated RAM memory.

8.4.3. Using VCToolkit for Distributed Simulations

VCToolkit, through its "dVS" run time environment has been designed specifically for computation parallelism. The VCT calls virtual object attributes (such as visual, audio or tactile features) Elements. Elements from different objects are grouped together and assigned a specific process or "Actor." As illustrated in Figure 8.14 [Grimsdale, 1991a], there are three categories of Actors, namely Sensing Actors, Control Actors, and Display Actors. Of interest here is the DGlove Actor, which reads input from sensing gloves (such as the DataGlove) and the TACT Actor, which is responsible for tactile feedback.

Various Actor processes can be distributed on several processors, either on a single parallel computer (as explained in Section 8.3.2), or on multiple computers

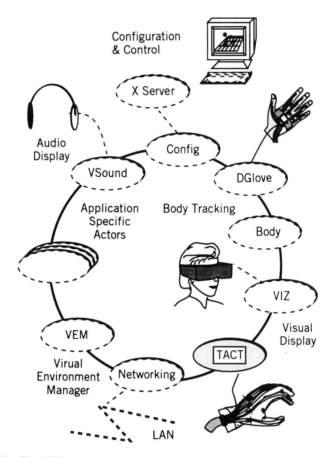

Figure 8.14 The dVS parallel run-time environment. Adapted from Grimsdale [1991a,b]. © Éditions Hermès. Reprinted by permission.

connected by an ethernet. Simulation distribution is realized through a shared data space maintained by special Actors called "Agents." Each computer connected to the network has its own Agent process that places Elements in the shared data space. Changes in Element states (or Instances) are monitored by Agents and transmitted to their Actors on a need-to-know basis. This reduces communication overhead and the chance for database access conflicts.

8.5. CONCLUSIONS

In this chapter, we discussed haptic interface control in terms of control laws, quality of haptic feedback, computation distribution, and simulation programming. Interface control can be done through force control, position control, or a combination of these fundamental methods. The quality of haptic feedback relates to the fidelity and range of sensations an interface can reproduce (namely the impedance range), as well as the system bandwidth and stability. In a digitally controlled system, high bandwidth requires small computation delays, which in turn call for computation distribution (locally or remotely over the network). The chapter ended with a brief description of commercial toolkit libraries that can be used to implement haptic feedback in a VR simulation.

CHAPTER 9

HUMAN FACTORS

In the preceding chapters, we described various haptic feedback interfaces and the way they are controlled during the VR simulation. We argued that realistic modeling (collision detection, surface deformation), good control (high bandwidth, reduced latency, and increased system stability), and good interface design (reduced friction and inertia, high stiffness) combine to produce quality haptic sensations. It is now time to measure the benefits brought by haptic feedback to the simulation realism and the user's sense of immersion. To do so, we refer to a number of pertinent human-factor studies performed to determine the positive (and negative) effects of haptic feedback.

Haptic feedback devices designed specifically for VR simulations have only recently become commercially available. Thus, there are few pertinent human-factors studies, usually with small subject populations. Therefore, statistical significance of the experimental results is not always high. Additionally, the underlying haptic feedback technology is constantly changing, making independent validation through repeated studies difficult. In view of these constraints, we also tap into the much richer literature describing human-factors in telerobotics. Their findings are relevant since many VR simulations use the same interface hardware (hand master) and control methods (force feedback).

Our discussion starts with an outline of performance criteria used in human-factor studies. Some of these criteria apply to VR simulations in general, whether haptic feedback is present or not. Other criteria are specific to simulations with haptic feedback. Subsequently, we describe human-factor studies of systems having either force feedback or tactile feedback. There are instances when force feedback is either unavailable or detrimental (when long time delays exist). In these cases sensorial substitution of force by tactile (or visual/auditory) feedback may be a solution. Thus we also describe studies of haptic sensorial substitution and of sensorial redundancy, in which force information is presented to the user through several simultaneous modalities (visual, auditory, and force feedback). Finally, we discuss simulation sickness and safety issues as they relate to haptic interfaces.

9.1. CRITERIA FOR ASSESSING TASK PERFORMANCE

Whenever a new interface device, system architecture, control method, or VR application is developed, it is necessary to measure performance. Experimental results are then used to fine tune the interface design, the control algorithm, or the application features. An intrinsic and key part of this evaluation process are human-factor studies, which measure the user's reactions to the simulation.

Task performance is measured based on objective and subjective criteria. *Objective criteria* refer to such variables as user's task completion time, error rates, and learning time. *Subjective criteria* refer to the user's expressed preference (or lack of it) for a given interface device, control modality, or application feature.

Task completion time represents the time span between the start and end of a given task. The time is measured from the moment the subject performs a given action, for example when first touching a virtual object, or when first seeing a moving target. The end of the experiment is also linked to an action, such as releasing the virtual object, hitting a target, and so on. Time can be measured on-line (with a stop watch, or using the computer clock) [Richard et al., 1994], or it can be obtained through off-line processing of a signal from a sensor actuated by the subject [Howe and Kontarinis, 1992].

Task error rate measures the type, size, and frequency of errors made by the user when performing the simulation task. What constitutes an error is of course task-dependent and is established by the experimental protocol. An error could be, for example, the breakage of a fragile virtual object manipulated by the subject, or it could be the placement of an object outside a given target area. For a given task, errors vary from trial to trial and from subject to subject. It is necessary to perform error averaging over all subjects and determine what is the standard deviation. The smaller the standard deviation, the more uniformly the subjects performed during the experiment.

When tasks are done repeatedly there is generally a decrease in error rates and completion time over all subjects. This reduction with the trial count represents the *task learning* process. The steeper the trial count-error rate curve, the quicker the learning process. Tasks that have flat learning curves have either very low difficulty (the subject already knows it) or are too difficult to perform. In such cases, the experimental protocol needs to be changed to alter the task difficulty accordingly.

Task completion time, error rate and learning time represent performance criteria that are applicable to VR simulations in general. There are, however, performance measurements that are specific to haptic feedback. One example is the *average contact force/torque* [Das et al., 1992] when interacting with the virtual or (remote) real object. High averages represent a forceful manipulation that may not be adequate for delicate tasks. The average force is given by

$$\text{Average force} = \frac{\sum_{i=1}^{N} \mathbf{f}_i}{N} \tag{9.1}$$

where N is the number of data samples in the contact phase and $\mathbf{f}_i$ is the magnitude of the ith force. Related performance criteria are the peak contact force and the force variance [Hannaford and Wood, 1989].

Another measurement specific to haptic feedback is the *cumulative contact force/torque*. This is obtained by multiplying the force/torque magnitude by the sampling interval, over the contact time, as in

$$\text{Cumulative force} = \sum_{i=1}^{N} \mathbf{f}_i \Delta t \tag{9.2}$$

where Δt is the sampling interval and N is the number of data samples, as before. The higher the cumulative force/torque, the higher the user's muscle exertion. High cumulative forces can lead to user fatigue and to high haptic interface energy consumption and wear.

The preceding discussion described general and haptic feedback-specific performance criteria without limiting the spectrum of simulation tasks that are of interest. Lampton and his colleagues at the U.S. Army Research Institute [Lampton et al., 1994] developed a Virtual Environment Performance Assessment Battery (VEPAB) for the evaluation of basic simulation training tasks. Their motivation in developing VEPAB came from the understanding that users have wide variability in their initial simulation interaction skills. However, users have to achieve some minimum level of VE skill before training on more complex tasks can be attempted. The five VEPAB task categories were Vision, Locomotion, Manipulation, Tracking, and Reaction Time. Within the scope of this book, we are primarily interested in the VEPAB Manipulation category. Its grasping tasks (of a horizontal control bar, of a rotating dial, or of a virtual ball) were programmed using a Sense8 Co. WTK. They used as an input device either a trackball (SGI "Spaceball") or a joystick (Gravis Joystick). Since neither the joystick nor trackball had haptic feedback, grasping was simulated by overlapping a three-dimensional cursor with the virtual object of interest. Tests performed on 24 subjects showed that manipulation completion time when using the trackball was almost twice that when the joystick was used. Lampton and his colleagues argue that the lack of performance for the trackball users was due to slow graphics refresh rates (2–9 fps) combined with the lack of apparent motion of the trackball when force was applied.

Another three-dimensional object manipulation study using a trackball was performed by Zhai and Milgram [1993] at the University of Toronto. They compared a three-dimensional manipulation task performance for four control modalities. In the first two, a three-dimensional sensor (Ascension Bird [Scully, 1993]) controlled the virtual object's three-dimensional position (isotonic position), or velocity (isotonic rate). The other two control modalities used the forces applied on the trackball to change the virtual object position (isometric position), or velocities (isometric rate).

Results showed that the task completion time was smallest for isotonic position and isometric rate and largest for isometric position. Intersubject variability among the eight test participants was also largest for isometric position.

9.2. FORCE FEEDBACK

The results of these human-factor studies underscore the difficulty of interacting and manipulating virtual objects in the absence of proprioceptive position and force feedback. We begin our discussion of the benefits of haptic feedback with the study performed by Hannaford and Wood [1989] at the Jet Propulsion Laboratory. They used the JPL Generalized Hand Master [Bejczy and Salisbury, 1980] to teleoperate a remote Puma 560 robot equipped with a six-axis force sensor. Five test subjects were asked to perform several manipulation tasks, such as velcro attachment (Task 1), peg-in-hole insertion (Task 2), and mating–unmating of an electrical connector (Task 3). These tasks were performed under three control modes: manual operation, teleoperation without force feedback, and teleoperation with force feedback. Force feedback was generated by the Hand Master based on forces measured by the robot force sensor. Subjects' performance under these control methods was measured through task completion time, task error rates, and the sum-of-square forces (SOSF) sensed by the robot force sensor. Task-completion time was measured between spikes in the force-sensor data produced by taps on the experimental board at the beginning and end of the task. The error rate in this case consisted of the total number of errors performed during several trials. The SOSF was calculated with

$$\text{SOSF} = \sum_{i}^{N} \mathbf{f}_i^2 \, dt \tag{9.3}$$

where N in the number of data samples, $\mathbf{f}_i$ is the ith force/torque sample, and dt is the time sample (0.01 sec in these experiments). Figure 9.1 [Hannaford and Wood, 1989] shows the experimental results averaged over the three tasks. As expected, the best performance was obtained when direct manual control was used. The interesting findings are obtained when comparing control mode 1 (no force feedback) with mode 2 (when force feedback was present). Over the three manipulation tasks, force feedback reduced completion time by 30% (Figure 9.1a), and error rates by approximately 60% (Figure 9.1c). Furthermore, SOSF was reduced by a factor of seven (from 3500 down to 500 lb^2sec)! When no force feedback was provided, the subjects had to rely on visual feedback alone, resulting in a much more forceful and potentially damaging manipulative interaction.

Task performance depends not just on the presence or absence of force feedback but also on the quality of the haptic sensation. Howe and Kontarinis [1992] used a telemanipulation system to study the influence of force feedback bandwidth on task performance. The experimental system consisted of a pair of kinematically identical master and slave manipulators as illustrated in Figure 9.2. The master manipulator had two identical finger hands, each with two degrees of freedom. By grasping the

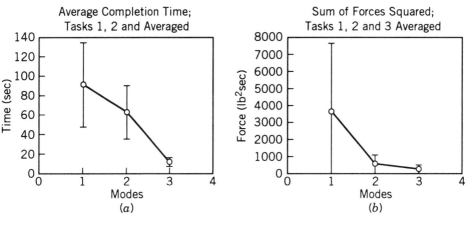

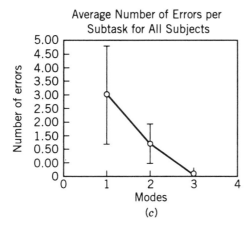

Figure 9.1 Evaluation of the JPL Generalized Hand Master in force reflecting teleoperation: (*a*) completion time; (*b*) sum-of-square forces; (*c*) error rates. Reprinted by permission from Hannaford and Wood [1989].

master with the thumb and index fingertips, the user could control positions and receive force feedback in a vertical plane. Thus, only planar manipulation tasks could be performed, such as the peg-in-hole insertion illustrated in Figure 9.2*b*.

The task studied in the experiments performed by Howe and Kontarinis consisted of the insertion of a round peg into a rectangular slot oriented perpendicular to the plane of motion. The peg-hole clearance was essentially zero, which made insertion

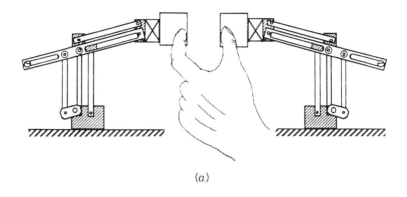

(a)

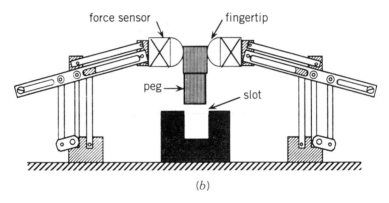

(b)

Figure 9.2 Telemanipulation experimental system: (a) master manipulator; (b) slave manipulator with peg-in-hole apparatus. Reprinted by permission from Howe and Kontarinis [1992].

more difficult and emphasized the role of force feedback in the task execution. The insertion task was performed in two modes. In the fast-insertion mode, the subjects were asked to perform the task as quickly as possible, regardless of the perceived contact forces. In the fragile-insertion mode subjects were asked to minimize contact forces. If the forces measured by the slave force sensors exceeded a force threshold of 1.6 N the manipulator motors were disabled. A low-pass filter was used to alter the bandwidth of the force-feedback signal from 100 Hz down to 32, 8, 2, and 0 Hz (no feedback). Five subjects were asked to perform the task under both fast- and fragile-insertion modes while the task completion time was recorded. Error rates (% failure) were recorded only for the fragile-insertion mode. Figure 9.3 shows the experimental results for the peg-in-hole insertion telemanipulation task [Howe and Kontarinis, 1992].

There was a clear reduction in task completion time with the increase in force-feedback bandwidth, with the longest time taken when only visual feedback (Vis) was

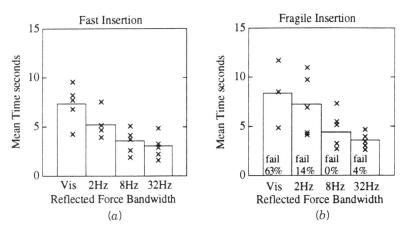

Figure 9.3 Task-completion time as a function of force-feedback bandwidth: (a) fast-insertion mode; (b) fragile-insertion mode. Reprinted by permission from Howe and Kontarinis [1992].

provided. Furthermore, this reduction is more significant from 0 to 8 Hz, and levels off afterward. In other words, for this telemanipulation task, there is little benefit when force-feedback bandwidth is increased from 8 to 32 Hz. A similar reduction was observed in the fragile insertion error rates with the increase in force-feedback bandwidth. Again, the worst case was that of visual feedback with no force feedback, when more than half of the trials ended in errors. There were very few errors once bandwidth was 8 Hz or above. The interesting result here is that even very low force-feedback bandwidth (2 Hz) reduced the error rates from 63% to 14%! Contact forces in the vertical direction (load forces) were also reduced by approximately 50% by the addition of force feedback to visual feedback. Even low force-feedback bandwidth helped avoid jamming the peg during the insertion in a hole with very tight tolerances. Grasping forces in the horizontal direction were much higher than the minimum value required to prevent peg slippage. This force overexertion was observed regardless of the force-feedback bandwidth. Howe and Kontarinis concluded that force feedback without tactile feedback is not sufficient to permit fine tuning of the grasping forces to prevent slippage.

Another variable influencing the task performance during virtual object manipulation is the weight of the object of interest. Ishii and Sato [1994b] performed human-factor studies using a SPIDAR haptic interface (see also Section 4.1.3) connected with a graphics workstation. The task being studied was a pick-and-place of a virtual cube of varying weights. The cube weight was set at either 20, 35, 50, 70, 100, and 150 gram-force, while its dimensions were kept constant ($5 \times 5 \times 5$ cm^3). The task consisted of picking up the cube at a given location, then moving it approximately 30 cm to a target, and finally placing it on the target as accurately as possible. During the task, subjects felt the grasping reaction forces, the weight and inertia of the cube, and the contact force between the cube and the target surface. The target used in these experiments was a circle with the diameter of 1 cm. Accuracy was measured by the height of the cube bottom from the target plane when the subject released it. Figure 9.4 presents experimental results for the pick-and-place task performed by three subjects. It can be seen that subjects took longer to manipulate the heavier cubes. This result may be explained by the slower speeds during the intermediate phase when the cube was moved to the target. Accuracy was best for cubes weighing 35 to 50 gram-force and degraded for the heavier cubes. Furthermore, there was a decrease in accuracy for very light cubes, which lack stability during manipulation.

In the above human-factor studies, task performance was measured solely based on objective criteria (task completion time, error rates, average contact forces, etc.). Adachi and his colleagues [1994] used subjective criteria to evaluate the realism of haptic sensations in a virtual push-button simulation. The push-button model was given by

$$\mathbf{F} = K_1(x - x_t) + K_2(x - x_b) + D_2 x + IL \tag{9.4}$$

where K_1 is the stiffness of the resistive spring in the first portion of the button travel, K_2 and D_2 are the stiffness and virtual damper in the second part of the button travel, IL is the initial resistance (load) (when x_t is zero), and x is the current button position. Subjects interacted with the virtual push button rendered on an SGI 420 VGX workstation using a SPICE haptic interface (see Fig. 4.18). After each trial the test subjects had to fill out a questionnaire (shown in Table 9.1) rating the feel of the simulation.

A statistical analysis was then performed to decompose the rating data into principal factors such as evaluation factor or stiffness factor. The button impedance parameters (stiffness and damping) were then mapped to these principal factors. In the first part of the study, seven subjects performed eight trials each. During the tests the parameters K_1 and IL in Eq. (9.4) were kept fixed, while K_2 and D_2 were varied.

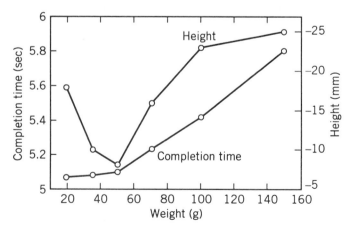

Figure 9.4   Completion time and accuracy as a function of manipulated object weight for a pick-and-place task. From Ishii and Sato [1994b]. Reprinted by permission of ASME.

TABLE 9.1   Subjective Rating Questionnaire for Push-Button Simulation

Reliable	1–2–3–4–5–6–7	Unreliable
Blur	1–2–3–4–5–6–7	Sharp
Durable	1–2–3–4–5–6–7	Fragile
Familiar	1–2–3–4–5–6–7	Unfamiliar
Solid	1–2–3–4–5–6–7	Fluid
Not easy to use	1–2–3–4–5–6–7	Easy to use
Agreeable	1–2–3–4–5–6–7	Disagreeable
Frail	1–2–3–4–5–6–7	Robust

Source: Adachi et al. [1994]. Reprinted by permission of the ASME.

In the second part of the study ten subjects performed eight trials each with varying IL and K_1, while K_2 and D_2 were fixed. Experimental results are shown in Figure 9.5 [Adachi et al., 1994]. In the low viscosity zone (D_2 of 100 to 500 N-sec/m) the "Stiffness Factor" grows linearly with the spring stiffness K_2. In general, evaluation was more favorable for buttons with high stiffness, as long as instabilities were not introduced. Virtual push buttons with small initial load IL received a low evaluation factor because they did not convey the crispiness of the button surface at the moment of contact. Buttons with very large IL were also ranked low according to the evaluation factor.

9.3. TACTILE FEEDBACK

Object manipulation and target acquisition tasks may also benefit from another haptic feedback modality, namely tactile feedback. Target acquisition is commonly done in today's window-based GUIs where users frequently select two-dimensional menus and icons by superimposing a cursor and pressing a mouse button. Visual and (sometimes) auditory feedback are used as a confirmation of the user's action after the mouse button was pressed. Akamatsu and his colleagues [1995] studied the influence of tactile feedback produced by a Multi-Modal Mouse (Fig. 6.11a) on GUI target acquisition time. They modified the GUI interface so that tactile feedback was provided while the cursor overlapped the target icon. The tactile feedback to the user's fingertip was turned off only after pressing the mouse button or after the cursor was moved outside of the target area. Subsequently, ten subjects were asked to perform a target acquisition task by moving the cursor from a start position to the target and clicking on it as quickly as possible. Each subject performed the task under five feedback conditions, namely normal (standard GUI mode), auditory (a 2-kHz tone

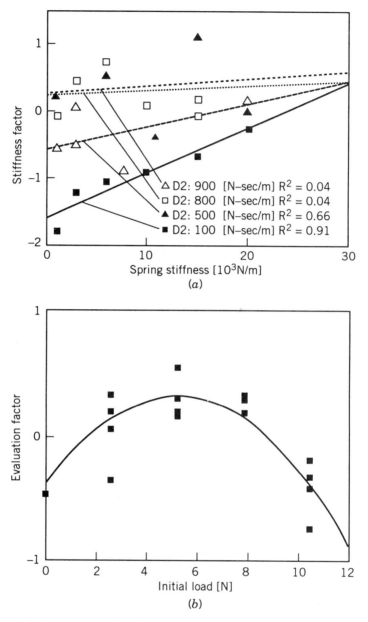

Figure 9.5 Subjective evaluation of a virtual pushbutton: (*a*) stiffness factor; (*b*) evaluation factor. From Adachi et al. [1994]. Reprinted by permission of the ASME.

was heard while the cursor was inside the target area), tactile (as explained above), visual (change in the target shading while the cursor overlapped it), and combined (all of the above feedback stimuli). Results showed that the final positioning time, which is the time to complete the trial once the cursor entered the target region, was smallest for the tactile feedback modality. When normal feedback was provided, subjects tended to move the cursor to the center of the target before selecting it. When additional feedback was provided, the on-target condition was sensed earlier, which is equivalent to a wider target. Figure 9.6 shows a histogram of the pixel Y coordinates when the target was selected, for (*a*) normal and (*b*) tactile feedback modes. The flatter histogram in Figure 9.6*b* indicates the subjects' tendency to use more of the target area when selecting it.

> When tactile sensations are exploited, wider targets also permit greater response noise (spatial variability) without loss of feedback. This is important, for example, if the operator's visual focus shifts away from the target.
>
> —Akamatsu et al. [1995]

The experiments presented above used a single actuator energized to provide tactile feedback. Another important category of tactile actuators are micro-pin arrays, which are used to present vibrotactile patterns to the user's fingertips. Weisenberger and Hasser [1996] studied the influence of the user's active and passive movement in the recognition of vibrotactile patterns produced by a 30-element SMM tactor array (see Fig. 6.14). The first part of the study used eight simple line patterns. The array tactors making up these lines had vibration frequencies of 5, 10, 20, 50, 100, and 200 Hz. The patterns where presented to six subjects in static, passive, and active scan modes. In the static presentation mode, all the tactors making up the various patterns were vibrated for 100 or 200 msec. In the passive scan mode, patterns were displayed in successive frames moving from right to left across the array. In active (or haptic) scan mode, the array was attached to an x/y digitizing tablet and the subjects had to move the array and actively scan the pattern(s). No time limit or scanning direction were specified under this display mode. Experimental results showed very high recognition rates (approximately 90%) for all presentation modes, regardless of the tactor vibratory frequency. Suspecting that ceiling effects were present (the patterns were too simple), Weisenberger and Hasser repeated their experiments, this time using more complex patterns. The new patterns were 10 letters of the alphabet (A, B, C, D, G, K, O, R, Q, and X). The pattern presentation modes were static, passive scan, and active scan, similar to those used in the first part of the study. Static patterns were displayed for 400 msec, whereas each frame of the passive scan mode had a duration of 100 msec. Again there was no time limit in the active (or haptic) scan mode. Test results are shown in Figure 9.7. The recognition rates across vibratory frequencies ranged from 46% to 71%, and were much lower than in the first experiment. The highest correct identification scores were for the letters C and X, whereas the lowest score was for the letter Q, which was often confused with the letter G. Over all the presentation modes, active (or haptic) scan produced the highest recognition rates. This was a possible result of the multiple scans and directions available for this pattern presentation mode.

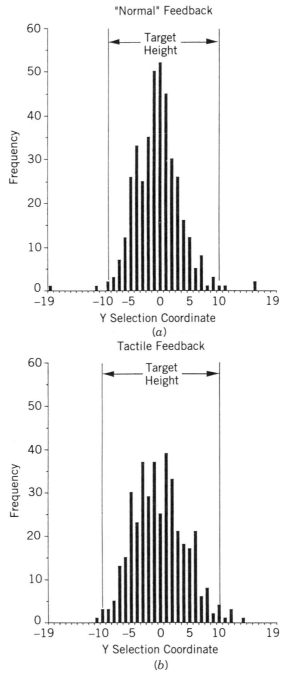

Figure 9.6 Two-dimensional target acquisition histogram using the Multi-Modal Mouse: (*a*) normal mode and (*b*) tactile feedback mode. From Akamatsu et al. [1995]. Reprinted by permission.

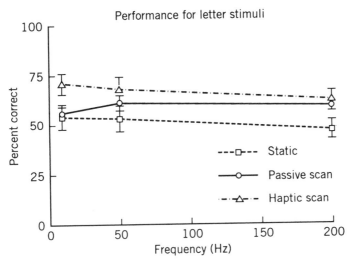

Figure 9.7 Vibrotactile pattern recognition performance as a function of presentation mode and vibratory frequencies. From Weisenberger and Hasser [1994]. Reprinted by permission.

The above results are in agreement with the pattern-recognition experiments performed by Kontarinis and his colleagues [1995]. In their first experiment, subjects rested their index fingertip on a stationary 6 × 4 actuator array and were asked to recognize three patterns. The first pattern was a point (single tactor raised), the second was a line (three tactors raised) and the last was a plane (all tactors energized). Experimental results showed 100% recognition rates for all subjects and all patterns. The second experiment used four patterns consisting of vertical, horizontal, or diagonal lines. Recognition rates were again 100%. It seems that simple patterns such as those used by Weisenberger and Hasser [1996] and by Kontarinis et al. [1995] can be reliably recognized with today's sparse tactile arrays. However, higher tactor densities and better control methods are needed for the recognition of complex vibrotactile patterns.

9.4. SENSORIAL SUBSTITUTION AND REDUNDANCY FOR FORCE FEEDBACK

Sensorial substitution occurs whenever information that is usually in one sensorial domain (e.g., vision) is presented to the brain through another sensory system (e.g., tactile) [Bach-y-Rita et al., 1987]. Sensorial substitution for the visually impaired is widely used by presenting text through Braille displays. Similarly, communication with the hearing-impaired is done by replacing auditory feedback with visual feedback (sign language).

In teleoperation or VR applications, sensorial substitution for force feedback means presenting contact force information through visual, auditory, or tactile feedback. NASA experimented with sensorial substitution of force by auditory display in their pioneering work on the Virtual Interface Environment Workstation (VIEW). Here, users controlled a remote virtual robot with a DataGlove and contact forces at the robot gripper were displayed as sounds. Tactile feedback was also used to substitute for the lack of direct force sensation when using heavy space suit gloves [Tan, 1988].

Massimino and Sheridan [1993] studied the influence of tactile and auditory substitution of force feedback in a teleoperation system with and without time delay. Their experimental system consisted of kinematically identical master and slave manipulator arms with six degrees of freedom each. Test subjects were provided with one of four feedback modalities. Visual feedback of the remote task was provided by a television monitor, whereas force feedback was produced by the master actuators. Auditory feedback presented a tone with loudness proportional to the contact force magnitude. Tactile feedback was applied to the thumb and index finger with a vibration magnitude proportional to the force. In the first part of the study, four subjects were asked to alternately tap with the tip of the remote manipulator between two objects attached to either a fixed or a movable base. When the base was fixed, only the presence of contact force had to be detected. However, when the base was movable the magnitude of the contact force became important, since for every 0.25 in. of object displacement a penalty of one tap was recorded. The force thresholds to move the remote objects (and platform) were either 0.5 lb or 2 lb. The taps had to be done as quickly as possible and the number of taps were recorded. Thus more taps indicated better performance. Experimental results are shown in Figure 9.8 [Massimino and Sheridan, 1993].

When the task was only to detect the presence of contact force, the best performance (largest number of taps) corresponded to audio feedback followed by vibrotactile feedback. The worst performance was measured when only visual feedback was provided (no ffb in Fig. 9.8*a*). Similar results were obtained when the 2-lb force threshold was used in the magnitude of contact force experiments (Fig. 9.8*b*). How-

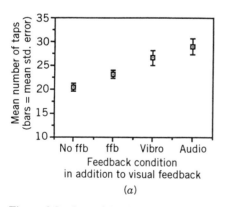 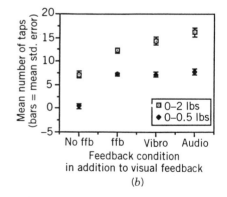

(a)   (b)

Figure 9.8 Sensorial substitution of force feedback in teleoperation: (*a*) contact force detection; (*b*) magnitude of contact force. From Massimino and Sheridan [1993]. Reprinted by permission of The MIT Press.

ever, when the force range was small (0.5-lb threshold) there were no differences in performance between actual force feedback and vibrotactile or auditory feedback. Thus, for perceiving small forces, sensory substitution worked as well as traditional force feedback.

In the second part of the study conducted by Massimino and Sheridan the task was a remote peg-in-hole insertion using the slave manipulator. This more complex task required a modification in the sensory substitution displays. The auditory display now presented different sounds to match the location, not just the intensity of contact forces. Force on the right side of the hole was presented as a medium pitch tone to the right ear, force on the left side as a medium pitch tone to the left ear, force on the bottom part of the hole as a low pitch to both ears, and so on. Similarly, the tactile feedback was enhanced by the addition of vibrotactile displays on the upper and lower parts of the palm. These were vibrated as a function of forces to the top and bottom of the hole, whereas displays on the index and thumb were mapped to forces on the left and right sides of the hole, respectively. Peg-in-hole insertion experiments were subsequently conducted with and without a 3-sec time delay in the feedback signal. The most significant findings occurred when time delay was present. Without sensory substitution, a 3-sec time delay would make such a task impossible to execute, because of system instabilities (as discussed in Chapter 8). Performance was measured by the task-completion time averaged over all subjects. Figure 9.9 illustrates the test results for both unobstructed and obstructed views of the remote scene. When the view was unobstructed, tactile and audio display of contact force information improved performance over visual display alone. When the view was obstructed, the test subjects had to insert the peg based solely on vibrotactile or auditory information. Under these conditions the auditory substitution of force information provided better performance than vibrotactile feedback, especially for a four-sided hole. Sensory substitution thus made possible the successful completion of a task that would normally have been impossible to execute.

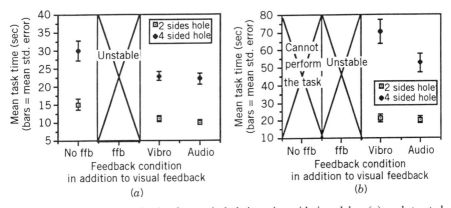

Figure 9.9   Sensorial substitution for peg-in-hole insertion with time delay: (*a*) unobstructed view; (*b*) obstructed view. From Massimino and Sheridan [1993]. Reprinted by permission of The MIT Press.

Another study of force feedback sensorial substitution was performed by Richard and his colleagues [1996] for a task involving dextrous manipulation of a deformable virtual object. The experimental system consisted of a partially immersive virtual environment (graphics workstation and shutter glasses), the Rutgers Master (shown in Figure 5.10) for force feedback to the subject's right hand and headphones for audio feedback. As illustrated in Figure 9.10 [Richard et al., 1996], subjects had to pick a virtual ball at location A and place it at location C by passing over location B. During this time, the ball had to be deformed no more than 10% of its radius, otherwise an error was recorded.

Force feedback sensorial substitution was realized either through visual display using the Rutgers Master interface LED bar graphs (subject group V), or through audio display on the headphones worn by the subjects (subject group A). Two additional feedback modalities had sensorial redundancy by presenting contact force information on either the Rutgers Master and LED displays (subject group H-V), or through the Rutgers Master and headphones (subject group H-A). Each group consisted of 14 subjects with a total of 84 subjects participating in the study. Figure 9.11 [Fabiani et al., 1996] shows the experimental results in terms of percentage ball deformation for curve "RM-I." It can be seen that, for nonredundant feedback modalities, the force feedback (group H) had the best performance (smallest ball deformation). This was probably due to the richer force information presented by the Rutgers Master (RM-I) than by auditory feedback alone. The addition of redundant visual and especially auditory force feedback improved performance further. Auditory feedback was able to give a cue of initial contact to supplement direct force feedback. Otherwise, the very small forces at the initial moment of ball deformation were masked by the static friction in the force feedback actuators. This conclusion was confirmed by recent tests

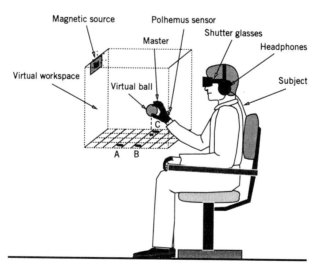

Figure 9.10 Experimental virtual environment configuration. From Richard et al. [1996]. Reprinted by permission of The MIT Press.

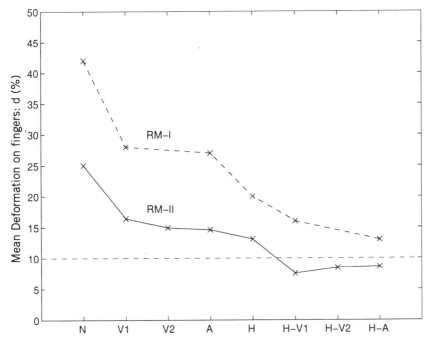

Figure 9.11   Manipulation task error rates for different force feedback modalities: N, none; V, visual; A, auditory; H, haptic. Reprinted by permission from Fabiani et al. [1996]. © 1996 IEEE.

performed by Fabiani and his colleagues [1996] using an improved Rutgers Master II (see Fig. 5.11) with low-friction actuators. Their results are illustrated in Figure 9.11 for curve "RM-II." This time, the performance of subject group H (only force feedback) was equal to that of group H-A in the study done by Richard et al. [1996]. Furthermore, the addition of redundant visual or auditory force information to the feedback produced by the RM-II decreased the ball deformation to less than 10%.

9.5. SIMULATION SICKNESS

The preceding human-factor studies substantiated the benefits brought by force and tactile feedback to the simulation task performance. Unfortunately, there are also detrimental effects brought about by haptic feedback. These relate to the so-called simulation sickness, more precisely motion sickness, that occurs whenever there are conflicting signals from the human vestibular and visual sensorial systems [Nemire, 1994]. Readers are probably familiar with simulation sickness associated with today's head-mounted displays. Symptoms include headache, nausea, and (in severe cases) vomiting. After-effects can last as many as 8 to 10 hours following the simulation session.

Within this book we are interested in cybersickness [McCauley and Sharkey, 1992] produced by haptic interfaces. Specifically, we are interested in VR systems, such as military or commercial flight simulators, which attempt to provide vestibular and proprioceptive cues by using motion platforms. A hydraulic motion platform typically has a ±2-m linear translation, ±35° rotation, and bandwidth of approximately 4 Hz [McCauley and Sharkey, 1992]. More modern electropneumatic platforms, such as the PemRAM (see Fig. 4.22), have a smaller range of motion but higher bandwidth (up to 50 Hz). All platforms, regardless of their capabilities, are unlikely to match the aggressive dynamics encountered in combat flight. Additionally, all platforms need periodic negative subthreshold accelerations to restore them to a neutral posture. These combine with the reduced motion range to diminish the platform dynamic fidelity and induce motion sickness.

The incidence of motion sickness in military pilots is as high as 40%. McCauley and Sharkey [1992] state that the incidence among the users of video games incorporating motion cues is likely to be higher than for pilots. This is due to a number of factors, such as lower calibration standards for commercial systems and users of older age being in poorer health. Pausch and his colleagues in their survey article [1992] indicate that motion sickness effects may be reduced by limiting the time delay between the visual and motion (proprioceptive) cues to less than 35 msec. Further decrease in simulation sickness may be attained by giving the participant a higher degree of control of the motion platform. Copilots and passengers on a motion platform are likely to experience more simulation sickness because they are not able to anticipate the platform motion.

9.6. SAFETY

Another topic of concern to the user of haptic interfaces is safety. Although interaction is with a simulated virtual environment, the feedback forces to the user are real! The author is not aware of any studies involving haptic interface safety issues. Nevertheless, common sense dictates that force-feedback levels should not be too high. Realistic and convincing haptic sensations can be obtained without exceeding 25% of maximum human force (for a given posture). This has the advantage of reducing fatigue and indirectly increasing safety, as rested users are more responsive than tired ones. Mechanical stops should also be incorporated whenever possible. These have the advantage of reducing the risk of injury in the event of computer failure at the expense of a smaller work envelope. Hasser [1996] reccomends the use of a combination of low-level joint velocity speed limits and high-level workspace limits implemented in software. This strategy was used with good results on the FREFLEX exoskeleton (shown in Color Plate 2).

The risks involved when wearing a powered haptic interface will grow in the future from a corresponding increase in system complexity including feedback to the whole arm:

> In such a configuration the force feedback devices should provide a safety button, similar to that used with many present robots. If both arms wear master "sleeves", then the safety

button may become a safety pedal. If full-body feedback is provided (some time in the future!), then voice commands should be used to "freeze/unfreeze" the feedback suit.

—Burdea and Langrana, [1993]

Clearly the benefits of haptic feedback have to be balanced against the risks involved and a compromise reached. Many studies are needed to ascertain the best compromise. These studies will follow as the underlying haptic feedback technology progresses.

9.7. CONCLUSIONS

This chapter described various methods to measure human performance in VR simulations when haptic feedback is provided. Objective and subjective criteria were used to quantify the benefits of force feedback, tactile feedback, sensorial substitution of force feedback (through visual, auditory, and tactile feedback) and redundant force feedback. The benefits brought by haptic feedback (reduced task completion time, error rates, etc.) need to be balanced against simulation sickness and injury risks to the user. Many more studies are needed to find the balance between risks and rewards when using a haptic interface device.

CHAPTER 10

HAPTIC FEEDBACK APPLICATIONS

The previous chapters described various haptic feedback interfaces that provide force and tactile feedback to the user interacting with a virtual world. The discussion focused on hardware architectures (both portable and nonportable), on modeling techniques, and on related control methodologies. This was followed by human-factor studies that quantified the clear benefits of haptic feedback in improving task performance. These advantages have prompted developers to look for ways of harnessing the potential of newer haptic feedback technology for applications in various fields of life.

The first half of this decade has witnessed the emergence of VR technology performing real-time position measurements, graphics rendering, and visual/auditory feedback. It was also the time when haptic feedback research was conducted at a fast pace worldwide, as exemplified throughout this book. We are now in a transition period, which will produce widespread commercial applications of virtual haptic feedback in the second half of this decade. One of the domains where haptic feedback is already attracting significant interest (from both researchers and investors) is medical training, especially surgical training. Medical applications is in fact the first topic of this chapter, followed by Entertainment applications, Telerobotics applications, and Military applications.

10.1. MEDICAL APPLICATIONS

Medical knowledge has had an extraordinary increase in the last 30 to 40 years (over twentyfold according to Dr. C. Everett Koop, former U.S. Surgeon General [Schwartz, 1993]). This prompted medical schools to modernize their teaching methodology for topics ranging from human anatomy to physiology and pathology. Interactive CD-

ROM anatomy trainers have replaced earlier static atlases and are widely used today. More recently, the first VR-based teaching systems have been developed [Rosen et al., 1996]. Surgical training systems, especially for minimally invasive surgery (MIS) have also become commercially available [Virtual Reality Inc., 1993]. These systems use head-mounted displays (HMD) to immerse the student or resident inside a virtual patient, providing a very intuitive and powerful instruction environment. However, the present VR MIS training systems lack haptic feedback, which limits their usefulness. This deficiency makes advanced surgical training impractical or the teaching of related areas such as diagnosis, anesthesiology, or rehabilitation procedures. We subsequently present systems currently under development that provide force/tactile feedback and thus address the need for increased medical simulation realism.

10.1.1. Tissue Palpation

The first stage in providing medical care is the diagnosis of the patient's illness. Current medical practice routinely uses sophisticated diagnostic tests through computer tomography, magnetic resonance imaging, and ultrasound imaging. However, one of the oldest (maybe ancient) diagnosis procedures is the palpation of body organs and tissue. Palpation is used, among other things, to measure swelling, detect bone fracture, find and measure pulse, or locate a malignancy within the surrounding tissue. Palpation cannot be simulated realistically without the sense of touch.

Sukthankar and Reddy [1994] looked at ways to measure real forces experienced during tissue palpation and their mapping for modeling tissue deformation. Their approach was to measure the hand EMG signal for the contraction of certain muscle groups. A calibration was then obtained linking the mean square value of the EMG signal to various muscle forces. Force information was then fed into a Finite Element Model of the virtual tissue, with the simulation providing visual feedback on a two-dimensional screen. A force-feedback device to provide the feel of palpation is presently under development.

More realism is obtained when three-dimensional organs are palpated by simulation. Langrana and his colleagues [1994] developed a general-purpose palpation simulation using the Rutgers Master to provide force feedback to the user. A virtual knee model (13,494 polygons) was acquired from Viewpoint Datalabs and rendered by an HP 755-CRX workstation. User i/o (hand position and force feedback) was done by a Sun 4 workstation communicating over the ethernet with the graphics renderer. The intricate details of the knee model (bones, muscles, and cartilages) made a custom collision detection algorithm necessary. The geometry of the knee model was stored in a special data structure that dynamically allocated pointers to the model segments. Each segment had its polygon structure, the coordinates of its geometric centroid, and the distances from each vertex to this centroid. Because knee segments had an irregular shape, spherical bounding boxes of varying radii were used, as illustrated in Figure 10.1 [Langrana et al., 1994]. Once the fingertip penetrated a given segment sphere of contact, a more detailed collision detection routine was activated. This algorithm calculated the distance between the fingertip and a plane determined

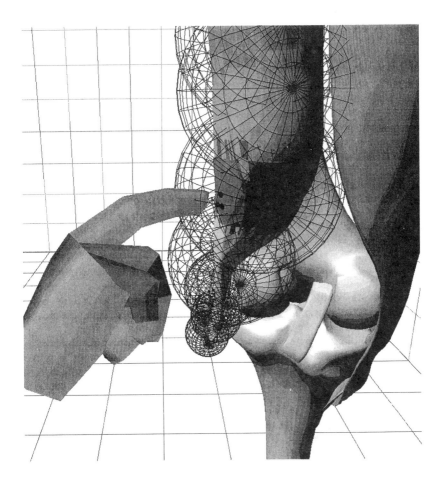

Figure 10.1 Collision detection during knee palpation. From Langrana et al. [1994]. Reprinted by permission of Elsevier Science BV.

by the closest three vertices on the segment surface. When contact was detected, the segment surface deformed up to its specified maximum penetration. Segments representing soft tissue (muscles) had large assigned maximum penetration distances and small maximum forces. Conversely, segments representing hard tissue (bones) had very small maximum penetration. Color Plate 9 shows a Gouraud-shaded muscle being deformed, with contact forces calculated in real-time based on Hooke's law. The bounding spheres were made transparent to increase simulation realism.

Another diagnostic procedure is the use of palpation to locate arteries and detect blood flow. Surgeons performing classical (open) surgery rely on their tactile sense to detect arteries located in the proximity of the surgical site and hidden behind other tissue. When procedures are done remotely (as in MIS) the surgeon is incapable of palpating the tissues of interest before they are cut. This increases the risk of life-threatening exsanguination. Peine and his colleagues [1994] developed a palpation system for artery localization in laparoscopic surgery. It consists of a tactile array sensor located at the end of a long probe with a grip housing the interface electronics, as illustrated in Figure 10.2 [Peine et al., 1994]. The sensor uses a matrix of 64 force-sensitive elements that form a thin, compliant layer. Force measurements obtained when pressing the probe against a hidden artery are processed by a computer that performs a power-spectrum analysis to infer the artery location. A two-dimensional plot is then displayed on a video monitor. Howe and his colleagues [1995] later integrated a 6×4 SMM tactile-feedback array (see Figure 6.16) in the above system. A more elaborate signal-processing scheme presently being developed uses an external pulse monitor. By correlating the anticipated pulse waveform with the sensor signal, the response time is reduced, and signal noise rejection is improved.

Howe and his colleagues [1995] integrated the tactile array with their force-feedback telerobotic system (see Figure 9.2) to study the detection of tumors through remote palpation. Their proof-of-concept experiments used a phantom consisting of a piece of hard rubber 4 mm in diameter embedded 5 mm beneath the surface of a softer foam rubber block. The vertical location of the phantom was changed randomly between trials within a ±20 mm range. During the tumor localization experiments the test subjects had force feedback from the remote palpation, but no visual feedback was provided. Some trials used a single row of the tactile array for additional tactile feedback. Results from 60 trials performed by three subjects

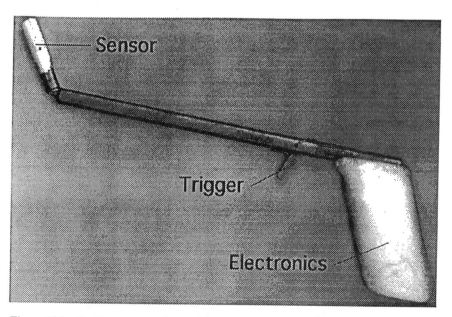

Figure 10.2   Tactile sensing probe used for artery localization during laparoscopic surgery. Reprinted by permission from Peine et al. [1994].

showed that force feedback alone produced mean absolute positional errors of 13 mm. When subjects had additional tactile feedback the tumor-localization accuracy increased significantly, and errors were 3 mm or less 95% of the time. This underscores the importance of small-scale shape information provided by the tactile-feedback actuators.

10.1.2. Anesthesia

Once the patient's illness has been diagnosed, the patient may have to undergo surgery. If surgery is required, then the patient needs to be anesthetized first. Certain procedures require general anesthesia, whereas others can be performed under local anesthesia.

Epidural or spinal anesthesis is a form of local anesthesia routinely used in obstetrics to lessen the pain of delivery. The procedure involves a delicate lumbar puncture in which a catheter is inserted into the spine with the help of a long needle. The needle insertion is complex owing to the lack of any visual cues, the long insertion distance and the proximity to the spine. If performed incorrectly, it can be very painful, even dangerous to the patient. Thus careful training of medical residents has to be done before good haptic skills are perfected. Figure 10.3 shows the anatomy in the needle insertion region and the corresponding force signature. At first there is a slight force increase as the needle penetrates the skin and dermal regions of the back. Then resistance grows as the harder intervertebrae ligament is traversed. If the needle orientation is correct, the resident will feel a sudden drop in resistance once the ligament has been fully traversed. There is a final force spike when the dural membrane is punctured, prior to penetrating the cerebral-spinal fluid and nerve fibers in the central spine region. If the needle orientation is incorrect, the needle tip lodges into the spine

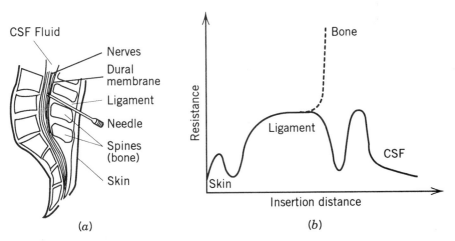

Figure 10.3 Epidural anesthesia: (*a*) anatomic cross section of the lumbar region; (*b*) resistive force signature during needle insertion. Reprinted by permission from Bostrom et al. [1993]. © 1993 IEEE.

and resistance increases sharply (and so does the pain felt by the patient). In such cases the needle needs to be fully extracted and the lumbar puncture attempted again.

Bostrom and his colleagues at Dartmouth College [1993] developed a prototype lumbar-puncture simulator using a specially designed three-degree-of-freedom haptic interface. As illustrated in Figure 10.4, this device had a long shaft simulating the needle, that was located coaxial to a dc linear actuator. The assembly was supported by a two-degree-of-freedom platform that allowed the shaft orientation within a 60° cone. The shaft orientation could be locked on demand using two brake disks on the same platform. Needle tip position was determined based on readings from three revolute sensors integrated in the haptic interface. Position accuracy for the needle tip was approximately 1 mm, and maximum resistive force produced by the dc motor was 10 N. A force sensor (strain gauge) provided data on actual forces that was used for closed-loop force control. The controller was housed in a separate interface box that also housed signal conditioning electronics for the position sensors, and a RS 232 line for communication with a graphics workstation. During the simulation, a three-dimensional model of the spine was displayed by the host computer (SGI Indi) at approximately 2 fps [Singh et al., 1994]. This low refresh rate was due to the complex graphical model and low rendering speed. To avoid system instabilities, it was necessary to decouple the graphics loop from the low-level force-feedback control. This, however, introduced time delays that affected the speed with which the needle insertion could be performed.

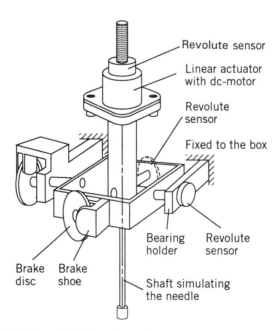

Figure 10.4 Epidural anesthesia simulator with haptic feedback. Reprinted by permission from Bostrom et al. [1993]. © 1993 IEEE.

Another simulator for epidural analgesia was developed recently by McDonald and his colleagues at the Ohio State University Hospital [McDonald et al., 1995]. It uses a one-degree-of-freedom haptic interface manufactured by Immersion Co. to provide resistive forces coaxial with the needle. The overall simulation system includes a high-performance graphics workstation and a voice-activated interface. Voice recognition is very useful, because the trainee has to keep his hand on the haptic interface. Before insertion, the virtual needle projects a shadow, which helps residents determine its proximity to the patient's back. Once the needle penetrates the virtual patient, force feedback is provided matching various tissue resistance (as explained previously). Residents can request additional visual feedback during the procedure (a section containing the current needle location). During section presentation, the needle is locked to prevent dependency on the visual display.

The above systems were designed specifically for lumbar puncture simulation. Training in other local anesthetic procedures could also benefit. Bostrom et al. [1993] state that

> Other regional anesthetic techniques which could be simulated include brachial plexus blocks, stellate ganglion blocks, and cervical plexus blocks. Similarly various vascular insertion techniques could be simulated. These might include central venous and/or pulmonary artery cannulation via the internal jugular or subclavian approach. Only the software need change, the hardware would be applicable to any of the above possibilities.
>
> —Bostrom et al. [1993]

10.1.3. Minimally Invasive Surgery

Once anesthetized, the patient is ready for the actual surgical procedure. Surgery involves delicate maneuvers in confined spaces, excellent hand–eye coordination, and above-average hand dexterity and positional accuracy. The present cadaver-based training cannot possibly allow a resident to acquire all the necessary skills in medical school. A learning curve follows graduation, which puts patients at increased risk. Virtual reality has been proposed as a viable solution to the above problem by Col. Richard Satava, a U.S. Army surgeon:

> The ability for a resident to practice a surgical procedure repeatedly until perfect before performing it on a patient, or the opportunity for a researcher to attempt new surgical procedures repeatedly before the first attempts on an animal model suggests that it is possible to greatly enhance the teaching of surgical skills while exposing the surgeon or patient to less risks. . . .
>
> —Satava [1993]

The above observation was prompted by the extraordinary increase in minimally invasive surgery (MIS), which is replacing traditional open surgery. Gall bladders are currently removed laparoscopically, polyps in the intestinal tract are extracted by endoscope, and knee surgery is routinely performed through arthroscopy. Whether it is called laparoscopy, endoscopy, or arthroscopy, MIS uses long tools and tiny cameras inserted through small incisions in the body. The reduced hospital stay and faster patient recovery come at the price of a more stressful environment for the surgeon, who loses direct sight of the surgical area. The surgeon must look at video monitors and has poor tactile feedback from the remote cutting location inside the body. Under these circumstances, the need for better training in MIS techniques becomes paramount. Loftin and colleagues [1994] see a need to apply VR technology to surgical-training simulators, owing to the increased training interactivity, flexibility, and ability to measure the trainee's technical competence. Another justification for using VR training systems is the potential reduction of the length of surgical residency programs from the present five years down to three years.

The first MIS trainers were purely mechanical and consisted of a plastic replica of the anatomical region of interest, with incisions made to allow the insertion of mock-up surgical tools. Such training systems proved inadequate, because interactivity was low, there was no realistic visual (or haptic) feedback, and no real-time data-gathering capability to assess the training process. An increase in interactivity was provided by the system patented by Hon [1990], which introduced sensors inside the mannequin to monitor the progress of an endoscopic probe. These sensors were interfaced with a computer for data gathering and to provide sound feedback to the trainee. As illustrated in Figure 10.5, the system also provided visual feedback from a camera in the endoscopic probe. Resistive forces were produced by electromagnetic actuators that were placed at various locations along the endoscopic probe path. The above system has now become commercially available from Ixion Inc.

Recently, Ziegler and colleagues [1995] at Franhofer Institute for Computer Graphics (Germany) developed a training simulator for arthroscopic surgery. The system uses a plastic replica of the knee, with holes for the insertion of a real surgical arthroscopic camera and an exploratory probe. The knee posture (bending angle) and

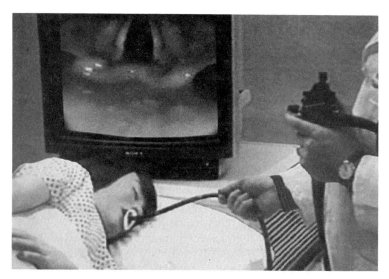

Figure 10.5   Endoscopic trainer patented by Hon [1990]. Photograph courtesy of Ixion Inc.

the position and orientation of the camera and probe are tracked by three position sensors. Their data is sent to a high-end graphics workstation, which displays virtual models of the knee and exploratory probe as seen by a virtual arthroscopic camera. The knee model was constructed based on MRI data, segmented and pruned down to 20,000 polygons. This was necessary to allow real-time rendering in response to the trainee's actions. The resulting graphics is similar to the image depicted in Color Plate 10. The system monitors the collisions between the exploratory probe and arthroscopic camera with the anatomical structure of the virtual knee. Collisions trigger an acoustic response and are counted as mistakes. Statistics on the number of collisions then give a measure of training progress. At the present time, the research team is working to enhance the simulation by integrating haptic feedback [Ziegler et. al., 1996].

Another computer-based training system that maps real surgical instruments to a virtual anatomic structure is the laparoscopic training workstation being developed by Cine-Med Inc. (Woodbury, CT) [Greenleaf, 1995]. The system compensates for the present lack of force feedback by providing highly realistic organ behavior during cutting, suturing, and other surgical tasks. Trackers and switches integrated with the surgical instruments are monitored by a graphics workstation, which displays a realistic stereo image, as illustrated in Figure 10.6. The system incorporates an artificial intelligence expert, which reproduces the patient's reactions during surgical procedures. If acceptable values for vital parameters are exceeded, the virtual patient may bleed excessively, the heart may fail, or in an extreme situation, the patient may die. This allows training in emergency surgical situations.

Another simulation authoring environment for MIS is the "Teleos" Virtual Environment Toolkit being developed by High Techsplanations (Rockville, MD). It is

Figure 10.6   The Virtual Clinic laproscopic simulator. Photograph courtesy of Cine-Med Inc.

designed to allow various medical specialists to author surgical training simulations without programming [Meglan et al., 1996].

The Teleos software uses CT, MRI, and the Visible Human dataset to build three-dimensional virtual organ models using OpenGL and OpenInventor running on SGI workstations. Its modeling centers around spatial spline formulations of tubes and their physical properties. Geometry is stored at several levels of detail, in order to optimize real-time rendering of complex models. Newtonian-based physical properties of texture-mapped models include collision detection, particle system behavior, fluid dynamics, tissue deformation, and cutting. High Techsplanations is now integrating haptic feedback into its training environment through i/o devices such as the PHANToM master or the Immersion Engine (discussed later in this chapter).

The lack of adequate tactile sensation in MIS procedures, compared to direct manipulation in open surgery, has been shown to degrade performance [Tendick et al., 1993]. To provide accurate haptic feedback to a MIS simulator, it is first necessary to measure the *real* forces experienced during surgery. Sukthankar and Reddy [1995] performed a study of the relationship between the forces at the tip of a laparoscopic forcep and those at its handle. The surgical instrument was retrofitted with ultraminiature strain gauges at both handle and tip and data read by a PC through a digitizer board. The instrumented forcep was then used to squeeze three classes of objects (soft, medium, and hard). Preliminary results indicated that the forces measured at the tip of the instrument were significantly different from those at its handle. Furthermore, there was a nonlinear relationship between the two sets of forces, which was also dependent on the hardness of the material being squeezed.

Measurement of cutting forces at the tip of a laparoscopic forceps can also be used to provide haptic feedback to the trainee. Fischer and colleagues at Kern-forschungszentrum Karlsruhe GmbH (Germany) have recently developed such a tactile-feedback system for MIS. The system consists of an instrumented laparoscopic forceps, an electronic interface, a PC computer, and a tactile-feedback array. The surgical tool was retrofitted with miniature strain gauges measuring three forces and a tactile sensor array installed at the cutting end, as illustrated in Figure 10.7a [Fischer et al., 1995]. The 12×15-mm array consisted of a foil sensor with a matrix of 64 measuring points. The array data was transmitted to the PC for real-time graphic visualization and to a tactile array actuator. As illustrated in Figure 10.7b, the feedback actuator incorporates three printer heads with 24 needles each. Each needle was actuated by an electromagnetic vibrator to a frequency of 600 Hz. The intensity of the tactile array signal was mapped to the needle vibrating frequency. Although the present system measures real contact forces in a telepresence arrangement, it could easily be adapted to a VR-based simulator without changing the feedback device.

A system specifically designed for force feedback in VR MIS simulations is the Laparoscopic Impulse Engine [Immersion Co., 1995; Rosenberg and Stredney, 1996]. As illustrated in Figure 10.8, this device allows surgical tools to be manipulated in five degrees of freedom within a $5 \times 9 \times 9$-in. workspace. The surgical tool can be tilted about the insertion port in two degrees of freedom by approximately 100° and translated in and out by 4 in. Computer-controlled torques up to 60 oz-in. can be applied about the pivot axes, whereas forces up to 2 lb resist the translation motion.

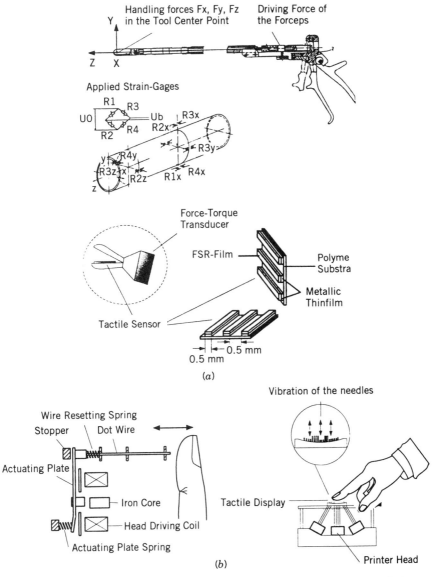

Figure 10.7 Instrumented laproscopic forceps with tactile feedback: (*a*) laparoscopic forceps with tactile sensor; (*b*) tactile feedback actuator. Reprinted by permission from Fischer et al. [1995].

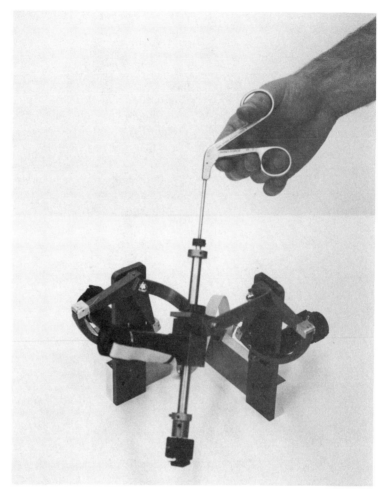

Figure 10.8 The Laparoscopic Impulse Engine. Photograph courtesy of Immersion Co.

The tool rotation angle about its longitudinal axis (360°) and the open–close motion of its handle are measured by the computer, but presently do not have force feedback. The two actuators providing tilting torques are connected to the tool handle through small diameter capstan pulleys and large diameter capstan drums. This mechanism insures low inertia and friction, high stiffness, and negligible backlash. The actuators (basket would dc servomotors) are connected to the tool by high-tension aircraft cables and use optical encoders for position feedback. The tool translation is done by a precision ground shaft which slides through Teflon-coated bearings. Tension is produced by a cable fixed to either side of the linear shaft and to a small diameter capstan pulley [Rosenberg and Stredney, 1996]. The simulation system has high position resolution (0.0009 in.), control bandwidth (120 Hz on the rotary axes and 650 Hz on the linear axis) and sampling rate (10 KHz). The current price of a Laparoscopic Impulse Engine is approximately $8000, which includes the interface card and power amplifiers.

10.1.4. Microsurgery

Another surgical specialty that can benefit from VR and telerobotic technologies is ophthalmic (eye) microsurgery. Such surgical procedures are extremely difficult for inexperienced surgeons owing to the very small forces and minute cutting distances involved, coupled with motor fatigue (hand tremor). If MIS skills can be acquired after 50 hours of training on advanced simulators [Cine-Med Inc., 1995], expert eye surgeons require thousands of hours of practice.

Salcudean and Yan [1994] observed that present microsurgery tasks are based on visual feedback alone (under microscope), because contact forces are too small (approximately 30 g). To improve the surgical outcome, they proposed a telerobotic system that provides tremor filtering and haptic feedback to the surgeon. This system uses three magnetically-levitated wrists, one as a joystick master (see Fig. 4.8) and the remaining two installed on a slave robot. They estimate that the force resolution at the slave could be as small as 0.002 N, for a maximum cutting force of 1.2 N. Forces sensed at the slave are amplified and fed to the trainee, while position commands sensed by the master are correspondingly scaled down and sent to the slave system.

The system proposed by Salcudean and Yan uses telerobotic surgery on real patients. It is implied that surgeons who will use the above system already possess the required skills. A system that addresses the training needs of ophthalmic surgery residents was developed by Hunter and colleagues [1993] at McGill University. Their simulator uses a pair of six-degree-of-freedom master–slave robotic manipulators, which read the surgeon's hand motion and apply force feedback. Position commands are scaled down by a factor of 100 when sent to the slave, and forces sensed at the slave are scaled up 100 times. The surgeon also receives audio feedback and visual feedback from the remote surgical site through a head-mounted display. The master and slave subsystems communicate through a pair of computers that perform low-level control (coordinate transforms, hand tremor filtering), image enhancement, and safety checking. When the system is used for training rather than actual surgery, the remote patient is replaced by a virtual model of the eye simulated by the master computer. This very detailed eye model was created in collaboration with Sagar and his colleagues [Sagar et al., 1994] at the University of Auckland (New Zealand). The complex eye geometry was created using nonuniform rational β-splines (NURBS), because they provide good geometrical continuity, minimal data sets, and fast collision detection with virtual surgical tools. As illustrated in Color Plate 11 [Hunter et al., 1993], the very realistic graphics includes blood vessels, light-sensitive retina reflexes, eyelashes, eyebrows, and eyelids that move. This model was rendered on an SGI Reality Engine at an update rate of 10 fps. Physical models of surface deformation and contact forces are being developed based on finite-element analysis. The large computational load involved (estimated at 10 Gflops [Hunter et al., 1993]) limit the present deformation model to only the cornea surface.

Another training system for eye surgery is being developed by Peifer and his colleagues at Georgia Institute of Technology [Peifer et al., 1994]. The surgeon in training interacts with a virtual eye model through a hand stylus mapped to four kinds of surgical instruments (knife, forceps, scissors, and phako emulsifier used to remove the lens in cataract surgery). The surgeon's hand position is tracked by a three-dimensional sensor in the stylus while force feedback is applied through three rigid bars connected to its tip. An additional dial and button box is used to select surgical instruments and to control the view to the simulation. The closing and opening of the surgical forceps and scissors is controlled by a switch on the stylus. The force feedback produced by three electrical actuators simulates the compliance of the eye sclera during its deformation. Once the knife penetrates the sclera, viscous resistance is felt in the cutting direction and compliant resistance is simulated in the direction orthogonal to the cutting direction. Force feedback is zeroed once interaction with the virtual eye ends.

10.1.5. Rehabilitation

Patients who have been disabled following accidents or surgery usually undergo a rehabilitation treatment designed to restore some of their lost sensory–motor capabilities. Within the context of this book, we are interested in the use of haptic feedback in the rehabilitation of the body mobility and force exertion capabilities. Brown and her colleagues at Dartmouth College [1993] describe a prototype exoskeleton used as a prosthetic device by patients who have lost muscular control of their hand. As illustrated in Figure 10.9, this device consists of a sensorized aluminum structure attached to the back of the hand wearing a Lycra glove. Hand position is measured by a PC host, which receives data from several rotary potentiometers integrated in the exoskeleton. Five cables routed to the palmar side of the hand are used to close the index and thumb in a pinching grasp. These cables are routed through low-friction Teflon tubing to five dc motors located on the patient's forearm. The motors, when energized, cause finger flexion, and restoring springs in the exoskeleton pull the fingers to a neutral position once the actuators are deenergized. Initial tests showed good range of motion, with the thumb being able to oppose the index and middle fingers. Although the system had good repeatability, calibration was needed for every new patient. Furthermore, cable static friction and the exoskeleton weight were judged to be too large, calling for prototype redesign.

Another computerized system designed for the rehabilitation of the hand was developed recently by Burdea et al. [1996]. This *unified* system consists of hand diagnosis and hand rehabilitation subsystems controlled by a single Sun 10-51 workstation. As illustrated in Figure 10.10, the diagnosis subsystem incorporates standard electromechanical measurement instruments, such as dynamometer, pinchmeter, and goniometer that are sampled by the host computer through an A/D/A board. A novel tactile measurement glove is also interfaced to the same board. This glove prototype consists of a DataGlove retrofitted with 16 ultrasonic force sensors (see Fig. 6.3) that measure the patient's grasping force distribution [1] [Burdea et al, 1995b]. Real-time force exertion and range-of-motion measurements are stored by an Oracle-based

---

[1] This glove was not used in later clinical trials due to large electronic noise that made calibration difficult.

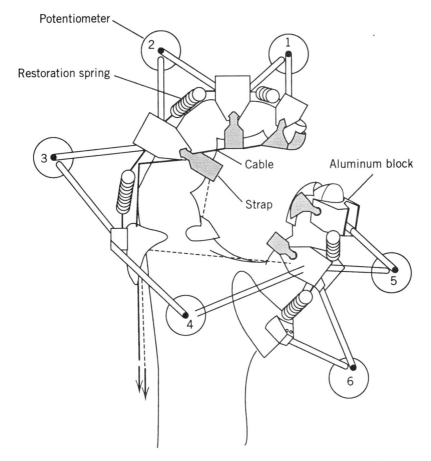

Potentiometer

Restoration spring

Cable   Aluminum block

Strap

Figure 10.9   The exoskeleton prototype for control of paralyzed hands. Reprinted by permission from Brown et al. [1993]. © 1993 IEEE.

patient's database [Oracle Inc., 1995]. A window-based GUI allows the physician or hand therapist to view force-and-displacement graphs and obtain other pertinent statistics (such as mean and standard deviation of the measured variable). The rehabilitation subsystem uses a Rutgers Master I to provide force feedback to the patient exercising in a virtual environment. A WorldToolKit package [Sense8 Co., 1995] was used to model three typical hand exercises, namely hand squeezing a rubber ball, a peg-in-hole insertion, and a Digi-Key exercise. The Digi-Key set contains five color-coded hand-held devices with four elastic springs each [North Coast Medical Inc., 1994]. Color Plate 12 shows a virtual Digi-Key that has been modified to provide resistance to the thumb instead of the little finger. This was required because the Rutgers Master I feedback actuators oppose the thumb, index, middle, and ring fingers. The same Oracle database is used to collect data during the rehabilitation exercise (such as number of squeezes, maximum force, etc.). This data can then

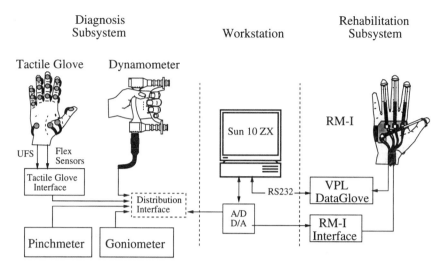

Figure 10.10   Unified system for hand diagnosis and rehabilitation. Reprinted from Burdea et al. [1996].

be used by the hand therapist to change the exercise difficulty as a function of the patient's rehabilitation progress.

Rehabilitation exercises using a VR simulation are by no means limited to the hand. Hogan and colleagues at MIT [Hogan et al., 1993] developed the "MIT–MANUS" workstation for manual therapy and training. The system consists of a five-degree-of-freedom robot manipulator and two PCs used for control and visual/auditory feedback to the patient. The robot has a custom brace which attaches to the patient's wrist, allowing both translation in a horizontal plane and rotation of the wrist (extension, abduction and pronation). A magnetic safety lock allows the patient to pull free from the manipulator without external assistance. The close proximity and interaction between the patient and robot made necessary an impedance control scheme that made the robot appear compliant. Recent clinical trials at Burke Rehabilitation Hospital (White Plains, NY) [Krebs et al., 1996] used this system for the neuro rehabilitation of patients with a paralyzed upper limb following stroke. The robot assisted and guided the patient's arm in performing a series of tasks such as, drawing circles, stars, squares, or diamonds. The robot trajectory was fed back visually to the patient and the technician conducting the trials. The trajectory and velocity profiles of the patient's wrist were used to objectively quantify the degree of recovery. Initial results showed faster motor rehabilitation for patients using the MIT–MANUS system in addition to conventional therapy, compared to patients that had only conventional therapy.

Takeda and Tsutsul [1993] at Nagasaki Institute of Applied Science have developed an orthosis for the exercising of the patient's upper arm. The device consists of a sensorized structure containing both position sensors (rotary encoders) and force-feedback actuators. As illustrated in Figure 10.11 [Takeda and Tsutsul, 1993], the actuators are light pneumatic muscles, which contract when pressurized. Two such

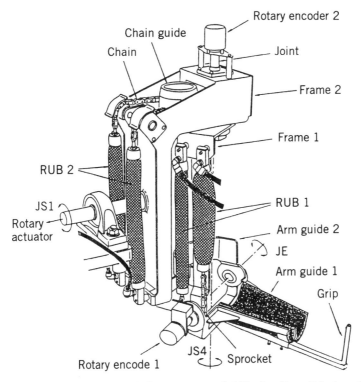

Figure 10.11 The prototype orthosis for upper arm rehabilitation. From Takeda and Tsutsul [1993]. Reprinted by permission of the ASME.

actuators (RUB 1 in the figure) working in opposition, control the elbow flexion–extension through a chain transmission mechanism. A similar actuator pair (RUB 2) is used for the lateral–median shoulder rotation. These actuators provide a force up to 260 kgf when pressurized to 5 kgf/cm^2. During the rehabilitation session, the patient places his arm on the orthosis arm guide and grasps its handle. A virtual environment consisting of a room with virtual exercising equipment (spring, dumbbell, etc.) is seen by the patient through a pair of head-mounted displays. The orthosis position is mapped by the computer running the simulation to a virtual upper body located in the exercising room. The patient controls the forward or reverse motion of the virtual body through a foot pedal. Force feedback is provided once collision is detected between the body arm extremity and the virtual exercising equipment. The dumbbell weight and spring compliance can be changed in order to increase or decrease the exercise difficulty. The haptic interface is lightweight, safe, provides a large range of motion and significant feedback-force levels. Unfortunately, the known nonlinearity and hysteresis associated with pneumatic muscle actuators remain a problem.

Another orthosis-based system, developed by Durfee and Goldfarb [1993] at Massachusetts Institute of Technology, is intended for paraplegic patients. Such individuals have lost their gait (walking) capability. Electrical stimulation used to restore gait has the disadvantage of induced leg-muscle fatigue. The system developed by Durfee and Goldfarb, called controlled-brake orthosis (CBO) uses an energized lower-limb support to reduce muscle stimulation cycles and fatigue. As illustrated in Figure 10.12, the CBO consists of an aluminum structure with hip and knee joints incorporating magnetic particle brakes (see Fig. 3.6). The knee and hip flexion–extension is constrained by controlled braking while the hip abduction–adduction is a free motion. As explained in Chapter 3, magnetic particle brakes have an excellent power-to-weight ratio. This explains why the hip brake weighing only 235 g produces a resistive torque of 29 Nm (256 lb-in.), whereas the knee brake produces a torque of 2.8 Nm (25 lb-in.) and weighs 335 g. The total CBO structure weighs 13.5 lb, approximately the same as commercial long legged braces. Durfee and Goldfarb report on a patient who could stand indefinitely using the CBO with the knee joint locked. With muscle stimulation alone, the same patient could only stand approximately 26 min. A subsequent study by Goldfarb and Durfee [1996] showed an 85% stimulation cycle

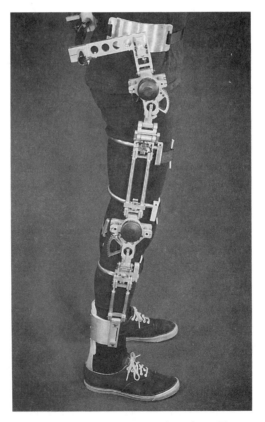

Figure 10.12   Controlled-brake orthosis for paraplegic patients. Photograph courtesy of Professor William Durfee, University of Minnesota.

for quadriceps during gait with electrical stimulation and no CBO. For CBO-assisted gait, the quadriceps were stimulated only 10% of the time (during swing motion). Furthermore, there was a significant reduction in stride-to-stride trajectory variation when CBO was used. Thus the patient could not just walk longer, but also more evenly.

10.2. ENTERTAINMENT APPLICATIONS

Another application domain for haptic feedback devices is VR entertainment. This is a multibillion dollar industry, which has traditionally used visual (graphics) and sound effects in response to the user's (player's) position input. At the present time, force and tactile feedback are being added to various video games to enhance their interactivity and realism. Haptic feedback, which was previously found only in expensive location-based entertainment or video arcades, is now starting to be incorporated in home-based systems too. Other kinds of entertainment benefiting from the use of force and tactile feedback are music, virtual excursions, and cybersex.

10.2.1. Haptic Feedback for Virtual Reality Arcades

Location-based entertainment (LBE) centers utilizing VR simulations have been in existence since 1990. Among the pioneers are the BattleTech Center in Chicago [Virtual World Entertainment, 1991] and the Legend Quest Center in England, which received the *CyberEdge Journal* 1992 VR Product of the Year Award [*CyberEdge Journal*, 1993a]. The game was played on a Virtuality Model 1000CS platform manufactured by W Industries Ltd. (now renamed Virtuality Entertainment Ltd.), integrating a head-tracked HMD, a three-dimensional mouse, and a 25-MHz Amiga computer. In 1992, W Industries obtained a patent on a sensorized glove used with Virtuality platforms [Holmes, 1992]. As illustrated in Figure 10.13, the glove has, on the back of each finger, flexible extensions that house position sensors. A number of ring-shaped finger attachments allow the passage of pressurized air to tactile actuators located on the palmar side. These feedback actuators are flexible membranes that are pressurized and vented through a computer-controlled valve assembly. Tactile feedback is provided when the player interacts with virtual objects during the game.

Another class of LBE game platforms incorporating haptic feedback are racing and flight simulators. One example is the Virtua Racing recently commercialized by SEGA of America. As shown in Color Plate 13, the driver's seat is located in front of a large monitor showing texture-mapped real-time graphics. Under the screen are located the steering wheel, stereo speakers, gear shift, and pedals for acceleration and braking. Haptic feedback is provided by the steering wheel, which produces resistive forces. These simulate the sluggishness of steering through mud, the shock of collisions with obstacles, or the centrifugal forces associated with high-speed turns. The coupling of high-quality graphics and haptic feedback made Virtua Racing quite a captivating experience for the author.

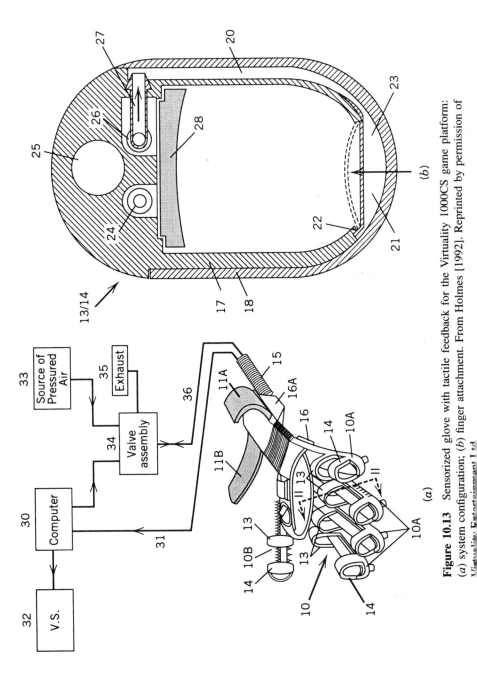

Figure 10.13 Sensorized glove with tactile feedback for the Virtuality 1000CS game platform: (a) system configuration; (b) finger attachment. From Holmes [1992]. Reprinted by permission of Virtuality Entertainment Ltd.

Flight simulators are another widespread type of LBE video games. Older platforms had rudimentary haptic feedback in the form of vibrating seats or resistive joysticks. Newer hardware attempts to replicate forces experienced during high-speed accelerations and turns. Such g forces are obtained with compact motion platforms designed for single or dual players. One example is the Hornet 1 simulator produced by Magic Edge Inc. [Robertson, 1994], which uses a three-degree-of-freedom hydraulic platform. The cockpit capsule supported by the motion platform has a pitch angle between $+45°$ and $-25°$ and a roll of $\pm60°$. The capsule also incorporates flight controls, surround-sound, and a 39×29 in. video screen. Six such simulators are interfaced with a single high-performance computer producing texture-mapped graphics. This interconnection allows multiplayer aerial dogfights.

Hydraulic motion platforms, such as the one used by the Hornet-1 simulator, have the disadvantage of high operating costs (due to large power consumption), expensive installation, and potential safety risks (due to high-pressure oil leaks) [Moog Inc., 1994]. An alternative is to use electropneumatic platforms that are clean, easy to install, and have much smaller operating costs, allowing for a faster investment payback. Such a platform is the Virtual Motion produced by Denne Developments Ltd. As illustrated in Color Plate 14, this simulator has a three-degree-of-freedom platform supporting a player on a surfboard. Its neutral posture can be accommodated without energizing the actuators. Motion effects such as vibrations and jolts of force felt when riding a virtual wave are produced by the three PemRAM platform actuators (see Fig. 4.22). By changing his body posture, the player can change the perspective of the simulation projected on his HMD, as well as the spatial orientation of a virtual surfboard.

10.2.2. Haptic Feedback for Home-Based Systems

The reduction in hardware costs has allowed the introduction in early 1995 of the first home-based immersive VR video games. These use low-cost HMDs and open-loop joysticks measuring the user's hand position. Force-feedback joysticks have previously been too expensive for the commercial video-game market. Recently EXOS Co. [1995b] has announced the PowerStick, a joystick capable of producing compliance, damping, and vibration effects. Companies such as Sierra On-Line, Microsoft, and Looking Glass are said to be developing games using the PowerStick which will cost about $100.

Another low-priced haptic feedback device for video-game use is the "Interactor" manufactured by Aura Systems [Long and Alexander, 1995]. As illustrated in Figure 10.14, the system consists of a plastic vest weighing approximately 4 lb and an electronics interface module that accepts input from a video-game sound track. Various tactile-feedback sensations are produced by a 50-W speaker actuator integrated in the vest. The interface module provides a power source for the vest, a signal filter (range 35–55 Hz), and amplitude adjustment for various feedback effects [*CyberEdge Journal*, 1994]. The interface also incorporates a channel-selection switch, which, in the future, will allow two players to participate (tactually) in the same video game [Lovett, 1994]. The low cost of the Interactor ($99) has attracted the attention of sev-

Figure 10.14 The Interactor tactile feedback vest. Photograph courtesy of Aura Systems Co.

eral game developers, such as Acclaim Entertainment, which has already integrated the vest with the *Mortal Kombat II* game. *Doom* is another well-known video game title using the Interactor.

Sound-based tactile feedback is also produced by the *ThunderSeat* manufactured by Thunderseat Technologies Co. [*VR World*, 1995]. This is a molded-plastic bucket seat with a 100-W subwoofer built into its base. Its retail price is approximately $160, excluding optional side consoles and keyboard holder. Interfacing with a PC-based video game requires a sound card and an amplifier.

10.2.3. Other Entertainment Applications

Virtual reality technology has benefited many other forms of entertainment, such as interactive art exhibits [Krueger, 1992], virtual museums [Miller et al., 1992], or virtual music [Sato et al., 1992]. Cadoz [1992] studied the integration of haptic feedback in simulations involving virtual musical instruments. Later on Gillespie and Cutkosky [1993] developed a model for the simulation of a grand piano using a synthesizer keyboard with haptic feedback. As illustrated in Figure 10.15, a single-key motorized keyboard was constructed using electromechanical voice-coil actuators.

The haptic keyboard was subsequently interfaced with a 486 PC through a motor control card. The keyboard was modeled using piece-wise continuous ordinary differential equations incorporating tuning parameters in the form of two virtual springs. The spring stiffness could be set up in software up to 100 N/m, allowing for a more natural simulation.

The last entertainment application using haptic feedback to be discussed here is *cybersex*, a term associated with computer-aided sexual gratification. While the soci-

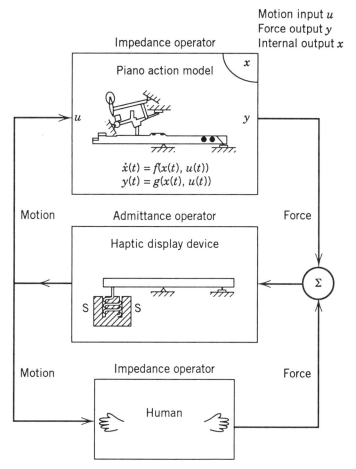

Figure 10.15 Virtual piano simulation with haptic feedback. From Gillespie and Cutkosky [1993]. Reprinted by permission of the ASME.

ological and psychological implications of cybersex are evident and quite important, the discussion here is limited to the underlying technology. Kirk Woolford at the Koln Academy of Media Arts [Woolford, 1994] has developed two tactile-feedback body-suits (for male and female partners) which he subsequently demonstrated in Paris in front of 300 people [Scallie, 1994]. The bodysuits, called "CyberSM III" were connected to two SGI graphics workstations over the ethernet. It was thus possible for two participants to experience intimate tactile vibratory stimulation transmitted over the network. What disturbs this author is that the bodysuits were also able to inflict pain through a 220-V electrical discharge.

10.3. TELEROBOTIC APPLICATIONS

In Chapter 4, we showed how robots can be used as haptic feedback devices in the form of robotic shape displays. A robot would move a turret and oppose the user's hand motion to simulate obstacles present in the virtual world [McNeely, 1993]. Another important application area is telerobotics, where haptic feedback can enhance the operator's telepresence, can overcome stability problems (due to arm dynamics or time delay), and can improve overall task performance (reducing error rates and completion times). Virtual haptic feedback can also help program the robot arm locally (off-line programming) or at a distance (teleprogramming).

10.3.1. Operator Telepresence

In a telerobotic system, the operator executes a task at a distance with the aid of a robot located in a remote or adverse environment. Telerobotics is currently being used in many fields including space repair (using the space shuttle manipulator), undersea or hostage rescue operations, or the maintenance of hot nuclear facilities. In all these applications, the operator needs to feel present at the remote location where the robot interacts with its surroundings. Thus, visual, auditory, and force-feedback information are essential in the successful completion of the remote task.

Force feedback is provided to the operator (user) through hand masters of the type previously described in Chapters 4 and 5. Tactile feedback is also being used, an example being the space telerobotic system presently being developed at NASA Johnson Space Center [Li, 1993]. As shown in Figure 10.16, the system consists of a dual arm repair robot, a computer and a tactile feedback suit worn by the operator. Tactile sensors in the robot arm and chest skin are sampled by the computer through an A/D converter, and feedback signals sent to the operator through a D/A board. The tactile-feedback suit (manufactured by Begej Co.) consists of arrays of small pneumatic bellows located on the forearm, upper arm, chest, and abdomen. The forearm and upper arm arrays have 64 microbellows each, whereas the chest and abdomen arrays have 128 microbellows each. Each stimulator array provides remote contact geometry and force information by spatial and temporal modulation of the microbellow pressure.

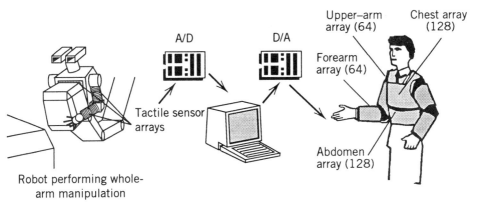

Figure 10.16 Space telerobotic application using a tactile feedback suit. Reprinted by permission from Li [1993].

10.3.2. Telerobotic System Stability

It was shown in Chapter 8 that system stability is negatively impacted by the interface dynamics (large inertia, friction, or mechanical compliance), as well as large system time delays. Robotic arm inertia, compliance, and communication delays have a similar negative effect on the stability of telerobotic systems. Underground storage tank cleanup, for example, uses longreach manipulators with long flexible links and large mass. Their large inertia prevents quick response when contact with the tank structure is detected by local (proximity or force) sensors. Such collisions can damage both the tank walls and the manipulator, requiring expensive repair. Anderson and Davies [1994] at Sandia National Laboratories, developed a VR simulation in which virtual force fields around objects are used to prevent such collisions. Figure 10.17 illustrates this approach. The remote cleaning robot and surrounding tank

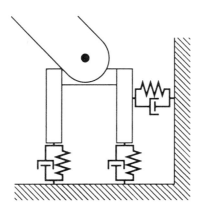

Figure 10.17 Utilizing virtual force barriers to prevent collisions when using a robotic arm with large inertia. Reprinted by permission from Anderson and Davies [1994]. © 1994 IEEE.

are first modeled graphically and integrated in the Sequential Modular Architecture for Robotics and Teleoperation (SMART) software environment also developed at Sandia. An Obstacle module added to SMART attaches virtual spring–damper combinations around the robot tool (in this case a gripper). The robot and tank models are decomposed in graphic primitives, which are then used to detect collisions. In such an event the spring–damper combinations provide repelling forces in the proximity of objects being protected. The researchers report experiments using a Puma 560 slave robot and a one degree-of-freedom master device with force feedback. When using a 58 convex-object virtual world the robot could track a planar surface smoothly, without collisions or chattering. Current work is extending the virtual force algorithm from just the tool to the whole robot arm. This will allow teleoperation in cluttered environments where arm (not just tool) collisions are likely.

Telerobotic systems where the distance between the master and slave is large (such as for orbital repair applications) are operating with large communication delays (of a second of more). As discussed previously, force feedback in the presence of large time delays leads to system instabilities. Kotoku [1992] attempted to solve this problem through the use of a virtual slave arm. As illustrated in Figure 10.18, the operator position commands arrive from the master arm to the slave arm with some communication delay (in this case 0.5 sec). The same master input is used by the computer running the simulation to move a virtual model of the remote slave manipulator. The virtual slave arm responds to the operator input without time delay. Contact forces are computed whenever collisions are detected between the virtual slave and the model of the remote environment. These forces are then fed back (again without time delay) to the operator through the master arm.

Initial experiments were conducted for a simple planar task in which the operator was asked to trace a rigid barrier while pushing with a constant force. The contact was considered frictionless and the remote slave was modeled as a point object, so that contact forces were always normal to the barrier surface. Subjects carried out the

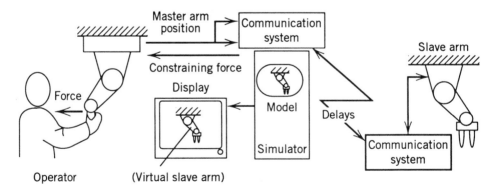

Figure 10.18 Telerobotic system using a virtual slave arm to overcome force-feedback instabilities due to transmission delays. Reprinted by permission from Kotoku [1992]. © 1992 IEEE.

task observing the virtual slave arm (and its modeled contact forces) on the graphics display and the real slave on a video monitor. The master arm trajectory was sent to the remote slave arm with a 0.5-sec transmission delay. Contact forces were fed back to the subjects in half of the trials. Results showed that the addition of force feedback produced a more stable control. Furthermore, the movement of the slave was three times faster when force feedback was present. When the master arm provided no force feedback subjects moved slower, because they used only the graphics display to gauge the contact force.

The approach developed by Kotoku [1992], although promising, suffers from several drawbacks. First, the virtual models of the slave and remote environment are oversimplified (planar surface, punctiform robot, nonfriction contact). Second, realistic tasks are more complex and cannot be performed under these simplified conditions. Third, the approach will fail if the robot and its remote environment are not modeled accurately. Thus, it will fail in unstructured remote environments where changes can occur randomly, and cannot be modeled in advance. Rosenberg [1993a], proposed an alternative method for solving the problem of teleoperation with time delay. He introduced the concept of *virtual fixtures*, which are abstract sensorial data overlaid on top of the remote workspace. More precisely:

> When overlaid on to a workspace, the fixtures only interact with the user and not with the workspace. Thus fixtures can occupy the same physical space as objects in the workspace. This means that the workspace geometry imposes no constraints upon the placement or configuration of virtual fixtures. What is more, virtual fixturing has no mass, no physical or mechanical constraints, requires no machining time or maintenance, can be easily prototyped and modified.
>
> —Rosenberg [1993a]

Later on Rosenberg [1993b, 1994] used virtual fixtures to enhance the performance of a peg-in-hole telerobotic task. Subjects donned a dual arm upper-body exoskeleton while controlling a remote robot arm. Visual information from the remote task was presented to the operator through a HMD. The robot end effector motion was scaled to match the operator's hand motion, but no force feedback was provided by the exoskeleton. A *fixture board* made of plastic was placed in front of the operator. Thus the subjects did not see the fixture board (due to the HMD), but felt it as real force feedback coming from the remote site. The three fixtures used in the experimental study are illustrated in Figure 10.19, but they could not be seen by the subjects. For each virtual fixture, the telerobotic task was executed without time delay, with a 250-msec time delay, and with a 450-msec time delay between master and slave. The performance degradation was measured as a percentage increase in movement time under time delay conditions, compared to the case when no delay existed. Results showed that movement time increased as much as 45% when no virtual fixtures were present and the time delay was 450 msec, compared to nondelayed teleoperation. Fixture 4 and especially fixture 6 had a beneficial effect by reducing this difference to only 3%. Thus the enhanced localization or guidance provided by the virtual fixtures succeeded in overcoming the adverse effects of communication time delay on task performance.

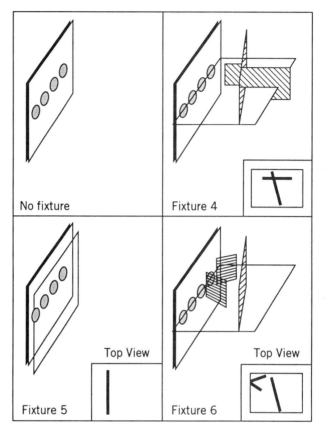

Figure 10.19   Virtual fixtures used in a peg-in-hole teleoperation task. From Rosenberg [1993b]. Reprinted by permission of the ASME.

10.3.3. Robot Teleprogramming

Virtual fixtures are also used in a form of telerobotics called *teleprogramming*, in which the master station (arm and computer) programs the slave robot by sending high-level commands, such as "move to location A," "pick part," and so on. In this way, it is possible to cope with low-bandwidth communication lines and with time delays. Sayers and Paul [1993, 1994] at the University of Pennsylvania developed a teleprogramming system in which the master arm is a Puma 250 robot equipped with six-axis wrist force sensor. The user applies forces on the robot arm, which are interpreted by the system as input, and the arm position response provides haptic feedback. A graphics workstation displays a virtual slave which responds to the user's input, as well as *synthetic fixtures* overlaid on the same graphics. These active fixtures are intended to guide the user in the teleoperation task by increasing precision and speed and decreasing the effect of uncertainties in the world model-and-command process.

The fixtures, such as point fixture, surface fixture, or face fixture are created automatically by the system and activated based on the location of the virtual slave end effector. They appear first visually in the simulation to provide a cue as to the system interpretation of the user's command. If the user moves the virtual robot closer to a fixture, the magnitude of the force cue increases, thus guiding the operator. If the end effector is closer to a fixture than the master arm positional uncertainty, then the system commands the remote slave to move in contact with the surface of interest. Certain fixtures attract the end effector (and are colored green on the screen), whereas others repel the virtual robot (and are colored red). The *face fixture*, for example, has a central attracting region, surrounded by a repelling region corresponding to the facet edge. In this way, the user is pushed away from uncertain contact at the edge of a facet and toward a more certain contact at the center of that facet. Color Plate 15 illustrates this concept for a virtual slave moving about two boxes. As the end effector approaches the top facet of the smaller box, the attracting synthetic fixture is activated. It rotates the end effector and brings it in contact with the top surface. A second face fixture is activated as the user translates the robot toward the larger box. Once he moves the robot away from the top surface and down to the corner between the two boxes, a repelling (red) fixture pushes the robot away from the edge of the top facet. Three face fixtures are activated once the end effector moves downward and slides on the bottom surface. Sayers and Paul [1993] explain the advantage of using synthetic fixtures as follows:

> ... by providing force clues which are task and configuration dependent, the system can take a very active role in assisting the operator to complete a given task. The advantage of such an approach is that it avoids the need for exact force simulation while increasing the amount of information available to the operator through force clues. The disadvantage is that it requires the system to have an understanding of the task.
>
> —Sayers and Paul [1993]

10.3.4. Teleoperation in the "Nano World"

The last force-feedback telerobotic application to be discussed here is the Nanomanipulator developed by Taylor and his colleagues at the University of North Carolina at Chapel Hill [Taylor et al., 1993; Taylor, 1994]. This is a telemanipulation system consisting of a force-reflecting Argonne III master manipulator controlling a scanning tunneling microscope (STM) tip. As illustrated in Figure 10.20, the STM consists of a piezoelectric positioning element supporting a metal tip in close proximity (a few tens of a nanometer) to the sample surface. The surface profile (Z height) is determined indirectly based on the tunneling current from the tip to the sample. Thus, unlike other microscopes, the STM data is an elevation map, rather than a projected image. A Pixel Planes 5 computer [Division Ltd., 1993c] is used to visualize the sample surface and render it as a virtual image displayed on the user's HMD. As the user moves the Argonne Arm, an icon is moved above the surface image. A linear restoring force is applied at the hand grip in the Z direction, allowing the user to feel the surface bumps and valleys. These feedback forces are simulated as spring forces

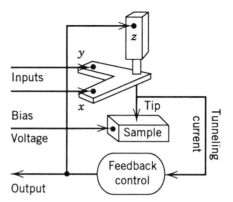

Figure 10.20 The scanning tunneling microscope and feedback control. Reprinted by permission from Taylor et al. [1993]. © 1993, Association for Computing Machinery.

based on the hand grip height at a given (X,Y) surface location. Color Plate 16 shows the user moving the STM above the sample surface by changing the position of the Argonne Arm. The yellow patches correspond to electrical pulses fired by the user by squeezing the master hand trigger. These pulses are used to actively modify the surface of the sample at a nanometer scale!

10.4. MILITARY APPLICATIONS

The end of the cold war resulted in tremendous downsizing budgetary pressures on the military. At the same time, the need for training became greater owing to increased complexity in weaponry and military tactics. Thus it became impractical to have simulators that are hardware-designed for a single type of tank, aircraft, submarine, and so on, owing to their rate of obsolescence. The multisensorial immersion capability of VR, coupled with its programming flexibility, have thus attracted the attention of military planners. In the early 1980s the Defense Advanced Research Projects Agency (DARPA) funded the development of the Simulation Network (SIMNET) [McDonough, 1993] for tank crew training. This distributed simulation could accommodate hundreds of tank crews simultaneously, training over virtual battlefields (both in Europe and the United States). In the meantime, the Air Force had been using traditional civilian-type flight simulators. These multimillion-dollar systems consist of a large back-projection dome, the crew station, instructor station, and simulation computer [Vince, 1994]. The whole structure is supported by a six-degree-of-freedom hydraulic motion platform that is used to provide motion cues. Acceleration and deceleration, for example, are simulated by tilting the platform backward or forward, respectively.

10.4.1. Fighter Aircraft Trainers

Single-seat military aircraft are better suited for smaller simulators, which replicate the reduced dimensions of a fighter aircraft cockpit. Haas and Heettinger [1993] at the Armstrong Laboratory of the Wright-Patterson Air Force Base are developing an F16 simulator using fusion interfaces. As shown in Figure 10.21, this enhanced-reality simulator consists of the airplane cockpit and surrounding back-projection screen. The pilot trainee wears a special see-through helmet that allows the superposition of data strings over the image displayed on the surrounding screen. Haptic feedback is obtained naturally by handling the cockpit controls and flight control stick. The control stick provides force feedback to respond to centrifugal forces when the airplane is in a rolling motion. Recent human-factor studies used the above system to quantify the benefits of a haptically augmented aircraft control stick during instrumented landings [Brickman et al., 1996]. Experimental results showed increased landing accuracy, reduced number of crashes, and reduced subjective workload, compared to simulations using a control stick with no force feedback. The haptically augmented stick was most useful during landings in turbulent weather.

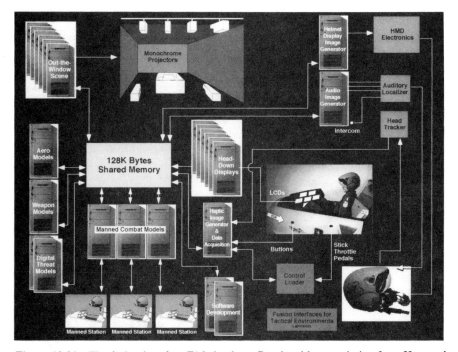

Figure 10.21   The fusion interface F16 simulator. Reprinted by permission from Haas and Heettinger [1993].

Providing natural haptic feedback through real cockpit controls (as opposed to virtual knobs and dials) has also been the design solution for the Real and Virtual Environment Configurable Training Aid (RAVECTA) system developed by Kalawsky [1993] at British Aerospace. As seen in Color Plate 17, the pilot wears an immersive HMD augmented by a pair of TV cameras. The pilot sees the cockpit interior and feels natural tactile feedback whenever he manipulates the controls. A nonstandard chroma processing is applied whenever the pilot looks up and through the windshield. Its blue color is detected by the camera and triggers the superimposition of a virtual image over the image showing the cockpit screen. This improves the simulation realism, while at the same time reducing simulator system complexity.

10.4.2. Individual Soldier Simulator

Another direction in recent military simulation tactics is the insertion of individual soldiers into the virtual battlefield. This is especially necessary for urban warfare and special forces training where there is great mission variability and need for intensive training. One example is the Virtual Stinger Trainer developed in Holland by TNO Physics and Electronics Laboratory [Jense, 1993]. The soldier trainee wearing a HMD held a real-size plastic mockup of a Stinger rocket launcher. Haptic feedback was provided naturally by the switches and trigger incorporated in the weapon mockup. A three-dimensional mouse integrated in the support handle was used for target tracking and firing.

Later, Pratt and his colleagues at the Naval Postgraduate School [1994] in collaboration with SARCOS Co. and the University of Pennsylvania demonstrated an *individual port* (I-Port) distributed interactive simulation for infantry and special forces training. As illustrated in Color Plate 18, the trainee wears a sensorized exoskeleton which measures the upper body position in real time. Head position is obtained through the tracker incorporated in an HMD, which displays the battlefield scene. A mobility platform with a seat and two pedals is used to control the direction and speed of motion in the virtual environment. Direction of motion is obtained based on the seat swivel angle, while speed is based on the user's pedaling velocity. Haptic feedback is provided by the pedal resistance (similar to common exercising bicycles). The physical interface hardware (exoskeleton, mobility platform, HMD) is controlled by a VME-based real-time computer called the Individual Soldier Mobility System Controller. The trainee's actions (walk, run, signal, fire, etc.) are mapped to those of a virtual soldier displayed in the simulation. The soldier's virtual model is based on the Jack animated articulated figure [Badler et al., 1993]. Simulation computations are distributed among several computers interconnected by an ethernet and using a combination of point-to-point Transmission Control Protocol/Internet Protocol (TCP/IP) and broadcast User Datagram Protocol (UDP/IP) communications [Hunt, 1992]. The complexity of the human geometrical model and actions require a significant amount of network traffic (equivalent to three simulated aircraft or eight tanks) [Pratt et al., 1994]. This limits the number of I-Ports that can be integrated over a given network.

10.5. CONCLUSIONS

This chapter presented a number of simulations using haptic feedback in application areas ranging from medicine and entertainment to telerobotics and the military. The addition of force and tactile feedback clearly benefited VR simulations through increased realism and task complexity. The above application list is by no means exhaustive. Other potential domains are education, business, architectural design, and mechanical design. The spectrum of VR simulations using haptic feedback will increase as the underlying technology matures and its price becomes more affordable. The future of haptic feedback for VR simulations is the subject of the next (and last) chapter of this book.

CHAPTER 11

THE FUTURE

This book presented various aspects of force and tactile feedback incorporated in today's VR simulations, from hardware and software to human factors and applications. It is now time to take a look at the foreseeable future of this technology. Major improvements in feedback actuators, sensors, and computing hardware will lead to miniaturization, less cumbersome haptic interface devices, and an increase in the user's safety and freedom of motion. These improvements should in turn lead to more natural, realistic, and useful simulations. Thus the last chapter of this book is dedicated to novel actuator technology, haptic feedback suits, and large-scale simulations that incorporate force and tactile feedback.

11.1. NOVEL ACTUATORS

The review of haptic feedback actuators presented in Chapter 3 underscored the limitations of the present technology. There is a clear need for a small, powerful, responsive, clean, silent, and safe actuator. Researchers are currently investigating a number of novel technologies that may result in such an actuator. These new technologies include metal hydrades [Shimizu et al., 1994], piezoelectric actuators [NASA, 1994], magnetostrictive actuators [Brimhall and Hasser, 1994] and polymeric gels [Brock, 1991; Shahinpoor, 1994]. Although present prototypes lack performance, it is important to discuss them here, in order to project what may very well become a revolution in haptic interface design.

11.1.1. Metal Hydrades

Shimizu and colleagues [1993a,b] at Hokkaido University have looked at metal hydrades as a possible power source for force-feedback devices. A metal hydrade is an alloy that has the ability to release large amounts of hydrogen when heated. When the alloy is cooled (below 300°C), the reaction reverses itself, and the hydrogen is absorbed back into the metal hydrate. Shimizu had the idea to enclose the metal hydrate in a small container that incorporates two Peltier heat pumps. It was then possible to control the pressure of the released gas as a function of the voltage supplied to the Peltier elements. This voltage in turn was controlled by a computer based on data from a thermocouple sensor placed inside the container. The capsule containing the metal hydrate was then connected through a steel tube to a metal bellow (linear) actuator, as shown in Figure 11.1a.

The overall weight of this actuator is relatively small (about 300 g), but its force output is 20 kgf [Shimizu et al., 1993a]. This large force (and force-to-weight ratio) is due to the large diameter bellow (20 mm) and the large hydrogen gas pressure. Additional advantages stem from the quietness of this actuator and its relative simplicity. The drawbacks are small actuator displacement for its dimensions (50-mm translation with precompression) and small speed (9 mm/sec). The actuator was subsequently integrated into the force-feedback device shown in Figure 11.1b. It consisted of an exoskeleton attached to the user's arm and forearm, and a grip handle, with the actuator placed diagonally between the two attachments. When the metal hydrade was heated the bellow was pressurized and the user's wrist pushed downward. Shimizu's report on human-factor studies using this experimental system showed good force discrimination [Shimizu et al., 1993b]. Later, two metal hydrade actuators were integrated in a single elbow exoskeleton [Shimizu et al., 1994]. Since the actuators were acting in opposition to each other, it was possible to vary the interface apparent compliance and to have a faster response.

11.1.2. Piezoelectric Actuators

Another class of actuators that may one day be used as part of haptic interfaces are piezoelectric motors. Schadebrodt and Salomon [1990] at AEG (Germany) developed an extremely compact and light rotary piezoelectric motor. As illustrated in Figure 11.2, the motor consists of a disk-shaped stator pressed against a laminated disk rotor. The stator is constructed of small elastic piezoelectric elements that oscillate in a state of resonance. These high-frequency oscillations produce a micro-slipping motion at the contact surface with the rotor. This results in a torque-to-speed ratio similar to that of dc shunt motors, with large stall torques and zero torque at high rotating speeds. Overall, piezoelectric motors have a 10-fold higher torque compared with conventional motors of the same volume, have very little inertia and high controllability, and are compact. They can weigh as little as 6 to 8 g, with power-to-weight and torque-to-mass ratios of 225 W/kg and 70 N-m/kg, respectively [Hasser, 1995a].

The ability of piezoelectric material to oscillate when electrically excited has been recently used for the design of a direct-drive robotic actuator [NASA, 1994]. The prototype, developed by Bonnevile Scientific Inc. under contract for NASA, is illustrated in Figure 11.3. It consists of two piezoelectric rotator actuators and two piezoelectric clamps that are assembled inside two finger segments. The two clamps,

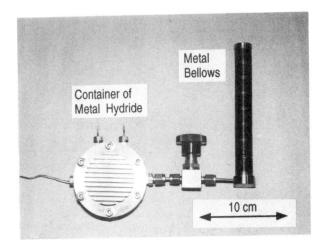

(a)

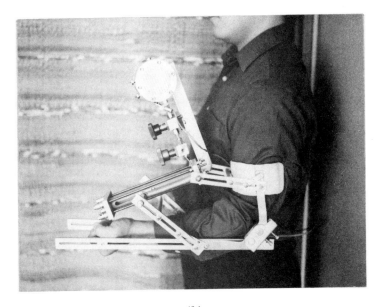

(b)

Figure 11.1   Force feedback interface using metal hydrade actuators: (a) actuator prototype. Reprinted by permission from Shimizu et al. [1993b]. © 1993 IEEE; (b) exoskeleton attached to the user's elbow. Photographs courtesy of Hokkaido Universiy.

Mechanical output: $\omega \cdot T$ (W)

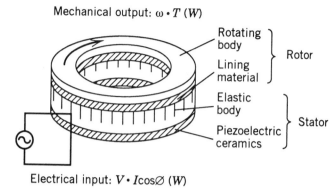

Electrical input: $V \cdot I\cos\varnothing$ (W)

Figure 11.2 The construction of a rotary piezoelectric actuator. From PCIM Staff [1987]. Reprinted by permission of Intertec International Inc.

when energized, press a concave shoe against the finger-joint shaft, while the two actuator beams push against the rotator. The combination of the small back-and-forth motion of the rotator and the clamping produces a rotation of finger segment 2 away from finger segment 1. Although the overall assembly is very light (approximately 10 g), its speed and power-to-weight ratios are large (18 cm/sec and 460 W/kg, respectively) [Hasser, 1995a]. Eventually, such an actuator could be miniaturized and placed at the finger joints of a hand master haptic interface.

11.1.3. Magnetostrictive Actuators

Whereas piezoelectric materials change dimensions when subjected to electrical voltages, magnetostrictive ones expand or shrink when immersed in strong magnetic fields. Such a material is Terfenol-D, which has an order of magnitude larger strain than that of available piezoelectric materials [Hasser, 1995a]. Brimhall and Hasser [1994] have proposed a linear inch-worm actuator that uses three rods of Terfenol-D. As illustrated in Figure 11.4, the magnetostrictive rods are surrounded by electric coils and placed in mechanical assemblies located coaxially with the actuator drive shaft. The upper, longer, assembly acts as a moving element, whereas the lower assemblies actuate mechanical brakes located at the motor extremities. Linear motion is created by controlling one of the brakes to clamp on the driving rod, then expanding the upper moving element, and finally clamping the second brake at the new position. At this point the upper rod retracts, and the whole assembly is ready for a new cycle. The direction of motion is determined by the sequence of braking, and linear speed is determined by the frequency of the motion cycle (brake-expand-brake).

The above design was used by Technical Research Associates to construct a magnetostrictive actuator under contract for the Air Force. The first prototype was rather bulky, owing to the large magnetic coils necessary to strain the Terfenol-D rods. It had a mass of 450 g, and a volume of $8.6\times4.5\times1.7$ cm. This earlier design was

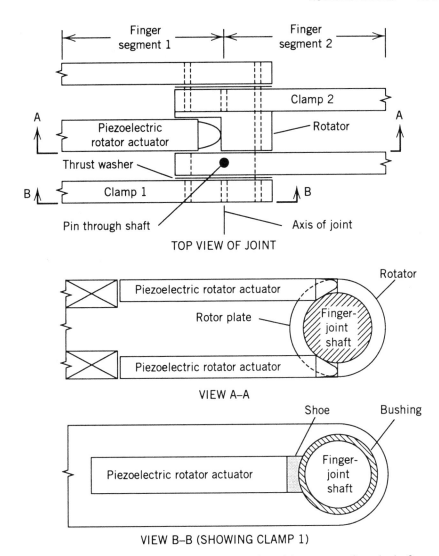

Figure 11.3 The construction of a piezoelectric direct-drive actuator for robotic fingers. Reprinted by permission from NASA [1994].

substantially improved in early 1995, resulting is a much smaller Prototype II actuator, as illustrated in Figure 11.5. Its weight was reduced to only 16 g, and its volume to $2.8 \times 2.2 \times 1.2$ cm. Its maximum force was 10 N, with a no-load maximum velocity of 14.5 cm/sec [Brimhall, 1995a]. Research is currently underway to integrate such small magnetostrictive actuators in force-reflecting hand exoskeletons [Brimhall, 1995b].

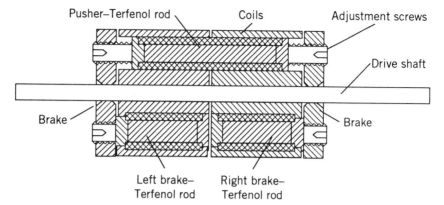

Figure 11.4 The construction of a magnetostrictive linear actuator. Reprinted by permission from Brimhall and Hasser [1994]. © SPIE.

11.1.4. Polymeric Gels

The last class of actuators to be discussed here, and probably the most speculative at this time, are polymeric gels. Such gels exhibit a quick volume change as a function of the pH of a surrounding liquid. They convert chemical into mechanical energy by shrinking up to 1000 times their original volume. Brock [1991] describes an artificial

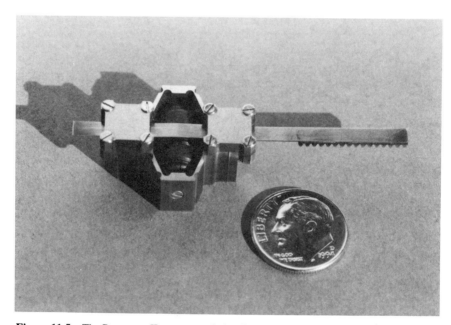

Figure 11.5 The Prototype II magnetostrictive linear actuator. Photograph courtesy of Capt. Christopher Hasser, AL/CFBA, Wright-Patterson AFB.

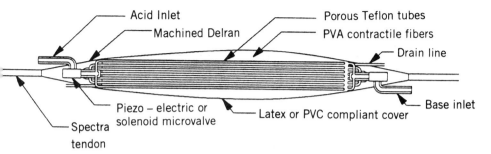

Figure 11.6 Artificial muscle made of Polyvinyl alcohol fiber bundles. Reprinted by permission from Brock [1991].

muscle using a bundle of polyvinyl alcohol (PVA) contractile fibers, as illustrated in Figure 11.6. Porous Teflon tubes surrounding the fibers allow the passage of fluids contained in a latex receptacle. Computer-controlled microvalves regulate the flow of acid and base fluids to change the pH of the fluid surrounding the PVA fibers. The advantages of such muscles are relatively large output forces (increasing with the number of fibers installed in parallel) and their long life cycle (over 65 years [Caldwell, 1992]). Disadvantages stem from the unidirectional output, low control bandwidth (< 2 Hz), and complex piping systems. Table 11.1 summarizes the characteristics of novel feedback actuators discussed in this section.

TABLE 11.1   Review of Novel Actuator Technology

Actuator Type	Power/mass (Power/volume)	Stall torque Stall force	Max. speed	Mass
Metal hydrades		196 N	1 cm/sec	300 g
Piezoelectric finger motor	225 W/kg	0.5 N-m	12.6 rad/sec	6–8 g
Magneto-strictive motor		10 N	14 cm/sec	16 g
Polymeric gels	6 W/kg			

Source: Adapted in part from Hasser [1995a].

11.2. HAPTIC FEEDBACK SUITS

The miniaturization of haptic feedback actuators will make possible the construction of light and comfortable full-body suits. These will replace present upper-body prototypes, which are very complex, heavy, and expensive. One concept for such a force amplification/feedback suit is the "Jedi" [Burdea et al., 1991]. As illustrated in Figure 11.7, the suit uses light plastic bellow-type actuators acting in pairs to control all major joints (shoulder, arms, lower back, hip, knee, and ankle). Each actuator ends with two support plates that distribute forces over the region of the user's body adjacent to the joint being controlled. Power to the pneumatic actuators is provided

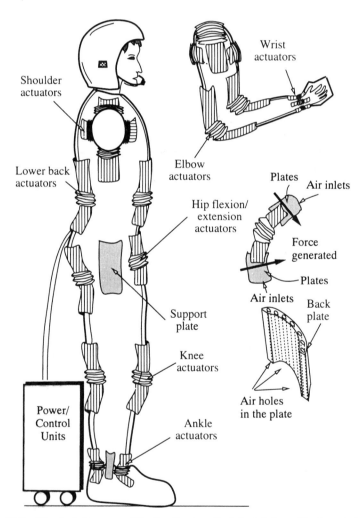

Figure 11.7 The Jedi force amplifier/feedback suit. Adapted from Burdea et al. [1991]. © Éditions Hèrmes. Reprinted by permission.

by an external power or control unit tethered to the back of the Jedi suit. From here low-pressure air is transmitted through channels in an ergonomically designed back plate. Heavy boots are used to transmit forces to the floor and to increase stability by lowering the center of gravity of the user wearing the suit.

Another full-body force-feedback suit called "Immerse" was proposed by Zechner [1993]. The device consists of a saddle platform supporting the user, who wears an exoskeleton. Each joint is powered by stepper motors with reduction gears. Pneumatic cuffs are used for an optimal fit of the exoskeleton on the user's body. Pneumatic pipes are routed together with electrical wires in a big hose from the back of Immerse to compressors and computers controlling the simulation. Visual feedback is provided through a HMD worn by the user. Figure 11.8 shows the various body postures that are accommodated by the Immerse suit.

Both Jedi and Immerse feedback suits use conventional pneumatic technology. Clearly the novel actuators presented in the previous section will allow further miniaturization and reduced power consumption, making it possible to replace a remote power source with a portable one. Furthermore, future simulation suits should integrate smart microprocessor-based controllers, and eventually portable and powerful computers,

11.3. LARGE-VOLUME SIMULATIONS

Basic technological advances in actuator miniaturization, light and long-life power sources, and miniature and wearable computers will make tethering of haptic feedback suits unnecessary. This will open the door for unencumbered and natural simulations over a large physical space and with multiple participants.

Data transmission to the suit computer will be done wirelessly, because only high-level, low-bandwidth communications will be necessary. Such wireless networks will extend the present sound-only environment to incorporate video, graphics, and haptic interactions [Schwartz, 1995]. The powerful suit computer will, at a minimum, perform data compression and decompression, and possibly even graphics and haptic rendering.

Navigating in a VR environment will require knowledge of the user's position inside the simulation room. Currently this is done by using multiple short-range electromagnetic trackers [Ascension Technologies, 1991], but these need to be replaced by single long-range trackers. Several possibilities for three-dimensional position measurements over large volumes include miniature infrared cameras and LEDs, smart floors, or inertial navigation. One project currently underway at the University of North Carolina at Chapel Hill uses a small camera on the user's head looking at a smart ceiling with multiple LEDs [Ward et al., 1992; Fuchs, 1995]. The camera image is then used to determine the user's head position and orientation and change the HMD image accordingly. Another possibility is to use smart floors of composite structure that incorporate arrays of pressure sensors [Speeter, 1993]. Such floors can detect the user's weight, speed of motion, even his possible locomotion

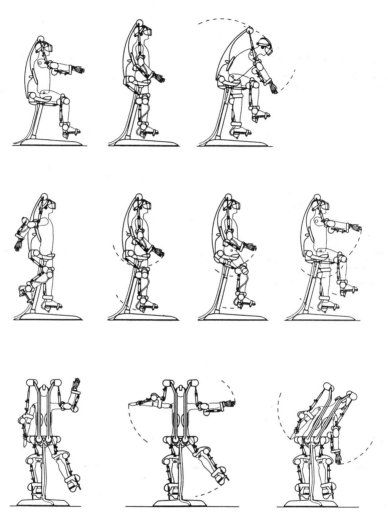

Figure 11.8 The Immerse force feedback suit. Reprinted by permission from Zechner [1993].

disability. Finally, inertial navigation may be possible owing to small and compact gyroscope-based trackers.

Voice commands will most probably be used in future simulation systems for a number of reasons. First, it will be difficult, if not impossible for the user wearing a haptic feedback suit to use his hands for typing on a keyboard. Second, new two- and three-dimensional microphone array technology [Lin et al., 1994] will allow hands-free voice pickup as well as speaker identification. Finally, voice and gesture-based input represent a more natural and faster method of interaction with the simulation.

11.4. CONCLUSIONS

The above discussion on the future of haptic feedback concentrated on technology advances and left out the sociological impact these may have. The whole area of force and tactile feedback is under active research worldwide, and it is difficult to predict exactly where the current advances will lead. Nevertheless, it is safe to say that, if used correctly and fully, force and tactile feedback should be very beneficial. It is the author's hope that this book will help make haptic feedback an integral and key part of the future VR simulation industry.

REFERENCES

Adachi, Y., 1993, "Touch and Trace on the Free-Form Surface of Virtual Object," *IEEE Virtual Reality Annual International Symposium (VRAIS)*, IEEE, New York, pp. 162–168, September.

Adachi, Y., 1994, "Development of a Haptic Interface for Virtual Reality," *2nd Japan-France Congress on Mechatronics*, Takamatsu, Japan, 4 pp., November.

Adachi, Y., T. Kumano and K. Ogino, 1994, "Sensory Evaluation of Virtual Haptic Push-Buttons," *Proceedings of ASME WAM*, DSC-Vol. 55-1, Chicago, pp. 361–368, November.

Adachi, Y., T. Kumano and K. Ogino, 1995, "Intermediate Representation for Stiff Virtual Objects," *IEEE Virtual Reality Anual International Symposium (VRAIS)*, IEEE, New York, pp. 203–210, March.

Adelstein, B. and M. Rosen, 1992, "Design and Implementation of a Force Reflecting Manipulandum for Manual Control Research," *Proceedings of ASME WAM*, DSC-Vol. 42, pp. 1–12.

Airpot, Co., 1982, "Airpot," Technical Bulletin P3-81, Norwalk, CT, 15 pp.

Akamatsu, M., S. Sato and S. MacKenzie, 1994, "Multimodal Mouse: A Mouse-Type Device with Tactile and Force Display," *Presence–Teleoperators and Virtual Environments*, Vol. 3, No. 1, MIT Press, Cambridge, MA, pp. 73–80.

Akamatsu, M., S. MacKenzie and T. Hasbroucq, 1995, "A comparison of tactile, auditory, and visual feedback in a pointing task using a mouse-type device," *Ergonomics*, Vol. 38, No. 4, Taylor & Francis, Basingstoke, Hants, pp. 816–827.

Akka, R., 1992, "Utilizing 6D head-tracking data for stereoscopic computer graphics perspective transformations," StereoGraphics Co., San Rafael, CA, 8 pp.

Allen, P. and P. Michelman, 1990, "Acquisition and Interpretation," *IEEE Transactions on Robotics and Automation*, Vol. 6, No. 4, pp. 397–404, August.

American National Standards Institute, 1988, "American National Standard for Information Processing Systems-Programmer's Hierarchical Interactive Graphics System (PHIGS)

Functional Description, Archive File Format, Clear-text Encoding of Archive File," ANSI, X3.144-1988, New York.

An, K-N., L. Askew and E. Chao, 1986, "Biomechanics and Functional Assessment of Upper Extremities," *Trends in Ergonomics/Human Factors III*, Elsevier Science Publishers, Amsterdam, pp. 573–580.

Anderson, R. and B. Davies, 1994, "Using Virtual Objects to Aid Underground Storage Tank Teleoperation," *Proceedings of 1994 IEEE International Conference on Robotics and Automation*, IEEE, New York, pp. 1421–1426, May.

Andrenucci, M., M. Bergamasco and P. Dario, 1989, "Sensor-based Fine Telemanipulation for Space Robotics," *NASA Conference on Space Telerobotics*, Vol. IV, NASA, Greenbelt, MD, pp. 101–107, February.

Appino, P., B. Lewis, L. Koved, D. Ling, D. Rabenhorst and C. Codella, 1992, "An Architecture for Virtual Worlds," *Presence–Teleoperators and Virtual Environments*, Vol. 1, No. 1, MIT Press, Cambridge, MA, pp. 1–17, March.

Arai, T., K. Cleary, T. Nakamura, H. Adachi and K. Homma, 1990, "Design, Analysis and Construction of a Prototype Parallel Link Manipulator," *IEEE International Workshop on Intelligent Robots and Systems (IROS)*, IEEE, New York, pp. 205–212, July.

ARTS Lab., 1994, "Virtual Environments and Teleoperation at the ARTS Lab," Technical Report, Pisa, Italy, 8 pp.

Ascension Technologies, 1991, "A Flock of Birds," Company brochure, Burlington, VT, 2 pp.

Atwood, D., 1995, Personal communication, SARCOS Co., Salt Lake City, April.

Autodesk Inc., 1993, "Cyberspace Developer Kit Concepts & Components," *CyTechnical Note # 1*, Sausalito, CA, 10 pp., June.

Bach-y-Rita, P., J. Webster, W. Tompkins and T. Crabb, 1987, "Sensory Substitution for Space Gloves and for Space Robots," *Proceedings of Workshop on Space Telerobotics*, Vol. 2, pp. 51–57.

Badler, N., M. Hollick and J. Granieri, 1993, "Real-Time Control of a Virtual Human Using Minimal Sensors," *Presence – Teleoperators and Virtual Environments*, Vol. 2, No. 1, MIT Press, Cambridge, MA, pp. 82–86.

Bardot, I., L. Bochereau, P. Bourgine, B. Heyd, J. Hossenlopp, N. Martin, M. Rogeaux and G. Trystram, 1992, "Cuisiner Artificial: Un Automate Pour la Formulation Sensorielle de Produits Alimentaires," *Proceedings of Interface to Real and Virtual Worlds Conference*, EC2, Paris, pp. 451–461, March.

Batter, J. and F. Brooks Jr., 1971, "GROPE-I: A computer display to the sense of feel," *Proceedings of ITIP Congress*, pp. 759–763.

Bejczy, A. and K. Salisbury, 1980, "Kinematic Coupling Between Operator and Remote Manipulator," *Advances in Computer Technology*, Vol. 1, ASME, New York, pp. 197–211.

Bejczy, A., 1993, "State-of-the-Art in Remote Manipulation Using Virtual Environment Display," *IEEE Workshop on Force Display on Virtual Environments and its Application to Robotic Teleoperation*, IEEE, New York, pp. 1–23, May.

Bergamasco, M., 1993a, "The GLAD-IN-ART Project," *Virtual Reality. Anwendungen und Trends*, in Forschung und Praxis, IPA/IAO Forum, Springer-Verlag, Berlin, pp. 251–258, February.

Bergamasco, M., 1993b, "Theoretical Study and Experiments on Internal and External Force Replication," *IEEE Workshop on Force Display on Virtual Environments and its Application to Robotic Teleoperation*, IEEE, New York, May, pp. 45–58.

Bergamasco, M., B. Allotta, L. Bosio, L. Ferretti, G. Parrini, G. Prisco, F. Salsedo and Sartini, 1994a, "An Arm Exoskeleton System for Teleoperation and Virtual Environments Applications," *Proceedings of the IEEE International Conference on Robotics and Automation*, San Diego, CA, pp. 1449–1454, May.

Bergamasco, M., P. Degl'Innocenti and D. Bucciarelli, 1994b, "A Realistic Approach for Grasping and Moving Virtual Objects," *Proceedings of IEEE/RSJ International Conference on Intelligent Robots and Systems (IROS'94)*, IEEE, New York, pp. 44–49, September.

Bergamasco, M., P. Degl'Innocenti, D. Bucciarelli and G. Rigucci, 1994c, "Grasping and moving objects in Virtual Environments: a preliminary approach towards a realistic behavior," *Proceedings of IEEE International Workshop on Robot and Human Communication (RO-MAN'94)*, IEEE, New York.

Bizio, C., 1994, "La Democrazia del Divertimento," *Virtual*, Vol. 2, No. 5, pp. 16–21, Italy.

Bostrom, M., S. Singh and C. Wiley, 1993, "Design of an Interactive Lumbar Simulator with Tactile Feedback," *Proceedings of IEEE Virtual Reality Annual International Symposium (VRAIS)*, IEEE, New York, pp. 280–286, September.

Bouzit, M., P. Richard and P. Coiffet, 1993, "LRP Dextrous Hand Master Control System," Technical Report, Laboratoire de Robotique de Paris, 21 pp., January.

Brickman, B., L. Hettinger, M. Roe, L. Lu, D. Repperger and M. Haas, 1996, "Haptic Specification of Environmental Events: Implications for the Design of Adaptive, Virtual Interfaces," *Proceedings of Virtual Reality Annual International Symposium*, IEEE, New York, pp. 147–153.

Brimhall, O. and C. Hasser, 1994, "Magnetostrictive linear devices for force reflection in dextrous telemanipulation," *Proceedings of SPIE*, Vol. 2190, pp. 508–519.

Brimhall, O., 1995a, "Advanced Development of New Actuators for Human Sensory Feedback," SBIR-Phase II 6th Quarterly Report, Technical Research Associates, Salt Lake City, UT, February.

Brimhall, O., 1995b, "Advanced Development of New Actuators for Human Sensory Feedback," SBIR-Phase II 7th Quarterly Report, Technical Research Associates, Salt Lake City, UT, May.

Brock, D., 1991, "Dynamic Model and Control of an Artificial Muscle Based on Contractile Polymers," M.I.T. AI Memo No. 1331, Cambridge, MA. 22 pp., November.

Brooks, F. Jr., M. Ouh-Young, J. Batter and A. Jerome, 1990, "Project GROPE—Haptic Displays for Scientific Visualization," *Computer Graphics*, Vol. 24, No. 4, pp. 177–185.

Brooks, T., 1990, "Telerobotic Response Requirements," *Proceedings of IEEE International Conference on Systems, Man and Cybernetics*, IEEE, New York, pp. 113–120, November.

Brown, P., D. Jones, S. Singh and J. Rosen, 1993, "The Exoskeleton Glove for Control of Paralyzed Hands," *Proceedings of 1993 IEEE International Conference on Robotics and Automation*, Atlanta, GA, pp. 642–647, May.

Burdea, G., 1989, "Human/Machine Interaction in Telerobotic Dextrous Feedback," *Symposium on Dynamics and Control of Biomechanical Systems*, 1989 ASME Winter Annual Meeting, ASME, New York, pp. 65–69.

Burdea, G., N. Langrana and W. You, 1991, "Supersuit Project-Report 2: Concepts," Rutgers University, Report for PSE&G, Piscataway, NJ, August.

Burdea, G., J. Zhuang, E. Roskos, D. Silver and N. Langrana, 1992a, "A Portable Dextrous Master with Force Feedback," *Presence–Teleoperators and Virtual Environments*, Vol. 1. No.1, MIT Press, Cambridge, MA, pp. 18–27, March.

Burdea, G., E. Roskos, D. Silver, F. Thibaud and R. Wolpov, 1992b, "A Distributed Virtual Environment with Dextrous Force Feedback," *Proceedings of Interface to Real and Virtual Worlds Conference*, Montpellier, France, pp. 255–265, March.

Burdea, G., 1993b, "Virtual Reality Systems and Applications," *Electro'93 International Conference*, Short Course, Edison, NJ, 164 pp., April 28.

Burdea, G., E. Roskos, D. Gomez and N. Langrana, 1993, "Distributed Virtual Force Feedback," *IEEE Workshop on Force Display in Virtual Environments and its Application to Robotic Teleoperation*, IEEE, New York, pp. 24–44, May 2.

Burdea, G. and N. Langrana, 1993, "Virtual Force Feedback – Lessons, Challenges and Future Applications," *Journal of Robotics and Mechatronics*, Vol. 5, No. 2, pp. 178–182, Japan.

Burdea, G. and P. Coiffet, 1994, *Virtual Reality Technology*, John Wiley & Sons, New York City, June.

Burdea, G. and R. Goratowski, 1994, "Calibration Tests of Force Sensors," Report to the Whitaker Foundation, Rutgers University, Piscataway, NJ, 33 pp., July.

Burdea, G. and D. Gomez, 1994, "Actuator System for Providing Feedback to a Portable Master Support," US Patent 5,354,162, October 11.

Burdea, G., D. Gomez, N. Langrana, E. Roskos, and P. Richard, 1995a, "Virtual Reality Graphics Simulation with Force Feedback," *International Journal in Computer Simulation*, ABLEX Publishing, Vol. 5, pp. 287–303.

Burdea, G., R. Goratowski and N. Langrana, 1995b, "A Tactile Sensing Glove for Computerized Hand Diagnosis," *The Journal of Medicine and Virtual Reality*, Vol. 1, No. 1, pp. 40–44, Spring.

Burdea, G., S. Dishpande, B. Liu, N. Langrana and D. Gomez, 1996, "A Virtual Reality-based System for Hand Diagnosis and Rehabilitation," *Presence–Teleoperators and Virtual Environments*, (in press).

Burke, J., 1992, "Exoskeleton Master Arm, Wrist and End Effector Controller with Force-Reflecting Telepresence," Technical Report AL/CF-TR-1994-0146, Odentics Inc., Anaheim CA, 104 pp., December.

Buttolo, P. and B. Hannaford, 1995, "Pen-Based Force Display for Precision Manipulation in Virtual Environments," *IEEE Virtual Reality Annual International Symposium (VRAIS)*, IEEE, New York, pp. 217–224, March.

Buzmatics, Inc., 1993, "SPCJR Unit Specifications," Company brochure, Indianapolis, IN, 4 pp.

Cadoz, C., 1992, "Interface de Communication Instrumentale: Clavier Retroactif Modulaire," *Proceedings of the Interface to Real and Virtual Worlds Conference*, EC2, Paris, pp. 43–47.

Caldwell, D., 1992, "Polymeric Gels: Pseudo Muscular Actuators and Variable Compliance Tendons," *Proceedings of 1992 IEEE/RSJ International Conference on Intelligent Robots and Systems*, IEEE, New York, pp. 950–957, July.

Caldwell, D. and C. Gosney, 1993, "Enhanced Tactile Feedback (Tele-Taction) using a Multi-Functional Sensory System," *Proceedings of the 1993 International Conference on Robotics and Automation*, IEEE, New York, pp. 955–960, May.

Caldwell, D., G. Medrano-Cerda and M. Goodwin, 1994a, "Characteristics and Adaptive Control of Pneumatic Muscle Actuators for a Robotic Elbow," *Proceedings of IEEE International Conference on Robotics and Automation*, IEEE, New York, pp. 3558–3563, May.

Caldwell, D., A. Wardle and M. Goodwin, 1994b, "Tele-Presence: Visual, Audio and Tactile Feedback and Control of a Twin Armed Mobile Robot," *Proceedings of IEEE International Conference on Robotics and Automation*, IEEE, New York, pp. 244–249, May.

Caldwell, D., G. Medrano-Cerda and C. Bowler, 1995a "Pneumatic Muscle Actuators as Low Weight Drive Units in a Robotic Exoskeleton," Technical Report, University of Salford, Manchester.

Caldwell, D., 1995b, Personal communication, University of Salford, Manchester, UK, July.

Caldwell, D., O. Kocak and U. Andersen, 1995c, "Multi-armed Dextrous Manipulator Operation Using Glove/Exoskeleton Control and Sensory Feedback," *Proceedings of IROS'95*, Pittsburgh PA, pp. 567–572, May.

Celinker, G. and W. Welch, 1992, "Linear Constraints for Deformable β-Spline Surfaces," *Proceedings of the 1992 Symposium on Interactive 3D Graphics*, ACM, New York, pp. 165–170.

Chapel, J., 1989, "Performance Limitations of Bilateral Force Reflection Imposed by Operator Dynamic Characteristics," *Proceedings of NASA Conference on Space Telerobotics*, NASA, Greenbelt, MD, Vol. IV, pp. 91–100, January.

Chen, E. and B. Marcus, 1994, "Exos Slip Display Research and Development," *Proceedings of ASME WAM*, DSC-Vol. 55-1, ASME, NY, pp. 265–270, November.

Cholewiak, R. and A. Collins, 1991, "Sensory and Physiological Bases of Touch,"in M. Heller and W. Schiff Eds., *The Psychology of Touch*, Lawrence Erlbaum Associates, Mahwah, NJ, pp 23–60.

Chou, C-P. and B. Hannaford, 1994, "Static and Dynamic Characteristics of McKibben Pneumatic Artificial Muscles," *Proceedings of IEEE International Conference on Robotics and Automation*, IEEE, New York, pp. 281–286, May.

Cine-Med Inc., 1995, "Virtual Reality in Surgical Training," *CinEvents*, Vol. 1, No.1, pp. 1. September.

Cohen, J., M. Lin, D. Manocha and M. Ponamgi, 1995, "I-COLLIDE: An Interactive and Exact Collision Detection System for Large-Scale Environments," *Proceedings of ACM Interactive 3D Graphics Conference*, ACM, NY, pp. 189–196.

Coiffet, P., M. Bouzit and G. Burdea, 1993, "The LRP Dextrous Hand Master," *VR Systems Fall 93 Conference*, Sig Advanced Applications, New York City, October.

Colgate, E. and B. Hannaford, 1993, "Force Reflecting Interfaces to Teleoperators and Virtual Environments," *Tutorial #5 for the IEEE Virtual Reality Annual International Symposium (VRAIS)*, IEEE, New York. 22 pp., September.

Colgate, E., P. Grafing, M. Stanley and G. Schenkel, 1993, "Implementation of Stiff Virtual Walls in Force-Reflecting Interfaces," *Proceedings of the IEEE Virtual Reality Annual International Symposium (VRAIS)*, IEEE, New York, pp. 202–208, September.

Colgate, E. and M. Brown, 1994, "Factors Affecting the Z-Width of a Haptic Display," *Proceedings of 1994 IEEE International Conference on Robotics and Automation*, IEEE, New York, pp. 3205–3210, May.

Colgate, E. and G. Schenkel, 1994, "Passivity of a Class of Sample-Data Systems: Application to Haptic Interfaces," *Proceedings of 1994 American Control Conference*, pp. 3236–3240, July.

Coquillart, S. and P. Jancene, 1991, "Animated Free-Form Deformation: An Interactive Animation Technique," *Computer Graphics*, Vol. 25, No. 4, pp. 23–26, July.

Cover, S., N. Ezquera, J. O'Brien, R. Rowe, T. Gadacz and E. Palm, 1993, "Interactively Deformable Models for Surgery Simulation," *IEEE Computer Graphics and Applications*, pp. 68–75, November.

Cutkosky, M. and R. Howe, 1990, "Human Grasp Choice and Robotic Grasp Analysis," in S. Venkataraman and T. Iberall Eds., *Dextrous Robot Hands*, Springer Verlag, New York, pp. 5–31.

Cutt, P., 1993, "Tactile Displays: Adding the Sense of Touch to Virtual Environments," *Proceedings of Virtual Reality Systems'93 Conference*, New York, pp. 120–122, March.

CyberEdge Journal, 1993a, "Product of the Year," Sausalito, CA, pp. 3–5, March/April.

CyberEdge Journal, 1993b, "The Virtual Lexicon," Special Edition, No. 1, Sausalito, CA, pp. 4, Fall.

CyberEdge Journal, 1994, "Industry Outlook," Sausalito, CA, pp. 26, September/October.

Cybernet Systems Co., 1995, Company brochure, Ann Arbor, MI.

Cyrus, M. and J. Beck, 1978, "Generalized Two- and Three-Dimensional Clipping," *Computers and Graphics*, Vol. 3, No. 1, pp. 23–28.

Dandekar, K. and M. Srinivasan, 1994, "Tactile Coding of Object Curvature by Slowly Adapting Mechanoreceptors," *Proceedings of ASME Advances, in Bioengineering*, BED-Vol. 28, ASME, New York, pp. 41–42.

Das, H., H. Zak, W. Kim, A. Bejczy and P. Schenker, 1992, "Operator Performance with Alternative Manual Control Modes in Teleoperation," *Presence – Teleoperators and Virtual Environments*, Vol. 1, No. 2, MIT Press, pp. 201–218.

Denavit, J. and R. Hartenberg, 1955, "A Kinematic Notation for Lower Pair Mechanisms Based on Matrices," *Journal of Applied Mechanics*, Vol. 77, pp. 215–221.

Denne Developments Ltd., 1994a, "PemRAM Type 3300/150," Company brochure, Wimborne, UK.

Denne Developments Ltd., 1994b, "PemRAM Type 306/6/1000," Company brochure, Wimborne, UK.

Denne P., 1994, "Virtual Motion," *Virtual Reality World*, pp. 41–44, May/June.

Denne Developments Ltd., 1995, Personal communication, Wimborne, UK.

Dinsmore M., N. Langrana and G. Burdea, 1994, "Issues Related to Real-Time Simulation of a Virtual Knee Palpation," *Proceedings of Virtual Reality and Medicine - The Cutting Edge*, SIG Advanced Applications, New York, pp. 16–20, September.

Dinsmore M., 1995, Personal communication, Rutgers University, CAIP Center, July.

Division Ltd., 1992, Company brochure, Bristol, UK.

Division Ltd., 1993a, "Amaze User manual," Bristol, UK.

Division Ltd., 1993b, "dVS 2.0 Virtual Reality Operating Environment," Bristol, UK., 4 pp.

Division Ltd., 1993c, "Pixel-Planes Defines New Price-Performance for Virtual Reality Graphics," Press Release, Bristol UK, 2 pp.

Donovan, J., 1993, "Market Overview and Market Forecasts for the VR Business," *Proceedings of Virtual Reality Systems '93 Conference*, SIG-Advanced Applications Inc., New York, NY, pp. 25–28, March.

Durfee, W. and M. Goldfarb, 1993, "Design of a Wearable Orthosis for Applying Controlled Dissipative Loads to the Lower Limbs," *Proceedings of ASME WAM*, Vol. DSC-Vol. 49, ASME, New York, pp. 11–14.

Edin B., R. Howe, G. Westling and M. Cutkosky, 1993, "A Physiological Method for Relaying Frictional Information to a Human Teleoperator," *IEEE Transactions on Systems, Man, and Cybernetics*, Vol. 23, No. 2, March/April, pp. 427–432.

Ellis, R., O. Ismaeil and M. Lipsett, 1993, "Design and Evaluation of a High-Performance Prototype Planar Haptic Interface," *Proceedings of ASME WAM*, DSC-Vol. 49, ASME, New York, pp. 55–64.

Ellis, S., 1995, "Human Engineering in Virtual Environments," *Proceedings of Virtual Reality World '95 Conference*, IDG Conferences, München, Germany, pp. 295–301, February.

EXOS Co., 1993a, "Force ArmMaster Specifications," Company brochure, Woburn MA, 1 pp., June.

EXOS Co., 1993b, "The Touch Master Specifications," Company brochure, Woburn MA, 1 pp., June.

EXOS Co., 1995a, "Sensing and Force Reflecting Exoskeleton (SAFIRE) Specifications," Woburn, MA, Company brochure, 1 pp.

EXOS Co., 1995b, Personal communication, Woburn, MA, April.

Fabiani, L., G. Burdea, N. Langrana and D. Gomez, 1996, "Human Performance Using the Rutgers Master II Force Feedback Interface," *IEEE Virtual Reality Annual International Symposium (VRAIS)*, IEEE, New York, pp. 54–59.

Farry, K. and I. Walker, 1993, "Myoelectric Teleoperation of a Complex Robotic Hand," *Proceedings of IEEE 1993 International Conference of Robotics and Automation*, IEEE, New York, pp. 502–509, May.

Fasse, E., N. Hogan, S. Gomez and N. Mehta, 1994, "A Novel Variable Mechanical-Impedance Electromechanical Actuator," *Proceedings of ASME WAM*, DSC-Vol 55-1, ASME, New York, pp. 311–318, November.

Fischer, H., B. Neisius and R. Trapp, 1995, "Tactile Feedback for Endoscopic Surgery," in K. Morgan, R. Satava, H. Sieburg, R. Mattheus and J. Christensen, Eds., *Interactive Technology and the New Paradigm for Healthcare*, IOS Press, Amsterdam, pp. 114–117, January.

Fitzgerald, A., C. Kingsley Jr. and S. Umans, 1983, *Electric Machinery*, McGraw-Hill Inc., New York.

Flogiston Co., 1994, Company brochure, Austin, TX, 1 pp.

Foley, J., A. van Dam, S. Feiner, and J. Hughes, 1990, *Computer Graphics. Principles and Practice*, Addison-Wesley Publishing Co., Menlo Park, CA.

Foley, J., A. van Dam, S. Feiner, J. Hughes, and R. Phillips, 1994, *Introduction to Computer Graphics*, Addison-Wesley Publishing Co., Menlo Park, CA.

Force Imaging Technologies, 1994, "FSR Integration Guide & Evaluation Parts Catalog," Company brochure, Chicago, IL, 16 pp.

Fowler, B., 1992, "Geometric Manipulation of Tensor Product Surfaces, *Proceedings of the 1992 Symposium on Interactive 3D Graphics*, ACM, New York, pp. 101–108.

Fu, K., R. Gonzalez and C. Lee, 1987, *Robotics: Control, Sensing, Vision and Intelligence*, McGraw Hill, New York.

Fuchs, H., J. Poulton, J. Eyles, T. Greer, J. Goldfeather, D. Ellsworth, S. Molnar, G. Turk, B. Tebbs, and L. Israel, 1989, "Pixel-Planes 5: A Heterogeneous Multiprocessor Graphics System Using Processor-Enhanced Memories," *Computer Graphics*, Vol. 23, No. 3, pp. 79–88, July.

Fuchs, H., 1995, Key-Note Address, *IEEE Virtual Reality Annual International Symposium (VRAIS)*, Research Triangle Park, NC, March.

Fukui, Y., 1995, Personal communication, Rutgers University, Piscataway, NJ. June.

Fulke, E., 1982, "Reading Braille," in W. Schiff and E. Foulke, Eds., *Tactile perception: a sourcebook*, Cambridge University Press, Cambridge, pp. 168–208.

Garcia, N., 1995, "Virtual reality creates a touching experience," *Sandia Lab News*, Albuquerque, NM, pp. 3, April 14.

Gembicki, M. and D. Rousseau, 1993, "Naval Applications of Virtual Reality," *Proceedings of Virtual Systems '93 Conference*, SIG Advanced Applications, New York, pp. 269–288, March.

Gharaybeh, M., 1992, "Dextrous Master with Force Feedback Using Shape Memory Metals," Master Thesis, Department of Electrical and Computer Engineering, Rutgers–The State University of New Jersey, Piscataway, NJ, August.

Gharaybeh, M. and G. Burdea, 1995, "Investigation of Shape Memory Alloy for Dextrous Force-Feedback Masters," *Advanced Robotics*, Holland, Vol. 9, No. 3, pp. 317–329.

Gillespie, B. and M. Cutkosky, 1993, "Interactive Dynamics with Haptic Feedback," *Proceedings of ASME WAM*, DSC-Vol. 49, ASME, New York, pp. 65–72.

Goertz, R. and R. Thompson, 1954, "Electronically controled manipulator," *Nucleonics*, pp. 46–47.

Goldfarb, M. and W. Durfee, 1996, "Design of a Controlled-Brake Orthosis for FES-Aided Gait," *IEEE Transactions on Rehabilitation Engineering*, Vol. 4, No. 1 (in press).

Gomez, D., 1993, "Pressure Controller Test: MPP-3-1/8 vs. SPCJr," Internal Report CAIP-IR-HMIL-001, Rutgers University, Piscataway, NJ, 13 pp., May.

Gomez, D., G. Burdea and N. Langrana, 1994, "The Second-Generation Rutgers Master (RM-II)," *The Third International Conference on Automation Technology*, Taipei, Taiwan, pp. 7–10, July.

Gomez, D., G. Burdea, and N. Langrana, 1995, "Integration of the Rutgers Master II in a Virtual Reality Simulation," *IEEE Virtual Reality Annual International Symposium (VRAIS)*, IEEE, New York, pp. 198–202, March.

Greenleaf, W., 1995, "Medical Applications of Virtual Reality Technology," V. Bronzio, Ed., CRC Press, *CRC Biomedical Handbook*, Boca Raton, FL, pp. 1165–1179.

Grimsdale, C., 1991a, "Virtual Reality - key technologies, problems and emerging solutions," Division Ltd., UK, 9 pp.

Grimsdale, C., 1991b, "Distributed Virtual Environment System dVS," Division Ltd, UK, 20 pp.

Haas, M. and L. Hettinger, 1993, "Applying Virtual Reality Technology to Cockpits of Future Fighter Aircraft," *Virtual Reality Systems*, Vol. 1, No. 2, pp. 18–26.

Hajian, A. and R. Howe, 1994, "Identification of the Mechanical Impedance of Human Fingers," *Proceedings of the ASME Winter Annual Meeting*, DSC–Vol. 55-1, pp. 319–328, November.

Hannaford, B., 1989, "A Design Framework for Teleoperators with Kinesthetic Feedback," *IEEE Transactions on Robotics and Automation*, Vol. 5, pp. 426–434.

Hannaford, B. and L. Wood, 1989, "Performance Evaluation of a 6 Axis High Fidelity Generalized Force Reflecting Teleoperator," *Proceedings of NASA Conference on Space Telerobotics*, Vol. II, NASA, Greenbelt, MD, pp. 87–96, January.

Hannaford, B., L. Wood, B. Guggisberg, D. McAffee and H. Zak, 1989, "Performance Evaluation of a Six-Axis Generalized Force-Reflecting Teleoperator," JPL Publication 89-18, California Institute of Technology, Pasadena, CA.

Hannaford, B. and S. Venema, 1995, "Kinesthetic Displays for Remote and Virtual Environments," in W. Barfield and T. Furness, Eds., *Virtual Environments and Advance Interface Design*, Oxford University Press, New York, pp. 415–436.

Hashimoto, H., M. Boss, Y. Kuni and F. Harashima, 1994, "Intelligent Cooperative Manipulation System Using Dynamic Force Simulator," *Proceedings of IEEE International Conference on Robotics and Automation*, IEEE, New York, pp. 2598–2603, May.

Hasser, C. and J. Weisenberger, 1993, "Preliminary Evaluation of a Shape-Memory Alloy Tactile Feedback Display," *Advances in Robotics, Mechatronics, and Haptic Interfaces*, DSC-Vol. 49, ASME-WAM, ASME, New York, pp. 73–80.

Hasser, C., 1995a, "Force-Reflecting Anthropomorphic Hand Masters," Armstrong Laboratory Technical Report AL/CF-TR-1995-0110, Wright–Patterson AFB, OH. 82 pp.

Hasser, C., 1995b, Personal communication, Wright–Patterson AFB, OH, June.

Hasser, C., 1996, Personal communication, Wright–Patterson AFB, OH, March.

Henri, P. and J. Hollerbach, 1994, "An Analytical and Experimental Investigation of a Jet Pipe Controlled Electropneumatic Actuator," *IEEE International Conference on Robotics and Automation*, IEEE, New York, pp. 300–306, May.

Hewlett-Packard, 1991, "Starbase Display List Programmer's Manual," 1st Edition, Fort Collins, CO , January.

Hirose, S., K. Ikuta and Y. Umetani, 1989, "Development of shape-memory alloy actuators. Performance assessment and introduction of a new composing approach," *Advanced Robotics*, Vol. 3, No. 1, pp. 3–16.

Hogan, N., 1989, "Controlling Impedance at the Man/Machine Interface," *Proceedings 1989 IEEE International Conference on Robotics and Automation*, IEEE, New York, pp. 1626–1631.

Hogan, N., H. Krebs, J. Charnnarong, P. Srikrishna and A. Sharon, 1993, "MIT–MANUS: a workstation for manual therapy and training II," *Proceedings SPIE Conference on Telemanipulator Technology*, SPIE, 1833, pp. 28–34.

Holland, R., 1989, *Microprocessors and their Operating Systems*, Pergamon Press, Oxford, UK.

Hollerbach, J., I. Hunter and J. Ballantyne, 1992, "A Comparative Analysis of Actuator Technologies for Robotics," in O. Khatib, J. Craig and T. Lozano-Perez Eds., *The Robotics Review 2*, MIT Press, Cambridge, MA, pp. 299–342.

Holmes, R., 1992, "Haptic Computer Input/Output Device," UK Patent GB 2,254,911 A, April 21.

Hon, D., 1990, "Expert System Simulator for Modeling Realistic Internal Environments and Performance," US Patent 4,907,973, March 13.

Howe R. and D. Kontarinis, 1992, "Task Performance with a Dextrous Teleoperated Hand System," *Proceedings of SPIE*, Vol. 1833, Boston, MA, pp. 199–207, November.

Howe R., W. Peine, D. Kontarinis, and J. Son, 1995, "Remote Palpation Technology for Surgical Applications," *The IEEE Engineering in Medicine and Biology Magazine*, Vol. 14, No. 3, pp. 318–323.

Hsu, W., J. Hughes and H. Kaufman, 1992, "Direct Manipulation of Free-Form Deformations," *Computer Graphics*, Vol. 26, No. 2, pp. 177–184, July.

Hunt, C. 1992, *TCP/IP Network Administration*, O'Reilly & Assoc., Sebastopol, CA.

Hunter, I., T. Doukoglou, S. Lafontaine, P. Charette, L. Jones, M. Sagar, G. Mallinson and P. Hunter, 1993, "A Teleoperated Microsurgical Robot and Associated Virtual Environment for Eye Surgery," *Presence–Teleoperators and Virtual Environments*, Vol. 2, No. 4, pp. 265–280, Fall.

Hutchings, B., A. Grahn and R. Petersen, 1994, "Multiple-Layer Cross-Field Ultrasonic Tactile Sensor," in *Proceedings of IEEE 1994 International Conference on Robotics and Automation*, IEEE, New York, pp. 2522–2528.

Iberall, T., G. Sukhatme, D. Beattie and G. Bekey, 1994, "On the Development of EMG Control for a Prosthesis Using a Robotic Hand," *Proceedings of IEEE 1994 International Conference on Robotics and Automation*, IEEE, New York, pp. 1753–1758, May.

IBM Co., 1995, "Project Elysium Professional Immersive Virtual Reality System," Company brochure, Greenford, UK. 8 pp.

Immersion Co., 1995, "Laparoscopic Impulse Engine," Company brochure, Santa Clara, CA, 2 pp., January.

Ino, S., T. Izumi, M. Takahashi and T. Ifukube, 1993a, "A Psychophysical Study on Tactile Sense Produced by Grasping for 'Hand with Sensory Feedback'," *Systems and Computers in Japan*, Vol. 24, No. 13, pp. 89–97.

Ino, S., S. Shimizu, T. Odagawa, M. Sato, M. Takahashi, T. Izumi and T. Ifukube, 1993b, "A Tactile Display for Presenting Quality of Materials by Changing the Temperature of Skin Surface," *IEEE International Workshop on Robot and Human Communication*, IEEE, New York, pp. 220–224.

Ishii, M. and M. Sato, 1993, "A 3D Interface Device with Force Feedback: A Virtual Work Space for Pick-and-Place Tasks," *IEEE Virtual Reality Annual International Symposium (VRAIS)*, IEEE, New York, pp. 331–335, September.

Ishii, M. and M. Sato, 1994a, "A 3D Spatial Interface Device Using Tensed Strings," *Presence–Teleoperators and Virtual Environments*, Vol. 3. No. 1, MIT Press, Cambridge, MA, pp. 81–86.

Ishii, M. and M. Sato, 1994b, "Force Sensations in Pick-And-Place Tasks," *Proceedings of ASME WAM*, DSC-Vol. 55-1, ASME, New York, pp. 339–344.

Ishii, M., P. Sukanya and M. Sato, 1994, "A Virtual Work Space for Both Hands Manipulation," Tokyo Institute of Technology, Technical Report, 6 pp.

Ismaeil, O. and R. Ellis, 1994, "Grasping Using the Whole Finger," *Proceedings of the 1994 IEEE International Conference on Robotics and Automation*, IEEE, New York, pp. 3111–3116, May.

Iwata, H., 1990, "Artificial Reality with Force-Feedback: Development of Desktop Virtual Space with Compact Master Manipulator," *Computer Graphics*, Vol. 24, No. 4, pp. 165–170.

Iwata, H., T. Nakagawa, and T. Nakashima, 1992, "Force Display for Presentation of Rigidity of Virtual Objects," *Journal of Robotics and Mechatronics*, Vol. 24, No. 1, pp. 39–42.

Iwata, H., 1993, "Pen-based Haptic Virtual Environment," *Proceedings of IEEE Virtual Reality Annual International Symposium*, IEEE, New York, pp. 287–292, September.

Iwata, H., 1994, "Desktop Force Display," *SIGGRAPH'94*, ACM, New York, July.

Jackson, B. and L. Rosenberg, 1995, "Force Feedback and Medical Simulation," in K. Morgan, R. Satava, H. Sieburg, R. Mattheus and J. Christensen Eds., *Interactive Technology and the New Paradigm for Healthcare*, IOS Press, Amsterdam, Chapter 24, pp. 147–151, January.

Jacobsen, S., E. Iversen, C. Davis, D. Poter and T. McLain, 1989, "Design of a multiple degree-of-freedom, force-reflective hand master/slave with a high mobility wrist," *Proceedings of ANS/IEEE/SMC 3rd Topical Meeting on Robotics and Remote Systems*, IEEE, New York, March.

Jacobsen, S., F. Smith, D. Backman and E. Iversen, 1991a, "High performance, high dexterity, force reflective teleoperator II," *ANS Topical Meeting on Robotics and Remote Systems*, ANSI, New York, February.

Jacobsen, S., F. Smith and D. Backman, 1991b, "High Performance, Dextrous Telerobotic Manipulator with Force Reflection," *Intervention/ROV'91*, Hollywood, FL, 6 pp., May.

Jandura, L. and M. Srinivasan, 1994, "Experiments on Human Performance in Torque Discrimination and Control," *Proceedings of 1994 ASME Winter Annual Meeting*, DSC–Vol. 55–1, ASME, New York, pp. 369–375, November.

Jau, B., 1992, "Man–Equivalent Telepresence Through Four Fingered Human-Like Hand System," *Proceedings of 1992 IEEE Robotics and Automation Conference*, IEEE, New York.

Jau, B., A. Lewis and A. Bejczy, 1994, "Anthropomorphic Telemanipulation System In Terminus Control Mode," *Proceedings of Ro-ManSy '94.*

Jense, H., 1993, Personal communication, TNO Physics and Electronics Laboratory, The Hague, The Netherlands, August.

Jex, H., 1988, "Four Critical Tests for Control-Feel Simulators," *23rd Annual Conference on Manual Control*, Cambridge, MA.

Johansson, R. and G. Westling, 1984, "Roles of glabrous skin receptors and sensorimotor memory in automatic control of precision grip when lifting rougher or more slippery objects," *Exp. Brain Res.*, Vol. 56, pp. 550–564.

Johnson, A., 1992, "Programmable Tactile Stimulator Array System and Method of Operation," U.S. Patent 5,165,897, November 24.

Jones, L. and J. Thousand, 1966, "Servo Controlled Manipulator Device," U.S. Patent 3,263,824, Northrop Corporation, Beverly Hills, CA, August 2.

Jones, L. and I. Hunter, 1992, "Human Operator Perception of Mechanical Variables and Their Effects on Tracking Performance," *Advances in Robotics*, DSC-Vol. 42, ASME WAM, ASME, New York, pp. 49–53.

Kaczmarek, K., M. Tyler and P. Bach-y-Rita, 1994, "Electrotactile Haptic Display on the Fingertips: Preliminary Results," *Proceedings of the 16th Annual International IEEE Conference on Engineering in Medicine and Biology*, IEEE, New York, 2 pp., November.

Kaczmarek, K. and P. Bach-y-Rita, 1995, "Tactile Displays," in W. Barfield and T. Furness III eds., *Virtual Environments and Advanced Interface Design*, Oxford University Press, New York, pp. 349–414.

Kalawsky, R., 1993, *The Science of Virtual Reality and Virtual Environments*, Addison-Wesley Ltd, UK.

Kazerooni, H., 1993, "Human Induced Instability in Haptic Interfaces," *Proceedings of ASME WAM*, DSC-Vol. 49, ASME, New York, pp. 15–27.

Keller P., R. Kouzes, L. Kangas and S. Hashem, 1995, "Transmission of Olfactory Information in Telemedicine," in K. Morgan, R. Satava, H. Sieburg, R. Mattheus and J. Christensen Eds. *Interactive Technology and the New Paradigm for Healthcare*, IOS Press, Amsterdam, Chapter 27, pp. 168–172, January.

Kilpatrick, P., 1976, "The Use of Kinesthetic Supplement in an Interactive System," Ph.D Thesis, Computer Science Department, University of North Carolina at Chapel Hill.

Kim, W. and A. Bejczy, 1991, "Graphical Displays for Operator Aid in Telemanipulation," *Proceedings of IEEE International Conference on Systems, Man and Cybernetics*, IEEE, New York, 9 pp, October.

Kobayashi, H. and J. Tatsuno, 1994, "Micro–Macro Manipulator with Haptic Interface," *Proceedings of 1994 ASME WAM*, DSC-Vol. 55–1, ASME, New York, pp. 329–337.

Kontarinis, D. and R. Howe, 1993, "Tactile Display of Contact Shape in Dextrous Telemanipulation," *Proceedings of ASME WAM*, DSC Vol. 49, ASME, New York, pp. 81–88.

Kontarinis, D. and R. Howe, 1995, "Tactile Display of Vibratory Information in Teleoperation and Virtual Environments," *Presence–Teleoperators and Virtual Environments*, Vol. 4, No. 4, MIT Press, Cambridge, MA, pp. 387–402.

Kontarinis, D., J. Son, W. Peine and R. Howe, 1995, "A Tactile Shape Sensing and Display System for Teleoperated Manipulation," *1995 IEEE International Conference on Robotics and Automation*, Vol. 1, IEEE, New York, pp. 641–646.

Kontarinis, D., 1995, "Tactile Display for Dextrous Telemanipulation," Ph.D. Thesis, Harvard University, Division of Applied Sciences, Cambridge, MA.

Kotoku, T., E. Husler, K. Tanie and A. Fujikawa, 1989, "The Development of a Direct Drive Master Arm," *Journal of Robotics and Mechatronics*, Vol. 2, No. 6, pp. 49–56.

Kotoku, T., 1992, "A Predictive Display with Force Feedback and its Application to Remote Manipulation System with Transmission Time Delay," *Proceedings of the 1992 IEEE/RSJ International Conference on Intelligent Robots and Systems*, IEEE, New York, pp. 239–246, July.

Kotoku, T., K. Komoriya and K. Tanie, 1992, "A Force Display System for Virtual Environments and its Evaluation," *Proceedings of IEEE International Workshop on Robot and Human Communication (RoMan'92)*, IEEE, New York, pp. 246–251, September.

Kotoku, T., K. Takamune and K. Tanie, 1994, "A Virtual Environment Display with Constraint Feeling Based on Position/Force Control Switching," *IEEE International Workshop on Robot and Human Communication (RoMan'94)*, IEEE, New York, pp. 255–260, July.

Kramer, J., P. Lindener and W. George, 1991, "Communication System for Deaf, Deaf-Blind, or Non-vocal Individuals Using Instrumented Glove," U.S. Patent 5,047,952, September 10.

Kramer, J., 1993, "Force Feedback and Texture Simulating Interface Device," U.S. Patent 5,184,319, February 2.

Krebs, H., N. Hogan, M. Aisen and B. Volpe, 1996, "Application of Robotics and Automation Technology in Neuro-Rehabilitation," *Japan–USA Symposium on Flexible Automation*, ASME, New York, (in press).

Krueger, M., 1991, *Artificial Reality II*, Addison-Wesley, Menlo Park, CA.

Krueger, M., 1992, "The 'Art' in Artificial Reality," *Proceedings of the Cyberarts Conference*, Miller Freeman Inc., San Francisco, pp. 245–254, October.

Kuni, Y. and H. Hashimoto, 1994, "Object Grasping in Virtual Environment Using Dynamic Force Simulation," *Proceedings of RoMan '94 Conference*, 4 pp.

LaMotte, R. and M. Srinivasan, 1987a, "Tactile Discrimination of Shape: Responses of Slowly Adapting Mechanoreceptive Afferents to a Step Stroke Across the Monkey Fingerpad," *The Journal of Neuroscience*, Vol. 7 (6), pp. 1655–1671, June.

LaMotte, R. and M. Srinivasan, 1987b, "Tactile Discrimination of Shape: Responses of Rapidly Adapting Mechanoreceptive Afferents to a Step Stroke Across the Monkey Fingerpad," *The Journal of Neuroscience*, Vol. 7 (6), pp. 1672–1681, June.

Lampton, D., B. Knerr, S. Goldberg, J. Bliss, M. Moshell and B. Blau, 1994, "The Virtual Environment Performance Assessment Battery (VEPAB): Development and Evaluation," *Presence–Teleoperators and Virtual Environments*, Vol. 3, No. 2, pp. 145–157.

Langrana, N., G. Burdea, K. Lange, D. Gomez and S. Deshpande, 1994, "Dynamic force feedback in a virtual knee palpation," *Artificial Intelligence in Medicine*, Vol. 6, Elsevier Science Publishers, Amsterdam, pp. 321–333.

Lawrence, D., 1988, "Impedance Control Stability Properties in Common Implementations," *IEEE International Conference on Robotics and Automation*, IEEE, New York, pp. 1185–1190, April.

Lawrence, A. and J. Chapel, 1994, "Performance Trade-Offs for Hand Controller Design," *1994 IEEE International Conference on Robotics and Automation*, IEEE, New York, pp. 3211–3216.

Levine, M., 1989, "Solid State Cooling with Thermoelectrics," *Electronic Packaging & Production*, Cahners Publishing Co., 4 pp., November.

Li, L., 1993, "Virtual Reality and Telepresence Applications in Space Robotics," *Virtual Reality Systems*, Vol. 1, No. 2, pp. 50–56, October.

Lin, M., 1993, "Efficient Collision Detection for Animation and Robotics," Ph.D. Thesis, University of California at Berkeley, Department of Electrical Engineering and Computer Science, Berkeley, CA.

Lin, Q., E-E. Jan and J. Flanagan, 1994, "Microphone Arrays and Speaker Identification," *IEEE Transactions on Speech and Audio Processing*, Vol. 2, No. 4, pp. 622–629, October.

Lindemann, R. and D. Tesar, 1989, "Construction and Demonstration of a 9-String 6 DOF Force Reflecting Joystick for Telerobotics," *Proceedings of NASA International Conference on Space Telerobotics*, NASA, Greenbelt, MD, Vol. 4, pp. 55–63.

Loftin, B., D. Ota, T. Saito and M. Voss, 1994, "A Virtual Environment for Laparoscopic Surgical Training," *Proceedings of Medicine Meets Virtual Reality II*, Aligned Management Assoc., San Diego, pp. 121–123, January.

Long, M. and J. Alexander, 1995, "In the Gut," *VR World*, pp. 55, January/February.

Lovett, C., 1994, "Interacting with the Interactor," *Pixelation*, No. 11, pp. 30–32, November.

Luecke, G. and J. Winkler, 1994, "A Magnetic Interface for Robot-Applied Virtual Forces," *ASME WAM*, DSC-Vol. 55-1, ASME, New York, pp. 271–276, November.

Makinson, B., 1971, "Research and development prototype for machine augmentation of human strength and endurance: Hardiman 1 project," Technical Reaport S-71-1056, General Electric Co., Schenectady, NY, May.

Marcus, B. and P. Churchill, 1989, "Human Hand Sensing for Robotics and Teleoperations," Arthur D. Little Technical Report, Cambridge, MA, November.

Marcus, B., T. Lawrence, and P. Churchill, 1991, "Hand Position/Measurement Control System," US Patent 4,986,280, 13 pp., January.

Marcus, B., 1993, "Sensing, Perception and Feedback for VR," *VR Systems Fall 93 Conference*, SIG Advanced Applications, New York.

Mark, W., M. Finch, S. Randolph and J. VanVerth, 1996, "UNC-CH Force Feedback Library," University of North Carolina at Chapel Hill, Technical Report TR96-012, 47 pp., October.

Mark, W., 1994, Personal communication, University of North Carolina at Chapel Hill, NC., July.

Massie, T. and K. Salisbury, 1994, "The PHANToM Haptic Interface: A Device for Probing Virtual Objects," *ASME Winter Annual Meeting*, DSC-Vol. 55-1, ASME, New York, pp. 295–300.

Massimino, M. and T. Sheridan, 1993, "Sensory Substitution for Force Feedback in Teleoperation," *Presence–Teleoperators and Virtual Environments*, Vol. 2, No. 4, pp. 344–352.

McCauley, M. and T. Sharkey, 1992, "Cybersickness: Perception of Self-Motion in Virtual Environments," *Presence–Teleoperators and Virtual Environments*, Vol. 1, No. 3, pp. 311–318.

McDonald J., L. Rosenberg and D. Stredney, 1995, "Virtual Reality Technology Applied to Anesthesiology," in K. Morgan, R. Satava, H. Sieburg, R. Mattheus and J. Christensen Eds., *Interactive Technology and the New Paradigm for Healthcare*, IOS Press, Amsterdam, Chapter 38, pp. 237–243, January.

McDonough, J., 1993, "Doorways to the Virtual Battlefield," *Proceedings of Virtual Reality '92*, San Diego, pp. 104–114.

McNeely, W., 1993, "Robotic Graphics: A New Approach to Force Feedback for Virtual Reality," *Proceedings of IEEE Virtual Reality Annual International Symposium (VRAIS)*, IEEE, New York, pp. 336–341, September.

Meglan, D., R. Raju, G. Merril, J. Merril, B. Nguyen, S. Swamy and G. Higgins, 1996, "The Teleos Virtual Environment Toolkit for Simulation-Based Surgical Education," in S.

Weghorst, H. Sieberg, and K. Morgan Eds., *Health Care in the Information Age*, IOS Press, Amsterdam, pp. 346–351.

MicroMo Electronics Inc., 1995, Personal communication, Clearwater, FL, March.

Miller, G., E. Hoffert, S. Chen, E. Patterson, D. Blackketter, S. Rubin, S. Applin, D. Yim and J. Hanan, 1992, "The Virtual Museum: Interactive 3D Navigation of a Multimedia Database," *Journal of Visualization and Computer Animation*, John Wiley and Sons, Vol 3, pp. 183–197.

Millman, P., M. Stanley and E. Colgate, 1993, "Design of a High Performance Haptic Interface to Virtual Environments," *IEEE Virtual Reality Annual International Symposium (VRAIS)*, IEEE, New York, pp. 216–222, September.

Milner, T., 1993, "Human Operator Adaptation to Machine Instability," *Proceedings of ASME WAM*, DSC-Vol. 49, ASME, New York, pp. 105–110.

Minsky, M., M. Ouh-young, O. Steele, F. Brooks Jr. and M. Behensky, 1990, "Feeling and Seeing: Issues in Force Display," *Computer Graphics*, ACM Press, Vol. 24, No. 2, pp. 235–243, March.

Mirtich, B. and J. Canny, 1994, "Easy Computable Optimum Grasps in 2-D and 3-D," *Proceedings of the IEEE International Conference on Robotics and Automation*, IEEE, New York, pp. 739–747, May.

Monkman, G. and P. Taylor, 1993, "Thermal Tactile Sensing," *IEEE Transactions on Robotics and Automation*, Vol. 9, No. 3, pp. 313–318, June.

Moog Inc., 1984, "High Performance Electromechanical Servoactuation Using Brushless DC Motors," Technical Bulletin 150, East Aurora, NY, 11 pp.

Moog Inc., 1994, "Motion Simulators: Electric vs. Hydraulic Issues," Technical Report, East Aurora, NY, 15 pp., July.

Moore, M. and J. Wilhelms, 1988, "Collision Detection and Response for Computer Animation," *Computer Graphics*, Vol. 22, No. 4, pp. 289–298.

NASA, 1994, "Piezoelectric Motor in Robot Finger Joint," *NASA Technical Briefs*, pp. 57–58, January.

Nemire, K., 1994, "Building Usable Virtual Environment Products," *CyberEdge Journal*, pp. 8–12, September/October.

Nissho Electronics Co., 1995, "Haptic Master," Company brochure, Tokyo, Japan, 2 pp., (in Japanese).

North Coast Medical Inc., 1994, "Digi-Key," Company brochure, San Jose, CA.

Oracle Inc., 1995, "User's Manual," Redwood City, CA.

Ouh-Young, M., M. Pique, J. Hughes, N. Srinivasan, and F. Brooks Jr., 1988, "Using a Manipulator for Force Display in Molecular Docking," *Proceedings of the 1988 IEEE International Conference on Robotics and Automation*, IEEE, New York, pp. 1824–1829, April.

Papper M. and M. Gigante, 1993, "Using Physical Constraints in a Virtual Environment," in *Virtual Reality Systems*, Academic Press, Orlando, FL, pp. 107–118.

Patrick, N., 1990, "Design, Construction, and Testing of a Fingertip Tactile Display for Interaction with Virtual and Remote Environments," Masters Thesis, Department of Mechanical Engineering, MIT, Cambridge, MA.

Pausch, R., T. Crea and M. Conway, 1992, "A Literature Survey for Virtual Environments: Military Flight Simulator Visual Systems and Simulator Sickness," *Presence–Teleoperators and Virtual Environments*, MIT Press, Vol. 1, No. 3, pp. 344–363.

PCIM Staff, 1987, "New Ideas in Motion," *PCIM*, Vol. 13, No. 4, pp. 37–38, April.

Peifer, J., M. Sinclair, R. Haleblian, M. Luxenberg, K. Green and D. Hull, 1994, "Virtual Environment for Eye Surgery Simulation," *Proceedings of Medicine Meets Virtual Reality II*, Aligned Management Assoc., San Diego, CA, pp. 166–169, January.

Peine, W., J. Son and R. Howe, 1994, "A Palpation System for Artery Localization in Laparoscopic Surgery," *Proceedings of the First International Symposium on Medical Robotics and Computer-Assisted Surgery*, Shadyside Hospital, Pittsburgh, pp. 250–253, September.

Piantanida, T., D. Boman and J. Gille, 1993, "Human Perceptual Issues and Virtual Reality," *Virtual Reality Systems*, Vol. 1, No. 1, pp. 43–52.

Pimentel, K. and K. Teixeira, 1994, *Virtual Reality: Through the New Looking Glass*, second edition, Windcrest McGraw-Hill, New York.

Ponamgi, M., D. Manocha and M. Lin, 1995, "Incremental Algorithms for Collision Detection between Solid Models," *Proceedings of ACM/SIGGRAPH Symposium on Solid Modeling*, ACM, New York, pp. 293–304.

Pratt, D., P. Barham, J. Locke, M. Zyda, B. Eastman, T. Moore, K. Biggers, R. Douglass, S. Jacobsen, M. Hollick, J. Granieri, H. Ko and N. Badler, 1994, "Insertion of an Articulated Human into a Networked Virtual Environment," *Proceedings of 1994 AI, Simulation and Planning in High Autonomy Systems*, Gainesville, FL, pp. 84–90, December.

Richard, P., G. Burdea, and P. Coiffet, 1993, "Performances Humaines dans des Taches Impliquant des Objets Virtuels avec Retour D'Effort," *Proceedings of the Interface to Real and Virtual Worlds Conference*, EC2, Paris, pp. 229–238, March, (in French).

Richard, P., P. Coiffet and G. Burdea, 1994, "Effect of Graphics Update Rate on Human Performance in a Dynamic Virtual World," *The Third International Conference on Automation Technology*, Taipei, Taiwan, Vol. 6, pp. 1–5, July.

Richard, P., G. Burdea, G. Birebent, D. Gomez, N. Langrana and P. Coiffet, 1996, "Effect of Frame Rate and Force Feedback on Virtual Object Manipulation," *Presence–Teleoperators and Virtual Environments*, Vol. 5, No. 1, pp. 95–108.

Rizzoni, G., 1993, *Principles and Applications of Electrical Engineering*, Richard D. Irwin, Burr Ridge, IL.

Robertson, G., S. Card and J. Mackinlay, 1993, "Nonimmersive virtual reality," *Computer*, IEEE, New York, pp. 81–83, February.

Robinett, W. and R. Holloway, 1992, *Implementation of Flying, Scaling and Grabbing in Virtual Worlds*, ACM, New York, pp. 189–192.

Rosen, J., A. Lasko-Harwill and R. Satava, 1996, "Virtual Reality and Surgery," in *Computer-Integrated Surgery*, R. Taylor, S. Lavallee, G. Burdea, and R. Möesges Eds., MIT Press, Cambridge, MA, pp. 231–244.

Rosenberg, L. and B. Adelstein, 1993, "Perceptual Decomposition of Virtual Haptic Surfaces," *Proceedings of IEEE 1993 Symposium on Research Frontiers in Virtual Reality*, San Jose, CA, pp. 46–53, October.

Rosenberg, L., 1993a, "Virtual Fixtures: Perceptual Tools for Telerobotic Manipulation," *Proceedings of IEEE Virtual Reality Annual International Symposium (VRAIS)*, Seattle, WA, pp. 76–82, September.

Rosenberg, L., 1993b, "The Use of Virtual Fixtures to Enhance Telemanipulation with Time Delay," *Proceedings of ASME WAM*, DSC-Vol. 49, ASME, New York, pp. 29–36.

Rosenberg, L., 1994, "Virtual Fixtures: Perceptual Overlays Enhance Operator Performance in Telepresence Tasks," Doctoral Thesis, Stanford University, Stanford, CA.

Rosenberg, L., 1995, "How to Assess the Quality of Force-Feedback Systems," Technical Report, Immersion Co., Santa Clara, CA, 3 pp.

Rosenberg, L. and D. Stredney, 1996, "A Haptic Interface for Virtual Simulation of Endoscopic Surgery," in S. Weghorst, H. Sieburg, and K. Morgan Eds., *Health Care in the Information Age*, IOS Press, pp. 371–387.

Rosenblum, L., 1994, *The Realization Report*, Issue 34, ONR, London, February.

Russo, M. and A. Tadros, 1992, "Controlling Dissipative Magnetic Particle Brakes in Force Reflective Devices," *Advances in Robotics*, DSC-Vol. 42, ASME WAM, ASME, New York, pp. 63–70.

Sagar, M., D. Bullivant, G. Mallinson, P. Hunter and I. Hunter, 1994, "A Virtual Environment and Model of the Eye for Surgical Simulation," *Computer Graphics Proceedings - SIGGRAPH'94*, ACM, New York, pp. 205–212.

Salcudean, S. and T. Vlaar, 1994, "On the Emulation of Stiff Walls and Static Friction with a Magnetically Levitated Input/Output Device," *Proceedings of ASME WAM*, DSC-Vol. 55-1, ASME, New York, pp. 303–309, November.

Salcudean, S. and J. Yan, 1994, "Towards a Force-Reflecting Motion-Scaling System for Microsurgery," *Proceedings of 1994 IEEE International Conference on Robotics and Automation*, IEEE, New York, pp. 2296–2301, May.

Salcudean, S., P. Drexel, D. Ben-Dov, A. Taylor and P. Lowrence, 1994, "A Six Degree-of-Freedom, Hydraulic, One Person Motion Simulator," *Proceedings of 1994 IEEE International Conference on Robotics and Automation*, IEEE, New York, pp. 2437–2443, May.

Salisbury, J. and M. Srinivasan, 1992, "Virtual Environment Technology for Training (VETT)," BBN Report No. 7661, VETREC, MIT, Cambridge, MA.

Salisbury, J., 1995, Panel on Haptic Interfaces, *IEEE Virtual Reality Annual International Symposium (VRAIS)*, IEEE, New York, pp. 226–227.

Satava, R., 1993, "Virtual Reality Surgical Simulator—The First Steps," *Proceedings of VR Systems '93 Conference*, SIG Advanced Applications, New York, pp. 41–49, March.

Sato, K., E. Igarashi and M. Kimura, 1991, "Development of Non-Constrained Arm with Tactile Feedback Device," *Proceedings of the International Conference on Advanced Robotics (ICAR'91)*, IEEE, New York, pp. 334–338, June.

Sato, A., S. Hashimoto, and S. Ohteru, 1992, "Virtual Singer & Virtual Band for Computer Music Performance," *Proceedings of the International Symposium on Musical Acoustics*, Tokyo, Japan, pp. 83–86, August.

Sayers, C. and R. Paul, 1993, "Synthetic Fixturing," *Proceedings of ASME WAM*, Vol. DSC-Vol. 49, ASME, New York, pp. 37–46.

Sayers, C. and R. Paul, 1994, "An Operator Interface for Teleprogramming Employing Synthetic Fixtures," *Presence–Teleoperators and Virtual Environments*, MIT Press, Vol. 3, No. 4., pp. 309–320.

Scallie, L., 1994, "High Voltage Entertainment," *Pixelation*, Vol. 10, pp. 4–7.

Schadebrodt, G. and B. Salomon, 1990, "The Piezo Traveling Wave Motor, a New Element in Actuation," *PCIM*, pp. 46–50, July.

Schlaroff, S. and A. Pentland, 1991, "Generalized Implicit Functions For Computer Graphics," *Computer Graphics*, Vol. 25, No. 4, pp. 247–250, July.

Schmidt, R., 1977, "Somatovisceral sensibility," in R. Schmidt Ed., *Fundamentals of sensory physiology*, Springer-Verlag, NY.

Schmult, B. and R. Jebens, 1993a, "A High Performance Force-Feedback Joystick," *Virtual Reality Systems'93 Conference*, SIG Advanced Applications, New York, pp. 123–129, March.

Schmult, B. and R. Jebens, 1993b, "Application Areas for a Force-Feedback Joystick," *Proceedings of ASME WAM*, DSC-Vol. 49, ASME, New York, pp. 47–54.

Schulte, R., 1962, "The Characteristics of the McKibben Artificial Muscle," *Applications of External Power in Prosthetics and Orthetics*, Publ. 874, pp. 94–115.

Schwartz, J., 1993, "A Computerized Cadaver to Aid Medical Students," *The New York Times*, NY, page D5, April 7.

Schwartz, M., 1995, "Network Management and Control Issues in Multimedia Wireless Networks," *IEEE Personal Communications*, Vol. 2, No. 3, pp. 8–16, June.

Scully, J., 1993, "Motion Tracking: The Ascension Flock of Birds," *Virtual Reality Systems*, Vol. 1, No. 1, pp. 40–42, March.

Sederberg, T. and S. Parry, 1986, "Free-Form Deformation of Solid Geometric Models," *Computer Graphics*, Vol. 20, No. 4, pp. 151–160.

Sense8 Co., 1992, "WorldToolKit Version 101," Technical Brief, Sausalito, CA, 52 pp., November.

Sense8 Co., 1995, "WorldToolKit Reference Manual Version 2.1b," Sausalito, CA.

SensAble Devices Inc., 1994, "PHANToM Master User's Manual," Cambridge, MA.

Seow, K., 1988, "Physiology of Touch, Grip and Gait," in J. Webster Ed., *Tactile Sensing for Robotics and Medicine*, John Wiley & Sons, New York, pp. 13–40.

Shahinpoor, M., 1994, "Eletro-Thermo-Mechanics of Resilient Contractile Fiber Bundles as Robotic Actuators," *IEEE International Conference on Robotics and Automation*, IEEE, New York, pp. 1502–1507, May.

Sheridan, T., 1992a, *Telerobotics, Automation, and Human Supervisory Control*, MIT Press, Cambridge, MA.

Sheridan, T., 1992b, "Musings on Telepresence and Virtual Presence," *Presence–Teleoperators and Virtual Environments*, Vol. 1, No. 1, MIT Press, pp. 120–126.

Sheridan, T., 1992c, "Defining our Terms," *Presence–Teleoperators and Virtual Environments*, Vol. 1, No. 2, MIT Press, pp. 272–274.

Sherrick, C. and J. Craig, 1982, "The Psychophysics of Touch," in W. Schiff and E. Foulke Eds., *Tactual Perception- A Source Book*, Cambridge University Press, New York, pp. 55–81.

Shimizu, S., S. Ino, T. Izumi, M. Takahashi and T. Ifukube, 1993a, "Development of Actuator Using Metal Hydride for Force Display to Elbow Joint," *Journal of Robotics and Mechatronics*, Vol. 5, No. 3, pp. 220–225.

Shimizu, S., S. Ino, M. Sato, T. Odagawa, T. Izumi, M. Takahashi and T. Ifukube, 1993b, "A Basic Study of a Force Display using a Metal Hydrade Actuator," *IEEE International Workshop on Robot and Human Communication*, IEEE, New York, pp. 211–215.

Shimizu, S., S. Ino, M. Sato, T. Izumi, T. Ifukube, M. Muro, H. Takeda and Y. Wakisaka, 1994, "A New Method of Variable Compliance for a Force Display System Using a Metal Hydrade Actuator," *IEEE International Workshop on Robot and Human Communication*, IEEE, New York, pp. 265–270.

Shimoga, K., 1992, "Finger Force and Touch Feedback Issues in Dextrous Telemanipulation," *Proceedings of NASA-CIRSSE International Conference on Intelligent Robotic Systems for Space Exploration*, NASA, Greenbelt, MD, September.

Shimoga, K., 1993, "A Survey of Perceptual Feedback Issues in Dextrous Telemanipulation: Part II. Finger Touch Feedback," *Proceedings of IEEE Virtual Reality Annual International Symposium*, IEEE, New York, pp. 271–279, September.

Shreeve, J., 1993, "Touching the Phantom," *Discover*, pp. 35–54, June.

Silicon Graphics Inc., 1991, *Graphics Library Programming: Tools and Techniques*, Mountain View, CA.

Singh, S., M. Bostrom, D. Popa and C. Wiley, 1994, "Design of an Interactive Lumbar Puncture Simulator with Tactile Feedback," *Proceedings of IEEE International Conference on Robotics and Automation*, IEEE, New York, pp. 1734–1752, May.

Son, J., E. Monteverde and R. Howe, 1994, "A Tactile Sensor for Localizing Transient Events in Manipulation," *Proceedings of 1994 IEEE Robotics and Automation Conference*, IEEE, New York, pp. 471–476.

Song, G-J. and N. Reddy, 1995, "Tissue Cutting in Virtual Environments," K. Morgan, R. Satava, H. Sieburg, R. Mattheus and J. Christensen Eds., *Interactive Technology and the New Paradigm for Healthcare*, IOS Press, Amsterdam, Chapter 54, pp. 359–364, January.

Speeter, T., 1993, Personal communication, AT&T Bell Laboratories, Holmdel, NJ, June.

Srinivasan M. and J. Chen, 1993, "Human Performance in Controlling Normal Forces of Contact with Rigid Objects," *Advances in Robotics, Mechatronics, and Haptic Interfaces*, DSC-Vol. 49, ASME, New York, pp. 119–125.

Srinivasan M. and R. LaMotte, 1995, "Tactual Discrimination of Softness," *Journal of Neurophysiology*, Vol. 73, No.1, pp. 88–101.

Srinivasan M. and K. Dandekar, 1995, "An Investigation of the Mechanics of Tactile Sense using Two Dimensional Models of the Primate Fingertip," *Journal of Biomechanical Eng.* Vol. 118, pp. 48–55.

Stadler, W., 1995, *Analytical Robotics and Mechatronics*, McGraw-Hill, New York.

Stanley, M. and J. Colgate, 1993, "Real Time Simulation of Stiff Dynamic Systems via Distributed Memory Parallel Processors," *Proceedings of IEEE Virtual Reality Annual International Symposium (VRAIS)*, IEEE, New York, pp. 456–461, September.

Stewart, D., 1965, "A platform with 6 degrees of freedom," *Proceedings of the Institute of Mechanical Engineers*, Vol. 180, pp. 371–386.

Stone, H., 1982, *Microcomputer Interfacing*, Addison-Wesley, Reading, MA.

Stone, R., 1991, "Advanced Human-System Interfaces for Telerobotics Using Virtual Reality & Telepresence Technologies," *Proceedings of the Fifth International Conference on Advanced Robotics ('91 ICAR)*, IEEE, New York, pp. 168–173.

Stone, R., 1992, "Virtual Reality Tutorial," *MICAD Conference*, Micado, Paris, France.

Stone, R. and J. Henequin, 1992, "Manipulator Interaction Simulation System," International Patent WO 92/05519.

Sturman, D., 1992, "Whole-hand Input," Ph.D Thesis, School of Architecture and Planning, MIT, Cambridge, MA.

Sukthankar, S. and N. Reddy, 1994, "Towards Virtual Reality of 'Tissue Squeezing': A Feasibility Study," *Proceedings of Medicine Meets Virtual Reality II*, Aligned Management Assoc., San Diego, CA., pp. 182–184, January.

Sukthankar, S. and N. Reddy, 1995, "Force Feedback Issues in Minimally Invasive Surgery," in K. Morgan, R. Satava, H. Sieburg, R. Mattheus and J. Christensen Eds., *Interactive Technology and the New Paradigm for Healthcare*, IOS Press, Amsterdam, Chapter 56, pp. 375–379, January.

Sutherland, I., 1965, "The Ultimate Display," *Proceedings of International Federation of Information Processing '65*, pp. 506–508.

Sutter, P., J. Iatridis and N. Thakor, 1989, "Response to Reflected-Force Feedback to Fingers in Teleoperation," *Proceedings of NASA Conference on Space Telerobotics*, Vol. IV, NASA, Greenbelt, MD, pp. 65–74, February.

Tachi, S., T. Maeda, R. Hirata, and H. Hoshino, 1994, "A Construction Method of Virtual Haptic Space," *Proceedings of The Fourth International Conference on Artificial Reality and Tele-Existence (ICAT'94)*, Tokyo, Japan, pp. 131–138, July.

Tadros, A., 1990, "Control System Design for a Three Degree of Freedom Virtual Environment Simulator Using Motor/Brake Pair Actuators," Master Thesis, Department of Mechanical Engineering, MIT, Cambridge, MA.

Takeda, T. and Y. Tsutsul, 1993, "Development of a Virtual Training Environment," *Proceedings of ASME WAM*, DSC-Vol. 49, ASME, New York, pp. 1–10.

Tan, B., 1988, "Sensor Application to the Space-Suit Glove," in J. Webster Ed., *Tactile Sensors for Robotics and Medicine*, John Wiley & Sons, New York, pp. 331–340.

Tan, H., X. Pang and N. Durlach, 1992, "Manual Resolution of Length, Force, and Compliance," *Advances in Robotics*, DSC-Vol. 42, ASME-WAM, pp. 13–18.

Tan, H., N. Durlach, Y. Shao and M. Wei, 1993, "Manual Resolution of Compliance when Work and Force Cues are Minimized," *Advances in Robotics, Mechatronics and Haptic Interfaces*, DSC-Vol. 49, ASME-WAM, pp. 99–104.

Tan, H., M. Srivasan, B. Eberman and B. Cheng, 1994, "Human Factors for the Design of Force-Reflecting Haptic Interfaces," *Proceedings of ASME WAM*, DSC-Vol. 55–1, ASME, New York, pp. 353–360.

Tanie, K. and T. Kotoku, 1993, "Force Display Algorithms for Virtual Environments," *IEEE Workshop on Force Display in Virtual Environments and Application to Robotic Teleoperation*, IEEE, New York, pp. 60–78, May.

Taylor, R., W. Robinett, V. Chi, F. Brooks Jr., W. Wright, S. Williams and E. Snyder, 1993, "The Nanomanipulator: A Virtual-Reality Interface for a Scanning Tunneling Microscope," *Computer Graphics*, ACM Press, New York, pp. 127–134.

Taylor, R., 1994, "The Nanomanipulator: A Virtual-Reality Interface to a Scanning Tunneling Microscope," Ph.D. Thesis, Department of Computer Science, The University of North Carolina, Chapel Hill, NC.

Taylor, R., S. Lavallee, G. Burdea and R. Möesges, Eds., 1996, *Computer-Integrated Surgery*, MIT Press, Cambridge, MA.

Tendick, F., R. Jennings, G. Tharp and L. Stark, 1993, "Sensing and Manipulation Problems in Endoscopic Surgery: Experiment, Analysis, and Observation," *Presence–Teleoperators and Virtual Environments*, Vol. 2, No. 1, pp. 66–81.

Tiersten, H., 1969, *Linear Piezoelectric Plate Vibrations*, Plenum Press, New York.

Vertut, J. and P. Coiffet, 1986, *Teleoperations and Robotics: Evolution and Development*, Robot Technology Series, Vol. 3A, Prentice Hall, Englewood Cliffs, NJ.

Viewpoint Datalabs, 1993, *Dataset Catalog*, Volume II, Orem, UT.

Vince, J., 1994, "Flying in Virtual Worlds," in MacDonald and Vince Eds., *Interacting with Virtual Environments*, John Wiley & Sons, New York, pp. 257–269.

Virtual Reality Inc., 1993, "MIS Training & Rehearsal System 323," Company brochure, Pleasantville, NY.

Virtual Technologies Inc., 1995, Press release, Palo Alto, CA, December.

Virtual World Entertainment Inc., 1991, "Bettlemech Operations Manual," Second Edition, Chicago, IL.

VPL Research Inc., 1987, *DataGlove Model 2 User's Manual*, Redwood City, CA.

VR World, 1995, "ThunderSeat: A New Gaming Experience," pp. 10, March/April.

Ward, M., R. Azuma, R. Bennett, S. Gottschalk, and H. Fuchs, 1992, "A Demonstrated Optical Tracker with Scalable Work Area for Head-Mounted Display Systems," *1992 Symposium on Interactive 3D Graphics*, ACM, pp. 43–52.

Webster, M., 1985, *Webster's Ninth New Collegiate Dictionary*, Merriam-Webster Inc., Springfield, MA.

Weisenberger, J. and C. Hasser, 1996, "Role of Active and Passive Movement in Vibrotactile Pattern Perception," *Journal of Experimental Psychology: Applied*, (submitted).

Welch, R. and D. Warren, 1986, "Intersensory Interactions," *The Handbook of Perception and Human Performance*, John Wiley & Sons, New York.

Wenzel, E., 1992a, "Localization in Virtual Acoustic Display," *Presence–Teleoperators and Virtual Environments*, Vol. 1, No. 1, MIT Press, pp. 80–107, March.

Wenzel, E., 1992b, "Launching Sounds Into Space," *Proceedings of Cyberarts Conference*, Miller Freeman, Inc., San Francisco, pp. 87–93, October.

Wiker, S., E. Hershkowitz and J. Zik, 1989, "Teleoperator Comfort and Psychometric Stability: Criteria for Limiting Master-Controller Forces of Operation and Feedback During Telemanipulation," *Proceedings of NASA Conference on Space Telerobotics*, Vol. I, NASA, Greenbelt, MD, pp. 99–107, February.

Wittenstein Motion Control GmbH, 1993, "Artificial Muscle," Technical brochure, Igersheim, Germany, 4 pp., November.

Woolford, K., 1994, Personal communication, University of North Carolina, Chapel Hill, NC, September.

Yamamoto, K., A. Ishiguro and Y. Uchikawa, 1993, "A Development of Dynamic Deformation Algorithms for 3D Shape Modeling with Generation of Interactive Force Sensation," *Proceesings of IEEE Virtual Reality Annual International Symposium (VRAIS)*, IEEE, New York, pp. 505–511, September.

Yamashita, J., H. Yokoi, Y. Fukui and M. Shimojo, 1994, "A Virtual Surface Modeler for Direct and Regional Free Form Manipulation," *Proceedings of The Fourth International Conference on Artificial Reality and Tele-Existence (ICAT'94)*, Tokyo, Japan, pp. 35–42, July.

Yokoi, H., J. Yamashita, Y. Fukui and M. Shimojo, 1994, "Development of the Virtual Shape Manipulating System," *Proceedings of The Fourth International Conference on Artificial Reality and Tele-Existence (ICAT'94)*, Tokyo, Japan, pp. 43–48, July.

Zarudiansky, A., 1981, "Remote Handling Device," U.S. Patent 4,392,138, November 24.

Zechner, S., 1993, "Immerse—Input and Force-Feedback Device for Applications in Virtual Environments," Master Thesis, Austria.

Zerkus, M., B. Becker, J. Ward and L. Halvorsen, 1993, "Temperature Sensing in Virtual Reality and Telerobotics," *Virtual Reality Systems*, Vol. 1, No. 2, pp. 88–90.

Zhai, S. and P. Milgram, 1993, "Human Performance Evaluation of Manipulation Scheme in Virtual Environments," *IEEE Virtual Reality Annual International Symposium (VRAIS)*, IEEE, New York, pp. 155–161, September.

Zhu, H., 1988, "Electrotactile Stimulation," in J. Webster Ed., *Tactile Sensors for Robotics and Medicine*, John Wiley & Sons, New York, pp. 341–353.

Ziegler, R., W. Mueller, G. Fischer and M. Goebel, 1995, "A Virtual Reality Medical Training System," Fraunhofer Institute for Computer Graphics, Darmstadt, Germany, 5 pp.

Ziegler, R., C. Brandt, C. Kunstmann and H. Werkhäuser, 1996, "Haptic Display of the VR Arthroscopy Training Simulator," *Proceedings of Eurographics '96 Conference*, (submitted).

LIST OF COMPANIES AND RESEARCH LABORATORIES

Advanced Research Projects Agency
North Fairfax Dr.
Arlington, VA 22203-1714, USA
tel: 1-703-696-2265
fax: 1-703-552-2668

Advanced Robotics Research Ltd.
University Rd.
Salford, England M5 4PP, UK
tel: 44-161-745-7384
fax: 44-161-745-8264
email: BOB@advanced-robotics-research-
centre.salford.ac.uk

AEA Technology Telerobotic Systems
10.2 Harwell, Didcot
Oxfordshire OX11 0RA, UK
tel: 44-1235-435571
fax: 44-1235-436138

Airmuscle Ltd.
12 Orchard Close
Cranfield, Bedfordshire MK43 0HX, UK
tel: 44-1234-750-791
fax: 44-1234-750-451

Airpot Co.
27 Lois St.
Norwalk, CT 06851, USA
tel: 1-203-846-2021
fax: 1-203-849-0539

Armstrong Laboratory USAF (AL/CFBA)
Crew Systems Directorate
2610 Seventh St.
Wright-Patterson AFB, OH 45433-7901, USA
tel: 1-513-255-2683
fax: 1-513-476-7617
email: c.hasser@ieee.org

AT&T Bell Laboratories
Machine Perception Research
Department
Crowfords Corner Rd.
Holmdel, NJ 07733, USA
tel: 1-908-949-3262
fax: 1-908-949-0399
email: bcs@vax135.att.com

Audiological Engineering Inc.
35 Medford St.
Somerville, MA 02143, USA
tel: 1-617-623-5562
fax: 1-617-666-5228

Autodesk Inc.
2320 Marinship Way
Sausalito, CA 94965, USA
tel: 1-415-332-2344
fax: 1-415-491-8303

Aura Systems Co.
2335 Alaska Ave.
El Segundo, CA 90245, USA
tel: 1-310-643-5300
fax: 1-310-643-8846

Avatar Partners
13000 Central Ave.
Boulder Creek, CA 95006, USA
tel: 1-408-338-6460
fax: 1-408-338-6462

Begej Co.
5 Claret Ash Rd.
Littleton, CO 80127, USA
tel: 1-303-932-2186
fax: 1-303-932-2186

BioControl Systems Inc.
430 Cowper St.
Palo Alto, CA 94301, USA
tel: 1-415-329-8494
fax: 1-415-329-8498

Boeing Computer Services Research and Technology
P.O. Box 24346, MS 7L-22
Seattle, WA 98124-0346, USA
tel: 1-206-655-1131
email: wmcneely@espreso.boeing.com

Bonneville Scientific Inc.
1849 W. North Temple
Salt Lake City, UT 84116, USA
tel: 1-801-359-0402
fax: 1-801-359-0416

Brigham Young University
Computer Science Dept.
3361 TMCB
Provo, UT 84602, USA
tel: 1-801-378-3027
fax: 1-801-378-7775

British Aerospace Brough Laboratory
Military Aircraft Division
North Humberside, HU15 1EQ, UK
tel: 44-1482-667-121
fax: 44-1482-664-203

Buzmatics Inc.
4361 W 96th St.
Indianapolis, IN 46268, USA
tel: 1-317-876-3413
fax: 1-317-876-3450

C & M Research
2437 Bay Area Boulevard, Suite 234
Houston, TX 77058, USA
tel: 1-713-488-3598
fax: 1-713-488-3599

Carnegie Mellon University
School of Computer Science
Schenley Park
Pittsburgh, PA 15213, USA
tel: 1-412-268-2565
fax: 1-412-268-5576
email:william.welch@cs.cmu.edu

Carnegie Mellon University
The Robotics Institute
Schenley Park
Pittsburgh, PA 15213, USA
tel: 1-412-268-3016
fax: 1-412-268-5570
email:Karun.Shimoga@j.gp.cs.cmu.edu

Cine-Med Inc.
127 Main St.
Woodbury, CT 06798, USA
tel: 1-203-263-0006
fax: 1-203-263-4839
email: cinemed127@delphi.com

CyberEdge Journal
1 Gate Six Rd., Suite G
Sausalito, CA 94965, USA
tel: 1-415-331-3343
fax: 1-415-331-3643

Cybernet Systems Co.
727 Airport Boulevard
Ann Arbor, MI 48108, USA
tel: 1-313-668-2567
fax: 1-313-668-8780
email: heidi@cybernet.com

Dartmouth College
Thayer School of Engineering
Hanover, NH 03755, USA
tel: 1-603-646-2230
fax: 1-603-646-3856
email: sunil.singh@dartmouth.edu

Denne Developments Ltd.
Unit 4, Cedar Park, Cobham Rd.
Wimborne, BH21 7SB, UK
tel: 44-1202-861-661
fax: 44-1202-861-233

Digital Equipment Co.
Cambridge Research Lab.
One Kendall Square
Cambridge, MA 02139, USA
tel: 1-617-692-7600
fax: 1-617-692-7650
email: hsu@crl.dec.com

Digital Image Design, Inc.
170 Claremont Ave.
New York, NY 10027, USA
tel: 1-212-222-5236
fax: 1-212-864-1189

Division Ltd.
19 Apex Court
Woodlands, Almondsbury
Bristol, BS12 4JT, UK
tel: 44-1454-615554
fax: 44-1454-615532

EXOS Co.
2A Gill St.
Woburn, MA 01801, USA
tel: 1-617-933-0022
fax: 1-617-933-0303
email: exos@exos.com

Fachhochschule Regensburg
Fachbereich Elektronik
Seyboth Strasse, 8400 Regensburg

Germany
tel: 49-941-954-42

Flogiston Co.
16701 Westview Trail
Austin, TX 78737, USA
tel: 1-512-894-0562
fax: 1-512-894-0562
email: floman@bga.com

Force Imaging Technologies
3424 Touhy Ave.
Chicago, IL 60645, USA
tel: 1-708-674-7665
fax: 1-708-674-7355

Fraunhofer Institute for Computer Graphics
Department of Visualization and Simulation
Wilhelminenstrasse 7
D-64283 Darmstadt, Germany
tel: 49-6151-155-310
fax: 49-6151-155-199
email: ziegler@igd.fhg.de

General Electric Co.
Research and Development Center
1 River Rd.
Schenectady, NY 12309, USA
tel: 1-518-387-5000
fax: 1-518-387-6170

Georgia Institute of Technology
Bioengineering Center
Mail Code 020
Atlanta, GA 30332, USA
tel: 1-404-894-7028
fax: 1-404-894-7025
email: john.peifer@berc.gatech.edu

Georgia Institute of Technology
College of Computing
Mail Code 0280
Atlanta, GA. 30084, USA
tel: 1-404-853-0672
fax: 1-404-853-0673
email: norberto@cc.gatech.edu

Greenleaf Medical Systems
3145 Porter Dr., Bldg. A
Palo Alto, CA 94304, USA

tel: 1-415-843-3640
fax: 1-415-843-3645
email: walterg@netcom.com

Harvard University
Division of Applied Sciences
Pierce Hall, 29 Oxford St.
Cambridge, MA 02138, USA
tel: 1-617-496-8359
fax: 1-617-495-9837
email: howe@arcadia.harvard.edu

High Techsplanations
6001 Montrose Rd.
Rockville, MD 20852, USA
tel: 1-301-984-3706
fax: 1-301-984-2104
email: dwight@ht.com

Hokkaido University
Research Institute for Electronic Science
Nishi 6, Kita 13, Kita-ku
Sapporo, 060, Japan
tel: 81-11-757-1250
fax: 81-11-757-1250
email: INO%ae%hines@xmail-gw.
sys.hokudai.ac.jp

Hokkaido Tokai University
School of Engineering
5-1 Minaminosawa, Minami-ku
Sapporo, 005, Japan
tel: 81-11-571-5111
fax: 81-11-571-7879
email: takashi_izumi@ae.hines
hokudai.ac.jp

Hosei University
Department of Electrical and Electronic
 Engineering
3-7-2 Kajino-cho, Koganei
Tokyo, 184 Japan
tel: 81-423-87-6187
fax: 81-423-87-6122
email: hisato@csl.hosei.ac.jp

I.B.M. UK Ltd.
P.O. Box 7, Rockware Ave.
Greenford, Middlesex, UB6 0DW, UK
tel: 44-181-575-7700
fax: 44-181-575-8015
email: COLLINSB@VNET.IBM.COM

Immersion Co.
2158 Paragon Dr.
San Jose, CA 95131, USA
tel: 1-408-467-1900
fax: 1-408-467-1901
email: louis@immerse.com

I.N.R.I.A.
Domanie de Voluceau
78153 Le Chesnay, France
tel: 33-1-39-635-711
fax: 33-1-39-635-423
email: sabine.coquillart@inria.fr

**Intelligent Systems
 Solutions Ltd.**
University Rd.
Salford M5 4PP, UK
tel: 44-161-745-7384
fax: 44-161-745-8264

Iowa State University
Department of Mechanical Eng.
2096 H. M. Black Eng. Bldg.
Ames, IA 50011, USA
tel: 1-515-294-5916
fax: 1-515-294-6778
email: grluecke@iastate.edu

Ixion Inc.
1335 North Northlake Way
Seattle, WA 98103, USA
tel: 1-206-282-6809
fax: 1-206-547-8802

**Kernforschungszentrum
 Karlsruhe GmbH**
Department of Enginering
 Technology
P.O. Box 3620
D76021 Karlsruhe, Germany
tel: 49-7247-823.072
fax: 49-7247-822.289
email: hafi@hdi.kfk.de

**Kunsthochschule fur
 Medien Koln**
Peter Welter Platz 2
D50676 Koln, Germany
tel: 49-221-201-89204
fax: 49-221-201-8917
email: kwolf@khm.uni-koeln.de

Laboratoire de Robotique de Paris
10-12 Avenue de L'Europe
78140 Velizy, France
tel: 33-1-3925-4965
fax: 33-1-3925-4967
email: richard@robot.uvsq.fr

Lockheed Martin
Astronautics Group
P.O.Box 179
Denver, CO 80201, USA
tel: 1-303-977-3000

Logitech Inc.
6505 Kaiser Dr.
Freemont, CA 94555, USA
tel: 1-510-795-8550
fax: 1-510-792-8901

Magic Edge Inc.
1245 Space Parkway
Mountain View, CA 94043, USA
tel: 1-415-254-5500
fax: 1-415-965-2703

Massachusetts Institute of Technology
Artificial Intelligence Laboratory
545 Technology Square
Cambridge, MA 02139, USA
tel: 1-617-253-5834
fax: 1-617-253-5060
email: jks@ai.mit.edu

Massachusetts Institute of Technology
Media Labs
20 Ames St.
Cambridge, MA 02139, USA
tel: 1-617-253-0300
fax: 1-617-258-6264
email:sandy@media.mit.edu

Massachusetts Institute of Technology
Mechanical Engineering Department
Cambridge, MA 02139, USA
tel: 1-617-253-2228
fax: 1-617-258-6575
email: sheridan@mit.edu

Materials Electric Products Co. (MELCOR)
1040 Spruce St.
Trenton, NJ 08648, USA
tel: 1-609-393-4178
fax: 1-609-393-9461

Matsushita Electric Industrial
26th Floor, World Trade Center
4-1 Hamamatsu-Cho 2-Chome
Minato-Ku, Tokyo, 105 Japan
tel: 81-3-3435-4556
fax: 81-3-3435-4585

McGill University
Biorobotics Laboratory
3775 University St.
Montreal, H3A 2B4, Canada
tel: 1-514-398-6740
fax: 1-514-398-8244

McGill University
School of Physical and Occupational
    Therapy
3654 Drummond St.
Montreal, H3G 1Y5, Canada
tel: 1-514-398-4499
fax: 1-514-398-8193
email: lyn@biorobotics.mcgill.ca

Mechanical Engineering Laboratory
Bio-Robotics Division, MITI
Tsukuba Science City
Ibaraki, 305 Japan
tel: 81-298-58-7088
fax: 81-298-58-7201
email: toku@mel.go.jp

MicroMo Electronics Inc.
14881 Evergreen Ave.
Clearwater, FL 34622-3008, USA
tel: 1-813-572-0131
fax: 1-813-573-5918

Mitsui Engineering & Shipbuilding Co., Ltd.
Head Office 6-4
Tsukiji 5-Chome, Chuo-Ku
Tokyo, 104 Japan
tel: 81-3-3544-3221
fax: 81-3-3544-3041

Mondo-tronics Inc.
524 San Anselmo Ave., #107
San Anselmo, CA 94960, USA
tel: 1-415-455-9330
fax: 1-415-455-9333
email: info@mondo.com

Monterey Technologies Inc.
1143 Executor Circle
Cary, NC 27511, USA
tel: 1-919-481-0565
fax: 1-919-481-0310

Moog Inc.
Motion Systems Division
East Aurora, NY 14052-0018, USA
tel: 1-716-652-2000
fax: 1-716-687-4467

Nagasaki Institute of Applied Science
Department of Mechanical Engineering
536 Aba, Nagasaki-city
Nagasaki, 851-01 Japan
tel: 81-958-38-5170
fax: 81-958-30-2089

Nagoya University
Department of Information Electronics
Furo-cho, Chikusa-ku
Nagoya, 464-01 Japan
tel: 81-52-781-5111
fax: 81-52-781-9263
email: yamamoto@uchikawa.
nuem.nagoya-u.ac.jp

NASA Ames Research Center
MS. 262-2, Moffett Field, CA 94035, USA
tel: 1-415-604-3937
tel: 1-415-604-3953
email: bda@eos.arc.nasa.gov

NASA Jet Propulsion Laboratory
California Institute of Technology
4800 Oak Grove Dr.
Pasadena, CA 91109, USA
tel: 1-818-306-6182
tel: 1-818-306-6912
email: tupman@isd.jpl.nasa.gov

NASA Johnson Space Center
Mail Code PT4

Houston, TX 77058, USA
tel: 1-713-483-8070
fax: 1-713-244-5698
email: bowen@gothamcity.jsc.nasa.gov

National Institute of Bioscience and Human Technology, MITI
1-1 Higashi, Tsukuba
Ibaraki, 305 Japan
tel: 81-298-54-6760
fax: 81-298-54-6762
email: fukui@nibh.go.jp

Naval Postgraduate School
Code CS/ZK
Monterey, CA 93943-5100, USA
tel: 1-408-656-2305
fax: 1-408-656-2814
email: zyda@siggraph.org

Nissho Electronics USA Co.
18201 Von Karman Ave., Suite 350
Irvine, CA 92715, USA
tel: 1-714-261-8811
fax: 1-714-261-8819
email: niki@nelco.com

Nissho Electronics Co.
Tsukiji 7-3-1, Chuoo-ku
Tokyo, 103 Japan
tel: 81-3-3544-8452
fax: 81-3-3544-8284
email: vr-info@nissho-ele.co.jp

Northwestern University
Department of Mechanical Engineering
2145 Sheridan Rd.
Evanston, IL 60208 USA
tel: 1-708-491-4264
fax: 1-708-491-3915
email: ed_colgate.me@plato.nwu.edu

NTT Human Interface Laboratories
1-2356 Take, Yokosuka-Shi
Kanagawa, 238-03 Japan
tel: 81-468-59-2329
fax: 81-468-59-2332

Odetics Inc.
1515 S. Manchester Ave.
Anaheim, CA 92802, USA

tel: 1-714-758-0300
fax: 1-714-491-9885

Ohio State University
Department of Speech and Hearing Science
1070 Carmack Rd.
Columbus, OH 43210, USA
tel: 1-614-292-1281
fax: 1-614-292-7504
email: jan+@osu.edu

Ohio State University Hospital
Department of Anesthesiology
410 W. 10th Ave.
Columbus, OH 43210, USA
tel: 1-614-293-8487
fax: 1-614-293-8153

Queen's University
Kingston, Ontario,
K7L 3N6 Canada
tel: 1-613-545-2938
fax: 1-613-545-6300

**Royal Melbourne Institute
of Technology**
Advanced Computer Graphics Centre
723 Swanson St.
Melbourne, 3053, Australia
tel: 61-3-282-2461
fax: 61-3-663-7873
email: bmfowler@godzilla.
cgl.citri.edu.au

**Rutgers—The State University
of New Jersey**
CAIP Center, P.O.Box 1390
Piscataway, NJ 08855-1390, USA
tel: 1-908-445-3443
fax: 1-908-445-4775
email: burdea@caip.rutgers.edu

Sandia National Laboratories
7011 East Ave.
Livermore, CA 94551, USA
tel: 1-510-294-3606
fax: 1-510-294-1377
email: rfrenzi@sandia.gov

SARCOS Research Co.
360 Wakara Way
Salt Lake City, UT 84108, USA

tel: 1-801-581-0155
fax: 1-801-581-1151

**Schlumberger Laboratory for
Computer Science**
P.O. Box 200015
Austin, TX 78720, USA
tel: 1-512-331-3000
fax: 1-512-331-3760
email: celniker@slcs.slb.com

Scuola Superiore Santa Anna
The ARTS Laboratory
Via Carducci 40
56127 Pisa, Italy
tel: 39-50-560-108
fax: 39-50-883-215
email: bergamasco@sssup1.sssup.it

SEGA of America
P.O. Box 8097
Redwood City, CA 94063, USA
tel: 1-800-872-7342/237
fax: 1-415-802-1338

Sense8 Co.
100 Shoreline Highway, Suite 282
Mill Valley, CA 94941, USA
tel: 1-415-331-6318
fax: 1-415-331-9148
email: info@sense8.com

SensAble Devices Inc.
University Park at MIT
26 Landsdowne St.
Cambridge, MA 02139, USA
tel: 1-617-621-0150
fax: 1-617-621-0135
email: thm@ai.mit.edu

Shilling Omega, Inc.
1633 da Vinci Court
Davis, CA 95616, USA
tel: 1-916-753-6718
fax: 1-916-753-8092

Simon Fraser University
School of Kinesiology
Burnaby, BC V5A 1S6, Canada
tel: 1-604-291-3499
fax: 1-604-291-3040
email: tmilner@sfu.ca

SRI International
Bioengineering Research Department
333 Ravenswood Ave.
Menlo Park, CA 94025, USA
tel: 1-415-859-2882
fax: 1-415-859-2658

Stanford University
Center for Design Research 551, Terman
 Engineering Bldg.
Stanford, CA 94305, USA
tel: 1-415-725-1588
fax: 1-415-723-3521
email: cutkosky@sunrise.stanford.edu

STX Systems Co.
4400 Forbes Boulevard
Lanham, MD 20706, USA
tel: 1-301-306-1000

Suzuki Motor Co.
Technical Research Center
2-1 Sakura-Namiki, Midori-Ku
Yokohama, 226 Japan
tel: 81-45-943-7111
fax: 81-45-943-7100
email: adachi@yrd.suzuki.co.jp

Technical Research Associates, Inc.
2257 South 1100 E St.
Salt Lake City, UT 84106, USA
tel: 801-485-4991
fax: 801-485-4997

TeleTechnologies
1621 Bardale Ave.
San Pedro, CA 90371, USA
tel: 818-832-3218
fax: 818-393-5009

ThunderSeat Technologies
6330 Arizona Circle
Los Angeles, CA 90045, USA
tel: 1-310-410-0022
fax: 1-714-851-1185

TiNi Alloy Co.
1621 Neptune Dr.
San Leandro, CA 94577, USA
tel: 1-510-483-9676
fax: 1-510-483-1309

TNO Physics & Electronics Laboratory
P.O. Box 96864
2509 JG The Hague, The Netherlands
tel: 31-70-326-4221
fax: 31-70-328-0961

Tokyo Institute of Technology
4259 Nagatsuda, Midori
Yokayama, 227 Japan
tel: 81-45-924-5050
fax: 81-45-921-0898
email: mishii@pi.titech.ac.jp

Toshiba Corporation
Nuclear Engineering Laboratory
Shinsugita 8, Isogo-ku
Yokohama, 210 Japan
tel: 81-45-770-2370
fax: 81-45-770-2308

Toyota Technological Institute
2 Hisakata, Tempaku
Nagoya, 468 Japan
tel: 81-52-802-1111
fax: 81-52-802-6069
email: yamada@toyota-ti.ac.jp

Unitech Research Inc.
582 Grand Canyon Dr.
Madison, WI 53719, USA
tel: 1-608-833-1148
fax: 1-608-833-1149
email: metyler1@facstaff.wisc.edu

University of Akron
Department of Biomedical Engineering
Akron, OH 44325, USA
tel: 1-216-972-6653
fax: 1-216-374-8834
email: npreddy@guts.biomed.uakron.edu

University of Auckland
Department of Mechanical Engineering
P.B. 92019, Auckland, New Zealand
tel: 64-9-3737599
fax: 64-9-3737468
email: ma.sagar@auckland.ac.nz

University of British Columbia
Department of Electrical Engineering

Vancouver, BC, V6T 1Z4, Canada
tel: 1-604-822-3243
fax: 1-604-822-5949
email: tims@ee.ubc.ca

University of California at Berkeley
Department of Electrical Engineering and
  Computer Science
529 Soda Hall
Berkeley, CA 94720, USA
tel: 1-510-642-9955
fax: 1-510-642-5775
email: jfc@cs.berkeley.edu

University of California at Berkeley
Department of Mechanical Engineering
Human Engineering Laboratory
  Etcheverry Hall
Berkeley, CA 94720, USA
tel: 1-510-642-2964
fax: 1-510-643-5599
email: kazeroon@me.berkeley.edu

**University of California
  at Santa Cruz**
Computer Graphics & Imaging Lab.
255 Applied Sciences
Santa Cruz, CA 95064, USA
tel: 1-408-459-2320
fax: 1-408-459-4829

University of Colorado
Department of Aerospace
  Engineering Sciences
Boulder, CO 80309, USA
tel: 1-303-492-6417
fax: 1-303-492-7881

University of Guelph
Department of Computing and Human
  Technology
Guelph, Ontario
N1G 2W1, Canada
tel: 1-519-824-6402
fax: 1-519-837-0323

University of Hull
Robotics Research Unit
Electronic Engineering Dept.
Cottingham Rd.
Hull HU6 7RX, UK

tel: 44-1482-346-311
fax: 44-1482-466-664
email:R.D.Macredie@computer-science
hull.ac.uk

University of Minnesota
Department of Mechanical Engineering
111 Church St., S.E
Minneapolis, MN 55455, USA
tel: 1-612-625-0099
fax: 1-612-624-1398
email: wkdurfee@maroon.tc.umn.edu

University of New Mexico
Structures and Systems Laboratory
School of Engineering
Albuquerque, NM 87131, USA
tel: 1-505-277-5521
fax: 1-505-277-1142

University of North Carolina
Department of Computer Science
Chapel Hill, NC 27599, USA
tel: 1-919-962-1700
fax: 1-919-962-1799
email: brooks@cs.unc.edu

University of Pennsylvania
Department of Computer and Information
  Science
3401 Walnut St.
Philadelphia, PA 19104, USA
tel: 1-215-898-0339
fax: 1-215-573-2048
email: sayers@grip.cis.upenn.edu

University of Salford
Department of Electronic and Electrical
  Engineering
Manchester, M5 4WT, UK
tel: 44-161-745-5000
fax: 44-161-745-5999
email: d.g.caldwell@eee.salford.ac.uk

University of Texas at Austin
Department of Mechanical
  Engineering
ETC 4.146C,
Austin, TX 78712, USA
tel: 1-512-471-3039
fax: 1-512-471-3987

University of Toronto
Ergonomics in Telerobotics and Control
  Laboratory
Department of Industrial Engineering
Toronto, Ontario,
M5S 1A4, Canada
tel: 1-416-978-3662
fax: 1-416-978-3453
email: milgram@ie.utoronto.ca

University of Tokyo
Institute of Industrial Science
7-22-1 Roppongi, Minato-ku
Tokyo, 106 Japan
tel: 81-3-3479-2766
fax: 81-3-3423-1484
email: martin@ics.iis.u-tokyo.ac.jp

University of Tokyo
RCAST
4-6-1 Komaba, Meguro-ku
Tokyo, 153 Japan
tel: 81-3-3481-4467
fax: 81-3-3481-4469
email: tachi@tansei.cc.u-tokyo.ac.jp

University of Tsukuba
Institute of Engineering Mechanics
Tsukuba, 305 Japan
tel: 81-298-53-5362
fax: 81-298-53-5207
email: iwata@k2.tsukuba.ac.jp

University of Umea
Department of Physiology
S-901 87 Umea, Sweden
tel: 46-90-165-497
fax: 46-90-166-683

University of Utah
Center for Engineering Design
3176 Merrill Engineering Building
Salt Lake City, UT 84112, USA
tel: 1-801-581-6499
fax: 1-801-581-5304
email: Jacobsen@ced.utah.edu

University of Virginia
Department of Computer Science
School of Engineering
Charlottesville, VA 22903, USA

tel: 1-804-924-7605
fax: 1-804-982-2214

University of Washington
Department of Electrical
  Engineering
Seattle, WA 98195, USA
tel: 1-206-543-2197
fax: 1-206-543-3842
email: blake@ee.washington.edu

University of Wisconsin—Madison
Center for Space Automation and Robotics
1415 Engineering Dr.
Madison, WI 53706, USA
tel: 1-608-262-5524
fax: 1-608-262-9458

University of Wisconsin-Madison
Department of Rehabilitation Medicine
1300 University Ave.
Madison, WI 53706, USA
tel:1-608-265-3756
fax:1-608-265-3757
email: kurtkacz@macc.wisc.edu

U.S. Army Research Institute
Simulator Systems Research Unit
12350 Research Parkway
Orlando, FL 32826, USA
tel: 1-407-380-4319
fax: 1-407-380-8536

Viewpoint Datalabs
870 W Center St.
Orem, UT 84057, USA
tel: 1-801-224-2222
fax: 1-801-224-2272

Virtual Reality Inc.
485 Washington Ave.
Pleasantville, NY 10570, USA
tel: 1-914-769-0900
fax: 1-914-769-7106

Virtual Technologies (Virtex)
P.O. Box 5984
Stanford, CA 94309, USA
tel: 1-415-321-4900
fax: 1-415-321-4912

Virtual Entertainment Ltd.
3 Oswin Rd.
Brailsford Industrial Park
Leicester, LE3 1HR, UK
tel: 44-116-2542-127
fax: 44-116-2471-855

**VRASP—The VR Alliance of Students
and Professionals**
P.O. Box 4139
Highland Park, NJ 08904-4139, USA
tel: 1-908-463-8787
fax: 1-908-580-0092

VR News
P.O. Box 2515
London, N4 4JW, UK
tel: 44-181-292-1498
fax: 44-181-292-1436
email: mike@vrnews.demon.co.uk

Wittenstein Motion Control GmbH
Herrenwiesenstrasse 4-9
P.O. Box 1163, D-97997 Igersheim Germany
tel: 49-79-316-032
fax: 49-79-315-1975

Xtensory Inc
140 Sunridge Dr.
Scotts Velley, CA 95066, USA
tel: 1-408-439-0600
fax: 1-408-439-8845

Zechner & Zechner
Stumpergasse 14-23
Wien 1060, Austria
tel: 222-597-0336
fax: 222-597-0339

INDEX

Absolute threshold, 16
Absolute tracking error, 27
Acceleration feedback gains, 52
Acclaim Entertainment, 266
Accumulator tank, 64
Accuracy, significance of, 11
Action potential, 14
Active Environment Display, 105
Active surfaces, surface deformation, 178–180
Actors, distributed Virtual Environment System
　(dVS), 214, 221
Actuators:
　band-width, 71–73
　ceiling-mounted, 106
　direct current (dc) linear, 29
　direct-drive:
　　generally, 100
　　robotic, 280, 283
　ξ-array, 56
　electrical, 42–57
　fatigue and, 71
　force feedback, 73
　friction and, 42, 66–67
　haptic, 71
　high-bandwidth, 10
　hydraulic, 57–62
　linear, 59, 66–68
　Lorenz, 85
　magnetostrictive, 282–284
　micro-pin, 147–155
　Moog, 73
　muscles and, 42
　novel, 279–285
　PemRAM, 67–69, 73, 265
　in PHANToM Master, 41
　piezoelectric, 280, 282
　pneumatic, 10, 62–71
　power-to-volume ratio, 41–42, 68, 73
　power-to-weight ratio, 68, 74
　Pyrex glass-graphite linear, 66
　rotary, 59
　in Rutgers Master II, 67, 71
　single-action, 59, 66
　thermal-feedback, 162
　voice-coil, 267
Adachi, Y., 97, 101–102, 196–197, 208, 232–234
Adaptation:
　force control, 21–22
　sensorial, 14–17
Adelstein, B., 77–79, 193
Advanced Research Projects Agency, 313
Advanced Robotics Research Ltd., 8, 143, 313
AEA Technology Telerobotic Systems, 313
Aeronautics, 203
Air filter, 63
Air jets, 142

Air rings, 142
Airmuscle Ltd., 143, 313
Airpot, 66–67
Airpot Co., 66–67, 313
Akamatsu, M., 148–150, 233, 235–236
Alexander, J., 265
Allen, P., 135
AM-20, 47–48
American National Standards Institute, 219
An, K-N., 22, 24
Analog/digital/analog (A/D/A) boards, 27, 29,
　33, 93, 258
Anchor, physical constraint, 194–195
Anderson, R., 269
Andrenucci, M., 120, 124
Anesthesiology, 249–251
Angular joint error, 20
Angular velocity, 28
Animated Free-Form Deformation (AFFD),
　184–185
Anthropomorphic mechanical device, 4
Appino, P., 141
Application Programmer Interface (API), 218
Arai, T., 83
Arcades, virtual reality, 263–265
Architectures:
　multicomputer, 215–217
　multiprocessor, 213–214
Argonne Arm:
　function of, 5–6, 11, 273
　multi-user systems, 218
Argonne National Laboratory, 5, 11
Armature winding, 43–45
Arm exoskeletons:
　EXOS Force, 117, 131
　GLAD-IN-ART, 115–116, 123, 131
　overview, 114–115
　from University of Salford, 117–119, 131
Armstrong Laboratory, Wright-Patterson Air
　Force Base, 112, 152, 275, 284, 313
Artery localization, 247–248
Art exhibits, interactive, 266
Arthroscopic surgery, 252–253
ARTS Glove, 215
ARTS Hand Force Feedback System, 121, 123,
　131
ARTS Lab., 115, 120–121
Ascension Bird, 227
Ascension Technologies, 287
AT&T Bell Laboratories, 79, 313
Auditory feedback, 238–240
Atwood, D., 73, 109
Audiological Engineering Inc., 145, 314
Aura Systems Co., 265–266, 314
Austenitic phase, shape memory metals, 52–53,
　56

324